S/NVQ Leve

WITHDRAWN

Revised
New evidence
and assessment
features

Health &
Social Care
(Adults)

Yvon

with Neil Moonie and

Heinemann

Heinemann is an imprint of Pearson Education Limited, a company incorporated in England and Wales, having its registered office at Edinburgh Gate, Harlow, Essex, CM20 2JE. Registered company number: 872828

www.heinemann.co.uk

Heinemann is a registered trademark of Pearson Education Limited

Text © Yvonne Nolan, Neil Moonie, Sian Lavers 2005, Revisions ©Yvonne Nolan, Jane Kellas 2008
First published 2005

CD Text © Nicki Pritchatt, Debby Railton 2006
First published 2006

12 11 10 09 08
10 9 8 7 6 5 4 3 2

British Library Cataloguing in Publication Data is available from the British Library on request.

ISBN 978 0 435466 99 2

Edited by Jan Doorly
Designed by Wooden Ark
Typeset by HL Studios

Original illustrations © Pearson Education Limited 2008
Illustrated by Graham Cameron Illustration (Steph Dix) and The Art Collection (Ben Croft)

Cover design by Wooden Ark
Cover photo/ Getty Images
Printed in China by South China Printing Company

Acknowledgements
Every effort has been made to contact copyright holders of material reproduced in this book. Any omissions will be rectified in subsequent printings if notice is given to the publishers.

Websites
The websites used in this book were correct and up-to-date at the time of publication. It is essential for tutors to preview each website before using it in class so as to ensure that the URL is still accurate, relevant and appropriate. We suggest that tutors bookmark useful websites and consider enabling students to access them through the school/college intranet.

Contents

Acknowledgements

Expert advice and guidance was provided during the preparation of this book by: **Anne Eaton**, Associate Director of Programmes, Skills for Health; **Linda Nazarko**, NVQ trainer and assessor for the NHS; **Dee Spencer-Perkins**, independent trainer and consultant for social services with a particular interest in disability issues; **Tim Thomas** and **Denise Knight**, Leicestershire Care Development Group (Tim Thomas is a member of the TOPSS England Occupational Standards and Qualifications Committee)

The authors and publisher would like to thank the following:

Jane Kellas and colleagues at Venus Training & Consultancy Ltd, for providing expertise in preparing the Key Specification links and Performance Criteria analysis.

All at the Fremantle Trust, especially Mark Kingham, Yvonne Peace, Lorraine McGinley and the staff and residents at Farnham Common House and Seabrook Court, for their kindness and invaluable assistance (www.fremantletrust.org)

All the staff and residents at Pendine Park, Wrexham, with special thanks to Jan Wood

Rachel Bunn at Lowestoft College for advice and assistance

Mencap for permission to reproduce a page from its website www.mencap.org.uk (page 268)

Crown copyright material is reproduced under Class License No. C01W0000141 with the permission of the Controller of HMSO and the Queen's Printer for Scotland

The authors and publisher would like to thank the following for permission to reproduce photographs:

© Alamy/Enigma page 142/ Nikreates page 334 /SHOUT page 312

© Corbis pages 275, 336 / Steve Prezant page 14

© David Hoffman Photo Library page 274

© Getty images page 230/ /Chris Baker page 126/ Photonica page 166

© Pearson Education Ltd p pages 38, 66, 144, 371/Gareth Boden pages 11, 24/ Lord & Leverett pages 3, 6, 23, 28, 75, 136, 148, 317, 185, 195, 357/ Mindstudio page 61 / Jules Selmes pages 57, 105, 296, 365/ Richard Smith pages 96, 110, 227, 235, 239, 269, 273, 286/ Studio pages 129, 146, 148, 173, 214, 250, 369, 370 /Tudor Photography page 184

© Photofusion Picture Library pages 245, 323/ Alamy pages 20, 263, 178

© Sally and Richard Greenhill page 332

© Westholme page 102

Introduction

This new edition of *Level 3 Health & Social Care* comes at a time of change in the sector. So much has happened, both in terms of new legislation, guidelines and policies and in the way that issues are approached and addressed, that some changes to the National Occupational Standards were absolutely essential. Greater regulation of the care sector has been an important factor in continuing improvement, creating higher quality services and giving better protection to vulnerable people who use the services of the sector.

The new standards reflect the changes in the profession, such as the emphasis on quality services, the focus on tackling exclusion, and the influence of the culture of rights and responsibilities. There has been a huge increase, too, in understanding in all parts of the sector, and a recognition of the satisfaction that comes from working alongside service users as partners and directors of their own care, rather than as passive receivers of services.

Those users of this book who are working towards the achievement of an S/NVQ at Level 3 will be taking on a hugely demanding, but very fulfilling job role. The standards and quality of service provision continue to rise and the demands on the workforce increase continually. It is of course those who take responsibility for their own work, or who provide support and supervision to others, who often find that the most is expected of them.

However, it is clear from feedback since the introduction of S/NVQs and the massive improvement in practice shown by those who have achieved such qualifications, that all their hard work and study have played a huge part in providing a better service for the very vulnerable people who benefit.

Not everyone reading this book will be undertaking a qualification; some will use it for reference or to keep up with new developments. I hope that the content encourages you to think and reflect on your own practice.

The revised NVQ Level 3 in Health and Social Care qualification has **eight** units: **four** core units and **four** options chosen from a wide selection. In this book we have included all four core units, five of the most popular option units and two other option units on CD, therefore providing a choice. For details of further units, go to the Heinemann website (see below). Each NVQ unit is presented in the same way:

- **Elements of Competence** divide the unit to make it more manageable
- **About this unit** tells you the subject matter of the unit; it also spells out the **scope** of the work and the **values** relating to the unit
- **Performance Criteria** tell you what you have to do at work to achieve the standard
- **Knowledge Specification** tells you what you need to know and understand.

You will find that this book follows the structure of the NVQ units closely and gives you the knowledge for each unit. You also will find that the knowledge specifications are highlighted against the main headings for each section throughout all units. In some sections this may also relate to knowledge from other units, your assessor will be able to support you to identify this where appropriate. Don't forget that you will always need to demonstrate that you have applied this knowledge in your practice.

Each unit contains a number of 'evidence boxes' and indicates how they relate to the performance criteria for that element. Your assessor will need to make the final judgement and will also record where this relates to performance and knowledge from other units. Look out for the 'keys to good practice', as these will also help you to satisfy the performance criteria.

The section at the end of each unit directs you to further research and reading. You will find a helpful glossary of terms on page 379, a list of useful references on page 381, and a grid detailing coverage of the Knowledge Specification points on page 383. The CD is held on the inside back cover.

For more information about learning materials and resources for S/NVQs in Health and Social Care, visit the Heinemann website at www.heinemann. co.uk/vocational and follow the links.

I wish all who use this book the very best in their future career.

Yvonne Nolan

Key features

Look out for the following special features as you work through the book.

Knowledge specifications

All the main headings in each unit link to the knowledge specifications of the S/NVQ elements helping you develop the knowledge and understanding required for the qualification

Performance criteria

Highlighted against the evidence you need to collect and show to help identify the skills you need for the qualification

Case study

Real-life situations that you may come across when working in health and social care

Evidence

Shows what you can do to collect evidence for your portfolio ... don't forget that you will always need to demonstrate that you have applied this knowledge in your practice

Did you know?

Additional information to illustrate points covered in the unit

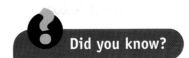

Active knowledge

Opportunities for you to research a topic further

Key term

Clear definitions of words and phrases you need to know

Remember

Reminders of important information

Keys to good practice

Checklists of points covered in the unit and aids to satisfying the performance criteria

Test yourself

Questions to test your knowledge

Test yourself

Further reading and research

Recommended books, journals and websites to develop your knowledge on subjects covered in the unit

FURTHER READING AND RESEARCH

Promote effective communication for and about individuals

Communication is all about the way people reach out to one another. It is an essential part of all relationships, and the ability to communicate well with service users, colleagues and others is a basic requirement for doing your job.

Communication is not just talking – we use touch, facial expressions and body movements when we are communicating with people personally, and there are many means of written and electronic communication in today's society.

It is important that you learn to communicate well even where there are differences in individuals' abilities and methods of communication; you will also need to be able to communicate effectively on complex and sensitive issues.

Recording information is important and serves many valuable purposes. You need to understand the significance of what you record and how it is recorded, in order to be sure that you are doing the best you possibly can for the individuals you work with.

This unit will help you to understand how all of these aspects of communication can be used in order to build and develop relationships and to improve your practice as a professional care worker.

What you need to learn

- Communication differences
- How to find out about likely communication problems
- Overcoming difficulties in communication
- Communicating about difficult issues
- Undertaking difficult, complex and sensitive communications
- How to identify the support individuals need
- Ways in which people communicate
- Barriers to communication
- Listening effectively
- Ways of receiving and passing on information
- Confidentiality
- Looking after information
- How to record information

HSC 31a Identify ways to communicate effectively

Communication differences

 KS ① ② ③ ⑥ ⑦ ⑧ ⑨ ⑩ ⑬ ⑭

This element deals with communication where there are differences between the worker and an individual that can cause problems. Communication differences include:

- people speaking different languages
- either the worker or the individual having a sensory impairment
- distress, where somebody is so upset that he or she is unable to communicate
- a physical illness or disability, such as a stroke or confusion
- cultural differences.

Using appropriate language

Speaking is about much more than just passing information between people. For example, many people can speak with different degrees of formality or informality. This is called the **register** of language.

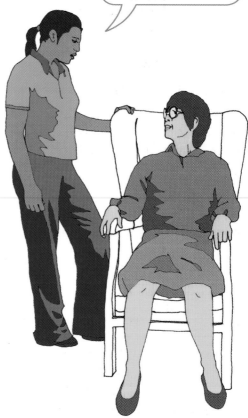

> Don't look so miserable, love – it may never happen!'

If you went to a hospital reception, you might expect the person on duty to greet you with a formal phrase, such as: 'Good morning, how can I help you?'. An informal greeting of the kind used by white males in the south-east of England might be: 'Hello mate, what's up then?' or 'How's it going?'.

It is possible that some people might prefer the informal greeting in many situations. An informal greeting could put you at ease; you might feel that the speaker is like you. But in some situations, the informal greeting might make people feel that they are not being respected.

The degree of formality or informality establishes a context. At a hospital reception you are unlikely to want to spend time making friends and chatting things over with the receptionist. You may be seeking urgent help; your expectations of the situation might be that you want to be taken seriously and put in touch with professional services as soon as possible. You might see the situation as a very formal encounter. If you were treated informally, you might interpret this as not being taken seriously, or not respected.

Informality and informal humour may be perceived as disrespect

Styles of speaking

People from different localities, different ethnic groups, different professions and work cultures all have their own special words, phrases and speech patterns. Where communities or groups of people have particular ways of speaking we call this a **speech community**. An elderly middle-class woman is very unlikely to start a conversation with the words 'Hello mate'.

Some service users may feel threatened or excluded by the kind of language they encounter. However, merely using formal language will not solve this problem. The technical terminology used by social care workers may also create barriers for people who are not part of that speech community.

Active knowledge

I come about getting some help around the house, you know, 'cause it's getting 'ard nowadays, what with me back an' everything.

Well, you need to speak to the Community Domiciliary Support Liaison Officer who can arrange an assessment in accordance with our statutory obligations.

The two statements above use different levels of formality, but they also represent speech from different speech communities. Can you work out what each person is saying? How do you think the service user will feel given such a response? Will the service user feel respected and valued?

Different languages

Where an individual speaks a different language from those who are providing care, it can be an isolating and frustrating experience. The individual may become distressed and frightened as it is very difficult to establish exactly what is happening and he or she is not in a position to ask or to have any questions answered. The person will feel excluded from anything happening in the care setting and will find making relationships with care workers extremely difficult. There is the possibility that misunderstanding will occur.

People communicate differently, but establishing good communication is vital

Hearing loss

A loss or reduction of ability to hear clearly can cause major differences in the ability to communicate.

Communication is a two-way process, and it is very difficult for somebody who does not hear sounds at all or hears them in a blurred and indistinct way to be able to respond and to join in. The result can be that people become withdrawn and feel very isolated and excluded from others around them. This can lead to frustration and anger. People may present some quite challenging behaviour.

Profound deafness is not as common as partial hearing loss. People are most likely to suffer from loss of hearing of certain sounds at certain volumes or at certain pitches, such as high sounds or low sounds. It is also very common for people to find it difficult to hear if there is background noise – many sounds may jumble together, making it very hard to pick out the voice of one person. Hearing loss can also have an effect on speech, particularly for those who are profoundly deaf and are unable to hear their own voices as they speak. This can make communication doubly difficult.

 Keys to good practice: Hearing impairments

When communicating with people with hearing impairments:

✓   make sure the person can see you clearly

✓   face both the light and the person at all times

✓   include the person in your conversation

✓   do not obscure your mouth

✓   speak clearly and slowly – repeat if necessary, or rephrase your words

✓   do not shout into a person's ear or hearing aid

✓   minimise background noise

✓   use your eyes, facial expressions and hand gestures, where appropriate.

(Points adapted from Hayman, 1998.)

Visual impairment

Visual impairment causes many communication difficulties. Not only is an individual unable to pick up the visual signals which are being given out by someone who is speaking, but, because he or she is unaware of these signals, may also fail to give appropriate signals in communication. This lack of non-verbal communication and lack of ability to receive and interpret non-verbal communication can lead to misunderstandings about a person's attitudes and behaviour. It means that communications can easily be misinterpreted, or it could be thought that he or she is behaving in an inappropriate way.

For people with limited vision it may be important to use language to describe things that a sighted person may take for granted, such as non-verbal communication or the context of certain comments. Touch may be an important aspect of communication; some registered blind people can work out what you look like if they can touch your face in order to build an understanding of your features.

Physical disability

Depending on the disability, this can have various effects. People who have suffered strokes, for example, will often have communication difficulties such as dysphasia – a problem with finding the right words or interpreting the meanings of words said to them. This condition is very distressing for the individual and for those who are trying to communicate. Often this is coupled with a loss of movement and a difficulty in using facial muscles to form words.

In some cases, the communication difficulty is a symptom of a disability. For example, many people with cerebral palsy and motor neurone disease have difficulty in controlling the muscles that affect voice production, and speaking in a way which can be readily understood becomes very difficult. Other disabilities may have no effect at all upon voice production or the thought processes that produce spoken words, but the lack of other body movements may mean that non-verbal communication may be difficult or not what you would expect.

Remember

Communication differences can result as much from differences in attitude as they can from differences in language or abilities.

Learning disabilities

These may, depending on their severity, cause differences in communication in terms of the level of understanding of the individual and his or her ability to respond appropriately to any form of communication. This will vary depending on the degree of learning disability of the individual, but broadly the effect of learning disabilities is to limit the ability of an individual to understand and process information given to him or her. It is also possible that individuals will have a short attention span, so this may mean that communications have to be repeated several times or perhaps paraphrased in an appropriate form. It will be very important to use words and phrases that the service user is familiar with.

Dementia/confusion

This condition is most prevalent in older people and the most common type is caused by Alzheimer's disease. People with Alzheimer's can ultimately lose the ability to communicate, but in the early stages it involves short-term memory loss to the extent of being unable to remember the essential parts of a conversation or a recent exchange.

People with memory disorders often substitute inappropriate words. A 90-year-old service user may say: 'My mother visited me yesterday'. On the surface, such

Key terms

Dementia: A condition involving a loss of mental powers, in particular of memory.

a statement appears to be irrational. From a care perspective it is very important not to challenge the rationality of what is being said; the most important thing is to make the older person feel valued and respected. Perhaps you know that the visitor was in fact, a daughter, and the service user has simply used an incorrect word. The important thing is that the service user feels safe and respected.

Sometimes a service user may be disorientated and make statements about needing to go to work or to go home to look after the children. Once again, it is important not to argue, but rather to try to divert the conversation in a way that interests and values the person. For example:

Service user: I must go home and get the tea ready for my children.

Care worker: All right, shall we walk to your room, then? You might want your coat.

Service user: Yes, that's right, you're so kind.

Care worker [now in service user's room]:
Is this photograph of your son and daughter?

Service user: Yes, that's right.

Care worker: They've both got married now – aren't they both grown up?

Service user: Yes, I'm very proud of them – they're coming to visit me tomorrow.

Care worker: That's wonderful. Why don't we go downstairs and have a cup of tea?

Service user: Yes, that would be very nice – you're so kind to me.

In the exchange above, the care worker has avoided arguing about logic, and instead has gently helped the service user to remember the age her children are now. Throughout the conversation, the care worker has shown respect for the service user.

The most important aspect of communication is to show that you value and respect individuals

Cultural differences

People's communication differences can result from differences in culture and background. Culture is about more than language – it is about the way that people live, think and relate to each other. In some cultures, for example, children are not allowed to speak in the presence of certain adults. Other cultures do not allow women to speak to men they do not know.

Some people may have been brought up in a background or in a period of time when challenging authority by asking questions was not acceptable. Such people may find it very hard to ask questions of doctors or other health professionals and are unlikely to feel able to raise any queries about how their care or treatment should be carried out.

It is important to be able to identify the different interpretations that words and body language can have in different cultures. This is not a straightforward issue; words and signs can mean different things depending on their context.

Taking account of context

Making sense of spoken language requires knowledge of the context and intentions of the speaker. Understanding **non-verbal communication** involves exactly the same need to understand the circumstances and cultural context of the other person. For example, in Britain the hand gesture with palm up and facing forwards means: 'Stop, don't do that.' In Greece it can mean 'You are dirt' and is a very rude gesture.

Communication is always influenced by cultural systems of meaning, and different cultures interpret body language differently. An almost infinite variety of meanings can be given to any type of eye contact, facial expression, posture or gesture. Every culture develops its own special system of meanings. Care workers have to understand and show respect and value for all these different systems of sending messages.

No one can learn every system of non-verbal communication, but it is possible to learn about the ones used by people you are working with. This can be done first by noticing and remembering what others do – the non-verbal messages they are sending. The next step is to think about the messages the person is trying to give you. Finally, check your understanding with the person.

Remember

The word 'wicked', can have different meanings. If an older person used this phrase to describe his or her experience of the Second World War, the phrase would mean 'horrific' or 'terrible'. In a TV comedy from 15 years ago, the phrase would mean 'cool' – something very desirable. In a religious context, 'wicked' might relate to the concept of sin.

Key terms

Non-verbal communication: A way of communicating without words, through body language, gestures, facial expression and eye contact.

Keys to good practice: Skilled communication

Skilled communication involves:

✓ observing the person with whom you are communicating

✓ noticing facial expressions and movements

✓ interpreting what words and actions mean and then checking your understanding with the person

✓ never relying on your own understanding, you may be wrong.

For example, you may be working with a man who has very poor speech following a stroke. He is making noises and is clearly trying to indicate something to you. He is moving his hand and eyes in the direction of the window:

- You ask if he wants the window open – he gets more agitated and shakes his head
- You ask if he wants the curtains drawn – he shakes his head again
- You think about what you were talking about before he started to try to tell you something – it was about his family, and his children and grandchildren coming to visit
- You ask if it is the photo on the window sill he wants – he nods and smiles
- You then sit with him for a few more minutes and talk about the people in the photograph, making sure that any questions just need a nod or shake of the head.

Effects of communication differences

A major effect of communication differences is for people to feel frustrated and isolated. It is an important part of your job to do everything in your power to reduce the effect of communication differences and to try to lessen the feelings of isolation and frustration that people experience.

Evidence   PC 2 3

Think of a situation at work when you have communicated with an individual you did not know well.

How did you decide on the best methods of communicating with them?

Did you need to change your communication to suit them?

Did you need to seek advice to help you?

How to find out about likely communication problems

KS 1 3 4 5 6 7 10 19

You can discover likely communication issues by simply observing an individual. You can find out a great deal about how a person communicates and what the differences are between his or her way of communicating and your own.

Observation should be able to establish:

- which language is being used
- if the service user experiences any hearing or visual impairment
- if there is any physical illness or disability
- if there is a learning disability.

Any of these factors could have a bearing on how well you will be able to communicate with someone, and what steps you may need to take to make things easier. Observation will give you some very good clues to start with, but you should work with the individual to establish exactly what is needed to assist communication. You may also consider:

- discussing with colleagues who have worked with the individual before and who are likely to have some background information and advice
- consulting other professionals who have worked with the individual and may have knowledge of means of communication which have been effective for them
- reading previous case notes or case histories
- finding out as much as you can about an individual's particular illness or disability, where you have been able to establish this – the most useful sources of information are likely to be the specialist agencies for the particular condition
- talking to family or friends. They are likely to have a great deal of information about what the differences in communication are for the individual. They will have developed ways of dealing with communication, possibly over a long period of time, and are likely to be a very useful source of advice and help.

How to record information

There would be little point in finding out about effective means of communication with someone and then not making an accurate record so that other people can also communicate with that person.

You should find out your employer's policy on where such information is to be recorded – it is likely to be in the service user's case notes.

Be sure that you record:

- the nature of the communication differences

- how they show themselves
- ways which you have found to be effective in overcoming the differences.

Information recorded in notes may look like this:

Communication plan for Mr Groves

Mr Groves has communication difficulties following surgery to remove a tumour from his tongue. His speech is slurred, but possible to understand with care. He is inclined to get frustrated when he cannot make himself understood.

Recommended actions:

- involve his key worker, Jessie, in information exchanges where possible
- provide communication flashcards to help him communicate
- ensure key conversations take place on a one-to-one basis, especially when providing information
- his own room is the best place for communication
- in the dining room, seat him by the window where it is quieter.

 Keys to good practice: Communicating effectively

✓ Check what the differences in communication are.

✓ Remember they can be cultural as well as physical.

✓ Work with individuals to understand their preferred methods of communication and language.

✓ Use all possible sources to obtain information and advice where you have difficulty communicating.

Evidence   PC 3 6

Think of a service user you have worked with who has communication difficulties. Write notes that would be useful for your colleagues, describing:

- the communication difficulties involved
- the approaches you use to promote effective communication.

Keep your notes for your portfolio.

Overcoming difficulties in communication

KS 2 3 6 7 8 9 10 11 12 13 14 15

Language differences

Where you are in the position of providing care for someone who speaks a different language from you, it is clear that you will need the services of an interpreter for any serious discussions or communication.

- Your work setting is likely to have a contact list of interpreters.
- Social services departments and the police have lists of interpreters.
- The embassy or consulate for the appropriate country will also have a list of qualified interpreters.

You should always use professional interpreters wherever possible. It may be very tempting to use other members of the family – very often children have excellent language skills – but it is inappropriate in most care settings. This is because:

- their English and their ability to interpret may not be at the same standard as a professional interpreter, and misunderstandings can easily occur
- you may wish to discuss matters which are not appropriate to be discussed with children, or the individual may not want members of his or her family involved in very personal discussions about health or care issues.

It is unlikely that you would be able to have a full-time interpreter available throughout someone's period of care, so it is necessary to consider alternatives for encouraging everyday communication.

Be prepared to learn words in the individual's language which will help communication. You could try to give the person some words in your language if he or she is willing and able to learn them.

There are other simple techniques that you may wish to try which can help basic levels of communication. For example, you could use flashcards or sign language, as you would for a person who has suffered a stroke.

Sign language and gestures can help with basic levels of communication

The suggestions shown on the previous page are not exhaustive and you will come up with many which are appropriate for the individual and for your particular care setting. They are a helpful way of assisting with simple communication and allowing people to express their immediate physical needs.

The most effective way of communicating with a person who speaks a different language is through non-verbal communication. A smile and a friendly face are understood in all languages, as are a concerned facial expression and a warm and welcoming body position.

However, be careful about the use of gestures – gestures which are acceptable in one culture may not be acceptable in all. For example, an extended thumb in some cultures would mean 'great, that's fine, OK', but in many cultures it is an extremely offensive gesture. If you are unsure which gestures are acceptable in another culture, make sure that you check before using any which may be misinterpreted.

CASE STUDY: A universal language

A Russian teacher accompanied a group of students on a visit to England. All of the party were staying with host families and the teacher was placed with a woman of similar age (early forties) who was a single parent with a teenage son. Neither woman spoke any of the other's language.

On the first morning the organiser of the trip spoke to the host family on the telephone and asked how the two women had got on the previous evening. He was amazed to be told that, despite not speaking a word of each other's language, they had spent the evening sitting either side of the fire with a bottle of wine and that both knew each other's life stories. They had managed to tell each other of their marriages, divorces and problems with their children. They had laughed and cried together, and had achieved all of this by using family photographs, gestures and facial expressions, and by speaking in their own language had managed to communicate their entire life histories. The two women had ended the evening firm friends and this continued throughout the rest of the visit.

1 *How do you think the women managed to communicate?*

2 *What methods of communication would you have used if you were in that situation?*

3 *Do you think it is significant that they were both middle-aged women with no disabilities? Why?*

4 *Can you think of a situation in your workplace which has any similarities to this?*

Hearing difficulties

- Ensure that any means of improving hearing which an individual uses, for example a hearing aid, is working properly and is fitted correctly, that the batteries are working, that it is clean and that it is doing its job properly in terms of improving the individual's hearing.
- Ensure that you are sitting in a good light, not too far away and that you speak clearly, but do not shout. Shouting simply distorts your face and makes it more difficult for a person with hearing loss to be able to read what you are saying.

- Be prepared to write things down if the service user prefers you to do this in order to communicate clearly.

Some people may be able to lip read, while many will use a form of sign language for understanding. This may be BSL (British Sign Language). The British Deaf Association states that BSL is a first or preferred language for nearly 70,000 people in the UK. Some deaf people may use MAKATON, a system for developing language that uses speech, signs and symbols to help people with learning difficulties to communicate and to develop their language skills. It may involve speaking a word and performing a sign using hands and body language. There are a large range of symbols that may help people with a learning difficulty to recognise an idea or to communicate with others.

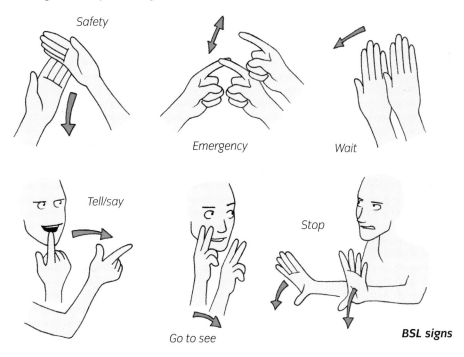

BSL signs

Other services which are extremely helpful to people who have hearing difficulties are telecommunication services, such as using a minicom or typetalk service. These allow a spoken conversation to be translated in written form using a form of typewriter, and the responses can be passed in the same way by an operator who will relay them to the hearing person. These services have provided a major advance in enabling people who are hard of hearing or profoundly deaf to use telephone equipment. For people who are less severely affected by hearing impairment, there are facilities such as raising the volume on telephone receivers to allow them to hear conversations more clearly.

Visual difficulties

One of the commonest ways of assisting people who have visual impairment is to provide them with glasses or contact lenses. You need to be sure that these are clean and that they are the correct prescription. You might advise older people to have their eyes tested every year, in order to check for diseases such as glaucoma. Younger people might be advised to have their eyes checked every two years. A person whose eyesight and requirements for glasses have changed will obviously have difficulty in picking up many of the non-verbal signals which you will be giving out when you are communicating with him or her.

For people with more serious loss or impairment, you will need to take other steps to ensure that you minimise the differences that will exist in your styles of communication.

People should have their eyes tested regularly in order to check their prescription and health

 Keys to good practice: Communicating with people who have visual impairment

✓ Do not suddenly begin to speak to someone without first of all letting him or her know that you are there. One way to do this is to touch him or her, but check that the service user is comfortable with this approach.

✓ Make sure that you introduce yourself when you come into a room. It is easy to forget that someone cannot see. A simple 'hello John, it's Sue' is all that is needed so that you don't 'arrive' unexpectedly.

✓ You may need to use touch more than you would in speaking to a sighted person, because the concerns that you will be expressing through your face and your general body movements will not be seen. So, if you are expressing concern or sympathy, it may be appropriate to touch someone's hand or arm, at the same time that you are saying you are concerned and sympathetic.

Continued

Keys to good practice: Communicating with people who have visual impairment (cont.)

✓ Ask the individual what system of communication he or she requires – do not impose your idea of appropriate systems on the person. Most people who are visually impaired know very well what they can and cannot do, and if you ask they will tell you exactly what they need you to do.

✓ Do not decide that you know the best way to help. Never take the arm of someone who is visually impaired to help him or her to move around. Allow the person to take your arm or shoulder, to ask for guidance and tell you where he or she wishes to go.

Physical disabilities

Physical disability or illness has to be dealt with according to the nature of the disability or the illness. For example, if you were communicating with someone who had a stroke you would have to work out ways of coping with his or her dysphasia (speech difficulties). This is best dealt with by:

● using very simple, short sentences, speaking slowly and being prepared to wait while the individual processes what you have said and composes a reply

● using gestures – they are helpful in terms of making it easier for people to understand the ideas you are trying to get across

● using drawing, writing or flashcards to help understanding

● using very simple, closed questions which only need a 'yes' or 'no' answer. Avoid long, complicated sentences with interrelated ideas. For example, do not say: 'It's getting near tea time now, isn't it? How about some tea? Have you thought about what you would like?' Instead, say: 'Are you hungry? Would you like fish? Would you like chicken?' and so on, until you have established what sort of meal the individual would prefer.

Other illnesses, such as motor neurone disease or cerebral palsy, can also lead to difficulties in making speech, although not in understanding it.

● The individual will understand perfectly what you are saying to him or her but the difficulty will be in communicating with you.

● There is no need for you to speak slowly, although you will have to be prepared to allow time for a response owing to the difficulties that the individual will have in producing words.

● You will have to become familiar with the sound of the individual's voice and the way in which he or she communicates. It can be hard to understand people who have illnesses which affect their facial, throat or larynx muscles.

Learning disabilities

Where people have a learning disability, you will need to adjust your methods of communicating to take account of the level of disability that they experience. You should have gathered sufficient information about the individual to know the level of understanding that he or she has – how simply and how often you need to explain things and the kinds of communication which are likely to be the most effective.

Many people with a learning disability respond well to physical contact and are able to relate and communicate on a physical level more easily than on a verbal level. This will vary between individuals and you should be prepared to use a great deal of physical contact and hugs when communicating with people who have a learning disability.

Cultural differences

Communication is about much more than words being exchanged between two people – it is influenced by a great many factors. The way in which people have been brought up and the society and culture that they live in has a great effect on the way in which they communicate.

For example, some cultures use gestures or touch much more than others. In some cultures it is acceptable to stand very close to someone, whereas in others people feel extremely uncomfortable if others stand too close. You need to find out about the person's background when you are thinking about how you can make communication work for him or her.

To find out the information you need, ask the individual if possible, and/or:
- look in the person's records
- speak to a member of the family or a friend, if this is possible
- ask someone else from the same culture, either a colleague or through the country's cultural representatives (contact the embassy or consulate and ask for the information) – alternatively you could try a local multicultural organisation
- use reference books, if necessary.

It is also important that you communicate with people at the correct intellectual level. Make sure that you communicate with them at a language level which they are likely to understand, but not find patronising. For example, older people and people who have disabilities have every right to be spoken to as adults and not patronised or talked down to. One of the commonest complaints from people with physical disabilities is that people will talk to their carers about them rather than talk to them directly – this is known as the 'does he take sugar' approach.

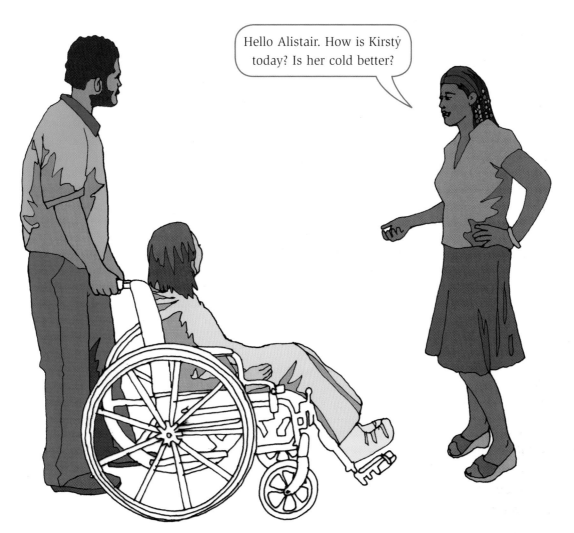

CASE STUDY: Communicating about cultural differences

Mrs Khan came to live in Britain about eight years ago. She came with her son and daughter-in-law from a small village in Afghanistan. She has always lived quietly with her family and has not needed to adapt her way of life to fit in with the different ways of doing things in her adopted country.

Now 86, Mrs Khan has mobility problems, and a domiciliary care worker has recently begun to visit to help with daily living tasks. One day Mrs Khan had a fall, which has left her with a leg wound that needs regular dressing.

1 *What communication issues would be involved in providing care for Mrs Khan?*

2 *What cultural differences might need to be addressed?*

3 *If you were supervising staff responsible for caring for Mrs Khan, how would you prepare them to deal with this situation successfully?*

Evidence   PC ① ③ ⑥

Find out the policy in your workplace for checking on people's cultural preferences. Ask who establishes the information about the cultural background of people who use your service, and what the policies are to ensure their needs are met. Make notes for your portfolio.

Making sure you have been understood

Although it is unacceptable to talk down to people, it is pointless trying to communicate with them by using so much jargon and medical terminology that they don't understand anything you have said. You must be sure that your communication is being understood. The most straightforward way to do this is to ask someone to recap on what you have discussed.

You could say something like: 'Can we just go over this so that we are both sure about what is happening – you tell me what is happening tomorrow'. Alternatively you can rephrase what you have just said and check with the individual that he or she has understood. For example:

'The bus is coming earlier than usual tomorrow because of the trip. It will be here at eight o'clock instead of nine – is that OK?'

'Yes.'

'So, you're sure that you can be up and ready by eight o'clock to go on the trip?'

Remember

If you are planning communication with somebody who has a sensory impairment or who has a learning disability, you will need to take account of this and adjust your communication so that it is at a level he or she is able to understand and make sense of. The single most important factor in communicating is that you are understood.

Communication through actions

For many people, it is easier to communicate by actions than by words. You will need to make sure that you respond in an appropriate way by recognising the significance of a touch or a sudden movement from someone who is ill and bedridden, or a gesture from someone who speaks a different language. A gesture can indicate what his or her needs are and what sort of response the person is looking for from you.

You may be faced with a young person with challenging behaviour who throws something at you – this is a means of communication. It may not be a very pleasant one, but nonetheless, it expresses much of the person's hurt, anger and distress. It is important that you recognise this for what it is and respond in the same way you would if that person had been able to express his or her feelings in words.

Encouraging communication

The best way to ensure that someone is able to communicate to the best of his or her ability is to make the person feel as comfortable and as relaxed as possible. There are several factors to consider when thinking about how to make people feel confident enough to communicate. They are summarised in the table on the next page.

Communication difference	Encouraging actions
Different language	• Smile • Have a friendly facial expression • Use gestures • Use pictures • Show warmth and encouragement – repeat their words with a smile to check understanding
Hearing impairment	• Speak clearly, listen carefully, respond to what is said to you • Remove any distractions and other noises • Make sure any aids to hearing are working • Use written communication where appropriate • Use signing where appropriate • Use properly trained interpreter if high level of skill is required
Visual impairment	• Use touch if appropriate to communicate concern, sympathy and interest • Use tone of voice rather than facial expressions to communicate mood and response • Do not rely on non-verbal communication i.e. facial expression or nodding head • Ensure that all visual communication is transferred into something which can be heard, either a tape or somebody reading
Confusion or dementia	• Try to make sense of communication by interpreting non-verbal behaviour • Focus on showing respect and maintaining the dignity of the other person • Do not challenge confused statements with logic • Re-orientate the conversation if you need to • Remain patient • Be very clear and keep conversation short and simple • Use simple written communication or pictures where they seem to help
Physical disability	• Ensure that surroundings are appropriate and accessible • Allow for difficulties with voice production if necessary • Do not patronise • Remember that some body language may not be appropriate
Learning disability	• Judge appropriate level of understanding • Make sure that you respond at the right level • Remain patient and be prepared to keep covering the same ground • Be prepared to wait and listen carefully to responses

Use signing where it is appropriate and understood

 Keys to good practice: Responding appropriately

✓ The single most important thing that you need to remember is that you must tailor your response to the individual person, not the condition.

Dealing with problems

You will be better able to anticipate and deal with any problems if you are well informed about the issues on which you are communicating, and have a good idea of the potential reactions of the individual. If you are in any doubt, make sure you check this information with your supervisor and the appropriate key people – remembering to respect confidentiality.

You must also be alert to the fact that individuals' needs do change, and that a method of communication which was effective in the past may not continue to be appropriate. Be prepared to change your approach and to seek additional help if necessary.

The risk of stereotyping

It can be very hard to really understand people's needs. Sometimes it can be tempting to make life easier by relying on fixed ideas to explain 'what people are like'. When a person has fixed ideas that he or she uses and regards certain types of people as all being the same, this is called **stereotyping**. Skilled caring starts from being interested in people's individual differences.

Stereotypes of people with disabilities are common. Disabled people are often understood as damaged versions of 'normal' people. When disabled people are negatively stereotyped in this way, they may be pitied or ignored.

Older people are often negatively stereotyped. Old age is sometimes thought of as a time of decline and decay. The individual potential of a person is ignored and he or she becomes just another 'problem'.

A negative stereotype of old people might include concepts such as the ones below:

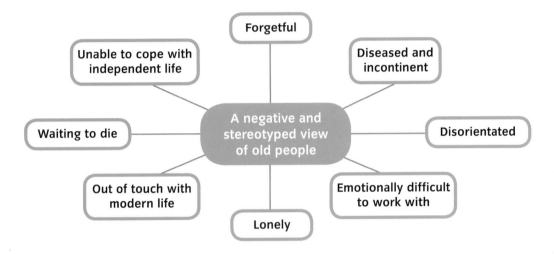

Stereotyped thinking might result in a care worker ignoring a service user's rights. For example, a worker might think 'I won't offer this person a choice because she's old – old people don't remember, so it doesn't matter what I do'.

In working with a service user you will need to be aware of the potential views of others and be ready to counteract any stereotyping or labelling which may be taking place. Be aware of the fact that assumptions may be made about the abilities of the service user.

For example, it is not uncommon to underestimate what people with learning difficulties can achieve. There is also a commonly held belief that people with Alzheimer's disease need round-the-clock protection. This is not always the case and many people who have Alzheimer's are capable of achieving a great deal of independence, provided that the environment in which they live is suitably adapted.

You will need to be aware of the assumptions that may be made, and the ways in which stereotyping and labelling can affect individuals.

Test yourself

1 Why is it important to pass on information about an individual's communication needs and preferences?

2 What steps could you take to improve communication with someone following a stroke? List three.

3 An 80-year-old woman brought up in an industrial town is living in a care home. One of the care assistants is the 25-year-old son of an Indian consultant cardiac surgeon. What would you expect to be the cultural differences between them?

4 What would you need to do if an issue to be communicated was outside your area of expertise?

5 What factors would you take into account when judging the best way to communicate with someone from a different country?

6 What do you need to do to encourage someone with visual impairment to feel confident about communicating?

7 What is the most important purpose of communication?

HSC 31b Communicate effectively on difficult, complex and sensitive issues

Communicating about difficult issues

 KS 15 16

The individual and his or her needs should be at the centre of the care process. Your role is to make sure that service users have every opportunity to state exactly how they wish their needs to be met, and this is especially important when the issues are difficult, sensitive or complex. Some service users will be able to give this information personally; others will need an advocate who will support them in expressing their views.

Developing relationships

Communication is the basis of all relationships, regardless of whether the relationships are personal or professional. As individuals communicate, a relationship is formed. This is usually a two-way process as each individual involved gets to know the other through a process of communicating and sharing information.

When you provide care for someone, you will get to know and talk to him or her, and a relationship will grow. This is not easy with all individuals you care for. When there appears to be little communication, you may find that forming a relationship is difficult.

Stages of an interaction

Communication between individuals in called an 'interaction'. As you spend time in communication with someone, the nature of the interaction will go through changes.

- *Stage 1:* Introduction, light and general. At first, the content of the communication may be of little significance. This is the stage at which both parties decide whether they want to continue the discussion, and how comfortable they feel. Body language and non-verbal communication are very important at this stage.

Body language and non-verbal communication are always important

- *Stage 2:* Main contact, significant information. The middle of any interaction is likely to contain the 'meat', and this is where you will need to use active listening skills to ensure that the interaction is beneficial.
- *Stage 3:* Reflect, wind up, end positively. People often have the greatest difficulty in knowing how to end an interaction. Ending in a positive way where all participants are left feeling that they have benefited from the interaction is very important. You may find that you have to end an interaction because of time restrictions, or you may feel that enough has been covered – the other person may need a rest, or you may need a break!

At the end of an interaction you should always try to reflect on the areas you have covered, and offer a positive and encouraging ending, for example: 'I'm glad you've talked about how unhappy you've been feeling. Now we can try to work at making things better.'

Even if the content of an interaction has been fairly negative, you should encourage the individual to see the fact that the interaction has taken place as being positive in itself.

If you are called away before you have had a chance to properly 'wind up' an interaction with an individual, make a point of returning to end things in a positive way. If you say 'I'll be back in a minute', make sure that you do go back.

Communication with service users

The principles of good communication are an important part of making sure that the individual is fully involved in dealing with any issues or difficult situations. The impact of dealing with situations in a way which makes people feel valued is enormous. Often the steps are small and do not take a great deal of effort or demand major changes – but the results are so effective that any effort you have made will be repaid many times over by the positive benefits for the individuals you care for.

CASE STUDY: Service users' beliefs

Hafsah is from Somalia in Africa and is a devout Muslim. She had her first baby in hospital in the UK. Following the delivery, Hafsah refused to get out of bed, and would press the buzzer every time she wanted anything, including asking staff to take her baby from the cot and give him to her to feed. This was in accordance with her own culture in which a new mother remains in bed for ten days after giving birth. During that time everything is done for her and her baby, and all she does is feed the baby. It is usually her mother-in-law or another female relative who takes control during this time.

The ward staff became resentful of the demands that Hafsah was making. They were not always as pleasant as they might be when they were called into her room. Hafsah became very distressed and was agitated and nervous each time she needed assistance. She began to have problems feeding the baby. There was a great deal of concern about this and about her refusal to get out of bed, and she was encouraged to do so. The midwives explained to her that she ran the risk of thrombosis or other circulatory problems if she continued to lie in bed.

A solution was eventually found by allowing her mother-in-law to remain with her in a side room to provide the care needed. But Hafsah could still not be persuaded to get out of bed. As she had been provided with all the information about possible consequences, and she had made an informed choice consistent with her own beliefs, her decision to stay in bed had to be respected.

1 *What were the issues presented by Hafsah's beliefs?*

2 *Do you think the situation was handled correctly?*

3 *What would you have done?*

Keys to good practice: Communicating on difficult or complex issues

✓ Arrange the immediate environment to ensure privacy, make communication easier and aid understanding.

✓ Check that individuals have the appropriate support to communicate their views and preferences.

✓ Use styles and methods of communication that are appropriate to the individual and the subject matter.

✓ Give individuals sufficient time to understand the content of the communication.

✓ Observe and respond appropriately to their reactions.

Life stages and development

 KS 8

One of the most significant influences on communication and the way people deal with difficult or stressful issues is the life stage they are at. The chart below will help you to understand the life stages service users are either at, or have experienced.

	Intellectual/cognitive	Social/emotional	Language	Physical
Infant, birth–1 year	Learns about new things by feeling with hands and mouth objects encountered in immediate environment	Attaches to parent(s), begins to recognise faces and smile; at about 6 months begins to recognise parent(s) and expresses fear of strangers, plays simple interactive games like peekaboo	Vocalises, squeals, and imitates sounds, says 'dada' and 'mama'	Lifts head first then chest, rolls over, pulls to sit, crawls and stands alone. Reaches for objects and rakes up small items, grasps rattle
Toddler, 1–2 years	Extends knowledge by learning words for objects in environment	Learns that self and parent(s) are different or separate from each other, imitates and performs tasks, indicates needs or wants without crying	Says some words other than 'dada' and 'mama', follows simple instructions	Walks well, kicks, stoops and jumps in place, throws balls. Unbuttons clothes, builds tower of 4 cubes, scribbles, uses spoon, picks up very small objects

Continued

	Intellectual/cognitive	Social/emotional	Language	Physical
Pre-school, 2–5 years	Understands concepts such as tired, hungry and other bodily states, recognises colours, becomes aware of numbers and letters	Begins to separate easily from parent(s), dresses with assistance, washes and dries hands, plays interactive games like tag	Names pictures, follows directions, can make simple sentences of two or three words, vocabulary increases	Runs well, hops, pedals tricycle, balances on one foot. Buttons clothes, builds tower of 8 cubes, copies simple figures or letters, for example 0, begins to use scissors
School age, 5–12 years	Develops understanding of numeracy and literacy concepts, learns relationship between objects and feelings, acquires knowledge and understanding	Acts independently, but is emotionally close to parent(s), dresses without assistance, joins same-sex play groups and clubs	Defines words, knows and describes what things are made of, vocabulary increases	Skips, balances on one foot for 10 seconds, overestimates physical abilities. Draws person with 6 parts, copies detailed figures and objects
Adolescent, 12–18 years	Understands abstract concepts like illness and death, develops understanding of complex concepts	Experiences rapidly changing moods and behaviour, interested in peer group almost exclusively, distances from parent(s) emotionally, concerned with body image, experiences falling in and out of love	Uses increased vocabulary, understands more abstract concepts such as grief	May appear awkward and clumsy while learning to deal with rapid increases in size due to growth spurts

Continued

	Intellectual/cognitive	Social/emotional	Language	Physical
Young adult, 18–40 years	Continues to develop the ability to make good decisions and to understand the complexity of human relationships – sometimes called wisdom	Becomes independent from parent(s), develops own lifestyle, selects a career, copes with career, social and economic changes and social expectations, chooses a partner, learns to live co-operatively with partner, becomes a parent	Continues to develop vocabulary and knowledge of different styles of language use	Fully developed
Middle age 40–65 years	Continues to develop a deeper understanding of life – sometimes called wisdom	Builds social and economic status, is fulfilled by work or family, copes with physical changes of ageing, children grow and leave nest, deals with ageing parents, copes with the death of parents	Vocabulary may continue to develop	Begins to experience physical signs of ageing
Older adult, 65+ years	Ability may be influenced by health factors; some indviduals will continue to develop 'wisdom'	Adjusts to retirement, adjusts to loss of friends and relatives, copes with loss of spouse, adjusts to new role in family, copes with dying	Ability may be influenced by health factors; some individuals may continue to develop language skills	Experiences more significant physical changes associated with ageing

It will be important to communicate with children in a different way from adults. Children will have different emotional, social, intellectual and language needs. They may not understand some of the long words that adults might use. Children will also think differently from adults; conversation may not work in the same way. If you ask children to tell you about their past life, they might only be able to tell you about very practical, concrete experiences such as a birthday party or where they went on holiday. Adults might be able to organise their life story into themes about jobs, relationships and aspirations.

Working with younger people, and working with adults with a learning difficulty, may mean that care workers have to support service users to organise their thoughts. You might find out about a child's past life by starting a scrapbook and gradually talk through different events in order to learn about the child's thoughts and feelings. Some adults may not need this kind of support – they can think abstractly and organise their thoughts in response to your questions.

Communicating with older adults

Older adults may also have quite different emotional, social, intellectual and conversational needs compared with young adults.

Imagine you are talking with Mrs Hemshore. She is 85 years old and has been telling you her life story. She then says: 'Now you won't understand this – you're too young to understand this – but I've had my life, and it's been a good life. I've done everything I wanted to do, and now I'm ready to die. It's not that I want to be dead, it's just that I'm very tired and it's right and proper that my life should end now. I'm not depressed and I'm not ill. What I really appreciate is just having you here to listen to me. There isn't anything for you to say – I just want someone to listen to me while I make sense of things. At your age, I guess you can't understand just how important this is for me.'

If a 25-year-old said something like this it might suggest a serious difficulty, but the needs of people in later life may be quite different from the needs of young adults. The ability to listen and provide a 'caring presence' may be central to meeting the needs and preserving the self-esteem of people in later life.

Encouraging conversation is a key way of supporting some service users

Physical effects of strong emotions

There are definite and measurable physical effects caused by strong emotional responses. It is useful to be aware of these effects of emotion as they can often be an early indicator of a potentially highly charged or dangerous situation. The physical effects of strong emotion can be:

- pupils dilate, the eyelids open wider than usual, and the eyes protrude
- speed and strength of heart beat is increased
- blood pressure is increased and blood is forced towards the surface of the body; this is clearly noticeable in flushing of the face and neck
- the hair can stand up, causing goose pimples
- breathing patterns will change
- the lung function alters to allow up to 25 per cent more oxygen to be absorbed
- more sweat is produced – this can often be identified as a 'cold sweat'
- the salivary glands are inhibited – resulting in the dry mouth feeling
- the digestive system is affected – the gastric fluids are reduced and blood is withdrawn from the digestive organs
- there is an increase in adrenaline – this reinforces all effects and increases blood clotting.

There are other very noticeable effects in people in a highly emotional state. They will often have what appears to be increased energy. For example, they don't speak, they shout; they don't sit or stand still, they run or walk about; they will slam doors and possibly throw furniture or objects around.

The additional energy and strength which result from powerful emotions can be extremely valuable and indeed essential in preserving life. There are many stories about people performing heroic feats of strength when in severe danger, as in the case of a fire, an accident or other life-threatening situation.

Another apparent effect of strong emotional responses is a temporary lessening of the awareness of pain. This often occurs when people act regardless of severe injury, as on the battlefield or in an accident or other emergency, and it is only when the immediate threat has passed that they become aware of their injuries.

Did you know?

These responses are said to prepare humans for 'fight or flight'. This is thought to be a basic human response to being under threat, in which the body physically prepares us to fight or run away.

How people control strong emotions

In growing and developing, most of us learn to control our powerful emotions. The sight of a two-year-old lying on the floor in a supermarket kicking and screaming is not uncommon – it is one which is accepted as normal behaviour for a child of that age. On the other hand, it is not socially acceptable for an adult to do the same thing, however much we may want to on occasions! We don't behave in this way in public because we have been socialised into behaviour which is accepted as the norm in society. However, some people do find it beneficial and therapeutic to have a tantrum in the privacy of their homes, to get relief from the rage they feel.

We can accept children having tantrums in public, but not adults

Active knowledge

Think about how you deal with emotions. Think of the occasions when you have felt strong and powerful emotions but managed to keep them under control and not show your distress publicly, and other occasions when you have shown public distress.

Try to identify the difference in circumstances and the factors which caused the two different responses.

Becoming distressed

 KS 9 15

Most people most of the time behave within the accepted norms of society. However, on occasions the emotions may become too powerful or the normal control which people exercise over their emotions may relax, resulting in a display of emotion which is recognised as distress. People can become distressed because of a wide range of causes, but some common causes of distress can be identified and it is helpful for you to be aware of situations and circumstances which can act as triggers. People commonly become distressed when:

- they are informed of the death or serious illness of someone close to them
- they receive bad or worrying news
- there are problems with a relationship that is important to them
- they become stressed through an overload of work or family pressures
- they have serious problems which worry them, to do with money, work or the family

- they are reacting to the behaviour of others towards them
- they are responding to something that they have heard, seen or read in the media
- they are in an environment that they find frustrating or restricting
- they are in an environment that they find intensely irritating, e.g. it is noisy or they are unable to find any personal space
- they are deprived of information and are fearful
- they have full information about a situation and they remain fearful of it
- they are anxious about a forthcoming event
- they are unable to achieve the objectives they have set themselves.

These are some of the more common triggers for distress. Clearly there are many others which you may come across depending on the setting in which you work.

Everyone has a breaking point

 Active knowledge

Identify six potential triggers for distress which relate to your own work setting.

How to identify when someone is becoming distressed

 KS 9 15

When you have a close working knowledge of an individual's behaviour over a period of time it becomes easy to identify when he or she is becoming distressed. You will find that you have become 'tuned-in' to individual behaviour and can recognise the small signs that indicate a change in mood. However, you will not always know your service users so well. Also, you may have to deal with distress not only in a service user, but also in a carer or a work colleague.

There are some general indications that an individual is becoming distressed which you can use in order to take immediate action. You are most likely to notice:

- changes in **voice** – it may be raised or at a higher pitch than usual
- changes in **facial expression** – this could be scowling, frowning, snarling
- changes in **eyes** – pupils could be dilated and eyes open wider
- **body language** would demonstrate agitation and people may adopt an aggressive stance, leaning forwards with fists clenched
- the **face and neck** are likely to be reddened
- there may be excessive **sweating**
- people's **breathing patterns** may change and they may breathe faster than normal.

You are likely to notice a significant change in normal behaviour when someone is becoming distressed. For example, someone who is normally talkative may become quiet and someone who is normally quiet may start to shout or talk very quickly. Other examples are someone who is normally lively becoming still and rigid, or someone who is normally relaxed starting to walk around waving his or her arms.

You need to be aware of changes in normal behaviour even if they are far less extreme than these examples. Sometimes a subtle change in behaviour can indicate someone is becoming distressed, and you are far more likely to notice subtle changes in individuals, colleagues or carers whom you know well and have worked with over a period of time.

CASE STUDY: Signs of distress

Liz is an elderly lady who has been in a residential home for the past three years. Like most of the residents she has her own chair and she likes to sit in a corner of the main lounge. Liz is normally bright and chatty and talks happily with the staff and other residents.

As with many residential settings there is a regular influx of new residents, who usually adapt to the setting extremely well. However, the previous week a new resident was admitted who, like Liz, was very talkative and friendly, but she would continue to talk at great length and quite loudly for long periods of time. For the first couple of days Liz appeared to join in and respond to the new lady's conversation, but staff noticed she gradually responded less and less and appeared to be becoming more unhappy. One morning a staff member went into the lounge, where the new lady was talking as usual, and noticed that Liz was sitting in her corner with her head down but bolt upright in her chair with her arms bent and fists clenched, and breathing faster than usual. When the staff member crouched down to talk to Liz she noticed she had bright red cheeks.

1 *What conclusions would you reach about Liz's state of mind from looking at the physical indications?*

2 *What would be the next step you would take?*

3 *What are the potential responses from Liz?*

4 *What would be a satisfactory outcome?*

Undertaking difficult, complex and sensitive communications

KS 15

If individuals are upset as the result of an outside event, such as the death of a close friend or relative, or because they have received some other bad news, there is probably little you can do to prevent the distress but the way you communicate with them on the topic and the way you handle the situation can often reduce it.

You must be careful not to pressurise individuals to discuss more than they want to. You could also offer them a choice of talking to another member of staff or a relative or friend, if they appear to be unwilling to discuss their worries with you.

Your acknowledgement and recognition of their distress may be sufficient for some people, and they may be able to resolve their distress themselves if they know that they can obtain additional support from you if necessary.

Jane, do you want to talk about why you're feeling so upset?

Care workers need to give individuals the chance to decide whether they want to talk about the causes of distress

The effects of your interactions

You need to be aware of the ways in which you are using your own communication skills to interact with someone who is distressed. While you are taking into account the person's body language and the clues of non-verbal communication, you will need to be conscious of the messages your own non-verbal communication is sending. You need to demonstrate openness with an open welcoming position, but don't encroach on an individual's personal space as this often heightens tension. Make eye contact in a way that demonstrates you are willing to listen.

It is important you approach any individual who is distressed or displaying anger or excitement in a calm and non-threatening way. This will minimise the risks to the individual, to any other people in the immediate area and to yourself. If at any point you feel your personal safety is at risk you should immediately summon help.

Getting help

No one is able to deal with every situation with which they are faced, and you may feel that a particular situation is beyond your capability. This is nothing to be ashamed of. Knowing your own limitations is important and demonstrates a higher degree of maturity and self-awareness than taking risks. Contact other members of your team or other professionals with the experience to deal with the situation – never hesitate to summon help when you feel unsure in dealing with an individual in distress.

A distressed person can become aggressive in some circumstances. If you observe a person becoming aggressive and potentially violent, as in the case of someone changing from crying or expressing anger to shouting or throwing things, then you should immediately summon help. Information on coping with aggression can be found in Unit HSC 336.

Anger is not always directed at others; it can be turned inwards to be directed against individuals themselves. You may be faced with a distressed, hurt and angry individual who makes it clear that he or she intends to self-harm. In this case you have a responsibility to take immediate action to protect the individual. You must also advise the individuals that you will have to take these steps to protect them and attempt to stop them from harming themselves.

Remember

It is never acceptable to allow someone to harm himself or herself.

How to identify the support individuals need KS ② ④ ⑤ ⑦ ⑧ ⑨ ⑩ ⑬ ⑭ ⑮

When communicating with someone who is distressed, one of the first things to do is decide on the support and assistance you need to offer. People in distress can benefit from a wide range of different forms of support.

Deciding the level of support

Sometimes all people need is having their hand held to enable them to go on coping with the distress themselves. You should therefore always establish with the individual the extent of the help needed and what you can usefully provide. Providing unwanted support can sometimes be as damaging and as unhelpful as too little or none. The risks of providing unwanted support are:

- people may feel they are disempowered and are no longer able to help or support themselves – this is not good for their self-esteem or self-confidence
- people may feel you have interfered and they have been forced to reveal more about themselves and their personal life than they would have wished to
- people may become over-dependent on you for help and support and it may reduce their ability to manage for themselves.

The General Social Care Council (GSCC) code of practice for social care workers in England states that care workers must support service users' rights to control their lives and make informed choices about the services they receive (principle 1.3). Unwanted attention might breach this principle.

All other UK countries also have codes of practice.

Offering too little or no help can have the following effects:
- people feel they are isolated and there is nobody who cares for them or is interested in their problems
- people may feel they are unworthy and not liked as individuals
- people may get very angry and frustrated at the apparent lack of care or interest from the rest of the world.

Not providing sufficient support may also breach the code of practice in your country.

The level of help and support you should offer is always best decided along with the individuals themselves. Wherever possible, this should be done through a process of discussion. Questions should be open-ended and clear, and designed to establish the correct level of support, such as 'I can see you're very upset – would it help to talk to me about it?' 'I can see you're very upset – would you like me to find you someone to talk to?'

There may be circumstances in which it is not possible to discuss this with individuals, perhaps because they are extremely agitated or angry or are in an exceedingly distressed state and unable to hold a calm conversation. It may even be that they are threatening to harm themselves or others. In these circumstances you will need to judge how best to intervene. You could try acting in the same way as you would when dealing with an individual who was calmer. For example, if you put your hand on the shoulder of someone who is sobbing and clearly very upset, the result could either be that the person shakes you off and walks away, or turns to you for a hug.

No! I don't want you to touch me. It won't help!

Attempts to comfort someone in distress may not always be welcome

Broadly, the necessary support you are likely to identify will probably fall into one of three categories, as shown in the table below.

Practical support	Giving information, offering a hug or hand holding, making a telephone call, providing transport or other practical assistance, contacting someone on behalf of the distressed person, or meeting an appropriate professional.
Emotional support	Using listening skills, using counselling skills.
Immediate emergency assistance	Summoning immediate help from a colleague, a senior member of staff, an appropriate professional, or the emergency services.

How to offer support

The types of support you might need to give are identified in the table above. You will need to ensure that you have access to sources of information and the appropriate resources that can be offered in particular circumstances. There are specialist organisations which will offer particular support for those who are bereaved, for those who are experiencing relationship difficulties or for those who are feeling depressed and may harm themselves. You should be sure that you can access all the relevant contact details.

Evidence   PC 4 6 8 9 10

Think about a situation at work when a service user has become distressed when you were communicating with them.

What action did you take to handle the situation sensitively?

Did you report the situation?

Check the information stored in your workplace about support for people in distress or at risk from self-harming. Make notes for your portfolio.

Using communication skills

When you have identified the most appropriate support, you will need to use your communication skills to the full. If you have undertaken a training programme in counselling skills you will find this invaluable. This will not make you a counsellor, but it will provide you with the basic skills you need in your work setting to assist people on a day-to-day basis. A therapeutic treatment programme could then be offered through a qualified counsellor.

In a training programme for counselling skills you will learn how to begin to establish a supportive relationship by using skills such as setting boundaries, active listening, paraphrasing, mirroring and reflecting, challenging, facilitating, and ending a relationship. Such training can be extremely valuable and will enable you to offer a more comprehensive level of service.

You should not attempt to offer counselling unless you have been adequately trained and had the opportunity for supervised practice. However, do not underestimate the support you will be able to provide by using good communication skills and a genuine empathy and care for your service users – you can encourage them to express how they feel about what is causing them worry, anxiety or distress.

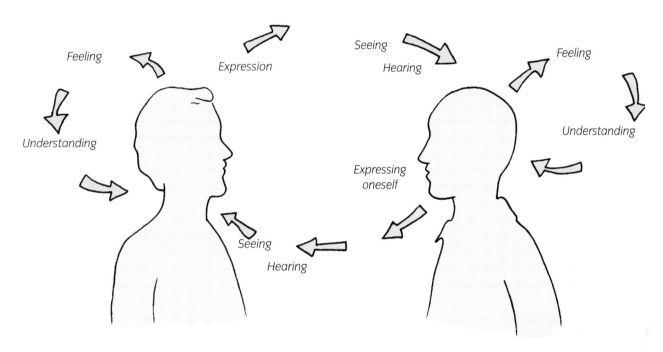

Feeling

Expression

Seeing

Hearing

Feeling

Understanding

Understanding

Expressing oneself

Seeing

Hearing

Developing a sense of empathy may involve a communication cycle of active listening

Empathy involves the skill of developing an accurate understanding of the feelings and thoughts of another person. It involves being able to understand the world of another person and the feelings that he or she may have. Empathising with another person is a skill that develops from good active listening, and it is a characteristic of a caring attitude, where an individual can see beyond his or her own assumptions about the world and can imagine the thoughts and feelings of someone who is quite different. It means that you can 'walk a mile in someone's shoes'.

Many situations can be resolved and the distress significantly reduced if the individual can talk to someone who has good listening skills and can offer clear, practical advice and information. Or it can simply be a matter of showing that someone cares enough to sit and hold his or her hand for half an hour, or to offer a big hug!

Simply showing someone you care can help in many situations

If, however, you feel the situation calls for more support than you can offer, it is important that you recognise this and make an appropriate referral.

CASE STUDY: Breaking bad news

Mrs Zalokovitz, who comes originally from Poland, has been in residential care for several years with deteriorating mobility due to Parkinson's disease. She has lost contact with her Polish friends but has been visited regularly by her only daughter, who lives nearby and is her pride and joy. One day the care manager receives a phone call from the police to say that Mrs Zalokovitz's daughter has been killed in a car crash. The manager realises that she will need to plan very carefully how to break this news to Mrs Zalokovitz and that she will need to put in place a support system for Mrs Zalokovitz in her bereavement.

1   *How could the care manager prepare to break the news to Mrs Zalokovitz?*

2   *How might Mrs Zalokovitz feel and react when she hears the news?*

3   *How best could the care manager respond?*

4   *What could the care manager do immediately to support Mrs Zalokovitz?*

5   *What support might Mrs Zalokovitz need in the longer term?*

6   *Try role playing the conversation between Mrs Zalokovitz and the care manager.*

How distress can affect you

It can be very upsetting to deal with someone who is displaying powerful emotions. People's stories or experiences can be so moving and distressing that you may feel very grateful, or perhaps even guilty, for your own happier circumstances. On the other hand, if you are having difficulties yourself, you could find these echoed or brought to the surface by dealing with an individual in distress. In this case it is important to talk to your supervisor or line manager as soon as possible and arrange for someone else to continue to offer support to the individual.

Feeling concerned, upset or even angry after a particularly emotional experience with a service user is normal. You should not feel that such a response is in any way a reflection on the quality of your work or your ability as a care worker. After such an experience most people are likely to continue to think about it for some time. One of the best ways to deal with this is to discuss it with your line manager or supervisor or with a close friend or relative, always bearing in mind the principles of confidentiality. After a period of time you may come to terms with what happened; but if you find it is interfering with your work, either with the individual or with other service users, there are plenty of sources of help available to you, both within and outside your workplace. Talk to your line manager or supervisor for advice on gaining access to any help you need.

The distress of others, whether in the form of anger, sadness or anxiety, will always be upsetting for the person who works with them. However, if you are able to develop your skills and knowledge so that you can identify distress, work towards reducing it and offer effective help and support to those who are experiencing it, then you are making a useful and meaningful contribution to the provision of quality care.

Test yourself

1 How would you prepare to communicate difficult or complex issues to an individual?

2 What are the key factors which would indicate that someone is becoming distressed?

3 What steps could you take to reduce someone's distress?

4 What action should be taken if someone threatens to harm himself or herself?

5 What action should be taken if someone becomes a threat to others?

HSC 31c Support individuals to communicate

Ways in which people communicate

 KS 8 10 12 15

This element is about supporting people to communicate with each other. Communication is much more than talking – it is about how people respond to each other in many different ways: touch, facial expression, body movements, dress, not to mention using written communication, the telephone or electronic messages!

Remember

You are the most important tool you have for doing your job. Care managers do not have carefully engineered machinery or complex technology – your own ability to relate to others and to understand them is the key you need!

More than talking

Any relationship comes about through communication. In order to be an effective care worker, you must learn to be a good communicator. You will have to know how to recognise what is being communicated to you, and to be able to communicate with others without always having to use words.

Active knowledge

Do this with a friend or colleague.

1 Write the names of several emotions (such as anger, joy, sadness, disappointment, fear) on pieces of paper.

2 One of you should pick up a piece of paper. Your task is to communicate the emotion written on the paper to your partner, without saying anything.

3 Your partner then has to decide what the emotion is and say why.

4 Change places and repeat the exercise. Take it in turns, until all the pieces of paper have been used. Make sure that you list all the things which made you aware of the emotion being expressed.

5 Discuss with your partner what you have discovered about communication as a result of this exercise.

When you carried out the exercise above, you will have found out that there are many things which told you what your partner was trying to communicate. It is not only the expression on people's faces which tells you about how they feel, but also the way they use the rest of their bodies.

This area of human behaviour is referred to as **non-verbal communication** (see page 7). It is very important for developing the ability to understand what people are feeling. If you understand the importance of non-verbal communication, you will be able to use it to improve your own skills when you communicate with someone.

Signs and signals

When we meet and talk with people, we will usually be using two language systems. We will use a verbal or spoken language, and non-verbal communication or body language.

Effective communication in care work requires the ability to analyse your own and other people's non-verbal behaviour. Our bodies send messages to other people – often without us meaning to send those messages. Some of the most important body areas that send messages are shown on the next page.

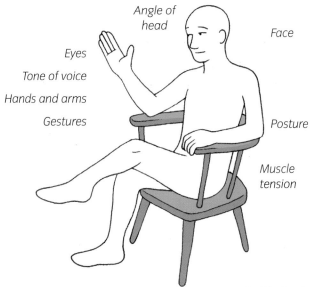

Angle of
head

Face

Eyes

Tone of voice

Hands and arms

Gestures

Posture

Muscle
tension

Non-verbal behaviour sends messages

The eyes

We can guess the feelings and thoughts that another person has by looking at their eyes, often called 'the windows of the soul'. We can sometimes understand the thoughts and feelings of another person by eye-to-eye contact. Our eyes get wider when we are excited, or when we are attracted to or interested in someone. A fixed stare may send the message that the person is angry. Looking away is often interpreted as showing boredom in European cultures.

The face

Faces can send very complex messages and we can read them easily – even in diagram form.

Our faces often indicate our emotional state. When a person is sad, he or she may look down, there may be tension in the face, and the mouth will be closed. The muscles in the person's shoulders are likely to be relaxed, but his or her face and neck may show tension. A happy person will have wide-open eyes that make contact with you, and will smile.

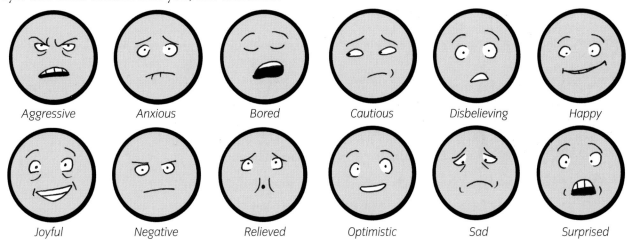

| Aggressive | Anxious | Bored | Cautious | Disbelieving | Happy |
| Joyful | Negative | Relieved | Optimistic | Sad | Surprised |

We can read facial expressions easily, even in diagram form

Voice tone

If we talk quickly in a loud voice with a fixed tone, people may see us as angry. A calm, slow voice with varying tone may send a message of being friendly.

Body movement

The way we walk, move our heads, sit, cross our legs and so on send messages about whether we are tired, happy, sad or bored.

Posture

Sitting with crossed arms can mean 'I'm not taking any notice'. Leaning back or to one side can send the message that you are relaxed or bored. Leaning forward can show interest.

Muscle tension

The tension in our feet, hands and fingers can tell others how relaxed or how tense we are. If people are very tense their shoulders might stiffen, their face muscles might tighten and they might sit or stand rigidly. A tense face might have a firmly closed mouth with lips and jaws clenched tight. A tense person might breathe quickly and become hot.

Gestures

Gestures are hand and arm movements that can help us to understand what a person is saying. Some gestures carry a generally agreed meaning of their own within a culture. When people are excited they may move their arms or hands quickly.

Touch

Touching another person can send messages of care, affection, power over them, or sexual interest. The social setting and other body language usually help people to understand what touch might mean. Care workers should not make assumptions about touch; even holding someone's hand might be interpreted as trying to dominate.

Proximity and personal space

The space between people can sometimes show how friendly or intimate the conversation is. Different cultures have different assumptions about how close people should be (their proximity) when they are talking.

In Britain, when talking to strangers we may keep an arm's length apart. The ritual of shaking hands indicates that you have been introduced – you may come closer. When you are friendly with someone you may accept the person coming even closer to you. Relatives and partners may not be restricted in how close they can come.

Did you know?

Research shows that people pay far more attention to facial expressions and tone of voice than they do to spoken words. For example, in one study, words contributed only 7 per cent towards the impression of whether or not someone was liked, tone of voice contributed 38 per cent and facial expression 55 per cent. The study also found that if there was a contradiction between facial expression and words, people believed the facial expression.

Personal space is a very important issue in care work. A care worker who assumes it is acceptable to enter a service user's personal space without asking or explaining may be seen as being dominating or aggressive.

Face-to-face positions (orientation)

Standing or sitting face to face can send a message of being formal or being angry. A slight angle can create a more relaxed and friendly feeling.

Responding to others

How do you work out what another person might be feeling? Look at a person's facial expression. Much of what you will see will be in his or her eyes, but the eyebrows and mouth also tell you a lot about what someone is feeling.

Notice whether someone is looking at you, or at the floor, or at a point over your shoulder. Lack of eye contact should give a first indication that all may not be well. It may be that the individual is not feeling confident. He or she may be unhappy, or feel uneasy about talking to you. You will need to follow this up.

Look at how a person sits. Is he or she relaxed and comfortable, sitting well back in the chair, or tense and perched on the edge of the seat? Is he or she slumped in the chair with the head down? People who are feeling well and cheerful tend to hold their heads up, and sit in a relaxed and comfortable way. An individual who is tense and nervous, who feels unsure and worried, is likely to reflect that in the way he or she sits or stands. Observe hands and gestures carefully. Someone twisting his or her hands, or fiddling with hair or clothes, is signalling tension and worry. Frequent little shrugs of the shoulders or spreading of the hands may indicate a feeling of helplessness or hopelessness.

CASE STUDY: Recognising body language

Mr Jarvis has just been admitted to a residential care home. He has severe arthritis and his mobility is very poor. He has some incontinence of urine. The arthritis in his hands, elbows and shoulders means that he is not able to carry out basic domestic tasks, but he can wash and dress, although he is slow and sometimes cannot manage the buttons.

He had been cared for at home by his wife until last week, when she suffered a massive stroke and died. Mr Jarvis has one son who lives 200 miles away. The son came at once when his mother died, and has stayed all week with his father. However, he now has to return to work and has arranged for his father to be admitted into residential care as a matter of urgency.

1 *What would you expect Mr Jarvis's facial expression to be?*
2 *Allowing for his physical difficulties, how do you think he would be sitting?*
3 *What do you think he would be doing with his hands?*
4 *What emotions and feelings is Mr Jarvis likely to be expressing through his body language?*
5 *How could Mr Jarvis's care worker support him to communicate?*

Giving out the signals

Being aware of your own body language is just as important as understanding the person you are talking to.

Keys to good practice: Communication skills

✓ Make sure that you maintain eye contact with the person you are talking to, although you should avoid staring! Looking away occasionally is normal, but if you find yourself looking around the room, or watching others, then you are failing to give people the attention they deserve.

✓ Be aware of what you are doing and try to think why you are losing attention.

✓ Sit where you can be comfortably seen. Don't sit where someone has to turn in order to look at you.

✓ Sit a comfortable distance away – not so far that any sense of closeness is lost, but not so close that you 'invade their space'.

✓ Make sure you are showing by your gestures that you are listening and interested in what people are saying – sitting half turned away gives the message that you are not fully committed to what is being said.

✓ Folded arms or crossed legs can indicate that you are 'closed' rather than 'open' to what someone is expressing.

✓ Nodding your head will indicate that you are receptive and interested – but be careful not to overdo it and look like a nodding dog!

✓ Lean towards someone to show that you are interested in what they are saying. You can use leaning forwards quite effectively at times when you want to emphasise your interest or support. Then move backwards a little at times when the content is a little lighter.

✓ Using touch to communicate your caring and concern is often useful and appropriate. Many individuals find it comforting to have their hand held or stroked, or to have an arm around their shoulders.

✓ Be aware of a person's body language, which should tell you if he or she finds touch acceptable.

✓ Always err on the side of caution if you are unsure about what is acceptable in another culture, for example with regard to touching.

Continued

Keys to good practice: Communication skills (cont.)

✓ Think about age and gender in relation to touch. An older woman may be happy to have her hand held by a female care worker, but may be uncomfortable with such a response from a man.

✓ Ensure that you are touching someone because you think it will comfort him or her, and not because you feel helpless and can't think of anything to say.

You can use the technique of leaning forwards at times when you want to emphasise your interest or support

Active knowledge

Do this with at least one other person – two or three is even better.

1 Think of an incident or situation which is quite important and significant to you. Stand still in the middle of a room and begin to tell your partner about your significant incident.

2 Your partner should start at the edge of the room and slowly move closer and closer to you.

3 At the point where you feel comfortable talking to your partner, say 'Stop'. Mark this point and measure the distance from where you are standing.

4 At the point where you feel that your partner is too close, say 'Stop'. Mark this point and measure the distance from where you are standing.

5 Change places and repeat the exercise.

You may find that you and your partner(s) have different distances at which you feel comfortable, but it is likely to be in the range of 3–5ft (1–1½ metres).

Intimate
zone
(touching)

Personal zone
(less than
1 metre)

Social zone
(1–2 metres)

Public zone
(2 metres +)

Barriers to communication

 KS 6 7 8 9 10 12 16

As you learned in the first element of this unit, there are many factors which can get in the way of good communication. You will need to understand how to recognise these and to learn what you can do to overcome them yourself, and to support individuals in overcoming them. Until you do this, your communication will always be less effective than it could be. It is easy to assume that everyone can communicate, and that any failure to respond to you is because of someone's unwillingness rather than inability. There are as many reasons why people find communication difficult as there are ways to make it easier.

Evidence   PC 2 4

Think of a service user who you work with regularly, who requires specific support/aids to enable them to communicate.

Describe the support/aid they need and your role to ensure they are able to communicate effectively.

Thinking about the obstacles

Never assume that you can be heard and understood and that you can be responded to, without first thinking about the individual and his or her situation. Check first to ensure you are giving the communication the best possible chance of success by dealing with as many barriers as possible.

Practical difficulties

If you need to communicate with someone who has a known disability, such as hearing loss, impaired vision, mobility problems or speech impairment, you must consider the implications for your communication.

If someone is profoundly deaf, you will need to establish what sort of assistance he or she needs. If he or she communicates by signing, you will need to have a sign language interpreter available. Do not assume that you can do this yourself – it is highly skilled and people train for a long time to do this. If someone uses a hearing aid, consider that it may not be operating efficiently if you seem to be having communication problems.

Consider the level of someone's hearing. Many people are hard of hearing, but this may not be a profound hearing loss. It can mean that they have difficulty hearing where there is background noise and other people talking.

If someone has a physical disability, you will need to consider whether this is likely to affect his or her non-verbal communication. Also, his or her body language may not be what you would expect.

Facial expressions may seem inappropriate

Hand and arm gestures may not be possible

Body posture may not give out the messages you would expect

The non-verbal communication of someone with a physical disability may be different from what you expect

CASE STUDY: Solving communication problems

Mr Talan lives alone. For many years he has been well known in the neighbourhood. He was never particularly chatty, but always said a polite 'Good morning' on his way to the shops, and had a smile and a kind word for the children. His wife died about 15 years ago. They had only one son, a soldier killed in action many years previously.

Recently, Mr Talan's health began to deteriorate. He had a bad winter with a chest infection and a nasty fall in the snow. This seemed to shake his confidence, and he accepted the offer of a home care assistant twice a week. Neighbours began to notice that Mr Talan no longer spoke to them, and he failed to acknowledge the children. His outings to the shops became less frequent. Jean, his home care assistant, was worried that he hardly responded to her cheerful chat as she worked. She realised that Mr Talan's hearing was deteriorating. After medical investigations, Mr Talan was provided with a hearing aid. He began to be much more like his old self – he spoke to people again, smiled at the children and enjoyed his visits to the shops.

1   *How do you think Mr Talan felt when he began to have problems hearing people?*
2   *Why do you think he reacted in the way he did?*
3   *What other factors might Jean have thought were causing Mr Talan's deterioration?*
4   *How are people likely to have reacted to Mr Talan?*

Individuals who have visual impairment to any significant degree will need to be addressed with thought and care. Do not rely on your facial expressions to communicate your interest and concern – use words and touch where appropriate. Remember to obtain any information they may need in a format they can use. Think about large print books, braille or audio tapes. If you need any further information, the Royal National Institute for the Blind (RNIB) will be able to advise you about local sources of supplies.

Hello. I'm Jeff and I'm going to be the person who is mainly responsible for looking after you while you are in here …

Good morning, Ralph. It's Solange. How are you?

The way you address people who have an impairment needs to be thought through carefully

Make sure that you know what language an individual is comfortable with – don't assume it is the same as yours without making certain! Find out if you need to provide any translation facilities, or written information in another language. If translation is needed, your team leader or manager should be able to help you to arrange it. Your local social services department will have a list of interpreters, as will the police or the consulate or embassy of their country. Many organisations provide information about where specialised assistance can be obtained.

Cultural differences

You will need to be aware of cultural differences between you and the person you are talking to. For example, using first names or touching someone to whom you are not related, or who is not a very close friend, can be viewed as disrespectful. Talking familiarly to someone of a different gender or age group can be unacceptable in some cultures. For example, some young Muslim women believe they should not talk at all to men to whom they are not related.

Many older men and women consider it disrespectful to address people by their first names. You will often find older people with neighbours they have known for 50 years, who still call each other 'Mrs Baker' or 'Mrs Wood'.

Did you know?

The Benefits Agency produces a catalogue of its leaflets, posters and information. This lists which items are available in other languages, braille, large print or on audio tape. Many other agencies and organisations do the same. Always make sure you ask if information is available in the format the individual needs. Being given information in an accessible format is far better than having to receive it second-hand.

Remember

The golden rule when you are communicating with someone from a different culture is to find out. Do not assume that you can approach everyone in the same way. It is your responsibility to find out the way to approach someone.

What words mean

Be aware that the words you use can mean different things to different people and generations – words like 'web', 'chip' or 'gay'. Be aware of particular local words which are used in your part of the country, which may not mean the same to someone from another area.

Think carefully about the subject under discussion. Some people from particular cultures, or people of particular generations, may find some subjects very sensitive and difficult to discuss. These days, it is not unusual among a younger age group to discuss personal income levels. However, people of older generations may consider such information to be highly personal.

Physical barriers

Communication can be hindered by physical and environmental factors. This may seem obvious, but they need to be considered when planning communication. Always provide a private situation if you have personal matters to discuss – it is rarely the case that the best that can be arranged is to pull the curtains around a bed. You need to think about the surroundings. People find it difficult to talk in noisy, crowded places. A communal lounge with a television on is not a good place for effective communication.

Remember the temperature – make sure it is comfortable. Think about lighting. Is it too dark or too bright? Is the sun in someone's eyes? Make sure that you do not sit with your face in shadow. It is very disconcerting not to be able to see someone's face when talking to him or her – remember what you have learned about non-verbal communication.

Remember

- Never take communication for granted.
- Not everyone communicates in the same way.
- It is your responsibility to support the individual to communicate.
- As far as possible, plan ahead and think what you will need to take into account.

It is important when communicating with someone that he or she can see your face and hear what you are saying

Listening effectively

 KS 2 10

Communication is a two-way process. This may sound obvious, but a great deal of communication is wasted because only one of the parties is communicating. Think about setting up communication between two radios – when a link is established, the question is asked 'Are you receiving me?' and the answer comes back 'Receiving you loud and clear'. Unfortunately, human beings don't do this exercise before they talk to each other!

If no one is listening and receiving the information a person is trying to communicate, it is just a waste of time. Learning how to listen is a key task for anyone working in care.

You may think that you know how to listen and that it is something you do constantly. After all, you are hearing all sorts of noises all day long – but simply hearing sounds is not the same thing as actively listening.

Active knowledge

Think about a time you have talked to someone you felt was really interested in what you were saying and listening carefully to you. Try to note down what it was that made you so sure he or she was really listening. Did the fact you thought the person was really listening to you make it easier to talk?

For most people, feeling that someone is really listening makes a huge difference to how confident they feel about talking. You will need to learn about ways in which you can show people you are listening to what they are saying.

Using body language

Although you may think that you do most of your communicating by speaking, you may be surprised to learn that over 80 per cent of what you communicate to others is understood without you speaking a word. Body language, or non-verbal communication, is the way in which we pick up most of the messages people are trying to give us – and some that they're not!

The way in which you use your body can convey messages about many things:

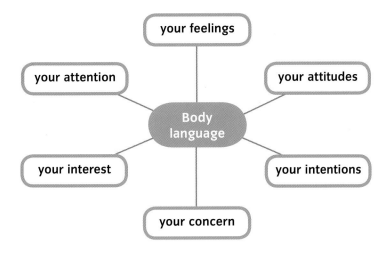

The messages are made clear by such things as facial expression, or maintaining eye contact; leaning forwards when you are listening; or having an open and relaxed posture.

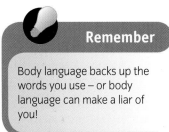

Remember

Body language backs up the words you use – or body language can make a liar of you!

Yes, I'm really interested, go on.

You can tell me anything. I'm very friendly and approachable.

No, it's fine. I've got plenty of time – don't feel you have to hurry.

Your body language will let people know that your are really listening to what they are saying. Practise your listening skills in just the same way you would practise any other skill – you can learn to listen well.

Always:
- look at the person who is talking to you
- maintain eye contact, without staring
- nod your head to encourage the person to talk and show that you understand
- use 'aha', 'mm' and similar expressions which indicate that you are still listening
- lean slightly towards the person who is speaking – this indicates interest and concern
- have an open and interested facial expression, which should reflect the tone of the conversation – happy, serious, etc.

Using verbal communication

Body language is one key to effective listening, but what you say in reply is also important. You can back up the message that you are interested and listening by checking that you have understood what has been said to you. Using sentences beginning 'So …' to check that you have got it right can be helpful. 'So … it's only since you had the fall that you are feeling worried about being here alone.' 'So … you were happy with the service before the hours were changed.'

You can also use expressions such as 'So what you mean is …' or 'So what you are saying is …'

Short, encouraging phrases used while people are talking can show concern, understanding or sympathy. Phrases such as 'I see', 'Oh dear', 'Yes', or 'Go on' all give the speaker a clear indication that you are listening and want him or her to continue.

Keys to good practice: Supporting individuals to communicate

✓ Support individuals to express how they want to communicate and to use their preferred methods of communication.

✓ Ensure that any aids to communication, such as hearing aids, are set up and working properly.

✓ Support others who are communicating with individuals to understand them and use appropriate methods of communication.

✓ Encourage individuals to respond, to express their feelings and emotions appropriately, and to overcome barriers to communication.

Using questions

Sometimes questions can be helpful to prompt someone who is talking, or to try to move a conversation forward. There are two different kinds of questions. Questions that can be answered with just 'yes' or 'no' are **closed questions**. 'Would you like to go out today?' is a closed question.

An **open question** needs more than 'yes' or 'no' to answer it. 'What is your favourite kind of outing?' is an open question. Open questions usually being with:

- what
- how
- why
- when
- where.

Depending on the conversation and the circumstances, either type of question may be appropriate. For example, if you are encouraging someone to talk because he or she has always been quiet, but has suddenly begun to open up, you are more likely to use open questions to encourage him or her to carry on talking. On the other hand, if you need factual information or you just want to confirm that you have understood what has been said to you, then you may need to ask closed questions.

Active knowledge

What type of question is each of the following?

- 'Are you feeling worried?'
- 'What sort of things worry you?'
- 'Do you want to join in the games tonight?'
- 'Is your daughter coming to visit?'
- 'Why were you cross with Marge this morning?'
- 'Were you cross with Marge this morning?'
- 'What have you got planned for when your daughter comes to visit?'
- 'Do you live here alone?'
- 'How do you feel about living alone?'

One of the main points to remember when listening is that whatever you say, there should not be too much of it! You are supposed to be listening, not speaking. Some DON'Ts for good listening are as follows.

- Don't interrupt – always let people finish what they are saying, and wait for a gap in the conversation.
- Don't give advice – even if asked. You are not the person concerned, so you cannot respond to questions beginning 'If you were me …'. Your job is to encourage people to take responsibility for their own decisions, not to tell them what to do!

- Don't tell people about your own experiences, unless you are doing this in order to encourage them to talk. Any conversation about yourself should support your role as a listener, not make people listen while you talk about yourself.
- Don't ever dismiss fears, worries or concerns by saying 'that's silly' or 'you shouldn't worry about that'. People's fears are real and should not be made to sound trivial.

Evidence   PC 1

Think about two particular occasions when you have been involved in communicating with service users. Write a brief description of the circumstances, and then write notes on how you showed the service users that you were listening to them. If you have not yet had enough experience of working with service users to be able to think of two occasions, think about times when you have listened effectively to a friend or relative and write about that instead.

Test yourself

1   What methods can you use to encourage individuals to communicate?

2   What environmental factors do you need to consider when planning communication?

3   Name three possible barriers to communication. How would you deal with each of them?

4   How would you deal with a staff member who was expressing his or her feelings in an unacceptable way?

HSC 31d Update and maintain records and reports

Updating and maintaining the accuracy of records and reports is vitally important for any care setting. The information in records or reports could be about an individual who is being cared for in your workplace, a relative or friend, or it could be about the organisation itself, about or for someone who works there, or for administrative purposes. The information could come to you in a range of ways:

- verbally, for example in a conversation either face to face or on the telephone
- on paper, for example in a letter, an individual's health record or instructions from a health professional
- electronically, by fax or on a computer.

Whatever the purpose of the information, it is important that you record it accurately. It is also important that you pass on any information correctly, in the right form and to the right person. Recording information is essential in health and care services, because the services that are provided are about people rather than objects, so it is vital that information is accurate, accessible and readable. Information about the communication and language needs of individuals is of daily importance.

Ways of receiving and passing on information

Today within health and care there are many ways in which information is circulated between agencies, colleagues, other team members, individuals receiving care, carers, volunteers and so on. The growth of electronic communication has meant a considerable change in the way that people receive and send information, in comparison to only a few years ago when information sharing was limited to face-to-face meetings, telephone calls or posted letters.

Telephone

One of the commonest means of communication is the telephone. It has advantages because it is instant, straightforward and is a relatively safe and accurate way of communicating and passing on information. However, there are some disadvantages to the telephone in that it can often be difficult to ensure that you have clearly understood what has been said. There can be problems with telephone lines which cause crackling and technical difficulties. It is also possible to misinterpret someone's meaning when you cannot pick up other signals, such as facial expression and body language. If you regularly take or place messages on the telephone, there are some very simple steps that you can take to ensure that you cut down the risk of getting a message wrong.

- Make sure that you check the name of the person who is calling. If necessary, ask the person to spell his or her name and repeat it to make sure you have it right. It is easy to mix up Thomas and Thompson, Williams and Wilkins, and so on. You may also need to take the person's address, and again it is worthwhile asking him or her to spell the details to ensure that you have written them correctly.

Always ask for a return telephone number so that the person who receives the message can phone back if necessary. There is nothing more infuriating than receiving a message on which you have some queries and no means of contacting the person who has left it for you. You should read back the message itself to the person who is leaving it to check that you have the correct information and that you have understood his or her meaning.

Texting

Texts are useful for passing on short communications, such as arranging meetings or letting someone know you will be late. Texts are not appropriate for transmitting detailed or confidential information.

Incoming post

If it is part of your role to open and check any incoming post, you must make sure that you:

- open it as soon as it arrives
- follow your own workplace procedures for dealing with incoming mail – this is likely to involve stamping it with the date it is received
- pass it on to the appropriate person for it to be dealt with or filed. See page 66 for advice on how to deal with confidential information.

Faxed information

The steps for dealing with an incoming fax message are as follows.

- Take the fax from the machine.
- Read the cover sheet – this will tell you who the fax is for, who it is from (it should include telephone and fax numbers) and how many pages there should be.
- Check that the correct number of pages have been received. If a fax has misprinted or has pages missing, contact the telephone number identified on the cover sheet and ask for the information to be sent again. If there is no telephone number, send a fax immediately to the sending fax number asking for the fax to be resent.
- Follow your organisation's procedure for dealing with incoming faxes. Make sure the fax is handed to the appropriate person as soon as possible.

E-mail

E-mail is a very frequently used means of communication within and between workplaces. It is fast, convenient and easy to use for many people. Large reports and complex information which would be cumbersome to post or fax can be transmitted as an attachment to an e-mail in seconds. However, not everyone in all workplaces has access to e-mail and not all electronic transmission is secure. Be aware of this if you are sending highly sensitive and confidential material. If you do send and receive information by e-mail you should:

- follow the guidelines in your workplace for using e-mail and the transmission of confidential material
- open all your e-mails and respond to them promptly
- save any confidential messages or attachments in an appropriate, password-protected file or folder, and delete them from your inbox unless that is also protected
- return promptly any e-mails you have received in error
- be careful not to give your password to anyone.

E-mail is a fast and efficient method of communication in most circumstances

Active knowledge

Your organisation should have a policy for dealing with the filing and storing of e-mails about service users. Check this policy to ensure it is up to date with the latest data protection legislation. If necessary, arrange training sessions for your team members.

Outgoing post

If you have to write information to send to another organisation, whether it is by letter or by fax or e-mail, you should be sure that the contents are clear, cannot be misunderstood and are to the point. Do not write a rambling, long letter which obliges recipients to hunt for the information they need.

It is likely that, within many organisations, you will need to show any faxes or letters to your supervisor or manager before they leave the premises. This safeguard is in place in many workplaces for the good reason that information being sent on behalf of your employer must be accurate and appropriate. As your employer is the person ultimately responsible for any information sent out, he or she will want to have procedures in place to check this.

Confidentiality

Confidentiality involves keeping information safe and only passing it on where there is a clear right to it and a clear need to do so. Confidentiality is an important right for all service users because:

- service users may not trust a care worker who does not keep information confidential

- service users may not feel valued or able to keep their self-esteem if their private details are shared with others
- service users' safety may be put at risk if details of their property and habits are shared publicly.

A professional service which maintains respect for individuals must keep private information confidential. There are legal requirements under the Data Protection Act 1998 to keep personal records confidential (see page 65).

Boundaries to confidentiality

Service users have a right to confidentiality, but also a responsibility in relation to the rights of others. Confidentiality often has to be kept within boundaries and the rights of others have to be balanced with the service user's rights. A care worker may have to tell his or her manager something learned in confidence. The information is not made public, so it is still partly confidential. Information may need to be passed to managers in the following situations.

Situation	Example of information that needs to be passed on
There is a significant risk of harm to a service user	An older person in the community refuses to put any heating on in winter; she may be at risk of harm from the cold.
A service user is in danger of being abused	A person explains that his son takes his money – he may be experiencing financial abuse.
There is a significant risk of harm to others	A person lives in a very dirty house with mice and rats, and may be creating a public health risk.
There is a risk to the care worker's health or well-being	A person is very aggressive, placing the care worker at risk.

Confidentiality and the need to know

Good care practice involves asking service users if we can let other people know things. It would be wrong to pass on even the date of a person's birthday without asking him or her first. Some people might not want others to celebrate their birthday – for example, Jehovah's Witnesses believe that it is wrong to do so. Whatever we know about a service user should be kept private unless the person tells us that it is acceptable to share the information. The exception to this rule is that information can be passed on when others have a right and a need to know it.

Some examples of people who have a need to know about work with service users are:

- managers – they may need to help make decisions which affect the service user

- colleagues – they may be working with the same person
- other professionals – they may also be working with the service user and need to be kept up to date.

When information is passed to other professionals, it should be on the understanding that they keep it confidential. It is important to check that people asking for information are who they say they are. If you answer the telephone and the caller says he or she is a social worker or other professional, you should explain that you must call back before giving any information. Phoning back enables you to be sure that you are talking to someone at a particular number or within a particular organisation. If you meet a person you don't know, you should ask for proof of identity before passing on any information.

Relatives will often say that they have a right to know about service users. Sometimes it is possible to ask relatives to discuss issues directly with the service user rather than giving information yourself, as shown in the illustration.

Sometimes it is possible to ask relatives to discuss issues directly with service users

Service users have a right to expect that information about them is accurately recorded. This and the right to confidentiality are backed by the Data Protection Act 1998. All services now have to have policies and procedures on the confidentiality of recorded information.

How you can maintain confidentiality

The most common way in which workers breach confidentiality is by chatting about work with friends or family. It is very tempting to discuss the day's events with your family or with friends over a drink or a meal. It is often therapeutic to discuss a stressful day, and helps get things into perspective. But you must make sure that you talk about issues at work in a way that keeps service user details confidential and anonymous.

For example, you can talk about how an encounter made you feel without giving any details of the other people involved. You can say: 'Today this service user accused me of stealing all their money – at first I was so angry I didn't know what to say! What would you have done?' The issue can be discussed without making reference to gender, ethnicity, age, physical description, location or any other personal information that might even remotely identify the person concerned. The issue is how you felt and what you should do, and you are always free to discuss yourself.

It might be considered a breach of the GSCC code of conduct to discuss service user details with people who do not have a need to know. The essential issue is trust; even if no one can identify the name of the person involved, others might perceive you as displaying a lack of respect if you talk about the personal characteristics of the people you work with in public places.

Did you know?

The Data Protection Act 1998 has been incorporated into the regulations used by the Commission for Social Care Inspection and the GSCC. For example, Standard 10 of the Commission for Social Care Inspection's National Minimum Standards for Care Homes for Younger Adults deals with this issue.

You never know who's listening!

CARELESS TALK COSTS LIVES

Imagine you were in a restaurant and you overheard staff from a local clinic saying: 'You wouldn't believe how ugly some of the patients are! The other day we had this 40-year-old, dark-haired woman – lives in Meadow Close – she had a face like the back of a bus. Well, the operation went wrong – but I mean, what's she got to live for anyway?' Now imagine that you were about to attend that clinic. Would you want those staff to look after you?

You will soon become used to maintaining confidentiality, even in relaxed situations with your colleagues

The principle of confidentiality is about trust and confidence in professional workers, not only about protecting the identity of individuals.

You also need to be sure that you do not discuss one person you care for with another whom you also care for. You may not think you would ever act in that way, but it is so easy to do, with the best of intentions.

Imagine the scene. Someone says 'Ethel doesn't look too good today', and your well-meant response is: 'No, she doesn't. She's had a bit of an upset with her son. She'd probably be really glad of some company later, if you've got the time'. This is the type of response which can cause great distress and, above all, distrust. If the woman you have spoken to later says to Ethel, 'Sue said you were a bit down because of the upset with your son', Ethel is not going to know how much you have said. As far as she knows, you could have given her whole life history to the woman who enquired. The most damaging consequence of this breach of confidentiality is the loss of trust. This can have damaging effects on an individual's self-esteem, confidence and general well-being.

In this case, the best way to respond to the woman's comment would have been: 'Don't you think so? Well, perhaps she might be glad of some company later if you've got the time'.

Active knowledge

Think of a time when you have told someone something in confidence and later discovered that they had told other people. Try to recall how you felt about it. You may have felt angry or betrayed. Perhaps you were embarrassed and did not want to face anyone. Note down a few of the ways you felt.

Policies of the organisation

Every health and caring organisation will have a policy on confidentiality and the disclosure of information. You must be sure that you know what both policies are in your workplace.

The basic rule is that all information an individual gives, or that is given on his or her behalf, to an organisation is confidential and cannot be disclosed to anyone without the consent of the individual. You will need to support individuals in contributing to and understanding records and reports concerning them, and ensure they understand how the rules of confidentiality affect them.

CASE STUDY: Security and confidentiality

Evergreens Care Home is a 14-bedded residential unit for elderly individuals with moderate care needs. It does not have a computerised record system. All the records on the residents, including their drug regime, are stored in folders which are kept in a filing cabinet behind the reception desk.

One day one of the residents, Mr Tedesco, is in great distress. He says he found his record folder lying on the reception desk and took a quick look inside. He saw that the doctor had recommended he have some tests for prostate cancer. Mr Tedesco had told the staff about his urinary problems, but had no idea there was a risk of cancer. He is very upset and also angry that 'the staff didn't tell me the truth'.

1   *What are the security and confidentiality issues in this situation?*
2   *How can the staff respond to Mr Tedesco's immediate distress?*
3   *What actions could be taken to improve security and confidentiality at Evergreens?*

Passing on information with consent

In many cases, the passing of information is routine and related to the care of the individual. For example, medical information may be passed to a hospital, to a residential home or to a private care agency. It must be made clear to the individual that this information will be passed on in order to ensure that he or she receives the best possible care.

But it is essential that only information which is required for the purpose is passed on. For example, it is not necessary to tell the hearing aid clinic that Mr Sampson's son is currently serving a prison sentence. However, if Mr Sampson became seriously ill and the hospital wanted to contact his next of kin, that information would need to be passed on.

Each organisation should have a policy which states clearly the circumstances in which information can be disclosed. Past government guidelines (Confidentiality of Personal Information 1988) required that the policy should identify:

- the members of senior management designated to deal with decisions about disclosing information

- what to do when urgent action is required
- the safeguards in place to make sure that the information will be used only for the purpose for which it is required
- arrangements for obtaining manual records and computer records
- arrangements for reviewing the procedure.

Current procedures are likely to follow this guidance and must also conform to the requirements of the Data Protection Act 1998.

Active knowledge

Check out the confidentiality policy in your workplace. Find the procedure and make sure you know how to follow it.

People who need to know

It can be difficult when people claim to have a right or an interest in seeing an individual's records. Of course, there are always some people who do need to know, either because they are directly involved in providing care for the individual or because they are involved in some other support role. However, not everyone needs to know everything, so it is important that information is given on a 'need to know' basis. In other words, people should be told what is necessary for them to carry out their role.

Relatives will often claim that they have a 'right to know'. The most famous example of this was Victoria Gillick, who went to court in order to try to gain access to her daughter's medical records. She claimed that she had the right to know whether her daughter had been given the contraceptive pill. Her GP had refused to tell her and she took the case all the way to the House of Lords, but the ruling was not changed and she was not given access to her daughter's records. The rules remain the same. Even for close relatives, the information is not available unless the individual agrees.

It is difficult, however, if you are faced with angry or distressed relatives who believe that you have information they are entitled to. One situation you could encounter is where a daughter, for example, believes that she has the right to be told about medical information in respect of her parent. Another example is where someone is trying to find out a person's whereabouts. The best response is to be clear and assertive (see Unit HSC 336 for a discussion of assertiveness), but to demonstrate that you understand it is difficult for them. Do not try to 'pass the buck' and give people the idea that they can find out from someone else. There is nothing more frustrating than being passed from one person to another without anyone being prepared to tell you anything. It is important to be clear and say, for example: 'I'm sorry. I know you must be worried, but I can't discuss any information unless your mother agrees', or 'I'm sorry, I can't give out any information about where Jennifer is living now. But if you would like to leave me a name and contact details, I will pass on the message and she can contact you'.

Looking after information

Once something is written down or entered on a computer, it becomes a permanent record. For this reason, you must be very careful what you do with any files, charts, notes or other written records. They must always be stored somewhere locked and safe. People should be very careful with files which leave the workplace. There are many stories about files being stolen from cars or left on buses!

Records kept on computers must also be kept safe and protected. Your workplace will have policies relating to records on computers, which will include access being restricted by a password, and the computer system being protected against the possibility of people 'hacking' into it.

Remember

- Generally you should only give information with consent.

- Only give people the information they need to know to do their job.

- Information should be relevant to the purpose for which it is required.

- Check the identity of the person to whom you give information.

- Make sure that you do not give information carelessly.

Computer records must be surrounded by proper security

Since the Access to Personal Files Act 1987, individuals can see their personal files. The Data Protection Act 1998 gives people a right to see the information recorded about them. This means that people can see their medical records, or social services files. Since January 2005 the Freedom of Information Act 2000 has provided people with a right to access general information held by public authorities, including local authorities and the National Health Service. Personal information about other people cannot be accessed and is protected by the Data Protection Act.

The information which you write in files should be clear and useful. Do not include irrelevant information, or opinions that are not backed up by facts, and write only about the individual concerned. Sign and date the information. Anything you write should be true and able to be justified, as the two examples on the next page show.

Name: A. Potter

Mr P settling back well after discharge from hosp. Fairly quiet and withdrawn today. Son to visit in am. Report from hosp included in file – prognosis not good. Not able to get him to talk today: for further time tomorrow.

Name: J. Soane

Joe visited new flat today. Very positive and looking forward to move. No access problems: delighted with purpose-built kitchen and bathroom. Further visit from OT needed to check on any aids required. Confirmed with housing assoc. that Joe wants tenancy. Will send tenancy agreement – should start on 1st.

Need to check: housing benefit, OT visit, notify change of address to Benefits Agency, PACT team, etc., shopping trip with Joe for any household items.

Information you record should be clear and factual

Keys to good practice: Recording information

The purpose of a file is to reflect an accurate and up-to-date picture of an individual's situation, and to provide an historical record which can be referred to at some point in the future. Some of it may be required to be disclosed to other agencies. Always think about what you write. Make sure it is ACES:

✓ Accurate

✓ Clear

✓ Easy to read

✓ Shareable.

All information, however it is stored, is subject to the rules laid down in the Data Protection Act 1998, which covers medical records, social service records, credit information, local authority information – in fact, anything which is personal data (facts and opinions about an individual).

The principles of data protection

Anyone processing personal data must comply with the eight enforceable principles of good practice. These say that data must be:
- fairly and lawfully processed
- processed for limited purposes

- adequate, relevant and not excessive
- accurate
- not kept for longer than necessary
- processed in accordance with the data subject's rights
- kept secure
- not transferred to countries without adequate protection.

Written records

The confidentiality of written records is extremely important. You will need to make sure that, when you receive information in a written form (perhaps intended for someone's file or a letter concerning someone you are caring for), the information is not left where it could be easily read by others.

Do not leave confidential letters or notes lying in a reception area, or on a desk where visitors or other staff members might see them. You should ensure that the information is filed, or handed to the person it is intended for, or that you follow your agency procedure for handling confidential information as it comes into the organisation.

You may need to stamp such information with a 'Confidential' stamp so that people handle it correctly.

Report writing must be done in a private place to keep information confidential

The dos and don'ts of dealing with information

Type of information	Do	Don't
Telephone calls, incoming	Check the identity of the caller	Give out any information unless you are sure who the caller is
Telephone calls, outgoing	Make sure that you are passing on information to which the caller is entitled	Give out details that the individual has not agreed to disclose
Texting	Use for arranging meetings and appointments	Give any detailed or confidential information
Written information	Check that it goes immediately to the person it is intended for	Leave written information lying around where it can be read by anyone
Receiving faxed material	Check your organisation's procedure for dealing with faxed material. Collect it as soon as possible from any central fax point	Leave it in a fax tray where it could be read by unauthorised people
Sending faxed material	Ensure that it is clearly marked 'Confidential' and has the name on it of the person to whom it should be given	Fax confidential material without clearly stating that it is confidential and it is only to be given to a named person If in doubt, do not use a fax to send confidential information
Receiving e-mailed information	Save any confidential attachments or messages promptly into a password-protected file Acknowledge safe receipt of confidential information	Leave an e-mail open on your screen
Sending e-mailed information	Ensure that you have the right e-mail address for the person who is receiving the information Clearly mark the e-mail 'Confidential' if it contains personal information Ask for the receipient to acknowledge receipt	Leave an e-mail open on your screen Send confidential information to an address without a named mailbox i.e. info@…

Choosing the best way to pass on information

Sometimes the method of communication is dictated by the circumstances. If the situation requires an immediate response, or you need to find essential information urgently, then you are unlikely to write a long letter, walk down to the post office, put it in the post and wait until next week to get a reply! You are far more likely to pick up the telephone and see if you can contact the person you need to speak to, or send a quick e-mail. Or you may choose to fax your request, or fax information in response to a telephone request from someone else. These methods are fast, almost instant, and relatively reliable for getting information accurately from one place to another.

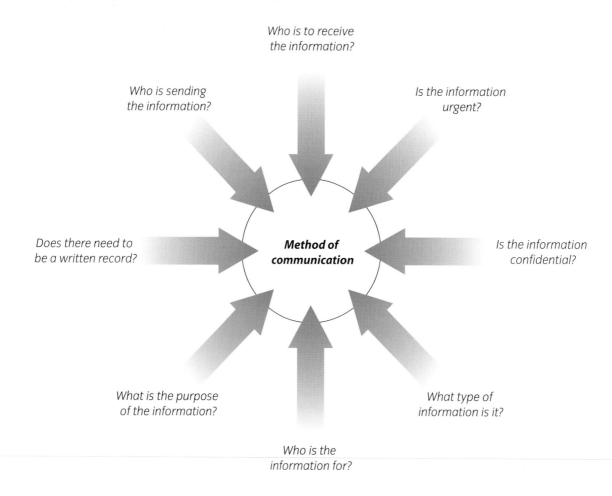

Who is to receive the information?

Who is sending the information?

Is the information urgent?

Does there need to be a written record?

Method of communication

Is the information confidential?

What is the purpose of the information?

What type of information is it?

Who is the information for?

Factors to consider when choosing a method of communication

There may be other occasions when, on the grounds of confidentiality, something is sent through the post marked 'Strictly confidential' and only to be opened by the person whose name is on the envelope. This method may be entirely appropriate for information which is too confidential to be sent by fax and would be inappropriate in a telephone conversation or to be sent by e-mail.

You will have to take a number of factors into account when deciding which method to use, as the diagram above shows.

The purpose of keeping records

In any organisation records are kept for a variety of different purposes. The type of record that you keep is likely to be dictated by the purpose for which it is required. It could be:

- information that is needed for making decisions
- information to provide background knowledge and understanding for another worker
- information about family and contacts of people who are important to an individual
- information to be passed to another professional who is also involved in providing a caring service
- information to be passed from yourself to a colleague over a short space of time to ensure that the care you provide offers an element of continuity
- information to help in planning and developing services.

The kind of information that you may record to pass on within your own organisation may well be different from the types of record that you would keep if you were going to send that information to another agency, or if it was going into someone else's filing system.

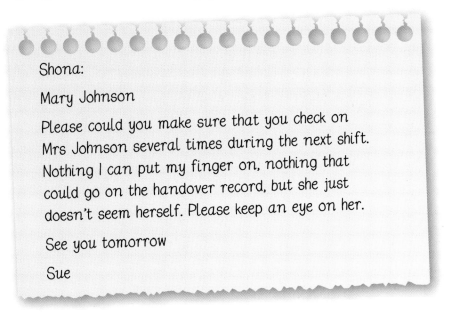

Shona:

Mary Johnson

Please could you make sure that you check on Mrs Johnson several times during the next shift. Nothing I can put my finger on, nothing that could go on the handover record, but she just doesn't seem herself. Please keep an eye on her.

See you tomorrow

Sue

An informal note like the one above is often used to pass on information which is not appropriate for a formal file or record sheet, but it is nevertheless important for a colleague to take note of. This is different from information which has to go outside the organisation – it would need to be formally written, and word processed using a more structured format.

Medical records

One of the very common means of transmitting information and keeping records in health and care is an observation chart recording temperature and blood pressure, like the one on the next page.

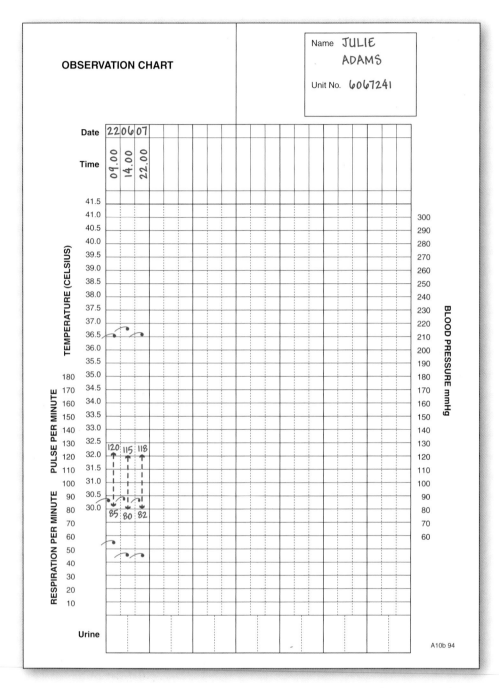

OBSERVATION CHART

Name JULIE ADAMS

Unit No. 6067241

An observation chart

This is done in a very simple form on a graph, so it is easy to see at a glance if there are any problems. The purpose of this record is simply to monitor a person's physical condition so that everybody who is caring for him or her is able to check on the person's well-being.

If you were to put a written record into someone's case notes or to write a report for another agency or another professional, it is unlikely that you would include the actual charts. It is far more likely that you would include a comment or an interpretation of the information on the charts similar to the one on the next page.

> Mrs J has shown no significant abnormalities in terms of raised temperature or blood pressure for the past week. It would seem to indicate her infection has now cleared up and her temperature has returned to normal after the very high levels of ten days ago.

Other types of record

Information which is likely to be used in making decisions about someone is very important. It may concern an older person who has been the subject of a protection conference, or someone with mental health problems where a background report is being provided to assist in decisions about how to best treat him or her.

Where such records are being kept for the purpose of assisting with decision making, it is important that reports are not written in such a way that people have to read through vast amounts of material before finding the key points. It may be necessary to include a significant amount of information in order to make sure that all of the background is there, but a summary at the beginning or the end is always useful for a reader in a hurry.

Evidence PC①③

Find out about the requirements and procedures for recording and reporting on individuals at your workplace.

Who do you need to go to for permission to access confidential records?

Why records are so important

If service user records are not managed in accordance with the Data Protection Act and Commission for Social Care Inspection regulations, service users might suffer a range of damaging consequences, including those shown below.

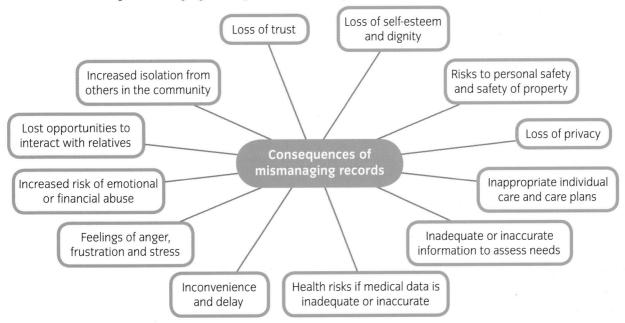

How to record information

 KS ① ⑰ ⑲

If you think about the purpose for which the information is to be used, this should help you to decide on the best way to record it. There would be little point in going to the trouble of typing out a piece of information that you were simply going to pass over to a colleague on the next shift. Alternatively, if you were writing something which was to go into someone's case notes or case file and be permanently recorded, then you would need to make sure that the information is likely to be of use to colleagues, or others who may need to have access to the file.

You may need to record and report:

- signs and symptoms indicating a change in the condition of an individual
- signs of a change in the care needs of an individual
- decisions you have made and actions you have taken relating to an individual's needs or condition
- difficulties or conflicts that have arisen, and actions taken to resolve them.

Active knowledge

Find out if your organisation has a policy about record-keeping and about where different types of information should be recorded and kept. Check whether there are clear guidelines on what should be handwritten and information that needs to be word processed.

You must make sure that you follow the guidelines and provide information in the format that your organisation needs. If you are unsure about how you should produce particular kinds of records, ask your manager.

Keys to good practice: Keeping records

There are certain golden rules which are likely to be included in any organisation's policy about keeping records and recording information:

✓ All information needs to be clear.

✓ It needs to be legible (particularly if you are handwriting it) – there is nothing more useless than a piece of information in a record file which cannot be read because someone's handwriting is poor.

✓ It should be to the point, not ramble or contain far more words than necessary.

✓ Any record should cover the important points clearly and logically.

Look at the following report on K by CS, K's key worker.

K has been bad this week. On Monday he wouldn't go to college. He said he felt ill but he didn't have a temperature or anything. I think he wanted to stay here and see his new girlfriend in the next lodge.

Tuesday 12 noon. After I had just fed him he vomited all over me. I know he can't help throwing up, but he could give me some warning so I didn't have to change all my clothes. I cleaned him up in the usual way.

Thursday we had archery in the lounge. K wanted to go in his wheelchair but he's supposed to use his sticks, so I told him he had to try with them. He got really stroppy and refused to go in the end. I think we ought to arrange some other activities for him that he can do in his own lodge. Then we won't have these fights about him getting about. What do you think?

1   *What is your opinion of this report? Consider the factual detail, the attitude shown towards K by his key worker, and the practical suggestions made.*

2   *List the improvements that you would make to this report.*

3   *What problems could be caused by poor report writing like this example?*

4   *If you were CS's manager, how would you respond to receiving a report like this?*

Methods of storing and retrieving records

Imagine going into a record shop which has thousands of CDs stored in racks but in no recognisable order; they are not filed by the name of the artist, nor by the title of the album. Imagine how much time it would take to trace the particular album that you are looking for. Anything from REM to the Rolling Stones to Mantovani would be all jumbled together! This is exactly what it is like with a filing system – unless there is a system that is easily recognisable and allows people to trace files quickly and accurately, it is impossible to use.

Records are stored in filing systems. These may be manual or computerised. All organisations will have a filing system, and one of the first jobs you must undertake is to learn how to use it.

Some organisations have people who deal specifically with filing, and they do not allow untrained people to access the files. This is likely to be the case if you work for a large organisation, such as an NHS trust. Smaller agencies are likely to have a general filing system to which everyone in the organisation has access. This is exactly the kind of situation where files and records are likely to go missing and to be misplaced.

If you learn to appreciate the importance of records and the different systems that can be used for their storage, then you can assist rather than hinder the process of keeping records up to date, in the right place and readily accessible when people need them.

Manual systems

In a manual filing system the types of file used can vary. The most usual type of file is a brown manila folder with a series of documents fastened inside. Other types include ring binders, lever arch files and bound copies of computer printouts.

All of the files have to be organised (indexed) and stored in a way which makes them easily accessible whenever they are required.

Alphabetical system

If there are not too many files, they can be kept in an alphabetical system in a simple filing cabinet or cupboard. In this sort of system, files are simply placed according to the surname of the person they are about. They are put in the same order as you would see names in a telephone directory, starting with A and working through to the end of the alphabet, with names beginning *Mc* being filed as *Mac* and *St* being filed as *Saint*. GPs' patient records are usually kept using an alphabetical system.

Numerical systems

Where there are large numbers of files an alphabetical system would not work. Imagine the numbers of M. Johnsons or P. Williamses who would appear as patients in a large hospital! In that situation an alphabetical filing system would become impossible to manage, so large organisations give their files numbers, and they are stored in number order. Clearly, a numerical system needs to have an index system so that a person's name can be attached to the appropriate number.

A hospital is likely to give a patient a number which will appear on all relevant documentation so that it is always possible to trace his or her medical notes. However, there still needs to be an overall record to attach that person's name and address to that particular set of case notes, and these days this is normally kept on a central computer.

Other indexing systems

It could be that, instead of files being organised alphabetically, they may be organised according to the different services an agency offers. For example, they could be kept under 'Mental health services', 'Care in the community services', 'Services for children' and so on. Within these categories files would be kept in alphabetical order. In a similar way, files may be organised under geographical areas.

Computerised systems

Your organisation is likely to use a computerised system, and there will be very clear procedures which must be followed by everyone who accesses the system. The procedures will vary depending on the system used, but usually involve accessing files through a special programme, which may well have been written either especially for your organisation, or specifically for record-keeping in health and care.

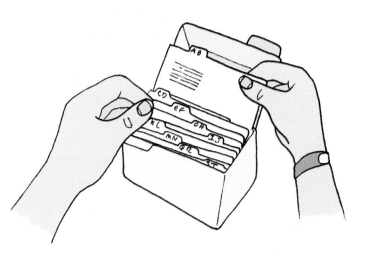

An alphabetical card index

You are unlikely to be able to delete or alter any information which is in someone's file on a computer. It is possible that you will only be able to add information in very specific places, or it could be that files are 'read only' and you cannot add any information to them. This process, because it will not allow people to change or alter files, does have the advantage that information is likely to remain in a clear format. It is less likely to become lost or damaged in the way that manual files are. After all, it is really not possible to leave a computer system on a bus!

With a computerised filing system, there will be clear procedures to be followed

A computerised system enables organisations to keep a great deal more information in much less space. Although they can be expensive to install and to set up, the advantages outweigh the disadvantages in the long run. It also means that everyone in the organisation has to learn how to operate the system and how to use the computer – this is a new skill for many people. It is, however, a skill worth learning if it enables you to record and use information more accurately and effectively.

Evidence   PC ⑥

Think of a situation when you have had difficulty accessing or updating records and reports.

Describe the problems you had and how you dealt with the situation.

Other types of records

Most organisations maintain electronic records for accounts, suppliers, personnel and all essential business records. There will be a back-up for any electronically held information; this may be a paper system or off-site electronic back-up.

Useful information about advice and support services in the area could be maintained in a resource area or filing system, so that helpful leaflets and information packs are not left in a heap on a shelf or a window sill! An electronic index of useful websites, with links, can be very valuable for service users and their families if they have computer access and are comfortable accessing information in this way.

Remember

Filing systems can work extremely well if they are properly run. They work efficiently and effectively in most organisations as long as a few basic rules are followed by everyone who uses them (see the table below).

Some basic rules about filing

Do	Don't
Leave a note or card (or something similar) when you borrow a file from a manual filing system	Remove an index card from a system
Return files as soon as possible	Keep files lying around after you have finished with them
Enter information clearly and precisely	Alter or move around the contents of a file, or take out or replace documents which are part of someone's file
Be sure that you access electronic files strictly within your permitted level of access	Make any changes to files unless permitted to do so
Make sure you log in and out correctly	Copy any part of an electronic record system
	Forget to log out

Test yourself

1 Name four reasons for keeping records on individuals.

2 Name three advantages and three disadvantages of a computerised filing system.

3 Why is it important to record and report changes of condition in an individual?

4 What might be the consequences of mismanaging records at your workplace?

5 Explain clearly the key principles of data protection and how these relate to your role at work.

HSC 31 FURTHER READING AND RESEARCH

In this section you have covered aspects of communication to help you build and develop relationships as well as ways to improve your practice as a professional care worker. Below are details of further opportunities to research this subject. The list is not exhaustive and some you may find more interesting and useful than others.

www.directgov.co.uk (Data Protection Act 1998, Rights and Responsibilities)

www.dh.gov.uk (Department of Health – Data Protection Act 1998, Patient choice, Sensory impairment

www.arcos.org.uk ARCOS (Association for Rehabilitation of Communication and Oral Skills) tel: 01684 576795

www.scie.org.uk (Social Care Institute of Excellence

www.rnib.org.uk (Royal Institute of Blind People)

www.sense.org.uk (Sense)

www.deafblind.org.uk, www.deafblindscotland.org.uk (Deafblind)

www.rnid.org.uk (RNID)

www.altzheimers.org.uk (Alzheimer's Society)

www.askmencap.info (Mencap – fact sheets on communication and people with learning disabilities)

Butler, S. (2004) *Hearing and Sight Loss* Age Concern and RNIB

Caldwell, P., Stevens, P. (2005) *Creative Conversations: Communicating with People with Learning Disabilities* Pavilion Publishers

Malone, C., Forbat, L., Robb, M., Seden, J. (2004) *Relating Experience: Stories from Health & Social Care: An Anthology about Communication and Relationships* Routledge

Moss, B (2007) *Communication Skills for Health & Social Care* Sage Publications Ltd

Thomson, H., Meggitt, C. (2007) *Human Growth and Development* Hodder Headline

Promote, monitor and maintain health, safety and security in the working environment

This unit is about the way you can contribute to making your workplace a safe, secure and healthy place for people who use it to meet their care needs, for those who work alongside you, and for yourself. Your workplace may be a home environment or any other facility which provides a health or care service.

In the first element you will need to learn about what needs to be done to ensure a safe workplace environment. In the second element you will be looking at how you may need to adapt the way you work to become more safety conscious and think about the way in which your work can affect others. The third element in this unit is about how to respond in an emergency.

What you need to learn

- What is safety?
- How to maintain security
- The legal framework
- Dealing with hazardous waste
- How to promote a safe work environment
- Safe manual handling
- How to contribute to infection control
- Challenging inappropriate practice
- How to maintain personal safety
- Fire safety
- Security issues
- Health emergencies.

HSC 32a Monitor and maintain the safety and security of the working environment

What is safety?

 KS 2 6 10 11 12 14 18

It sounds very simple and straightforward: make sure that the place in which you work is safe and secure. However, when you start to think about it – safe for whom or from whom? Safe from tripping over things? Safe from hazardous fumes? Safe from infection? Safe from intruders? Safe from work-related injuries? You can begin to see that this is a wide and complex subject. It may help if you think about safety and security in respect of the areas of responsibility shown in the table below.

Responsibilities for safety and security in the workplace

Employer's responsibilities	Employee's responsibilities	Shared responsibilities
Planning safety and security	Using the systems and procedures correctly	Safety of individuals using the facilities
Providing information about safety and security	Reporting flaws or gaps in the systems, equipment or procedures in use	Safety of the environment
Updating systems and procedures		

Safety in the workplace

You share responsibility with your employer for the safety of all the people who use your service. There are many hazards which can cause injury to people, especially if they are old, ill or disabled. You need to be aware of the following types of hazards.

Environmental hazards

These include:
- wet or slippery floors
- cluttered passageways or corridors
- re-arranged furniture
- worn carpets or rugs
- electrical flexes.

Hazards connected with equipment and materials

Examples of such hazards include:

- faulty brakes on beds
- worn or faulty electrical or gas appliances
- worn or damaged lifting equipment
- worn or damaged mobility aids
- incorrectly labelled substances, such as cleaning fluids
- leaking or damaged containers
- faulty waste-disposal equipment.

Hazards connected with people

This category of hazards includes:

- handling procedures
- visitors to the building
- intruders
- violent and aggressive behaviour.

Your role

Your responsibility to contribute to a safe environment means more than simply being aware of these potential hazards. You must take steps to check and deal with any sources of risk. If you are supervising staff, you must also ensure that they are aware of the possible risks and hazards and know how to deal with them, or how to ask for help or advice from a senior member of staff. Although it is ultimately your employer's responsibility you have a duty to ensure the safety of any staff you supervise.

Key terms

Hazard: Something which could possibly cause harm.

Risk: The likelihood of a hazard causing harm.

You can fulfil your role in two ways: you can deal directly with the hazard, or you can report it to your manager.

Dealing directly with the hazard

This means that you have taken individual responsibility. It will probably apply to obvious hazards such as:

- trailing flexes – you can roll them up and store them safely
- wet floors – you can dry them as far as possible and put out warning signs

After washing floors dry them as much as possible, and set out warning signs

- cluttered doorways and corridors – you can remove objects and store them safely or dispose of them appropriately; if items are heavy, use assistance or mechanical aids
- visitors to the building – challenge anyone you do not recognise; asking 'Can I help you?' is usually enough to establish whether a person has a good reason to be there
- fire – follow the correct procedures to raise the alarm and assist with evacuation.

Informing your manager

When you inform your manager, the hazard becomes an organisational responsibility. You should report hazards which are beyond your role and competence, such as:

- faulty equipment – fires, kettles, computers, etc.
- worn floor coverings
- loose or damaged fittings
- obstructions too heavy for you to move safely
- damaged or faulty aids – hoists, bed brakes, bathing aids, etc.
- people acting suspiciously on the premises
- fire.

How to maintain security

Most workplaces where care is provided are not under lock and key. This is an inevitable part of ensuring that people have choice and that their rights are respected. However, they also have a right to be secure. Security in a care environment is about:

- security against intruders
- security in respect of people's privacy and decisions about unwanted visitors
- security against being abused
- security of property.

Security against intruders

If you work for a large organisation, such as an NHS trust, it may be that all employees are easily identifiable by identity badges with photographs. Some of these even contain a microchip which allows the card to be 'swiped' to gain access to secure parts of the building. This makes it easier to identify people who do not have a right to be on the premises.

In a smaller workplace, there may be a system of issuing visitors' badges to visitors who have reasons to be there, or it may simply rely on the vigilance of the staff.

Some workplaces operate electronic security systems, like those in the NHS where cards are 'swiped' to open doors. Less sophisticated systems in small workplaces may use a keypad with a code number known only to staff and those who are legitimately on the premises. It is often difficult to maintain security with such systems, as codes are forgotten or become widely known. In order to maintain security, it is necessary to change the codes regularly, and to make sure everyone is aware.

Some workplaces still operate with keys, although the days of staff walking about with large bunches of keys attached to a belt are fast disappearing. If mechanical keys are used, there will be a list of named keyholders and there is likely to be a system of handover of keys at shift change. However, each workplace has its own system and you need to be sure that you understand which security system operates in your workplace.

The more dependent individuals are, the greater the risk. If you work with high-dependency or unconscious patients, people with a severe learning disability or multiple disabilities or people who are very confused, you will have to be extremely vigilant in protecting them from criminals.

Keys to good practice: Protecting against intruders

✓ Be aware of everyone you come across. Get into the habit of noticing people and thinking, 'Do I know that person?'

✓ Challenge anyone you do not recognise.

✓ The challenge should be polite. 'Can I help you?' is usually enough to find out if a visitor has a reason to be on the premises.

✓ If a person says that he or she is there to see someone:

✓ Don't give directions – escort him or her.

✓ If the person is a genuine visitor, he or she will be grateful. If not, he or she will disappear pretty quickly!

Workplaces where most or all service users are in individual rooms can also be difficult to make secure, as it is not always possible to check every room if service users choose to close the door. A routine check can be very time consuming, and can affect individuals' rights to privacy and dignity.

Communal areas are easier to check, but can present their own problems; it can be difficult to be sure who is a legitimate visitor and who should not be there. Some establishments provide all visitors with badges, but while this may be acceptable in a large institution or an office block, it is not compatible with creating a comfortable and relaxed atmosphere in a residential setting. Extra care must be taken to check that you know all the people in a communal area. If you are not sure, ask. It is better to risk offending someone by asking 'Can I help you?' or 'Are you waiting for someone?' than to leave an intruder unchallenged.

Remember

If you find an intruder on the premises, don't tackle him or her – raise the alarm.

CASE STUDY: Checking visitors

Fitzroy works in a secure residential unit for older people with dementia. All the entry and exit doors to the unit are operated by a swipe card, and all staff and visitors are required to wear their identity pass visibly at all times. The visitor passes cannot open the doors.

One day Fitzroy sees Mrs Gregory, a resident, standing at the exit door with a man Fitzroy does not recognise. The man has a swipe card and is about to open the door. Fitzroy quickly approaches and politely asks the man to identify himself. The man says he is Mrs Gregory's nephew and has come to take her out for a drive in his car. It is a cold day but Mrs Gregory is not wearing a coat.

1 *Was Fitzroy right to challenge the man?*

2 *What should Fitzroy do next?*

3 *What might have happened if Fitzroy had not challenged the man?*

4 *What are the management issues in this case study?*

Protecting people

If very dependent individuals are living in their own homes, the risks are far greater. You must try to impress on them the importance of finding out who people are before letting them in. If they are able to use it, the 'password' scheme from the utilities (water, gas and electricity companies) is helpful. There are many security schemes operated by the police in partnership with local authority services and charities such as Age Concern and Help the Aged, such as 'Safe as Houses' and 'Safer Homes', which provide security advice and items such as smoke alarms and door chains to older people.

Restricting access

People have a right to choose who they see. This can often be a difficult area to deal with. If there are relatives or friends who wish to visit and an individual does not want to see them, you may have to make this clear. It is difficult to do, but you can only be effective if you are clear and assertive. You should not make excuses or invent reasons why visitors cannot see the person concerned. You could say something like: 'I'm sorry, Mr Price has told us that he does not want to see you. I understand that this may be upsetting, but it is his choice. If he does change his mind we will contact you. Would you like to leave your phone number?'

Do not allow yourself to be drawn into passing on messages or attempting to persuade – that is not your role. Your job is to respect the wishes of the person you are caring for. If you are asked to intervene or to pass on a message, you must refuse politely but firmly.

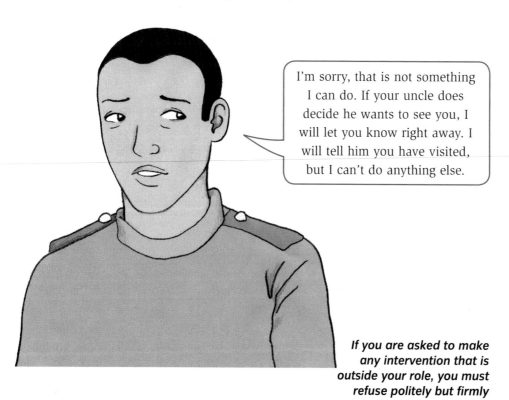

I'm sorry, that is not something I can do. If your uncle does decide he wants to see you, I will let you know right away. I will tell him you have visited, but I can't do anything else.

If you are asked to make any intervention that is outside your role, you must refuse politely but firmly

There may also be occasions when access is restricted for other reasons; possibly because someone is seriously ill and there are medical reasons for limiting access, or because of a legal restriction such as a court order. In either case, it should be clearly recorded on the individual's record and your supervisor will advise you about the restrictions. If you are working in a supervisory capacity, it will be part of your role to ensure that junior staff are aware of these restrictions.

Abuse is dealt with in depth in Unit HSC 35 (page 200), but it can never be repeated often enough that individuals have a right to be protected from abuse, and you must report immediately any abuse you see or suspect.

Active knowledge

You need a colleague or friend to try this role play. One of you should be the person who has come to visit and the other the care worker who has to say that a friend or relative will not see him or her. Try using different scenarios – angry, upset, aggressive, and so on. Try at least three different scenarios each. By the time you have practised a few times, you may feel better equipped to deal with the situation when it happens in reality.

If you cannot find anyone to work with you, it is possible to do a similar exercise by imagining three or four different scenarios and then writing down the words you would say in each of the situations.

Security of property

Property and valuables belonging to individuals in care settings should be safeguarded. It is likely that your employer will have a property book in which records of all valuables and personal possessions are entered.

There may be particular policies within your organisation, but as a general rule you are likely to need to:

- make a record of all possessions on admission
- record valuable items separately
- describe items of jewellery by their colour, for example 'yellow metal' not 'gold'
- ensure that individuals sign for any valuables they are keeping, and that they understand that they are liable for their loss
- inform your manager if an individual is keeping valuables or a significant amount of money.

Evidence   PC 1 2 3

Find out about the procedures relating to security at your workplace.

What action should you take to deal with people who do not have a right to enter, be in or around the premises and environment in which you work?

Make notes for your portfolio.

It is always difficult when items go missing in a care setting, particularly if they are valuable. It is important that you check all possibilities before calling the police.

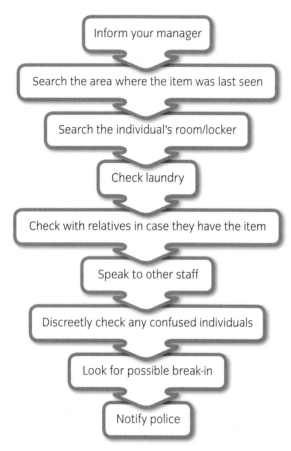

Action stages when property goes missing

Outside the usual care setting

There are always additional health and safety considerations when you are providing care or support to service users outside the care environment. For example, if you are planning a visit or holiday trip, you may need to consider the following:

- accessibility
- safety of premises and potential hazards
- accessibility and safety of transport
- provision of safe toilet facilities
- security of people, property and travel documents
- safety checks on any equipment
- instructions for using any unfamiliar equipment
- provision for special dietary arrangements
- insurance.

A change in environment can prove unsettling for some individuals, and extra vigilance may be needed to ensure that vulnerable people are not distressed by the changes.

The legal framework

The settings in which you provide care are generally covered by the Health and Safety at Work Act 1974 (HASAWA). This Act has been updated and supplemented by many sets of regulations and guidelines, which extend it, support it or explain it. The regulations most likely to affect your workplace are shown in the diagram below.

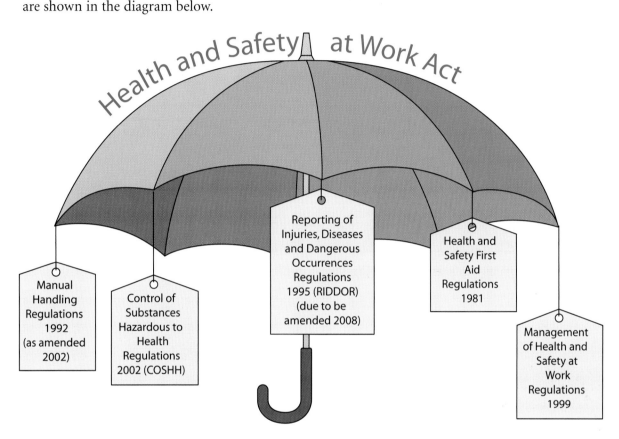

Health and Safety at Work Act

Manual Handling Regulations 1992 (as amended 2002)

Control of Substances Hazardous to Health Regulations 2002 (COSHH)

Reporting of Injuries, Diseases and Dangerous Occurrences Regulations 1995 (RIDDOR) (due to be amended 2008)

Health and Safety First Aid Regulations 1981

Management of Health and Safety at Work Regulations 1999

The Health and Safety at Work Act is like an umbrella

You and the law

There are many regulations, laws and guidelines dealing with health and safety. You do not need to know the detail, but you do need to know where your responsibilities begin and end.

The laws place certain responsibilities on both employers and employees. For example, it is up to the employer to provide a safe place in which to work, but the employee also has to show reasonable care for his or her own safety.

Employers have to:
● provide a safe workplace
● ensure that there is safe access to and from the workplace
● provide information on health and safety
● provide health and safety training
● undertake risk assessment for all hazards.

Workers must:

- take reasonable care for their own safety and that of others
- co-operate with the employer in respect of health and safety matters
- not intentionally damage any health and safety equipment or materials provided by the employer.

Both the employee and employer are jointly responsible for safeguarding the health and safety of anyone using the premises.

Each workplace where there are five or more workers must have a written statement of health and safety policy. The policy must include:

- a statement of intention to provide a safe workplace
- the name of the person responsible for implementing the policy
- the names of any other individuals responsible for particular health and safety hazards
- a list of identified health and safety hazards and the procedures to be followed in relation to them
- procedures for recording accidents at work
- details for evacuation of the premises.

Active knowledge

Find out where the health and safety policy is for your workplace and make sure you read it.

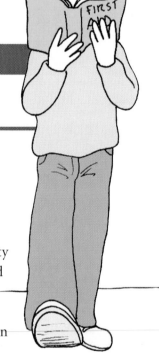

The Health and Safety Executive

Britain's Health and Safety Commission (HSC) and the Health and Safety Executive (HSE) are responsible for the regulation of almost all the risks to health and safety arising from work activity in Britain. The Health and Safety Commission is sponsored by the Department of Work and Pensions and is accountable to the Minister of State for Work.
The HSE's job is to help the Health and Safety Commission ensure that risks to people's health and safety from work activities are properly controlled.

The Health and Safety Executive (www.hse.gov.uk) states:

Our mission is to protect people's health and safety by ensuring risks in the changing workplace are properly controlled.

The HSC believes that prevention is better than cure, and two key roles are providing information and support to ensure that workplaces are safe and enforcement in order to ensure that legislation is adhered to. The HSE has the power to prosecute employers who fail in any way to safeguard the health and safety of people who use their premises.

Risk assessment

Risk assessment is designed for employers and self-employed people, who are required by law to identify and assess risks in the workplace. This includes any situations where potential harm may be caused. There are many regulations that require risks to be assessed and some are covered by European Community directives. These include:

- Management of Health and Safety at Work Regulations 1999
- Manual Handling Operations Regulations 1992 (amended 2002)
- Personal Protective Equipment at Work Regulations 1992
- Health and Safety (Display Screen Equipment) Regulations 1992 (amended 2002)
- Noise at Work Regulations 1989
- Control of Substances Hazardous to Health Regulations 2002 (COSHH)
- Control of Asbestos at Work Regulations 2002
- Control of Lead at Work Regulations 2002.

There are other regulations that deal with very specialised risks such as major hazards and ionising radiation. However, these are not considered to be common risks in most workplaces.

There are five key stages to undertaking a risk assessment, which involve answering the following questions.

- What is the purpose of the risk assessment?
- Who has to assess the risk?
- Whose risk should be assessed?
- What should be assessed?
- When should the risk be assessed?

The Management of Health and Safety at Work Regulations 1999 state that employers have to assess any risks which are associated with the workplace and work activities. This means all activities, from walking on wet floors to dealing with violence. Having carried out a risk assessment, the employer must then apply **risk control measures**. This means that actions must be taken to reduce the risks. For example, alarm buzzers may need to be installed or extra staff employed, as well as steps such as providing extra training for staff or written guidelines on how to deal with a particular hazard.

Risk assessments are vitally important in order to protect the health and safety of both you and the service user. You should always check that a risk assessment has been carried out before you undertake any task, and then follow the steps identified in the assessment in order to reduce the risk.

However, do not forget that you must balance the individual wishes and preferences of each individual who uses your service with your own safety and the safety of others. Some examples of this principle are discussed in the section on manual handling on page 100.

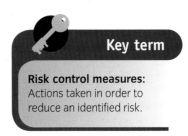

Key term

Risk control measures: Actions taken in order to reduce an identified risk.

Risks in someone's home

Of course, the situation is somewhat different if you work in an individual's own home. Your employer can still carry out risk assessments and put risk control measures in place, such as a procedure for working in twos in a situation where there is a risk of violence. What cannot be done is to remove environmental hazards such as trailing electrical flexes, rugs with curled up edges, worn patches on stair carpets or old equipment. All you can do is to advise the person whose home it is of the risks, and suggest how things could be improved. You also need to take care!

Control of Substances Hazardous to Health (COSHH)

What are hazardous substances? There are many substances hazardous to health – nicotine, many drugs, even too much alcohol! The COSHH Regulations apply to substances which have been identified as toxic, corrosive or irritant. This includes cleaning materials, pesticides, acids, disinfectants and bleaches, and naturally occurring substances such as blood, bacteria, etc. Workplaces may have other hazardous substances which are particular to the nature of the work carried out.

The Health and Safety Executive states that employers must take the following steps to protect employees from hazardous substances.

Step 1

Find out what hazardous substances are used in the workplace and the risks these substances pose to people's health.

Step 2

Decide what precautions are needed before any work starts with hazardous substances.

Step 3

Prevent people being exposed to hazardous substances, but where this is not reasonably practicable, control the exposure.

Step 4

Make sure control measures are used and maintained properly, and that safety procedures are followed.

Step 5

If required, monitor exposure of employees to hazardous substances.

Step 6

Carry out health surveillance where assessment has shown that this is necessary, or COSHH makes specific requirements.

Remember

- It may be your workplace, but it is the person's home. If you work in an individual's home or long-term residential setting, you have to balance the need for safety with the rights of people to have their living space the way they want it.

- Both you and the individuals using the service are entitled to expect a safe place in which to live and work, but remember their rights to choose how they want to live.

Step 7

If required, prepare plans and procedures to deal with accidents, incidents and emergencies.

Step 8

Make sure employees are properly informed, trained and supervised.

Every workplace must have a COSHH file, which should be easily accessible to all staff. This file lists all the hazardous substances used in the workplace. It should detail:

- where they are kept
- how they are labelled
- their effects
- the maximum amount of time it is safe to be exposed to them
- how to deal with an emergency involving one of them.

From April 2005 employers are required to focus on the following eight principles of good practice in the control of substances hazardous to health:

- Design and operate processes and activities to minimise emission, release and spread of substances hazardous to health.
- Take into account all relevant routes of exposure – inhalation, skin absorption and ingestion – when developing control measures.
- Control exposure by measures that are proportionate to the health risk.
- Choose the most effective and reliable control options which minimise the escape and spread of substances hazardous to health.
- Where adequate control of exposure cannot be achieved by other means, provide, in combination with other control measures, suitable personal protective equipment.
- Check and review regularly all elements of control measures for their continuing effectiveness.
- Inform and train all employees on the hazards and risks from the substances with which they work and the use of control measures developed to minimise the risks.

Ensure that the introduction of control measures does not increase the overall risk to health and safety.

If you have to work with hazardous substances, make sure that you take the precautions detailed in the COSHH file. This may be wearing gloves or protective goggles, or it may involve limiting the time you are exposed to the substance or only using it in certain circumstances.

The COSHH file should also give you information about how to store hazardous substances. This will involve using the correct containers as supplied by the manufacturers. All containers must have safety lids and caps, and must be correctly labelled.

Remember

Hazardous substances are not just things like poisons and radioactive material – they are also substances such as cleaning fluids and bleach.

Active knowledge

You must ensure that you and all staff know the location of the COSHH file in your workplace. Read the contents of the file, especially information about the substances you use or come into contact with and what the maximum exposure limits are. You do not have to know the detail of each substance but the information you need should be contained in the COSHH file, which must be kept up to date.

Never use the container of one substance for storing another, and *never* change the labels.

Symbol	Abbreviation	Hazard	Description of hazard
	E	explosive	Chemicals that explode
	F	highly flammable	Chemicals that may catch fire in contact with air, only need brief contact with an ignition source, have a very low flash point or evolve highly flammable gases in contact with water
	T (also Carc or Muta)	toxic (also carcinogenic or mutagenic)	Chemicals that at low levels cause damage to health and may cause cancer or induce heritable genetic defects or increase the incidence of these
	Xh or Xi	harmful or irritant	Chemicals that may cause damage to health, especially inflammation to the skin or other mucous membranes
	C	corrosive	Chemicals that may destroy living tissue on contact
	N	dangerous for the environment	Chemicals that may present an immediate or delayed danger to one or more components of the environment

The symbols above indicate hazardous substances. They are there for your safety and for the safety of those you care for and work with. Before you use *any* substance, whether it is liquid, powder, spray, cream or aerosol, take the following simple steps:

- check the container for the hazard symbol
- if there is a hazard symbol, go to the COSHH file
- look up the precautions you need to take with the substance
- make sure you follow the procedures, which are intended to protect you.

If you are concerned about a substance being used in your workplace which is not in the COSHH file, or if you notice incorrect containers or labels being used, report this to your supervisor. Once you have informed your supervisor, it becomes his or her responsibility to act to correct the problem.

Reporting of Injuries, Diseases and Dangerous Occurrences (RIDDOR)

Reporting accidents and ill-health at work is a legal requirement. All accidents, diseases and dangerous occurrences should be reported to the Incident Contact Centre. The Centre was established on 1 April 2001 as a single point of contact for all incidents in the UK. The information is important because it means that risks and causes of accidents, incidents and diseases can be identified. All notifications are passed on to either the local authority Environmental Health department, or the Health and Safety Executive, as appropriate.

Your employer needs to report:

- deaths
- major injuries (see below)
- accidents resulting in more than three days off work.
- diseases
- dangerous occurrences

Reportable major injuries and diseases

Reportable injuries	Reportable diseases
fracture other than to fingers, thumbs or toes	certain poisonings
amputation	
dislocation of the shoulder, hip, knee or spine	some skin diseases such as occupational dermatitis, skin cancer, chrome ulcer, oil folliculitis acne
loss of sight (temporary or permanent)	
chemical or hot metal burn to the eye or any penetrating injury to the eye	lung diseases including occupational asthma, farmer's lung, pneumoconiosis, asbestosis, mesothelioma
injury resulting from an electric shock or electrical burn leading to unconsciousness or requiring resuscitation or admittance to hospital for more than 24 hours	
any other injury which leads to hypothermia (getting too cold), heat-induced illness, or unconsciousness; requires resuscitation; or requires admittance to hospital for more than 24 hours	infections such as leptospirosis, hepatitis, tuberculosis, anthrax, legionellosis (Legionnaires' disease) and tetanus
unconsciousness caused by asphyxia (suffocation) or exposure to a harmful substance or biological agent	
acute illness requiring medical treatment, or leading to loss of consciousness, arising from absorption of any substance by inhalation, ingestion or through the skin	other conditions such as occupational cancer, certain musculoskeletal disorders, decompression illness and hand-arm vibration syndrome
acute illness requiring medical treatment where there is reason to believe that this resulted from exposure to a biological agent or its toxins or infected material.	

Dangerous occurrences

If something happens which does not result in a reportable injury, but which clearly could have done, then it may be a dangerous occurrence which must be reported immediately.

Accidents at work

If accidents or injuries occur at work, either to you, other staff or to an individual you are caring for, then the details must be recorded. For example, someone may have a fall, or slip on a wet floor. You must record the incident regardless of whether there was an injury.

Active knowledge

Check that you understand fully all the terms used in the table above.

Your employer should have procedures in place for making a record of accidents, either an accident book or an accident report form. This is not only required by the RIDDOR regulations, but also, if you work in a residential or nursing home, by the Commission for Social Care Inspection.

Any accident book or report form must comply with the requirements of the Data Protection Act 1998 by making sure that the personal details of those involved cannot be read by others using the book. This can be ensured by recording personal details on a tear-off part of the form so that only an anonymous description of the accident is left, or by using individual, numbered and recorded forms that are then logged at a central point. However it is done, it is a legal requirement that people's personal details are not available for others to see unless consent has been given.

Make sure you know where the accident report forms or the accident book are kept, and who is responsible for recording accidents. It is likely to be your manager. An example of an accident report form is given in the Appendix, on page 382.

You must report any accident in which you are involved, or which you have witnessed, to your manager or supervisor. It may be useful to make notes, as in the example below, as soon as possible after the incident so that details on the accident report form can be complete and accurate.

Date: 24.8.07   **Time:** 14.30 **hrs**   **Location:** Main lounge

Description of accident:

PH got out of her chair and began to walk across the lounge with the aid of her stick. She turned her head to continue the conversation she had been having with GK, and as she turned back again she appeared not to have noticed that MP's handbag had been left on the floor. PH tripped over the handbag and fell heavily, banging her head on a footstool.

She was very shaken and although she said that she was not hurt, there was a large bump on her head. P appeared pale and shaky. I asked J to fetch a blanket and to call Mrs J, deputy officer in charge. Covered P with a blanket. Mrs J arrived immediately. Dr was sent for after P was examined by Mrs J.

Dr arrived after about 20 mins and said that she was bruised and shaken, but did not seem to have any injuries.

She wanted to go and lie down. She was helped to bed.

Incident was witnessed by six residents who were in the lounge at the time: GK, MP, IL, MC, CR and BQ.

Signed: **Name:**

An example of notes for the completion of an accident report form

Any medical treatment or assessment which is necessary should be arranged without delay. If an individual has been involved in an accident, you should check if there is anyone he or she would like to be contacted, perhaps a relative or friend. If the accident is serious, and you cannot consult the individual – because he or she is unconscious, for example – the next of kin should be informed as soon as possible.

Complete a report, and ensure that all witnesses to the accident also complete reports. You should include the following in any accident report (see the example on the previous page):

- date, time and place of accident
- person/people involved – bearing in mind the Data Protection Act
- circumstances and details of exactly what you saw
- anything that was said by the individuals involved
- the condition of the individual after the accident
- steps taken to summon help, time of summoning help and time when help arrived
- names of any other people who witnessed the accident
- any equipment involved in the accident.

Evidence   PC ① ⑤ ⑦

Read back over the sections relating to COSHH and RIDDOR.

Describe how each of these regulations affects your work. Try to use real examples.

Dealing with hazardous waste  KS ⑪ ⑫ ⑱

As part of providing a safe working environment, employers have to put procedures in place to deal with waste materials and spillages. There are various types of waste, which must be dealt with in particular ways. The types of hazardous waste you are most likely to come across are shown in the table on the next page, alongside a list of the ways in which each is usually dealt with. Waste can be a source of infection, so it is very important that you follow the procedures your employer has put in place to deal with it safely.

Type of waste	Method of disposal
Clinical waste – used dressings	Yellow bags, clearly labelled with contents and location. This waste is incinerated.
Needles, syringes, cannulas ('sharps')	Yellow sharps box. Never put sharps into anything other than a hard plastic box. This is sealed and incinerated.
Body fluids and waste – urine, vomit, blood, sputum, faeces	Cleared and flushed down sluice drain. Area to be cleaned and disinfected.
Soiled linen	Red bags, direct into laundry; bags disintergrate in wash. If handled, gloves must be worn.
Recyclable instruments and equipment	Blue bags, to be returned to the Central Sterilisation Services Department (CSSD) for recycling and sterilising.

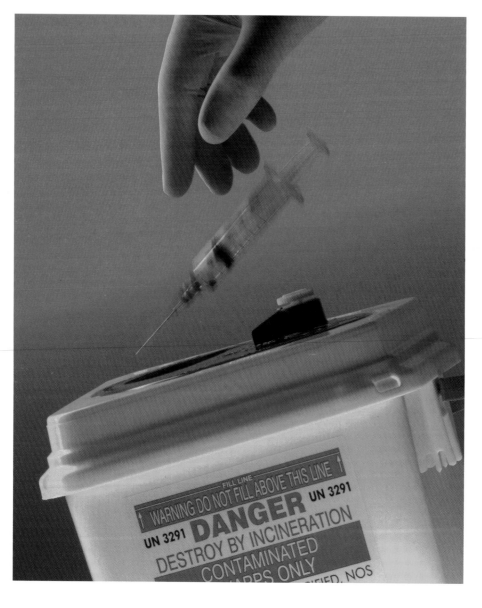

 Remember

- Other people will have to deal with the waste after you have placed it in the bags or containers.

- Make sure it is properly labelled and in the correct containers.

Needles and syringes should be put into a hard plastic box, which is sealed and incinerated

Test yourself

1 How many possible hazards and risks can you find in the illustration below?

   a List at least six.

   b Which of these are the responsibility of the employer?

   c Which are the responsibility of the care staff?

2 Why is it important to check someone's right to enter the premises?

3 What should you do if you see someone you do not recognise in your workplace?

4 What are your employer's responsibilities in respect of hazardous substances?

5 What are your responsibilities in respect of hazardous substances?

6 Name three reportable diseases and describe the process for reporting them in your workplace.

HSC 32b Promote health and safety in the working environment

This element is about what you actually do when you are working. In the previous element, you looked at the procedures and policies which have to be put in place to protect workers and people who use the service, and the laws which govern health and safety. Now you need to learn about the steps you should be following to ensure that the laws and policies work in practice.

How to promote a safe work environment

 KS ② ⑨ ⑪ ⑱

Care environments are places where accidents can quite often happen, not because staff are careless or fail to check hazards, but because of the vulnerability of the people who use the care facilities.

As people become frail or develop physical conditions which affect mobility such as arthritis or Parkinson's, they become susceptible to falls and trips because they are unsteady, and the slightest change in surface or level can upset their balance. Increasing age can also result in less flexibility of muscles and joints, meaning that people are less able to compensate for a loss of balance or a slip and are more likely to fall than younger people, who may be better able to save themselves by reacting more quickly.

Age is not the only factor to increase risk. Other factors, such as impaired vision, multiply the risk of accidents from trips, falls, touching hot surfaces and knocking into objects. Hearing loss can increase the risk of accidents where people have not heard someone, or perhaps something such as a trolley, approaching around a corner. Dementia can increase risks because people fail to remember to take care when they move about. They can also forget where they have put things down and fail to understand the consequences of actions such as touching hot liquids or pulling on cupboard doors.

Supporting individuals to assess and manage risks

It is important that you support individuals in your care in ensuring their own health and well-being. Wherever possible, encourage them to:

- express their needs and preferences in this area
- understand and take responsibility for promoting their own health and care
- assess and manage risks to their health and well-being
- identify and report any factors that may put themselves or others at risk.

Checklist for a safe work environment

It is important that you develop an awareness of health and safety risks and that you are always aware of any risks in any situation you are in. If you get into the habit of making a mental checklist, you will find that it helps. The checklist will vary from one workplace to another, but could look like the one below.

Hazards	Check
Environment	
Floors	Are they dry?
Carpets and rugs	Are they worn or curled at the edges?
Doorways and corridors	Are they clear of obstacles?
Electrical flexes	Are they trailing?
Equipment	
Beds	Are the brakes on? Are they high enough?
Electrical or gas appliances	Are they worn? Have they been safety checked?
Lifting equipment	Is it worn or damaged?
Mobility aids	Are they worn or damaged?
Substances such as cleaning fluids	Are they correctly labelled?
Containers	Are they leaking or damaged?
Waste disposal equipment	Is it faulty?
People	
Visitors to the building	Should they be there?
Handling procedures	Have they been assessed for risk?
Intruders	Have the police been called?
Violent and aggressive behaviour	Has it been dealt with?

One of the other factors to consider in your checklist may be what your colleagues do about health and safety issues. It is very difficult if you are the only person following good practice. You may be able to encourage others by trying some of the following options:

- always showing a good example yourself
- explaining why you are following procedures
- getting some health and safety leaflets from your trade union or environmental health office and leaving them in the staffroom for people to see

- bringing in any information you can about courses or safety lectures
- asking your supervisor if he or she can arrange a talk on health and safety.

See page 107 for what you should do in the situation where a colleague is behaving inappropriately or using unsafe practices.

What you wear

There are several reasons why what staff wear has an impact on health and safety, and why many employers issue uniforms to their employees. The uniform should be comfortable and well fitting with plenty of room for movement. Inappropriate clothing can be restrictive and prevent free movement when working with service users.

High-heeled or poorly supporting shoes are a risk to you in terms of foot injuries and very sore feet! They also present a risk to individuals you are helping, because if you overbalance or stumble, so will they.

Staff should be encouraged to tie up long hair. Hair can contain substantial amounts of bacteria, which could cause infection. In addition, loose long hair could be a safety hazard. Agitated or confused service users may grab hair, or it might get caught in equipment.

There may be restrictions on wearing jewellery or carrying things in your pocket which could cause injury. This can also pose a risk to you – you could be stabbed in the chest by a pair of scissors or ball-point pen! Wrist watches should not be worn. Apart from the possibility of scratching a service user when providing personal care, wearing a watch can prevent good hand-washing practice. Fob watches that pin onto the uniform are convenient and easily obtainable.

Many workplaces do not allow the wearing of rings with stones. Not only is this a possible source of infection, but they can also scratch people or tear protective gloves.

Keys to good practice: Reducing risk

 Simple precautions can often be the most effective in reducing the risk. Always look for the risk and take steps to reduce it.

THINK RISK → ASSESS → REDUCE → AVOID

Safe manual handling

Handling and moving individuals is dealt with in detail in Unit HSC 360 (page 351), but the implications for the safety of both the care worker and the service user are examined in this unit.

Did you know?

Lifting and handling individuals is the single largest cause of injuries at work in health and care settings. One in four workers take time off because of a back injury sustained at work.

The Manual Handling Operations Regulations 1992 require employers to avoid all manual handling where there is a risk of injury 'so far as it is reasonably practical'. Everyone from the European Commission to the Royal College of Nursing has issued policies and directives about avoiding lifting. Make sure you check out the policies in use in your workplace and that you understand them.

Lifting Operations and Lifting Equipment Regulations (1992) (LOLER)

These regulations came into effect on 5 December 1998 and apply to all workplaces. An employee does not have any responsibilities under LOLER but under the Management of Health and Safety at Work Regulations, employees have a duty to ensure that they take reasonable care of themselves and others who may be affected by the actions that they undertake.

Employers do have duties under LOLER. They must ensure that all equipment provided for use at work is:
- sufficiently strong and stable for the particular use and marked to indicate safe working loads
- positioned and installed to minimise any risks
- used safely – that is the work is planned, organised and performed by competent people
- subject to ongoing thorough examination and, where appropriate, inspection by competent people.

In addition employers must ensure:
- lifting operations are planned, supervised and carried out in a safe way by competent people
- equipment for lifting people is safe
- lifting equipment and accessories are thoroughly examined
- a report is submitted by a competent person following a thorough examination or inspection.

Lifting equipment designed for lifting and moving loads must be inspected at least annually, but any equipment that is designed for lifting and handling people must be inspected at least every six months. A nominated competent person may draw up an examination scheme for this purpose.

If employees provide their own lifting equipment, this is covered by the regulations.

Manual lifting

There is almost no situation in which manual lifting and handling could be considered acceptable, but the views and rights of the individual being lifted must be taken into account and a balance achieved.

Remember

- Always use lifting and handling aids.
- There is no such thing as a safe lift.
- Use the aids which your employer is obliged to provide.

On the rare occasions when it is still absolutely necessary for manual lifting to be done, the employer has to make a 'risk assessment' and put procedures in place to reduce the risk of injury to the employee. This could involve ensuring that sufficient staff are available to lift or handle someone safely, which can often mean that four people are needed.

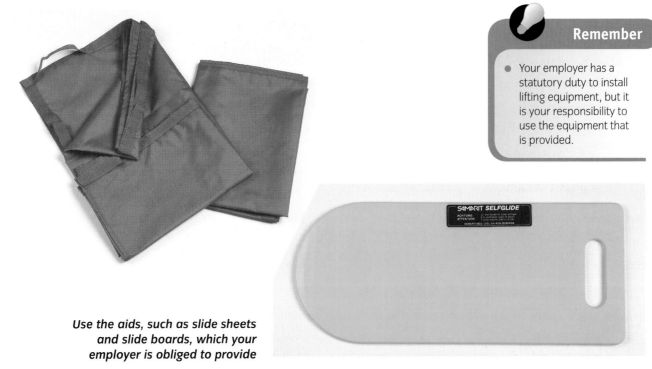

Use the aids, such as slide sheets and slide boards, which your employer is obliged to provide

CASE STUDY: Using safe lifting procedures

Kirsty is a new care assistant at a day centre for adults with disabilities. She was trained to use a hoist as part of a moving and handling course in her previous job. Although there is a mobile hoist at the day centre, Kirsty has noticed that none of the staff use it. On several occasions she has seen individuals being manually lifted from their wheelchairs by the staff, working in pairs.

One morning a service user, Valerie, asked Kirsty to accompany her to the toilet. Kirsty knew that Valerie would need to be helped from her chair onto the toilet, so she went to get the hoist. As she passed the other staff one of them said: 'Oh, you don't want to bother with that thing. Val isn't very heavy – it's much easier to just lift her yourself. Anyway, I don't think the hoist works any more.'

1 *What should Kirsty do next?*

2 *If the hoist does not work, what should Kirsty do?*

3 *What could be the consequences of lifting incorrectly:*

   a *to the staff*

   b *to the individuals they are attempting to lift?*

4 *What training and safety procedures would you recommend for this day centre?*

5 *Are you confident that your own moving and handling skills are up to date? If not, what steps are you taking to improve them?*

Your employer should arrange for all staff to attend a moving and handling course. You must attend one each year, so that you are up to date with the safest possible practices.

If you do have to lift, what should you do?

Encourage all individuals to help themselves – you would be surprised how much 'learned helplessness' exists. This can occur when care workers find it is quicker and easier to do things themselves rather than allowing a person to do it for himself or herself. If service users accept that someone else will take over all care, they may stop making the effort to maintain their independence – in short, they learn how to become helpless.

It is also essential that the views of the person being moved are taken into account. While you and your employer need to make sure that you and other staff are not put at risk by moving or lifting, it is also important that the person needing assistance is not caused pain, distress or humiliation. Groups representing disabled people have pointed out that blanket policies excluding any lifting may infringe the human rights of an individual needing mobility assistance. For example, individuals may in effect be confined to bed unnecessarily and against their will by a lack of lifting assistance. A High Court judgement (A & B vs East Sussex County Council, 2003) found in favour of two disabled women who had been denied access to lifting because the local authority had a 'blanket ban' on lifting regardless of circumstances. Such a ban was deemed unlawful. It is likely that similar cases will be brought under the Human Rights Act 1998, which gives people protection against humiliating or degrading treatment.

The Disability Discrimination Act 1995 came fully into force in October 2004. It was introduced in several stages to take account of the time needed to meet its requirements. This included allowing time for service providers to consider making reasonable changes to their premises so that they could be accessed by disabled users.

Since October 1999, service providers have had to consider making reasonable adjustments to the way they deliver their services so that disabled people can use them. The new duties will apply to service providers where physical features make access to their services impossible or unreasonably difficult for disabled people.

How to contribute to infection control

KS 2 3 11 12 18

The very nature of work in a care setting means that great care must be taken to control the spread of infection. You will come into contact with a number of people during your working day – an ideal opportunity for infection to spread. Infection which spreads from one person to another is called

'cross-infection'. If you work in the community, cross-infection is difficult to control. However, if you work in a residential or hospital setting, infection control is essential. There are various steps which you can take in terms of the way you carry out your work (wherever you work) which can help to prevent the spread of infection.

You do not know what viruses or bacteria may be present in any individual, so it is important that you take precautions when dealing with everyone. The precautions are called 'standard precautions' precisely because you need to take them with everyone you deal with. You must ensure that all staff are familiar with standard precautions and adhere to them.

Wear gloves

When	Any occasion when you will have contact with body fluids (including body waste, blood, mucus, sputum, sweat or vomit), or when you have any contact with anyone with a rash, pressure sore, wound, bleeding or any broken skin. You must also wear gloves when you clear up spills of blood or body fluids or have to deal with soiled linen or dressings.
Why	Because gloves act as a protective barrier against infection.

How

1 Check gloves before putting them on. Never use gloves with holes or tears. Check that they are not cracked or faded.

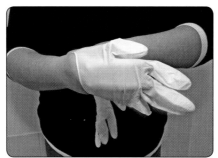

2 Pull gloves on, making sure that they fit properly. If you are wearing a gown, pull them over the cuffs.

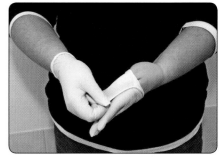

3 Take them off by pulling from the cuff – this turns the glove inside out.

4 Pull off the second glove while still holding the first so that the two gloves are folded together inside out.

5 Dispose of them in the correct waste disposal container and wash your hands.

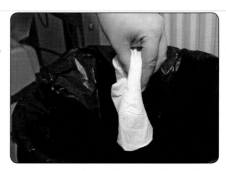

Wash your hands

When	Before and after carrying out any procedure which has involved contact with an individual, or with any body fluids, soiled linen or clinical waste. You must wash your hands even though you have worn gloves. You must also wash your hands before you start and after you finish your shift, before and after eating, after using the toilet and after coughing, sneezing or blowing your nose.
Why	Because hands are a major route to spreading infection. When tests have been carried out on people's hands, an enormous number of bacteria have been found.
How	Wash hands in running water, in a basin deep enough to hold the splashes and with either foot pedals or elbow bars rather than taps, because you can re-infect your hands from still water in a basin, or from touching taps with your hands once they have been washed. Use the soaps and disinfectants supplied. Make sure that you wash thoroughly, including between your fingers. This should take between 10 and 20 seconds.

How

1 Wet your hands thoroughly under warm running water and squirt liquid soap onto the palm of one hand.

2 Rub your hands together to make a lather.

3 Rub the palm of one hand along the back of the other and along the fingers. Then repeat with the other hand.

4 Rub in between each of your fingers on both hands and round your thumbs.

5 Rinse off the soap with clean water.

6 Dry hands thoroughly on a disposable towel.

Alcohol hand rub

Alcohol hand rubs can be useful for use when hands are socially clean and if you are not near a source of water. A small amount should be used and rubbed into the hands using the same technique as for washing with water. The hand rub should be rubbed in until the hands are completely dry.

This is not an alternative to hand washing and is only to be used alongside the proper handwashing technique. It is not effective against bacteria with a spore phase, such as *Clostridium difficile*, so handwashing is essential.

Wear protective clothing

When	You should always wear a gown or plastic apron for any procedure which involves bodily contact or is likely to deal with body waste or fluids. An apron is preferable, unless it is likely to be very messy, as gowns can be a little frightening to the individual you are working with.
Why	Because it will reduce the spread of infection by preventing infection getting on your clothes and spreading to the next person you come into contact with.
How	The plastic apron should be disposable and thrown away at the end of each procedure. You should use a new apron for each individual you come into contact with.

Tie up hair

Why	Because if it hangs over your face, it is more likely to come into contact with the individual you are working with and could spread infection. It could also become entangled in equipment and cause a serious injury.

Clean equipment

Why	Because infection can spread from one person to another on instruments, linen and equipment just as easily as on hands or hair.
How	By washing large items like trolleys with antiseptic solution. Small instruments must be sterilised. Do not shake soiled linen or dump it on the floor. Keep it held away from you. Place linen in the proper bags or hampers for laundering.

Deal with waste

Why	Because it can then be processed correctly, and the risk to others working further along the line in the disposal process is reduced as far as possible.
How	By placing it in the proper bags. Make sure that you know the system in your workplace. It is usually: • clinical waste – yellow • soiled linen – red • recyclable instruments and equipment – blue

Take special precautions

When	There may be occasions when you have to deal with an individual who has a particular type of infection that requires special handling. This can involve things like hepatitis, some types of food poisoning or highly infectious diseases.
How	Your workplace will have special procedures to follow. They may include such measures as gowning, double gloving or wearing masks. Follow the procedures strictly. They are there for your benefit and for the benefit of the other individuals you care for.

Prevention of infection is everyone's responsibility, so you must ensure that colleagues follow the appropriate guidelines.

Challenging inappropriate practice

 KS ② ⑨ ⑩ ⑱

You may have to deal with the situation where one of your colleagues is misusing equipment or behaving in an inappropriate way towards service users or other care workers, a way that fails to minimise risks to health, safety or security.

If you are faced with the situation where a colleague is behaving inappropriately or bad practice is being allowed to occur, you can respond in several ways. Depending on the severity of the problem, you should:

- challenge the behaviour, or the source of the bad practice
- have a one-to-one discussion with the colleague in question
- act as a mentor with whom your colleague can share problems and difficulties
- act as a role model of good practice.

Active knowledge

Working with your colleagues, discuss how inappropriate practice is challenged in your workplace. Explore any improvements in practice that could be introduced.

Motivation

One of the factors which is likely to maintain the motivation and therefore the performance of a team is shared responsibility. Responsibility for the outcome of the team's work is often a very important factor in motivating the team. Developing challenges and plans for their own team and being responsible for the outcome, rather than handing over responsibility to management, is likely to provide team members with the challenge and motivation necessary to maintain good performance, including excellent health and safety standards.

In order for your team to be able to accept responsibility for its actions, it will also need to have the authority to carry out the plans it has made. The team may need to approach management in order to gain this authority, and it may only be for specific events or plans that this is possible, but all the research into effective teams shows that those that have both responsibility and the authority to carry out their plans tend to maintain motivation over longer periods of time. This can only be beneficial in promoting health and safety in the working environment.

How to maintain personal safety

 KS ① ② ③ ④ ⑩ ⑮

There is always an element of risk in working with people. There is little doubt that there is an increase in the level of personal abuse suffered by workers in the health and care services. There is also the element of personal risk encountered by workers who visit people in the community, and have to deal with homes in poor states of repair and an assortment of domestic animals!

However, there are some steps which you can take to assist with your own safety.

 Keys to good practice: Steps to personal safety

✓ If you work alone in the community, always leave details of where you are going and what time you expect to return. This is important in case of accidents or other emergencies, so that you can be found.

✓ Carry a personal alarm, and use it if necessary.

✓ Ask your employer to provide training in techniques to combat aggression and violence. It is foolish and potentially dangerous to go into risky situations without any training.

✓ Try to defuse potentially aggressive situations by being as calm as possible and by talking quietly and reasonably. But if this is not effective, leave.

✓ If you work in a residential or hospital setting, raise the alarm if you find you are in a threatening situation.

✓ Do not tackle aggressors, whoever they are – raise the alarm.

✓ Use an alarm or panic button if you have it – otherwise yell – very loudly.

Your employer should have a written 'lone-working' policy which identifies steps to be taken to protect staff working alone. Make sure that you have read and understood the policy.

CASE STUDY: Risk in the community

Karinda was a home-care assistant on her first visit to a new service user, Mr West. She had been warned that his house was in a poor condition and that he had a large dog. She also knew that he had a history of psychiatric illness and had, in the past, been admitted to hospital compulsorily under the Mental Health Act. When Karinda arrived on her first morning, the outside of the house was in a very poor state – the garden was overgrown, and it was full of rubbish and old furniture. The front door was half open and she could see that half the floorboards in the hallway appeared to be missing – there were simply joists and a drop into the cellar below. Mr West's dog was in the hallway growling and barking, and Mr West was at the top of the stairs shouting 'Who are you? You won't get me out of here – I'll kill you first!'

1   *Q   What should Karinda do?*

   A   Leave! She should leave the house at once and report the situation to her manager.

2   *Q   When should she go back?*

   A   Only after a risk assessment has been carried out.

3   *Q   What sort of risks need to be assessed?*

   A   a   Mr West's mental health and whether any treatment or support is required.

   b   The safety of the house. Mr West will have to be consulted about whether he is willing for his house to be made safe and the floorboards repaired.

   c   The dog and whether it is likely to present a risk of attack on a visitor to the house.

4   *Q   If Mr West refuses to allow a risk assessment, or his house to be repaired, should Karinda go back anyway?*

   A   No. Karinda's job is to provide care, but not at the risk of her own safety.

5   *Q   Who should carry out the risk assessment?*

   A   Karinda's employer.

The General Social Care Council (GSCC), the Scottish Social Services Council, the Care Council for Wales and the Northern Ireland Social Care Council have produced standards of practice by which all social care workers must abide. In a situation such as that described in the case study above, Karinda has certain responsibilities under the standards of practice to provide care for Mr West. However, she also has the right to safety and security and this is also specified in the standards. In addition, Mr West has the right to refuse care, and his wishes must be respected.

Test yourself

1   Note down three safe techniques for moving and handling.

2   What steps would you take to encourage others to identify and report health and safety risks?

3   What are the most effective methods of infection control, and why are they effective?

4   What are the different ways of disposing of waste at your workplace?

5   What are the steps involved in carrying out a risk assessment?

HSC 32c Minimise risks arising from incidents and emergencies

Fire safety

 KS ③④⑥

Your workplace will have procedures which must be followed in the case of an emergency. All workplaces must display information about what action to take in case of fire. The fire procedure is likely to be similar to the one shown below.

Fire Safety Procedure

1 Raise the alarm.

2 Inform the telephonist or dial 999.

3 Ensure that everyone is safe and out of the danger area.

4 If it is safe to do so, attack the fire with the correct extinguisher.

5 Go to the fire assembly point (this will be stated on the fire procedure notice).

6 Do not return to the building for any reason.

Make sure that you know where the fire extinguishers or fire blankets are in your workplace, and also where the fire exits are.

Make sure you know where the fire extinguishers are in your workplace

Remember

Don't be a hero! Never attempt to tackle a fire unless you are confident that you can do so safely, for example:

- you have already raised the alarm

- you have a clear, unobstructed route away from the fire in case it grows larger

- you are confident of your ability to operate the extinguisher

- you have the correct type of extinguisher.

Your employer will have installed fire doors to comply with regulations – never prop them open.

Your employer must provide fire lectures each year. All staff must attend and make sure that they are up to date with the procedures to be followed.

The Fire Precautions (Workplace) (Amendment) Regulations 1999 require that all workplaces should be inspected by the fire authority to check means of escape, firefighting equipment and warnings, and that a fire certificate must be issued. A breach of fire regulations could lead to a prosecution of the employer, the responsible manager, or other staff members.

Which extinguisher?

There are specific fire extinguishers for fighting different types of fire. It is important that you know this. You do not have to memorise them as each one has clear instructions on it, but you do need to be aware that there are different types and make sure that you read the instructions before use.

Did you know?

All new fire extinguishers are red. Each one has its purpose written on it. Each one also has a patch of the colour previously used for that type of extinguisher.

Extinguisher type and patch colour	Use for	Danger points	How to use	How it works
Red Water	Wood, cloth, paper, plastics, coal, etc. Fires involving solids.	Do **not** use on burning fat or oil, or on electrical appliances.	Point the jet at the base of the flames and keep it moving across the area of the fire. Ensure that all areas of the fire are out.	Mainly by cooling burning material.
Blue Multi-purpose dry powder	Wood, cloth, paper, plastics, coal, etc. Fires involving solids. Liquids such as grease, fats, oil, paint, petrol, etc. but **not** on chip or fat pan fires.	Safe on live electrical equipment, although the fire may re-ignite because this type of extinguisher does not cool the fire very well. Do **not** use on chip or fat pan fires.	Point the jet or discharge horn at the base of the flames and, with a rapid sweeping motion, drive the fire towards the far edge until all the flames are out.	Knocks down flames and, on burning solids, melts to form a skin smothering the fire. Provides some cooling effect.
Blue Standard dry powder	Liquids such as grease, fats, oil, paint, petrol etc. but **not** on chip or fat pan fires.	Safe on live electrical equipment, although does not penetrate the spaces in equipment easily and the fire may re-ignite. This type of extinguisher does not cool the fire very well. Do **not** use on chip or fat pan fires.	Point the jet or discharge horn at the base of the flames and, with a rapid sweeping motion, drive the fire towards the far edge until all the flames are out.	Knocks down flames.

Continued

Extinguisher type and patch colour	Use for	Danger points	How to use	How it works
Cream AFFF (Aqueous film-forming foam) (multi-purpose)	Wood, cloth, paper, plastics, coal, etc. Fires involving solids. Liquids such as grease, fats, oil, paint, petrol, etc. but **not** on chip or fat pan fires.	Do **not** use on chip or fat pan fires.	For fires involving solids, point the jet at the base of the flames and keep it moving across the area of the fire. Ensure that all areas of the fire are out. For fires involving liquids, do not aim the jet straight into the liquid. Where the liquid on fire is in a container, point the jet at the inside edge of the container or on a nearby surface above the burning liquid. Allow the foam to build up and flow across the liquid.	Forms a fire-extinguishing film on the surface of a burning liquid. Has a cooling action with a wider extinguishing application than water on solid combustible materials.
Cream Foam	Limited number of liquid fires.	Do **not** use on chip or fat pan fires. Check manufacturer's instructions for suitability of use on other fires involving liquids.	Do not aim jet straight into the liquid. Where the liquid on fire is in a container, point the jet at the inside edge of the container or on a nearby surface above the burning liquid. Allow the foam to build up and flow across the liquid.	
Black Carbon dioxide CO_2	Liquids such as grease, fats, oil, paint, petrol, etc. but **not** on chip or fat pan fires.	Do **not** use on chip or fat pan fires. This type of extinguisher does not cool the fire very well. Fumes from CO_2 extinguishers can be harmful if used in confined spaces: ventilate the area as soon as the fire has been controlled.	Direct the discharge horn at the base of the flames and keep the jet moving across the area of the fire.	Vaporising liquid gas smothers the flames by displacing oxygen in the air.
Fire blanket	Fires involving both solids and liquids. Particularly good for small fires in clothing and for chip and fat pan fires, provided the blanket **completely** covers the fire.	If the blanket does not completely cover the fire, it will not be extinguished.	Place carefully over the fire. Keep your hands shielded from the fire. Take care not to waft the fire towards you.	Smothers the fire.

Security issues

As noted in the previous element, you need to be vigilant about security risks and know who to report any problems to.

Evacuating buildings

In an extreme case it may be necessary to help evacuate buildings if there is a fire, or for other security reasons, such as:

- a bomb scare
- the building has become structurally unsafe
- an explosion
- a leak of dangerous chemicals or fumes.

The evacuation procedure you need to follow will be laid down by your workplace. The information will be the same whatever the emergency is: the same exits will be used and the same assembly point. It is likely to be along the following lines.

- Stay calm, do not shout or run.
- Do not allow others to run.
- Organise people quickly and firmly without panic.
- Direct those who can move themselves and assist those who cannot.
- Use wheelchairs to move people quickly.
- Move a bed with a person in, if necessary.

Health emergencies  KS 16 17 18

Helping in a health emergency is about first aid, and you need to understand the actions you should take if a health emergency arises. The advice that follows is not a substitute for a first aid course, and will only give you an outline of the steps you need to take. Reading this part of the unit will not qualify you to deal with these emergencies. Unless you have been on a first aid course, you should be careful about what you do, because the wrong action can cause more harm to the casualty. It may be better to summon help.

What you can safely do

Most people have a useful role to play in a health emergency, even if it is not dealing directly with the ill or injured person. It is also vital that someone:

- summons help as quickly as possible
- offers assistance to the competent person who is dealing with the emergency
- clears the immediate environment and makes it safe – for example, if someone has fallen through a glass door, the glass must be removed as soon as possible before there are any more injuries
- offers help and support to other people who have witnessed the illness or injury and may have been upset by it. Clearly this can only be dealt with once the ill or injured person is being helped.

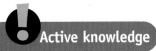

Active knowledge

1 Where are the main evacuation points in your workplace?

2 Which service users use each one?

3 Do any service users need assistance to reach evacuation points? If so, of what kind?

4 Who is responsible for checking your workplace is cleared in an emergency?

5 What are your personal responsibilities in an emergency situation?

Remember

Only attempt what you know you can safely do. Do not attempt something you are not sure of. You could do further damage to the ill or injured person and you could lay yourself and your employer open to being sued. Do not try to do something outside your responsibility or capability – summon help and wait for it to arrive.

How you can help the casualty in a health emergency

It is important that you are aware of the initial steps to take when dealing with the commonest health emergencies. You may be involved with any of these emergencies when you are at work, whether you work in a residential, hospital or community setting. Clearly, there are major differences between the different work situations.

- If you are working in a hospital where skilled assistance is always immediately available, the likelihood of your having to act in an emergency, other than to summon help, is remote.
- In a residential setting, help is likely to be readily available, although it may not necessarily be the professional medical expertise of a hospital.
- In the community you may have to summon help and take action to support a casualty until the help arrives. It is in this setting that you are most likely to need some knowledge of how to respond to a health emergency.

This section gives a guide to recognising and taking initial action in a number of health emergencies:

- severe bleeding
- cardiac arrest
- shock
- loss of consciousness
- epileptic seizure
- choking and difficulty with breathing
- fractures and suspected fractures
- burns and scalds
- poisoning
- electrical injuries.

Severe bleeding

Severe bleeding can be the result of a fall or injury. The most common causes of severe cuts are glass, as the result of a fall into a window or glass door, or knives from accidents in the kitchen.

Symptoms

There will be apparently large quantities of blood from the wound. In some very serious cases, the blood may be pumping out. Even small amounts of blood can be very frightening, both for you and the casualty. Remember that a small amount of blood goes a long way, and things may look worse than they are. However, severe bleeding requires urgent medical attention in hospital. Although people rarely bleed to death, extensive bleeding can cause shock and loss of consciousness.

Aims

- To bring the bleeding under control
- To limit the possibility of infection
- To arrange urgent medical attention

Action for severe bleeding

1   You will need to apply pressure to a wound that is bleeding. If possible, use a sterile dressing. If one is not readily available, use any readily available absorbent material, or even your hand. Do not forget the precautions (see 'Protect yourself' below). You will need to apply direct pressure over the wound for 10 minutes (this can seem like a very long time) to allow the blood to clot.

2   If there is any object in the wound, such as a piece of glass, *do not* try to remove it. Simply apply pressure to the sides of the wound.

3   Lay the casualty down and raise the affected part if possible.

4   Make the person comfortable and secure.

5   In a residential care setting, call for the senior registered nurse to assess the severity of the injury. He or she will make a decision regarding whether the wound is severe enough to call an ambulance.

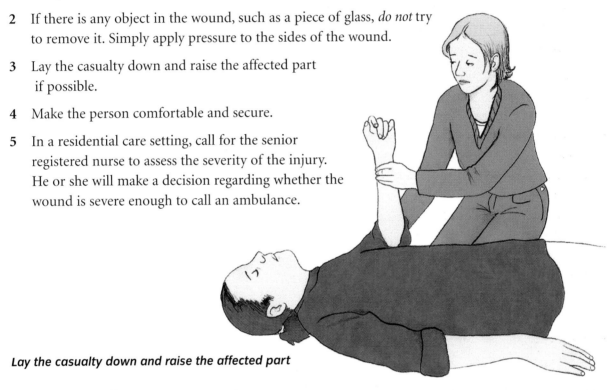

Lay the casualty down and raise the affected part

Protect yourself

You should take steps to protect yourself when you are dealing with casualties who are bleeding. Your skin provides an excellent barrier to infections, but you must take care if you have any broken skin such as a cut, graze or sore. Seek medical advice if blood comes into contact with your mouth, nose or gets into your eyes. Blood-borne viruses (such as HIV or hepatitis) can be passed only if the blood of someone who is already infected comes into contact with broken skin.

- If possible, wear disposable gloves.
- If this is not possible, cover any areas of broken skin with a waterproof dressing.
- If possible, wash your hands thoroughly in soap and water before and after treatment.

- Take care with any needles or broken glass in the area.
- Use a mask for mouth-to-mouth resuscitation if the casualty's nose or mouth is bleeding.

Cardiac arrest

Cardiac arrest occurs when a person's heart stops. Cardiac arrest can happen for various reasons, the most common of which is a heart attack, but a person's heart can also stop as a result of shock, electric shock, a convulsion or other illness or injury.

Symptoms
- No pulse
- No breathing

Aims
- To obtain medical help as a matter of urgency
- It is important to give oxygen, using mouth-to-mouth resuscitation, and to stimulate the heart, using chest compressions. This procedure is called cardio-pulmonary resuscitation – CPR. You will need to attend a first aid course to learn how to resuscitate – you cannot learn how to do this from a book. On the first aid course you will be able to practise on a special dummy.

Action for cardiac arrest

1 Check whether the person has a pulse and whether he or she is breathing.

2 If not, call for urgent help from a senior registered nurse who will assess the need for summoning emergency services.

3 Start methods of resuscitation if you have been taught how to do it.

4 Keep up resuscitation until help arrives.

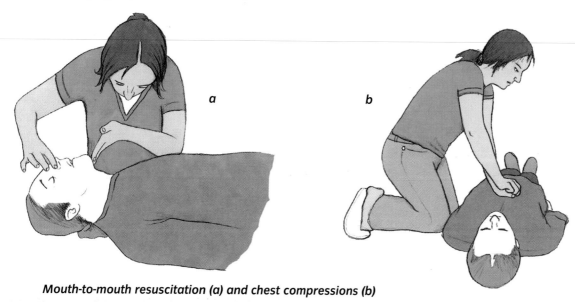

a   *b*

Mouth-to-mouth resuscitation (a) and chest compressions (b)

Shock

Shock occurs because blood is not being pumped around the body efficiently. This can be the result of loss of body fluids through bleeding, burns, severe vomiting or diarrhoea, or a sudden drop in blood pressure or a heart attack.

Symptoms

The signs of shock are easily recognised. The person:
- will look very pale, almost grey
- will be very sweaty, and the skin will be cold and clammy
- will have a very fast pulse
- may feel sick and may vomit
- may be breathing very quickly.

Aims
- To obtain medical help as a matter of urgency
- To improve blood supply to heart, lungs and brain

Action for shock

1 Summon expert medical or nursing assistance.

2 Lay the person down on the floor. Try to raise the feet off the ground to help the blood supply to the important organs.

3 Loosen any tight clothing.

4 Watch the person carefully. Check the pulse and breathing regularly.

5 Keep the person warm and comfortable, but *do not* warm the casualty with direct heat, such as a hot water bottle.

Raise the feet off the ground and keep the casualty warm

Do not:
- allow casualty to eat or drink
- leave the casualty alone, unless it is essential to do so briefly in order to summon help.

Loss of consciousness

Loss of consciousness can happen for many reasons, from a straightforward faint to unconsciousness following a serious injury or illness.

Symptom

A reduced level of response and awareness. This can range from being vague and 'woozy' to total unconsciousness.

Aims

- To summon expert medical help as a matter of urgency
- To keep the airway open
- To note any information which may help to find the cause of the unconsciousness

Action for loss of conciousness

1   Make sure that the person is breathing and has a clear airway.

2   Maintain the airway by lifting the chin and tilting the head backwards.

3   Look for any obvious reasons why the person may be unconscious, such as a wound or an ID band telling you of any condition he or she may have. For example, many people who have medical conditions which may cause unconsciousness, such as epilepsy or diabetes, wear special bracelets or necklaces giving information about their condition.

4   Place the casualty in the recovery position (see below), *but not if you suspect a back or neck injury*, until expert medical or nursing help or the emergency services arrive.

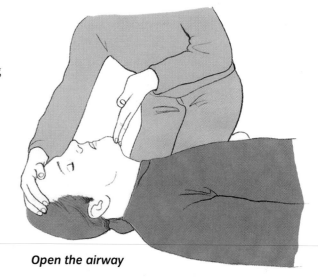

Open the airway

Do not:

- attempt to give anything by mouth
- attempt to make the casualty sit or stand
- leave the casualty alone, unless it is essential to leave briefly in order to summon help.

The recovery position

Many of the actions you need to take to deal with health emergencies will involve you in placing someone in the recovery position. In this position a casualty has the best chance of keeping a clear airway, not inhaling vomit and remaining as safe as possible until help arrives. This position should not be attempted if you think someone has back or neck injuries, and it may not be possible if there are fractures of limbs.

1   Kneel at one side of the casualty, at about waist level.

2   Tilt back the person's head – this opens the airway. With the casualty on his/her back, make sure that limbs are straight.

3   Bend the casualty's near arm as in a wave (so it is at right angles to the body). Pull the arm on the far side over the chest and place the back of the hand against the opposite cheek (**a** in the diagram opposite).

4   Use your other hand to roll the casualty towards you by pulling on the far leg, just above the knee (**b** in the diagram). The casualty should now be on his or her side.

5   Once the casualty is rolled over, bend the leg at right angles to the body. Make sure the head is tilted well back to keep the airway open (**c** in the diagram).

Epileptic seizure

Epilepsy is a medical condition that causes disturbances in the brain which result in sufferers becoming unconscious and having involuntary contractions of their muscles. This contraction of the muscles produces the fit or seizure. People who suffer with epilepsy do not have any control over their seizures, and may do themselves harm by falling when they have a seizure.

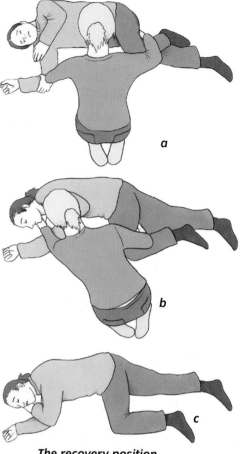

The recovery position

Aims

- To ensure that the person is safe and does not injure himself or herself during the fit
- To offer any help needed following the fit

Action for epileptic seizure

1   Try to make sure that the area in which the person has fallen is safe.

2   Loosen all clothing.

3   Once the seizure has ended, make sure that the person has a clear airway and place in the recovery position.

4   Make sure that the person is comfortable and safe. Particularly try to prevent head injury.

5   If the fit lasts longer than five minutes, or you are unaware that the casualty is a known epileptic, call an ambulance.

Do not:

- attempt to hold the casualty down, or put anything in the mouth
- move the casualty until he or she is fully conscious, unless there is a risk of injury in the place where he or she has fallen.

Choking and difficulty with breathing (in adults and children over 8 years)

This is caused by something (usually a piece of food) stuck at the back of the throat. It is a situation which needs to be dealt with, as people can quickly stop breathing if the obstruction is not removed.

Symptoms

- Red, congested face at first, later turning grey
- Unable to speak or breathe, may gasp and indicate throat or neck

Aims

- To remove obstruction as quickly as possible
- To summon medical assistance as a matter of urgency if the obstruction cannot be removed

Action for choking

1 Ensure any dentures are removed. Sweep the mouth with one gloved finger to clear any food, vomit or anything else from the mouth.

2 Try to get the person to cough. If that is not immediately effective, move on to step 3.

3 Bend the person forwards. Slap sharply on the back between the shoulder blades up to five times (**a** in the diagram opposite).

4 If this fails, use the Heimlich manoeuvre *if you have been trained to do so*. Stand behind the person with your arms around him/her. Join your hands just below the breastbone. One hand should be in a fist and the other holding it (**b** in the diagram).

5 Sharply pull your joined hands upwards and into the person's body at the same time. The force should expel the obstruction.

6 You should alternate backslaps and abdominal thrusts until you clear the obstruction.

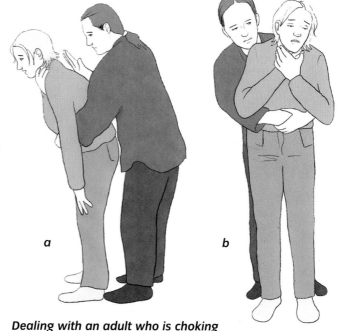

Dealing with an adult who is choking

Fractures and suspected fractures

Fractures are breaks or cracks in bones. They are usually caused by a fall or other type of injury. The casualty will need to go to a hospital as soon as possible to have a fracture diagnosed correctly.

Symptoms

- Acute pain around the site of the injury
- Swelling and discoloration around the affected area
- Limbs or joints may be in odd positions
- Broken bones may protrude through the skin

Action for fractures

1 The important thing is to support the affected part. Help the casualty to find the most comfortable position.

2 Support the injured limb in that position with as much padding as necessary – towels, cushions or clothing will do.

3 Take the person to hospital or call an ambulance.

Do not:

- try to bandage or splint the injury
- allow the casualty to have anything to eat or drink.

Support the injured limb

Burns and scalds

There are several different types of burn; the most usual are burns caused by heat or flame. Scalds are caused by hot liquids. People can also be burned by chemicals or by electrical currents.

Symptoms

- Depending on the type and severity of the burn, skin may be red, swollen and tender, blistered and raw or charred
- Usually severe pain and possibly shock

Aims

- To obtain immediate medical assistance if the burn is over a large area (as big as the casualty's hand or more) or is deep
- To send for an ambulance if the burn is severe or extensive. If the burn or scald is over a smaller area, the casualty could be transported to hospital by car
- To stop the burning and reduce pain
- To minimise the possibility of infection

Action for burns and scalds

1 For major burns, summon immediate medical assistance.

2 Cool down the burn. Keep it flooded with cold water for 10 minutes. If it is a chemical burn, this needs to be done for 20 minutes. Ensure that the contaminated water used to cool a chemical burn is disposed of safely.

Cool the burn with water

3   Remove any jewellery, watches or clothing which are not sticking to the burn.

4   Cover the burn if possible, unless it is a facial burn, with a sterile or at least clean non-adhesive dressing. If this is not possible, leave the burn uncovered. For a burn on a hand or foot, a clean plastic bag will protect it from infection until it can be treated by an expert.

If clothing is on fire, remember the basics: *stop, drop, wrap* and *roll* the person on the ground.

Do not:

- remove anything which is stuck to a burn
- touch a burn, or use any ointment or cream
- cover facial burns – keep pouring water on until help arrives.

Poisoning

People can be poisoned by many substances, drugs, plants, chemicals, fumes or alcohol.

Symptoms

Symptoms will vary depending on the poison.

- The person could be unconscious
- There may be acute abdominal pain
- There may be blistering of the mouth and lips

Aims

- To remove the casualty to a safe area if he/she is at risk, and it is safe for you to move him/her
- To summon medical assistance as a matter of urgency
- To gather any information which will identify the poison
- To maintain a clear airway and breathing until help arrives

Action for poisoning

1   If the casualty is unconscious, place him/her in the recovery position to ensure that the airway is clear, and that he/she cannot choke on any vomit.

2   Dial 999 for an ambulance.

3   Try to find out what the poison is and how much has been taken. This information could be vital in saving a life.

4   If a conscious casualty has burned mouth or lips, he or she can be given small frequent sips of water or cold milk.

Do not try to make the casualty vomit.

Remember

If a person's clothing is on fire, STOP – DROP – WRAP – ROLL:

- *Stop* him or her from running around.

- Get him/her to *drop* to the ground – push him/her if you have to and can do so safely.

- *Wrap* him/her in something to smother the flames – a blanket or coat, anything to hand. This is better if it is soaked in water.

- *Roll* him/her on the ground to put out the flames.

Describe a situation when you have had to deal with an emergency – either health related or environmental. What actions did you take throughout the situation?

How did you feel?

If you have not personally had to deal with an emergency speak to your friends, family and colleagues to see if they have examples.

Electrical injuries

Electrocution occurs when an electrical current passes though the body.

Symptoms

Electrocution can cause cardiac arrest and burns where the electrical current entered and left the body.

Aims

- To remove the casualty from the current when you can safely do so
- To obtain medical assistance as a matter of urgency
- To maintain a clear airway and breathing until help arrives
- To treat any burns

Action for electrical injuries

There are different procedures to follow depending on whether the injury has been caused by a high or low voltage current.

Injury caused by high voltage current

This type of injury may be caused by overhead power cables or rail lines, for example.

1 Contact the emergency services immediately.

2 *Do not* touch the person until all electricity has been cut off.

3 If the person is unconscious, clear the airway.

4 Treat any other injuries present, such as burns.

5 Place in the recovery position until help arrives.

Injury caused by low voltage current

This type of injury may be caused by electric kettles, computers, drills, lawnmowers, etc.

1 Break the contact with the current by switching off the electricity, at the mains if possible.

2 It is vital to break the contact as soon as possible, but if you touch a person who is 'live' (still in contact with the current) you too will be

injured. If you are unable to switch off the electricity, then you must stand on something dry which can insulate you, such as a telephone directory, rubber mat or a pile of newspapers, and then move the casualty away from the current as described below.

3   Do not use anything made of metal, or anything wet, to move the casualty from the current. Try to move him/her with a wooden pole or broom-handle, even a chair.

4   Alternatively, drag him/her with a rope or cord or, as a last resort, pull by holding any of the person's dry clothing which is *not* in contact with his/her body.

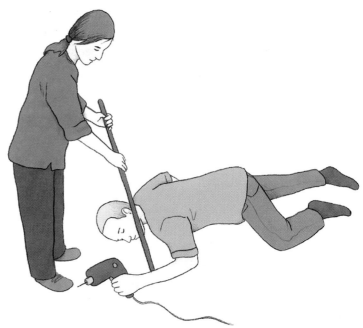

Move the casualty away from the current

5   Once the person is no longer in contact with the current, you should follow the same steps as with a high voltage injury.

Other ways to help

Summon assistance

In the majority of cases this will mean telephoning 999 and requesting an ambulance. It will depend on the setting in which you work and clearly is not required if you work in a hospital! But it may mean calling for a colleague with medical qualifications, who will then be able to make an assessment of the need for further assistance. Similarly, if you work in the residential sector, there should be a medically qualified colleague available. If you are the first on the scene at an emergency in the community, you may need to summon an ambulance for urgent assistance.

If you need to call an ambulance, try to keep calm and give clearly all the details you are asked for. Do not attempt to give information until it is asked for – this wastes time. Emergency service operators are trained to find out the necessary information, so let them ask the questions, then answer calmly and clearly.

Follow the action steps outlined in the previous section while you are waiting for help to arrive.

Assist the person dealing with the emergency

A second pair of hands is invaluable when dealing with an emergency. If you are assisting someone with first aid or medical expertise, follow all his or her instructions, even if you don't understand why. An emergency situation is not the time for a discussion or debate – that can happen later. You may be needed to help to move a casualty, or to fetch water, blankets or dressings, or to reassure and comfort the casualty during treatment.

Make the area safe

An accident or injury may have occurred in an unsafe area – and it was probably for precisely that reason that the accident occurred there! Sometimes, it may be that the accident has made the area unsafe for others. For example, if someone has tripped over an electric flex, there may be exposed wires or a damaged electric socket. Alternatively, a fall against a window or glass door may have left shards of broken glass in the area, or there may be blood or other body fluids on the floor. You may need to make the area safe by turning off the power, clearing broken glass or dealing with a spillage.

It may be necessary to redirect people away from the area of the accident in order to avoid further casualties.

Maintain the privacy of the casualty

You may need to act to provide some privacy for the casualty by asking onlookers to move away or stand back. If you can erect a temporary screen with coats or blankets, this may help to offer some privacy. It may not matter to the casualty at the time, but he or she has a right to privacy if possible.

Make accurate reports

You may be responsible for making a report on an emergency situation you have witnessed, or for filling in records later. Concentrate on the most important aspects of the incident and record the actions of yourself and others in an accurate, legible and complete manner.

CASE STUDY: Dealing with a health emergency

On the way to lunch one Tuesday, Miss Shaw, who sometimes experiences incontinence, had a little 'accident' in the main hallway. Another resident coming along behind called out, 'Oh look! She's done a puddle!' and stopped to stare. Miss Shaw, feeling embarrassed and distressed, turned quickly to go back to her room and slipped on the wet floor, falling heavily on her hip. The first staff member on the scene was Maria.

1　*List the actions that Maria should take, in order.*

2　*Could this accident have been prevented? If so, how?*

3　*What follow-up actions or discussions would you recommend to the management?*

How to deal with witnesses' distress – and your own

People who have witnessed accidents can often be very distressed by what they have seen. The distress may be as a result of the nature of the injury, or the blood loss. It could be because the casualty is a friend or relative or simply because seeing accidents or injuries is traumatic. Some people can become upset because they feel helpless and do not know how to assist, or they may have been afraid and then feel guilty later.

You will need to reassure people about the casualty and the fact that he or she is being cared for appropriately. However, do not give false reassurance about things you may not be sure of.

You may need to allow individuals to talk about what they saw. One of the commonest effects of witnessing a trauma is that people need to repeat over and over again what they saw.

What about you?

You may feel very distressed by the experience you have gone through. You may find that you need to talk about what has happened, and that you need to look again at the role you played. You may feel that you could have done more, or you may feel angry with yourself for not having a greater knowledge about what to do.

There is a whole range of emotions which you may experience; Unit HSC 35 covers in detail the different emotions that may arise in similarly difficult circumstances involving abuse, and describes ways to cope with such feelings (page 217). You should be able to discuss them with your supervisor and use any support provided by your employer.

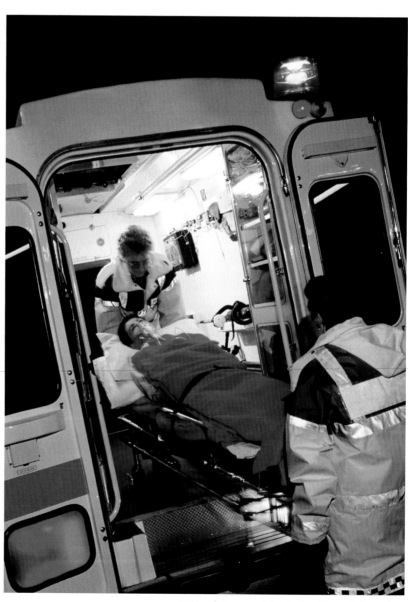

Witnessing accidents is often distressing

If you have followed the basic guidelines in this element, you will have done as much as could be expected of anyone at the scene of an emergency who is not a trained first aider.

Test yourself

1 In which conditions would it be safe for you to attempt to tackle a fire?

2 In what situations should you attempt first aid?

3 What is the single most important thing for an untrained person to do in a health emergency?

4 List three tasks you can carry out at the scene of a health emergency which do not necessarily involve first aid.

5 How would you talk to a casualty while you waited for help?

6 How would you support others who had witnessed an incident or accident?

HSC 32 FURTHER READING AND RESEARCH

Work place health, safety and security is an important and complex issue. This section has dealt with the key factors and below is details of opportunities to find out more.

www.dh.gov.uk (Department of Health – Health & safety, Emergency planning)

www.hse.gov.uk (Health and Safety Executive – HSE)
tel: 0845 345 0055

www.healthandsafetytips.co.uk (Health and Safety Tips)
tel: 01506 200109

www.nric.org.uk (National Resource for Infection Control)

www.neli.org.uk (National Electronic Library of Infection)

www.nice.org.uk ((National Institute for Health and Clinical Excellence)

Bowmen R. C., Emmett R. C. (1998) *A Dictionary of Food Hygiene* CIEH

Hartropp, H. (2006) *Hygiene in Health and Social Care* CIEH

Horner J. M. (1993) *Workplace Environment, Health and Safety Management; A Practical Guide* CIEH

Reflect on and develop your practice

The knowledge and skills addressed in this unit are the key to working effectively in all aspects of your practice. In order to work effectively, it is essential to know how to evaluate your work, how you can improve on what you do, and understand the factors which have influenced your attitudes and beliefs.

The care sector is constantly benefiting from new research, new developments, policies and guidelines. In order to offer the best possible level of service to those you care for, you need to make sure that you are up to date in work practices and knowledge, and aware of current thinking. As a worker in a care setting, you have a responsibility to constantly review and improve your practice. It is the right of service users to expect the best possible quality of care from those who provide it, and high quality care requires all practitioners to regularly reflect on their own practice and look at ways of improving.

Each organisation and each individual owes a **duty of care** to service users; this means that it is your responsibility to make sure that the service provided is the best it can possibly be. This is not an option, but a duty which you accept when you choose to become a professional care worker. The information in this unit will help you to identify the best ways to develop and update your own knowledge and skills.

What you need to learn

- How to explore your own values, interests and beliefs
- How your values, interests and beliefs influence your practice
- Reflective practice
- Support networks
- Learning from work practice
- Making good use of training/development opportunities
- Developing your own personal effectiveness
- Understanding new information
- How to ensure your practice is current and up to date
- Preparing a development plan.

HSC 33a Reflect on your practice

How to explore your own values, interests and beliefs

KS 2 3 7

Everyone has their own values, beliefs and preferences. They are an essential part of who you are. What you believe in, what you see as important and what you see as acceptable or desirable are as much a part of your personality as whether you are shy, outgoing, funny, serious, friendly or reserved.

Care workers work with vulnerable people so it is important to be able to make them feel safe and to be able to meet their self-esteem needs. The way in which you respond to people is linked to what you believe in, what you consider important and the things that interest you. You may find you react positively to people who share your values and less warmly to people who have different priorities. When you develop friendships it is natural to spend time with people who share your interests and values, those who are 'on your wavelength'.

Choosing your friends and meeting with others who share your interests is one of life's joys and pleasures; however, the professional relationships you develop with people you care for are another matter. As a professional carer you are required to provide the same quality of care for all, not just for those who share your views and beliefs. This may seem obvious, but knowing what you need to do and achieving it successfully are not the same thing.

Your friendships reflect your own values, interests and beliefs

Remember

If you were in a shop and asked the sales assistant a series of questions about a product that you were interested in, how would you feel if he or she was uninterested and unhelpful, so that you failed to get the information you needed? You would probably feel annoyed and perhaps you would decide to take your custom elsewhere.

If you were in hospital and had been told you have a serious illness, but the care workers seemed to be uninterested and unhelpful, how would this affect you? You are likely to feel angry but you are also likely to feel afraid. Your sense of self-esteem may be damaged. You might feel that you can't be worth much if people don't care about your health.

Being ignored in a caring setting may cause you much more damage than being ignored in a shop. Within the care setting you may feel vulnerable.

Working in the care sector, you are bound to come across service users and colleagues whose view you don't agree with, and who never seem to understand your point of view. Awareness of differences, your reaction to them and how they affect the care you give is a crucial part of personal and professional development. Fill in the table below and discuss it with your colleagues. Think as broadly as you can about these scenarios.

Your beliefs/values/interests	Situation	Possible effect
	A service user with limited English is unable to explain her dietary needs	
All young people wearing hoods are potential vandals and threats to society		
	You are with a colleague speaking to a new service user and his disabled companion. Your colleague turns to you and says 'Who is going to fill in the forms?'	

If you allow your own preferences to dominate your work with service users you may fail to perform to the standards of the Codes of Practice for Social Care Workers set out by the UK regulating bodies. All the codes require that care workers must respect and promote the individual views and wishes of service users. But how do you manage to make the right responses when there is a clash between your views and those of the people you are working for? The first step may be to identify and understand your own views and values.

Being aware of the factors that have influenced the development of your personality is not as easy as it sounds. You may feel you know yourself very well, but knowing who you are is not the same as understanding how your beliefs are influencing your reactions – understanding *how* you got to be you.

Active knowledge

Step 1

Take a range of items from a newspaper, about six or seven. Make a note of your views on each of them: say what your feelings are on each one – does it shock or disgust you, make you sad, or angry, or grateful that it hasn't happened to you?

Step 2

Try to think about why you reacted in the way you did to each of the items in the newspaper. Think about what may have influenced you to feel that way. The answers are likely to lie in a complex range of factors, including your upbringing and background, experiences you had as a child and as an adult, and relationships you have shared with others.

Unravelling these influences is never easy, and you are not being asked to carry out an in-depth analysis of yourself – simply to begin to realise how your development has been influenced by a series of factors.

Factors which influence our development

Everyone's values and beliefs are affected to different degrees by the same range of factors. These include:

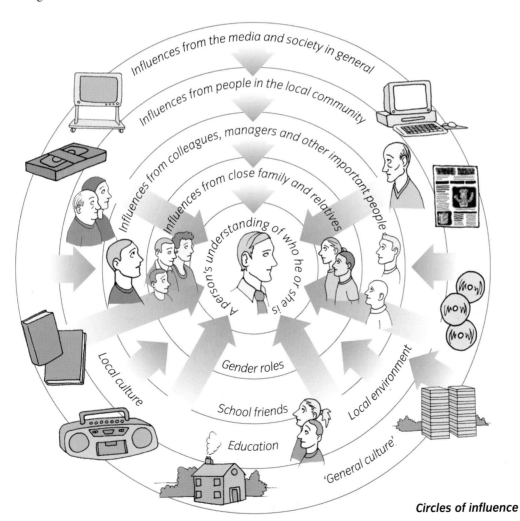

Circles of influence

Each of us will be influenced to a greater or lesser degree by these layers of influence. As each individual is different, the extent of the influences will be different for each person. It is therefore important that you have considered and reflect on the influences on your development so that you understand how you became the person you are.

Active knowledge

Think about the factors that have influenced your own development, and the values and beliefs that you now hold. Which factors have had the strongest effect in making you who you are? Which factors continue to influence you and the way you work?

Key influences on development

The following are some of the key factors associated with differences between people – the factors that can result in different people having different values.

You should be able to begin to trace some of the influences from your past environment on the development of your own attitudes and values.

We are strongly influenced by our contact with other people. But different people live very different lives and mix with communities that have very different beliefs. People have different cultures, family values, religions, social class backgrounds and so on. Men often grow up with very different expectations and experience of life from women. Older people are likely to have had different life experiences from those of younger people. Some ways in which people are different from each other (or diverse) are listed on the next page.

Age	People may be classified as being children, teenagers, young adults, middle aged or old. Discrimination can creep into our thinking if we see some age groups as being 'the best', or if we make assumptions about the abilities of different age groups.
Gender	In the past, men often had more rights and were seen as more important than women. Assumptions about gender such as what is women's work and what is men's work can still result in mistakes and discrimination.
Race	People understand themselves in terms of ethnic categories such as being black or white, as European, African or Asian. Many people have specific national identities such as Polish, Nigerian, English or Welsh. Assumptions about racial characteristics and beliefs, or thinking that some groups are superior to others, result in discrimination.
Class	People differ in their upbringing, the kind of work they do and the money they earn. People also differ in the lifestyle they lead and the views and values that go with different levels of income and spending habits. People may discriminate against others because their class or lifestyle is different.
Religion	People grow up in different traditions of religion. For some people, spiritual beliefs are at the centre of their understanding of life. For others, religion influences the cultural traditions that they celebrate; for example, many Europeans celebrate Christmas even though they might not see themselves as practising Christians. Discrimination can take place when people assume that their customs or beliefs should apply to everyone else.
Sexuality	Many people see their sexual orientation as very important to understanding who they are. Gay and lesbian relationships are often discriminated against. Heterosexual people sometimes judge other relationships as 'wrong' or abnormal.
Ability	People may make assumptions about what is 'normal'. People with physical disabilities or learning difficulties may become labelled, stereotyped and discriminated against as damaged versions of 'normal' people.
Relationships	People choose many different lifestyles and emotional commitments, such as marriage, having children, living in a large family, living a single lifestyle but having sexual partners, or being single and not being sexually active. People live within different family and friendship groups. Discrimination can happen if people start to judge that one lifestyle is 'right' or best.
Politics	People can develop different views as to how a government should act, how welfare provision should be organised and so on. Disagreement and debate are necessary; but it is important not to judge people as bad or stupid because their views are different from ours.

Problems arise because our own culture and life experience may lead us to make assumptions as to what is right or normal. When we meet people who are different it can be easy to see them as 'not right' or 'not normal'. Different people see the world in different ways. Look at the illustration on the next page. Which is the 'normal' front of the cube?

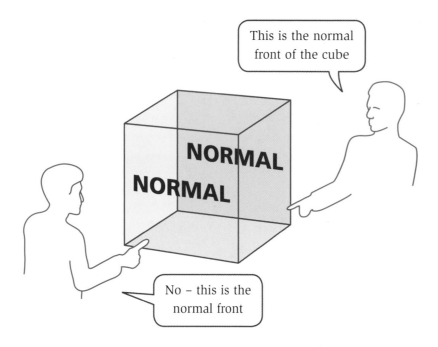

Which is the 'normal' front of the cube?

If a person was used to seeing this cube in one way, he or she might be sure that view was the right one. In the same way, our culture may lead us to think that some habits are more 'normal' than others, but in a multicultural, multifaith society such as the UK it is more difficult to define what 'normal' is.

Active knowledge

Take a piece of paper and draw a horizontal line, marking off each year of your life from the age of five so far. Then draw a vertical line at the left to create a scale of how happy your life has been. Try to reflect on your memories of the past, and draw a graph of your levels of happiness. What made particular years happy or unhappy for you? As you think back over your life, try to recall the people and the situations that affected you. Many of your beliefs and values have probably come about because of your interaction with these key people.

Try to imagine how you might have been different if you had lived in a different family or in a different community. Can you imagine how different life experiences create different belief systems? Can you see why it is vitally important not to make assumptions about what is right and wrong in different people's lives?

How your values, interests and beliefs influence your practice

KS 7 9 11

Once you have begun to identify the major factors that have influenced your development, the next stage is to look at how they have affected the way in which you work and relate both to service users and colleagues. This is the basis of developing into a 'reflective practitioner' – someone who evaluates what he or she does.

Working in care requires that in order to be effective and to provide the best possible service for those you care for, you need to be able to think about and evaluate what you do and the way you work, and to identify your strengths and weaknesses. It is important that you learn to think about your own practice in a constructive way. Reflection and evaluation should not undermine your confidence in your own work; rather you should use them in a constructive way to identify areas that require improvement.

The ability to do this is an indication of excellent practice. Any workers in care who believe that they have no need to improve their practice or to develop and add to their skills and understanding are not demonstrating good and competent practice, but rather an arrogant and potentially dangerous lack of understanding of the nature of work in the care sector.

Becoming a thoughtful practitioner is not about torturing yourself with self-doubts and examining your weaknesses until you reach the point where your self-confidence is at zero! But it is important that you examine the work you have done and identify areas where you know you need to carry out additional development. A useful tool in learning to become a reflective practitioner is to develop a checklist which you can use, either after you have dealt with a difficult situation or at the end of each shift or day's work, to look at your own performance.

Checklist to evaluate practice

1 How did I approach my work?

2 Was my approach positive?

3 How did the way I worked affect the service users?

4 How did the way I worked affect my colleagues?

5 Did I give my work 100 per cent?

6 Which was the best aspect of the work I did?

7 Which was the worst aspect of the work I did?

8 Was this work the best I could do?

9 Are there any areas in which I could improve?

10 What are they, and how will I tackle them?

Reflective practice

 KS 7 9 11

The purpose of reflective practice is to improve and develop your practice by thinking about what you are doing. What is reflection and what does a worker need to be able to do in order to be able to improve his or her own practice? Reflection involves thinking things over; you could visualise reflection as reflecting ideas inside the mind like light bouncing between mirrors. Reflection involves complex mental processing that discovers new ideas or new inter-relationships between ideas. Reflection helps us to realise new ideas and make new sense of practice issues.

Imagine that every morning a resident who lives in a supported housing complex comes to the office to complain. The complaints might be about anything: sinks that don't drain quickly enough, cars parked too close to a wall, light bulbs that need changing (even though they still work!). Naturally this behaviour is annoying for the people who work in the office. But why does this resident complain?

Reflecting on the situation might enable a professional care worker to come up with some answers. But reflection can involve different levels of thinking. The most basic kind of reflection is simply to remember something. Different ideas that could develop from reflection are listed below.

Reflecting can help you to understand feelings and the wider issues involved

Just noticing what happens

Perhaps the interaction with this resident always follows a pattern. The person will wait for a short period and then launch into a verbal outburst about what is wrong. During this outburst the resident is unresponsive to the reactions of others. Having completed the outburst, the resident will look for a reaction and then storm off.

Just noticing this detail might provide a start to the reflective process. It would be so easy to label the resident as 'difficult' or 'challenging', and then use this label as if it were an explanation – and no further thinking were required. Just noticing the detail of what happens may help us to avoid labelling.

Reflection in order to make sense of a situation

What does the resident's pattern of behaviour mean? Perhaps this confrontational exchange represents a release of tension. Perhaps the resident does not have the social and emotional skills to engage in more sociable conversations. Perhaps the resident is trying to create a sense of belonging within the housing complex, and confrontation is chosen as the method because of limited social skills.

Reflection may not give us the correct answer, but trying to make sense of a situation helps us to be open to new ideas.

Going deeper – trying to understand feelings

What does the resident feel like when he or she comes to complain? Like so many people, the resident may feel a little isolated – a little insecure. Perhaps, like so many people, this resident is thinking 'If I don't feel good, then someone else is to blame'. Perhaps these emotions become focused on trivia such as light bulbs.

Thinking about feelings might help to generate extra ideas about what could be happening.

Going deeper – reflecting on wider issues

A care worker thinking about the problems that service users experience might reflect on the significance of these feelings. There are people who always search for other people to blame whenever anything is perceived to be less than perfect. But maybe we all tend to do this! Maybe we feel that 'they' should do something about climate change, about house prices, or about holes in the road. Perhaps we all like to retreat into a childlike state, expecting a kind parent to make the world comfortable and perfect for us.

Reflection that takes a wide view can involve new thoughts that could, for example, help us to understand ourselves better. Perhaps the difference between the resident's behaviour in the example above and our own behaviour is that we are more skilled at knowing how, when and where it is safe to 'have a moan'.

Reflection that results in new ways of thinking

How far do we take responsibility for our own emotions? If you were a person who had assumed that your emotions were all caused by outside events, it could be a major shock to find that your own thinking can directly influence your feelings. Many of the assumptions we make about life are hard to change. Abandoning the belief that someone else should make my life better and deciding that I am responsible for my life could represent a huge shift in thinking.

Remember

The purpose of reflection is to improve and develop your own practice.

Reflection on our own assumptions is not something that can happen on a daily basis. This kind of reflection involves an extreme shift in thinking that could change people's lives.

How deeply does your own reflective thinking go? As long as you reflect enough to get beyond the labelling stage, you are on the right path. The important thing is to think positively about areas of your work that you can improve. Reflection that does not identify areas for improvement is of little value – in fact, it can be highly destructive.

CASE STUDY: Seeking constructive feedback

Lewis works in a large residential setting for elderly adults where one of the people he cares for is Mrs Kaur, an Indian woman who speaks very little English. Mrs Kaur has many relatives who visit her regularly, and has long and animated conversations with them. But when she has no visitors, Mrs Kaur is very quiet. She hardly responds at all when Lewis tries to talk to her and is unwilling to talk to the other residents or to take part in any of the activities on offer. Lewis is concerned that Mrs Kaur may feel isolated; he would like to be able to communicate with her better and to improve his own practice.

1   *What are the barriers to communication between Lewis and Mrs Kaur?*
2   *Who could Lewis speak to about the situation?*
3   *What other actions could he take to improve his practice?*

Learning

When you have identified skills you would like to improve, the next step is to set about learning them. One of the best-known theories about the way in which people learn is the Lewin/Kolb cycle of experiential learning.

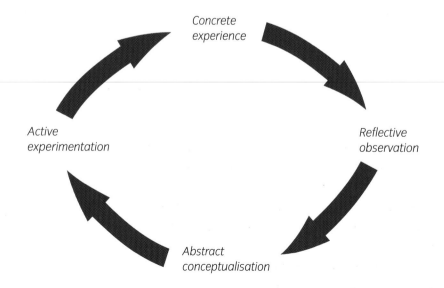

Kolb's cycle

Basically, this cycle means the following.

- Something happens to you or you do something; it can be an unusual event or something you do every day (**concrete experience**).
- You think about it (**reflective observation**).
- You work out some general rules about it, or you realise that it fits into a theory or pattern you already know about (**abstract conceptualisation**).
- Next time the same situation occurs, you apply your rules or theories (**active experimentation**).
- This will make your experience different from the first time, so you will have different factors to think about and different things to learn – so the cycle continues. You never stop learning.

Imagine that you are working with a man who has a learning difficulty. It is the first time you have met him and you are offering him a drink at lunchtime. You offer a glass of orange squash by placing it in front of him. He immediately pushes the glass away with a facial expression that you take to express disgust.

Within Kolb's learning cycle you have had a concrete experience.

Stage 1

Stage 1 of the learning cycle is the experience that this service user has rejected your offer of orange squash. But why has he reacted in this way?

Stage 2

Stage 2 involves thinking through some possible reasons for the reaction. Perhaps he doesn't like orange squash? Perhaps he doesn't like the way you put it in front of him? Perhaps he doesn't like to take a drink with his meal? Could it be an issue to do with social group membership? For example, could a cold drink symbolise childhood status for this individual? Does he see adult status as defined by having a hot drink? Reflection on the non-verbal behaviour of the service user may provide a range of starting points for interpreting his actions.

Stage 3

Kolb's third stage involves trying to make sense of our reflections. What do we know about different cultural interpretations of non-verbal behaviour? What are the chances that the way we placed the drink in front of the person has been construed as an attempt to control or dominate him? We didn't intend to send this message, but the service user may have interpreted our behaviour on an emotional level as being unpleasant. The more we know about human psychology and social group membership the more we can analyse the service user's reaction. We need to choose the most likely explanation for the service user's behaviour using everything we know about people.

Stage 4

Kolb's fourth stage involves 'experimenting', or checking out ideas and assumptions that we may have made. The worker might attempt to modify his or her non-verbal behaviour to look supportive. The worker might show the service user a cup and saucer to indicate the question: 'Is this what you would like'? If the service user responds with a positive non-verbal response, the worker would have been around the four stages of the cycle and would have solved the problem in a way that valued the individuality and diversity of the individual.

Workers might expect to have to go round this 'learning cycle' a number of times before they were able to correctly understand and interpret a service user's needs.

How quickly can you work through these four stages? Would you be able to think through these issues while working with the service user, or would you need to go away and reflect on practice? The answer to this question might depend on the amount of experience you have had in similar situations.

What is your learning style?

Honey and Mumford (1982) developed a theory based on this idea of a four-stage process of learning from experience. They theorised that some people develop a preference for a particular part of the learning cycle. Some people enjoy the activity of meeting new people and having new experiences, but these 'activists' may not get so much pleasure from reflecting, theorising and finding answers to individual needs. Some people mainly enjoy sitting down and thinking things through. These are 'reflectors'. Some people enjoy analysing issues in terms of established theoretical principles; these people are 'theorists'. Finally, some people prefer trying out new ideas in practice – these people are 'pragmatists'.

Active knowledge

Think about the ways in which *you* learn new things. Do you tend to use one part of the learning cycle more than others? Think about ways in which you could develop your skills in other parts of the cycle.

Honey and Mumford have argued that the ideal way to approach practical learning is to balance all the components of the learning cycle. Some people can achieve this more holistic approach. For other people it might be important to recognise their own biases and to try to compensate for an over-reliance on one style.

Honey and Mumford's theory of learning styles fits the four-stage learning cycle as follows:

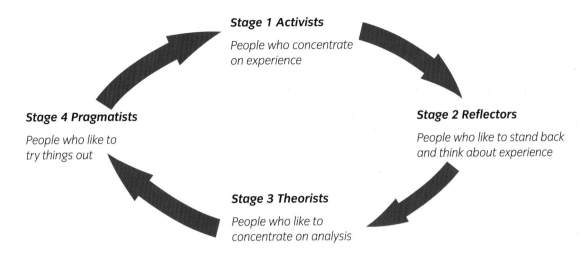

Stage 1 Activists

People who concentrate on experience

Stage 2 Reflectors

People who like to stand back and think about experience

Stage 4 Pragmatists

People who like to try things out

Stage 3 Theorists

People who like to concentrate on analysis

Honey and Mumford's theory of learning styles

You can test your own learning style preference or obtain further details of tests based on this theory at www.peterhoney.com.

One approach is to adopt this four-stage model of learning from experience and to actively monitor personal problem solving at work. For example, you might make records about an issue and records of practical action taken in an attempt to meet service user needs or solve other practical problems.

The 'four-stage' or 'cycle' theory of learning from experience is just one model of learning. This model may be useful in practice, especially as a way of approaching complicated non-routine problem solving. There are many other ways in which care workers might undertake personal development.

Which of these stages do you enjoy most, or do you enjoy each of these stages equally?

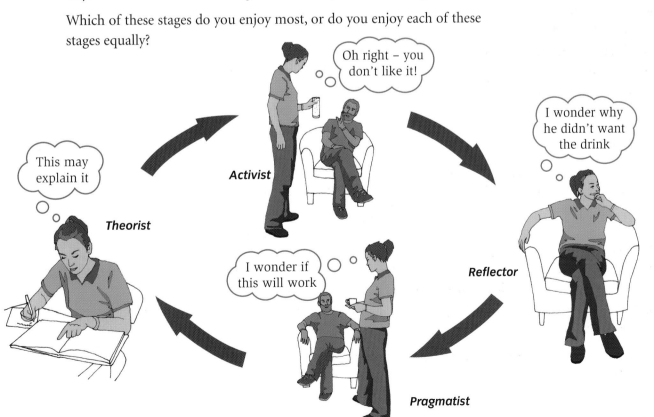

You can see how reflecting is closely connected with learning; you do something, then you reflect on it and learn from it, so that the next time you perform the same task you will be able to do it better and more effectively.

Active knowledge

Keep a reflective diary for a week. At the end of each working day, spend half an hour writing down one or two key issues that concerned you or irritated you – or even that you did well! How did you respond to these issues? How could you learn from this experience to take your own practice forward?

Examples might include an incident such as noticing a wastepaper basket placed where someone could trip over it, failing to move it because you were in a hurry, then returning with a jug of water and tripping over the basket yourself! The result might be that you had to spend much more time cleaning up your water spill than it would have taken to move the basket in the first place. Or perhaps there was a difficult interaction with an individual with whom you don't get along very easily – perhaps nothing significant, but a niggling feeling that you could have done better.

Different ways of learning

Formal training and development are not the only ways you can learn and expand your knowledge and understanding. There are plenty of other ways to keep up progress towards the goals you have set yourself.

Not everyone learns best from formal training. Other ways people learn are from:

- being shown by more experienced colleagues
- working and discussing issues as a team or group
- reading textbooks, journals and articles
- following up information on the Internet
- making use of local library facilities or learning resource centres
- asking questions and holding professional discussions with colleagues and managers.

Libraries and learning resource centres are wonderful sources of information and knowledge

Write down the different ways of learning that you have experienced. Have you, for example, studied a course at college, completed a distance learning programme or attended hands-on training sessions? Tick the learning methods which have been the most enjoyable and most successful for you.

Here is a checklist of ways of learning that you might find useful:

- watching other people
- asking questions and listening to the answers
- finding things out for yourself
- going to college and attending training courses
- studying a distance learning course or a course on the Internet.

How could you use this information about how you best like to learn in order to update your workplace skills?

Keep your notes as evidence for your portfolio.

Support networks

 KS ⑤ ⑥ ⑦ ⑧ ⑨ ⑪

Undertaking reflection alone is very difficult, so it is important to make use of your supervisor or mentor in order to get feedback on what you have done. Support networks, whether they are formal or informal, are one of the most effective means of identifying areas of your own practice which need further development. They will also help you to deal with any dilemmas or conflicts that you have identified.

Formal networks

These networks of support are usually put in place by your employer. They are likely to consist of your immediate supervisor and possibly other more senior members of staff on occasion. You are likely to have a regular system of feedback and support meetings, or appraisal sessions with your supervisor. These could be at differing intervals depending on the system in your particular workplace, but are unlikely to be less frequent than once a month.

These systems are extremely useful in giving you the opportunity to benefit from feedback from your supervisor, who will be fully aware of the work you have been doing, and able to identify areas of practice which you may need to improve and areas in which you have demonstrated strength.

The appraisal or supervision system in your workplace may also be the point at which you identify a programme of development which you need to undertake. Some employers identify this at six-monthly or 12-monthly intervals, and some more frequently. Your supervisor is likely to identify which of the available training programmes are appropriate for the areas of your practice which have been identified as needing development.

In discussion with your supervisor, programmes of development can be identified

Getting the most out of supervision

Make sure that you are well prepared for sessions with your supervisor so that you can get maximum benefit from them. This will mean bringing together your reflections on your own practice, using examples and case notes where appropriate. You will need to demonstrate to your supervisor that you have reflected on your own practice and that you have begun identifying areas for development. If you can provide evidence through case notes and records to support this, it will assist your supervisor greatly.

You will also need to be prepared to receive feedback from your supervisor. While feedback is likely to be given in a positive way, this does not mean that it will be uncritical. Many people have considerable difficulty in accepting criticism in any form, even where it is intended to be supportive and constructive. If you are aware that you are likely to have difficulty accepting

Active knowledge

Ask a colleague, or if you don't feel able to do that ask a friend or family member, to offer some constructive criticism on a task you have undertaken – a practical activity such as cooking a meal, or work you have undertaken in the garden or in the house, would be suitable.

If you are able to practise receiving feedback on something that is relatively unthreatening, you are likely to be able to use the same techniques when considering feedback on your working practices.

criticism, try to prepare yourself to view feedback from your supervisor as valuable and useful information which can add to your ability to reflect effectively on the work you are doing.

Your response to negative feedback should not be to defend your actions or to reject the feedback. You must try to accept and value it. A useful reply would be: 'Thank you, that's very helpful. I can use that next time to improve.' If you are able to achieve this you are likely to be able to make the maximum use of opportunities to improve your practice.

On the other hand, if criticism of any kind undermines your confidence and makes it difficult for you to value your own strengths, you should ask your supervisor to identify areas in which you did well, and use the positive to help you respond more constructively to the negative feedback.

Your supervisor's role

Your supervisor's role is to support and advise you in your work and to make sure that you know and understand:

- your rights and responsibilities as an employee
- what your job involves and the procedures your employer has in place to help you carry out your job properly
- the philosophy of care where you work – that is, the beliefs, values and attitudes of your employer regarding the way that service users are cared for, and how you can demonstrate values of care in the way you do your work
- your career development needs – the education and training requirements for the job roles you may progress into, as well as for your current job.

Evidence   PC 1 2 4

Ask your supervisor for a copy of the relevant policy or plan at work on the supervision of staff.

Read the plan and note down what it covers, for example how you will be supervised, how often you can expect to be formally supervised and what kinds of things your supervisor will be able to help you with in your work role and career.

If the plan is not clear, make a list of the things on which you would like your supervisor's support and agree a time and place to discuss these items with him or her. Keep your notes as evidence for your portfolio.

Training and development sessions

One of the other formal and organised ways of reflecting on your own practice and identifying strengths, weaknesses and areas for development is during training opportunities. On a course, or at a training day, aspects of your practice and areas of knowledge that are new to you will be discussed, and this will often open up avenues that you had not previously considered. This is one of the major benefits of making the most of all the training and education opportunities that are available to you.

CASE STUDY: Identifying opportunities to improve practice

Palvinder is a support worker in a unit for young adults with disabilities, run by a leading charity. He was aware that his knowledge of disability legislation was not as comprehensive as it ought to be and he felt uncertain about answering some of the questions that the young people put to him.

Palvinder raised this issue with his line manager, who immediately found that training days were provided by the local authority that would help Palvinder to learn about the relevant legislation. Following his training days, Palvinder felt far more confident, as not only had he learned a great deal during the course itself, he had also been given some handouts and been informed about useful textbooks and websites.

1 *How will Palvinder benefit personally from taking this training?*

2 *How will the individuals Palvinder works with benefit?*

3 *Are you confident about your knowledge of legislation relating to your own work? If not, what steps are you taking to improve it?*

Informal networks

Informal support networks are likely to consist of your work colleagues. These can be major sources of support and assistance. Part of the effectiveness of many teams in many workplaces is their ability to provide useful ideas for improving practice, and support when things go badly.

Informal networks can be major sources of support and assistance

Some staff teams provide a completely informal and ad-hoc support system, where people give you advice, guidance and support as and when necessary. Other teams will organise this on a more regular basis, and they may get together to discuss specific situations or problems which have arisen for members of the team. You need to be sure that you are making maximum use of all opportunities to gain support, advice and feedback on your practice.

Active knowledge

Identify the formal and informal support networks in your workplace. Note down the ways in which you use the different types of network and how they support your development. If you identify any gaps or areas where you feel unsupported, discuss this with your supervisor or manager.

Test yourself

1 List at least three factors which can influence the way you work.

2 What is the key difference between working in health and care and working in most other jobs?

3 Describe some of the different learning styles that people may use. Explain how each would be appropriate for different types of skills.

4 Describe the advantages that learning to be a thoughtful and reflective practitioner bring a) to the care worker and b) to the individuals he or she cares for.

HSC 33b Take action to enhance your practice

Learning from work practice

Everything you do at work is part of a process of learning. Even regular tasks are likely to be important for learning because there is always something new each time you do them. A simple task like taking a service user a hot drink may result in a lesson – if, for example, you find that the service user tells you he or she doesn't want tea, but would prefer coffee this morning, thank you! You will have learned a valuable lesson about never making assumptions that everything will be the same.

Learning from working is also about using the huge amount of skills and experience which your colleagues and supervisor will have. Not only does this mean they will be able to pass on knowledge and advice to you, but you have the perfect opportunity to discuss ideas and talk about day-to-day practice in the service you are delivering.

Talking about day-to-day practice with your colleagues is an ideal way to learn

Finding time to discuss work with colleagues is never easy; everyone is busy and you may feel that you should not make demands on their time. You may be in a position where you have to prioritise your time to provide supervision for others, and your manager has to prioritise time for your supervision.

Most supervision will take place at scheduled times but you may also be able to discuss issues in the course of hand-over meetings or team meetings, and other day-to-day activities. Use supervision time or quiet periods to discuss situations which have arisen, problems you have come across or new approaches you have noticed other colleagues using.

Evidence PC ① ② ④ ⑥

You have already begun the process of keeping a reflective diary (see page 142). Build on this to use your reflection to enhance your practice. Plan a feedback session with your manager. You may have straightforward questions, or more complicated issues to do with appropriate decisions about rights and risks, such as 'How did you make the decision that it was safe enough for Mr Jackson to go out to the shops by himself, when there are obvious risks?'

Try discussing such issues with different experienced colleagues – you may be surprised at what you learn. Keep your notes as evidence for your portfolio.

Using your mistakes

Everyone makes mistakes – they are one way of learning. It is important not to waste your mistakes, so if something has gone wrong, make sure you learn from it. Discuss problems and mistakes with your supervisor, and work out how to do things differently next time. It is important to reflect on both success and failure and you can use reflective skills in order to learn from situations which have not worked out the way you planned.

However, it is important that you consider carefully why things turned out the way they did and think about how you will ensure that they go according to plan next time. Unfortunately, there are real people on the receiving end of our mistakes in care, and learning how not to do it again is vitally important.

Using your successes

Talking to colleagues and supervisors is equally useful when things work out really well. It is just as important to reflect on why something worked, so that you can repeat it.

A key factor is to be organised in your approach to professional development. Thompson (1996) emphasises 'being systematic' as an important skill in care work. Practice is systematic when you know:

- what you are trying to achieve
- how you are you going to achieve it
- how you will tell when you have achieved it.

If, for example, you were planning to develop your communication skills, you might have the aim of establishing a degree of trust with a service user. You would not be able to plan a set strategy to produce trust – it is a feeling that might grow and develop within a caring relationship. But you could list some of the skills you would be using in your communication that would contribute to the development of a caring relationship.

You would have to have an understanding of relationships and trust in order to be able to explain the degree to which you have established a trusting relationship. You should use theory during the planning stage of your work in order to identify how you will know if you have achieved your aim.

Thompson (1996) argues that vague, unfocused care work can result in poor quality care and also in stress for the care worker. Some benefits of planned, systematic work, based on Thompson's analysis, are shown below.

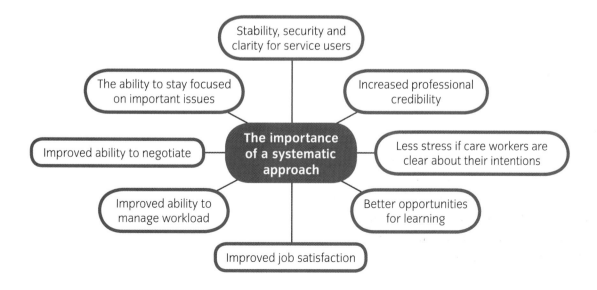

Look at the case study below.

CASE STUDY: Setting aims and objectives

Mr Gommer has been very unhappy since the death of his wife just over a year ago. He has stopped going out and has had no interest in meeting other people or becoming involved in activities. You provide domiciliary care to Mr Gommer and he has asked you to support him in re-establishing contact with other people. You make a plan so that you can check how well this has worked.

> **What needs to be achieved (the aim):**
> Improve Mr Gommer's social contacts
>
> **Goals which help to measure success (objectives):**
> Mr Gommer to agree to meet local organiser of Age Concern
> Mr Gommer to attend St Chad's luncheon club
>
> **How to do it (method):**
> 1 Talk to him about meeting the organiser and secure his agreement
> 2 Arrange the meeting at his home
> 3 Be there for the meeting
> 4 Be positive and encouraging
> 5 Offer to accompany him for his first visit to the luncheon club
> 6 Arrange transport for his first visit
> 7 Go with him

This type of plan will help you see if you are achieving your aim at each stage, by checking your progress. You will then know at which point something has not worked and can ask for help if necessary from your colleagues and supervisor. It will also help you to know when something has gone well and your plan has worked. Don't simply pat yourself on the back! Explore why your work went well. Use your supervision time and opportunities to talk with experienced colleagues.

Making good use of training/development opportunities  KS 3 4 6 7 8 9 11

Personal development is to do with developing the personal qualities and skills that everyone needs in order to live and work with others, such as understanding, empathy, patience, communication and relationship-building. It is also to do with the development of self-confidence, self-esteem and self-respect.

If you look back on the ways in which you have changed over the past five years, you are likely to find that you are different in quite a few ways. Most people change as they mature and gain more life experience. Important experiences such as changing jobs, moving home, illness or bereavement can change people. It is inevitable that your personal development and your professional development are linked – your personality and the way you relate to others are the major tools you use to do your job. Taking advantage of every opportunity to train and develop your working skills will also have an impact on you as a person.

Professional development is to do with developing the qualities and skills that are necessary for the workplace. Examples are teamwork, the ability to communicate with different types of people, time management, organisation, problem solving, decision making and, of course, the skills specific to the job.

Continuous professional development involves regularly updating the skills you need for work. You can achieve this through attending training sessions both on and off the job, and by making the most of the opportunities you have for training by careful planning and preparation.

Key terms

Personal development: Developing the personal qualities and skills needed to live and work with others.

Professional development: Developing the qualities and skills necessary for the workforce.

Legal requirements for training

Standards across the UK now lay down the number of trained staff which all residential care establishments must have, and they are periodically inspected by the regulator for each country within the UK. England is regulated by the Commission for Social Care Inspection under the Care Standards Act 2000. The same Act applies in Wales, and facilities are inspected and regulated by the Care Standards Inspectorate for Wales. In Scotland, regulation is by the Care Commission under the Regulation of Care (Scotland) Act 2001. The Social Services Inspectorate inspects social care services in Northern Ireland.

Acts of Parliament have resulted in the establishment of clear sets of standards that can be used by inspectors. These include standards relating to staff training and personal and professional development. All staff are required to demonstrate that they meet the requirements of induction standards when they first start working in care. There is also a requirement in England and Scotland that at least 50 per cent of staff delivering care must be qualified to NVQ level 2; in Wales, all staff are required to hold or be working towards a level 2 qualification. There are also requirements in the standards that staff receive supervision and are given a personal development plan for ongoing training. Paid training days must be provided. In Wales, there are specific requirements about how many supervision sessions each member of staff must receive during a year.

How to get the best out of training

Your supervisor will work with you to decide on the types of training that will benefit you most. This will depend on the stage you have reached with your skills and experience. There would be little point, for example, in doing a course in advanced micro-surgery techniques if you were at the stage of having just achieved your First Aid certificate! It may be that not all the training you want to do is appropriate for the work you are currently assigned to – you may think that a course in advanced therapeutic activities sounds fascinating, but your supervisor may suggest that a course in basic moving and handling is what you need right now. You will only get the best out of training and development opportunities if they are the right ones for you at the time. There will be opportunities for training throughout your career, and it is important that you work out which training is going to help you to achieve your goals.

Many different types of training opportunities will be open to you

CASE STUDY: Choosing appropriate training

Michelle is a health care support worker in a large hospital, on a busy ward. She was very aware of the fact that she lacked assertiveness in the way she dealt with both her colleagues and with many of her service users. Michelle was always the one who agreed to run errands and to cover additional tasks which others should have been doing. She knew that she ought to be able to say no, but somehow she couldn't and then became angry and resentful because she felt she was doing far more work than many others on her team. Her supervisor raised the issue during an appraisal and supervision session and suggested that Michelle should consider attending assertiveness training. Although initially reluctant, Michelle decided to take the opportunity. After six weeks of attending classes and working with the supportive group she met there, Michelle found that she was able to deal far more effectively with unfair and unreasonable requests from her colleagues and to deal in a firm but pleasant way with her service users.

1 *What difference is Michelle's training likely to make a) to the service users she works with, and b) to herself?*

2 *Have you ever said 'yes' to extra work or additional responsibility when you wanted to say 'no'? How did this make you feel?*

3 *What could you have done about it?*

How to use training and development

You should work with your supervisor to prepare for any training you receive, and to review it afterwards. You may want to prepare for a training session by:

- reading any materials which have been provided in advance
- talking to your supervisor or a colleague who has attended similar training, about what to expect
- thinking about what you want to achieve as a result of attending the training.

Keys to good practice: Training

Make the most of training by:

✓ preparing well

✓ taking a full part in the training and asking questions about anything you don't understand

✓ collecting any handouts and keeping your own notes of the training.

Think about how to apply what you have learned to your work by discussing the training with your supervisor later. Review the ways in which you have benefited from the training.

Evidence   PC ① ② ⑤ ⑥

Think about the last training or development session you took part in and write a short report.

- Describe the preparations you made beforehand so that you could benefit fully from it.

- Describe what you did at the session; for example, what and how did you contribute, and what did you learn? Do you have a certificate to show that you participated in the session? Do you have a set of notes?

- How did you follow up the session? Did you review the goals you had set yourself, or discuss the session with your supervisor?

- Describe how you have used what you learned at the session. For example, how has the way you work changed, and how have your service users and colleagues benefited from your learning?

Developing your own personal effectiveness

 KS ⑥ ⑨ ⑪

The health and social care sector is one which constantly changes and moves on. New standards reflect the changes in the profession, such as the emphasis on quality services, the focus on tackling exclusion, and the influence of the culture of rights and responsibilities. There has been a huge increase in understanding in all parts of the sector, and a recognition of the satisfaction that comes from working alongside service users as partners and directors of their own care, rather than as passive receivers of services.

Developments in technology have brought huge strides towards independence for many service users, thus promoting a changing relationship with care workers; at the same time, technological developments have brought different approaches to the way in which work in care is carried out and the administration and recording of service provision.

Legislation and the resulting guidelines are a feature of the work of the sector. Sadly, many of the new guidelines, policies and procedures result from enquiries and investigations which followed tragedies, errors and neglect.

Despite all this, much of what we do in the care sector will remain the same; the basic principles of caring, treating people with dignity and respect, ensuring they have choice and promoting independence will continue, and the skills of good communication remain as vital as ever.

Being aware of new developments

There are many ways in which you can ensure that you keep up to date with new developments in the field of care, and particularly those which affect your own area of work. You should not assume that your workplace will automatically inform you about new developments, changes and updates which affect your work – you must be prepared to actively maintain your own knowledge base and to ensure that your practice is in line with current thinking and new theories. The best way to do this is to incorporate an awareness of the need to constantly update your knowledge into all of your work activities. If you restrict your awareness of new developments to specific times, such as a monthly visit to the library, or a training course every six months, you are likely to miss out on a lot of information.

CASE STUDY: Researching sleep deprivation

Beth, a senior care assistant, has recently started to work nights on a rota system. Unfortunately, at first things didn't go as well as she had hoped. Everyone said she would get used to it, but that simply didn't happen. At 3 o'clock in the morning, no matter how busy she was, she found herself getting light-headed and feeling quite nauseous. The other major problem was that she found sleeping during the day quite difficult. She managed to get through her first week, but dreaded the next time it was her turn on nights. She felt that the quality of her care would be unsafe if she didn't learn to cope.

Beth mentioned her concerns to Paul, a nursing friend. It turned out that he had once researched sleep deprivation, and found that there are all sorts of ways of coping. He recommended that she look at one or two helpful websites, and also that she read some of the research on night working – she could use both the local trust library and her own local library. The websites he suggested were: www.sleepeducation.com and www.bbc.co.uk/science/humanbody/sleep.

Beth looked at the websites and the research, found them very helpful and followed some of the advice she received. She is now able to cope better and more safely with her night shifts.

1 *Was Beth right to be concerned and to follow up her concerns, or should she just have tried to get used to it?*

2 *Look at these websites, or find similar ones on sleep yourself. Can you identify three strategies that Beth could adopt to make her night working and daytime sleeping more effective?*

3 *How could she communicate what she finds out to her colleagues?*

Sources of information

The media

The area of health and care is always in the news, so it is relatively easy to find out information about new studies and research. You will need to pay attention when watching television and listening to radio news bulletins to find out about new developments, legislation, guidelines and reports related to health and care service users and workers.

Active knowledge

For one week keep a record of every item which relates to health and care services which you hear on a radio bulletin, see in a television programme, or read in a newspaper article. You are likely to be surprised at the very large number of references you manage to find.

Articles in newspapers and professional journals are excellent sources of information. When reporting on a recently completed study, they usually give information about where to obtain a copy of it.

Reports and reviews

You can read the findings of enquiries into the failures experienced within social work, health and social care, and this might provide you with a focus for reflection. In the past there have been many cases where children and adults have been neglected or abused and social services have failed to protect vulnerable people adequately. Currently there is great national concern about the cleanliness and safety of hospital wards. While you may not be involved in policy-making decisions with respect to these services, there may be many principles such as 'whistle blowing' that are relevant in your own work setting. Many past serious failings might have been preventable if people had been able to identify the issues and take action earlier.

As well as reflecting on failures of the service, it will be important to reflect on positive practice. The Commission for Social Care Inspection (CSCI) includes brief anecdotes that help to explain the positive role of standards and inspection in improving the quality of life for service users, in some of its documents designed for the public. The CSCI website at www.csci.org.uk might provide you with one starting point for exploring ideas on successful approaches to care practice.

Conferences

Professional journals also carry advertisements for conferences and training opportunities. You may also find such information in your workplace. There is often a cost involved in attending these events, so the restrictions of the training budget in your workplace may mean that you cannot attend.

However, it may be possible for one person to attend and pass on the information gained to others in the workplace, or to obtain conference papers and handouts without attending.

The Internet

The development of information technology, and in particular the Internet, has provided a vast resource of information, views and research.

There are clearly some limitations to using the Internet; for example, many people are reluctant to look for information through that route because they are not confident about using computers. However, the use of computers in the health and care sector is becoming increasingly widespread and important. If you have access to a computer, using the Internet is a simple process that you could easily learn.

The Internet provides a vast amount of information

Another disadvantage is that you need to be wary of the information you obtain on the Internet, unless it is from accredited sources such as a government department, a reputable university or college, or an established research centre. Make every effort to check the validity of what you are reading. The World Wide Web provides free access to vast amounts of information, but it is an unregulated environment – anyone can publish information on the Internet, and there is no requirement for it to be checked or approved. People can publish their own views and opinions, which may not be based on fact. These views and opinions from a wide range of people are valuable and interesting in themselves, but be careful that you do not assume anything to be factually correct unless it is from a reliable source.

Treated with care, the Internet can prove to be one of the speediest and most useful tools in obtaining up-to-date information.

Your supervisor and colleagues

Never overlook the obvious: one of the sources of information which may be most useful to you is close at hand – your own workplace supervisor and colleagues. They may have many years of experience and accumulated knowledge which they will be happy to share with you. They may also be updating their own practice and ideas, and may have information that they would be willing to share.

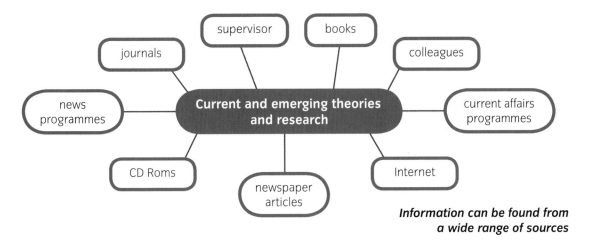

Information can be found from a wide range of sources

Understanding new information

Reading and hearing about new studies and pieces of research is all very well, but you must understand what it is that you are reading. It is important that you know how new theories are developed and how research is carried out.

Reliability and validity

There are specific methods of carrying out research to ensure the results are both reliable and valid. Research is judged on both of these factors, and you need to be able to satisfy yourself that the reports you read are based on reliable and valid research.

Reliability means the results would be repeated if someone else were to carry out the same piece of research in exactly the same way. **Validity** means that the conclusions that have been drawn from the research are consistent with the results, consistent with the way in which the research was carried out and consistent in the way in which the information has been interpreted.

The research process

You will need to understand some of the basic terms which are used when discussing research in any field.

- **Primary research** refers to information or data which is obtained directly from the research carried out, not from books or previously published work.
- **Secondary research** refers to information obtained from books, previously published research and reports, CD Roms, the Internet, etc. – any information obtained from work carried out by others. For example, if you were asked to write an assignment you are most likely to find the information from secondary sources such as textbooks or the Internet, rather than carry out a research project yourself in order to establish the information you need.

The information obtained from research is often referred to as **data**. It is called data regardless of whether it is in numbers or in words.

There are two broad areas of approach to research and they determine both the way in which the research is carried out and the type of results that are obtained. The first is referred to as **quantitative**, the second is **qualitative**.

Quantitative research

This approach has developed from the way in which scientists carry out laboratory experiments. The method produces statistical and numerical information. It provides hard facts and figures, and uses statistics and numbers to draw conclusions and make an analysis.

Many researchers in the field of health and care use quantitative approaches and produce quantitative data. They may carry out 'experiments' using many of the rules of scientific investigation. In general, if you are reading research which provides statistics and numerical information and is based purely on facts, it is likely to have used one of the quantitative approaches.

Many government publications are good examples of quantitative research – they give statistics in relation to the National Health Service, for example, such as the numbers of patients on waiting lists, the numbers having a particular operation, or the numbers of residents in nursing homes throughout the country.

Qualitative research

A qualitative approach looks at the 'quality' rather than the 'quantity' of something. It would be used to investigate the feelings of people who have remained on the waiting list for treatment, or people's attitudes towards residential care, or the relationships between those in residential care and those who care for them. Generally, qualitative data is produced in words rather than figures and will consist of descriptions and information about people's lives, experiences and attitudes.

Active knowledge

By using any of the methods for finding up-to-date information, such as newspapers, journals, reports, television, the Internet or textbooks, find two pieces of research carried out within the past two years. One should be quantitative and one qualitative. Read the results of both pieces of research and make a note of the differences in the type of information provided.

How to ensure your practice is current and up to date
KS 6 7 9 10 11

There is little point in reading articles, watching TV programmes and attending training days if your work practice is not updated and improved as a result. With the enormous pressures on everybody in the health and care services, it is often difficult to find time to keep up to date and to change the practices you are used to. Any form of change takes time and is always a little uncomfortable or unusual to begin with. So when we are under pressure because of the amount of work we have to do, it is only normal that we tend to rely on practices, methods and ways of working which are comfortable, familiar and can be done swiftly and efficiently.

You will need to make a very conscious effort to incorporate new learning into your practice. You need to allocate time to updating your knowledge, and incorporating it into your practice. You could try the following ways to ensure that you are using the new knowledge you have gained.

Keys to good practice: Applying new skills and knowledge in practice

✓ Plan out how you will adapt your practice on a day-to-day basis, adding one new aspect each day. Do this until you have covered all the aspects of the new information you have learned.

✓ Discuss with your supervisor and colleagues what you have learned and how you intend to change your practice, and ask for feedback.

✓ Write a checklist for yourself and check it at the end of each day.

✓ Give yourself a set period of time, for example one month, to alter or improve your practice, and review it at the end of that time.

New knowledge is not only about the most exciting emerging theories. It is also often about mundane and day-to-day aspects of your practice, which are just as important and can make just as much difference to the quality of care you provide for your service users. It is also about taking your practice forward by developing your knowledge across a range of situations.

CASE STUDY: Opportunities for self-directed training

Meena works as a care worker at a big, busy day centre and meets the families of service users of all ages. One day she was chatting to the daughter of a service user and mentioned the problem of teenage pregnancy, expressing her disapproval of the extreme youth of some new mothers. 'It's funny you should say that', replied the woman, 'but my daughter Louise is pregnant. I'm not that happy – she's only 16 – but what can you do?' Meena felt embarrassed, but decided she needed to be better informed on the issue. She got in touch with the local family planning clinic and spoke to the manager, explaining that she would like to learn more about the sexual health services available to young people. She arranged to spend some time on a self-directed 'work experience' placement at the clinic, and is now a volunteer there, helping to run the crèche. In her reflective diary she writes:

'Really tired tonight. All day at work and then 2 hours at the clinic. Spent half an hour with a young girl who was crying because her Dad has threatened to kick her out. Helped her fill in some forms and arrange to see social services. All this is making me more aware, and I hope a better all-round carer.'

1 *What benefits to Meena's 'day job' do you think will come from her self-directed training?*

2 *How can training help to overcome prejudice?*

Active knowledge

Think about an occasion when you have been able to reflect on an area of your own practice or knowledge which needed improvement, and the steps you took to achieve the improvement. Record what you did and also how you incorporated the new knowledge into your practice. Once you have identified this and recorded it in detail, you should include it in your NVQ portfolio as part of the evidence that you will need to achieve this unit.

Preparing a development plan

It is a requirement of many organisations that their staff have personal development plans. A personal development plan is a very important document as it identifies a worker's training and development needs and, because the plan is updated when the worker has taken part in training and development, it also provides a record of participation.

A personal development plan should be worked out with your supervisor, but it is essentially your plan for your career. You need to think about what you want to achieve, and discuss with your supervisor the best ways of achieving your goals.

There is no single right way to prepare a personal development plan, and each organisation is likely to have its own way. However, it should include different development areas, such as practical skills and communication skills, the goals or targets you have set – such as learning to manage a team – and a timescale for achieving them. Timescales must be realistic; for example, if you were to decide that you needed to achieve competence in managing a team in six months, this would be unrealistic and unachievable. You would inevitably fail to meet your target and would therefore be likely to become demoralised and demotivated. But if your target was to attend a training and development programme on team building during the next six months and to lead perhaps two team meetings by the end of the six months, those goals and targets would be realistic and you would be likely to achieve them.

When you have set your targets, you need to review how you are progressing towards achieving them – this should happen every six months or so. You need to look at what you have achieved and how your plan needs to be updated.

Development plans can take many forms, but the best ones are likely to be developed in conjunction with your manager or workplace supervisor. You need to carefully consider the 'areas of competence' and understand which ones you need to develop for your work role. Identify each as either an area in which you feel fully confident, one where there is room for improvement and development, or one where you have very limited current ability. The headings in the table on the next page are suggestions only.

Development plan		
Area of competence	Goals	Action plan
Time management and workload organisation	Learn to use computer recording and information systems	Attend 2-day training and use study pack. Attend follow-up training days. Use computer instead of writing reports by hand

Review date: 3 months

Professional development priorities	
My priorities for training and development in the next 6 months are:	IT and computerised record systems
My priorities for training and development in the next 6–12 months are:	As above and NVQ assessor training

Repeat this exercise in: 6 months
and review the areas of competence and priorities.

Once you have completed your plan you can identify the areas on which you need to concentrate. You should set some goals and targets, and your line manager should be able to help you ensure they are realistic. Only you and your line manager can examine the areas of competence and skills which you need to achieve. This is a personal development programme for you and you must be sure that it reflects not only the objectives of your organisation and the job roles they may want you to fulfil, but also your personal ambitions and aspirations.

When you have identified the areas in which you feel competent and chosen your target areas for development, you will need to design a personal development log which will enable you to keep a record of your progress. This can be put together in any way that you find effective.

In your plan you may wish to include things as varied as learning sign language, learning a particular technique for working with service users with dementia, or developing your potential as a manager by learning organisational and human resources skills. You could also include areas such as time management and stress management. All of these are legitimate areas for inclusion in your personal and professional development plan.

Evidence

PC 1 2 3 4 7

Your task is to prepare a Personal Development Plan. You should use a computer to do this, even if you print out a hard copy in order to keep a personal portfolio.

Step 1

Use the model on the following pages to prepare your plan.

Step 2

Complete the plan as far as you can at the present time. Note where you want your career to be in the short, medium and long term. You should also note down the training you want to complete and the skills you want to gain. You should do this on a computer if possible, otherwise complete a hard copy and keep it in a file.

Step 3

Update the plan regularly. Keep on reviewing it with your supervisor.

Personal Development Plan

Name:

Workplace:

Supervisor:

Long-term goals (1–5 years)

Medium-term goals (6–12 months)

Short-term goals (next 6 months)

Areas of strength

Areas of weakness

Training and development

This section of your plan helps you to look at what you need to do in order to reach the goals you recorded in the first section. You should make a note of the training and development you need to undertake in order to achieve what you have identified.

Short-term goals	Development needed
Medium-term goals	Development needed
Long-term goals	Development needed

Milestones and timescales

In this section you should look at the development you have identified in the previous section and plan some timescales. Decide what the 'milestones' will be on the way to achieving your goal. Make sure that your timescales are realistic.

Development	Milestone	By when

Reviews and updates

This section helps you to stay on track and to make the changes which will be inevitable as you progress. Not all your milestones will be achieved on target – some will be later, some earlier. All these changes will affect your overall plan, and you need to keep up to date and make any alterations as you go along.

Milestone	Target date	Actual achievement/revised target

Test yourself

1 Why are personal development plans important?

2 Who would you ask to help you to prepare a personal development plan?

3 Do you agree with the requirements in the Care Standards for training? Give reasons for your answer.

4 Name three ways of finding out current and up-to-date information about care practice.

5 Why does it matter that you keep your practice up to date?

6 How could you make sure that you get the most benefit from new knowledge after a training session?

HSC 33 FURTHER READING AND RESEARCH

The introduction to this section highlights your duty to make sure that the service provided is the best it can possibly be. In order to do this it is essential that you are constantly reflecting on your practice and striving to develop the way you work. Here are some suggestions of further reading and research to help you to do this.

www.gscc.org.uk (General Social Care Council (GSCC) – training and learning)

www.dh.gov.uk (Department of Health – human resources and training)

www.skillsforcare.org.uk (Skills for Care – workforce development for UK social care sector)

www.skillsforhealth.org.uk (Skills for Health – workforce development for UK health sector)

www.cwdcouncil.org.uk (Children's Workforce Development Council) tel: 0113 2446311

www.scie.org.uk (Social Care Institute of Excellence)

Hawkins, R., Ashurst, A. (2006) *How to be a Great Care Assistant* Hawker Publications

Knapman, J., Morrison, T. (1998) *Making the Most of Supervision in Health & Social Care* Pavilion Publishers Shakespeare, P. (DATE) *Learning in Health and Social Care* Blackwell Publishing

Promote choice, well-being and the protection of all individuals

Caring for individuals is about making sure that you value everyone you work with as an individual, and that you treat them with respect and make sure they can enjoy life with the dignity that every individual deserves. It is also about making sure you promote individuals' rights and preferences.

Well-being is about much more than just health; it is about every part of people's lives including feeling safe, valued and respected. Choice, as much independence as possible and the opportunity to reach your own potential are the key factors in achieving individual well-being.

Feeling safe is also an important part of well-being and everyone has the right to be protected from abuse and harm. You have an important role in noticing and reporting any signs of abuse, neglect or other harm.

What you need to learn

- Relationships
- Choices and empowerment
- Individuals' rights
- Providing support to meet the needs and preferences of individuals
- Active support
- Dealing with conflicts
- Treating people as individuals
- How to recognise your own prejudices
- Anti-discriminatory practice
- Forms of abuse
- Signs and symptoms which may indicate abuse
- Who can abuse?
- How to respond to abuse and neglect
- The effects of abuse
- How the law affects what you do.

HSC 35a Develop supportive relationships that promote choice and independence

Relationships

Being able to develop effective working relationships with individuals is an essential skill for a professional care worker. Making a working relationship with an individual is about using all your communication skills, but it also means establishing a two-way process and making a connection with the other person. We all experience many types of relationships, and you need to understand what makes them work so that you can make useful relationships with the individuals you work with.

Different types of relationships

Everyone has a wide range of relationships with different people, ranging from family to work colleagues. Each of the different types of relationship is important and plays a valuable role in contributing to the overall well-being of each of us. The needs and demands of different types of relationships are varied, as are the effects that relationships can have on individuals' views of themselves and the confidence with which they deal with the world.

We all develop relationships that are important to our lives

Professional caring relationships  KS 14 2 8 11 12

As a professional working in a care setting, the relationships you form with service users and work colleagues are essential to providing an effective service.

You will need to make use of all the communication skills you have learned in order to develop relationships which make service users feel valued as individuals, respected and treated with dignity. The caring relationship must provide support and, most importantly, should empower the individual to become as independent as possible.

Working relationships with colleagues should be based on a professional respect for the skills and work of others, and consideration for the demands that work roles place on others. Workloads and responsibility should be shared as appropriate, and so should information and knowledge where this does not conflict with the principles of confidentiality.

The government is concerned that service users should be treated as individuals. The Department of Health has established a National Service Framework for Older People. This is a 10-year programme aimed at improving the delivery of health and care services for older people. Standard 2 of this framework is entitled 'Person-centred care', and it stresses the importance of choice, respect and dignity in meeting the needs of service users.

Choice and empowerment  KS 12 15 22

One of the vitally important aspects of relationship-building in your job is making sure that people make choices and take control over their own lives. You must do everything you can in your own practice and in your own work setting to recognise that people have the power to do this through Direct Payments or managing an Individual Budget.

Many people who receive care services were often unable to make choices about their lives. This was because of a range of different circumstances, but often because of the way essential services were provided.

Active knowledge

Make a list of four or five people you work with or are responsible for, and think about five normal activities of living over which they had limited or no choices. It could be:

- which music to listen to
- access to shops or facilities
- meals
- entertainment
- daily relationships
- bath/shower time
- dependence on a carer.

Think about how you would feel if your choices were limited in the same way. How would you rank these issues in order of importance? How has this choice changed since people were placed in control of their own services?

In order to understand the importance of the effects of placing people in control you must understand what can happen to people who feel that they are powerless in relation to their day-to-day activities. How much we value ourselves – our **self-esteem** – is a result of many factors, but a very important one is the extent of control, or power, we have over our lives.

Of course, many other factors influence our self-esteem, such as:

- the amount of encouragement and praise we have had from important people in our lives, such as parents, partners and friends
- whether we have positive and happy relationships with other people, such as family and work colleagues
- the amount of stimulation and satisfaction we get from our work – paid or unpaid.

Individuals who are unable to exercise choice and control may very soon suffer lower self-esteem and lose confidence in their own abilities. Unfortunately, this means they may become convinced that they are unable to do many tasks for themselves, and that they need help in most areas of their day-to-day lives. It is easy to see how such a chain of events can result in people becoming dependent on others and less able to do things for themselves. Once this downward spiral has begun it can be difficult to stop, so it is far better to avoid the things that make it begin.

Active knowledge

Look at the illustration above. This situation is not untypical – there are more women in care than men, not everyone likes cricket and this care worker clearly had not bothered to remember Jack's needs. What could she have done, even at the last moment, to support Jack? How could this situation have been avoided in the first place? Have you ever been guilty of the 'one size fits all' attitude towards service users?

Self-esteem has a major effect on people's health and well-being. People with a confident, positive view of themselves, who believe that they have value and worth, are far more likely to be happy and healthy than someone whose self-esteem is poor and whose confidence is low.

People who have a positive and confident outlook are far more likely to be interested and active in the world around them, while those lacking confidence and belief in their own abilities are more likely to be withdrawn and reluctant to try anything new. It is easy to see how this can affect someone's quality of life and reduce his or her overall health and well-being.

Control for service users

It was often the case that individuals were told the level of support they would receive and the days on which they would receive it. They may even have been told the times at which they would receive such help. The White Paper 'Our Health Our Care Our Say' 2005 set out to change these practices dramatically. Putting power and control in the hands of people who use services was the key message of the White Paper. People are encouraged to control their own services through 'self directed support' where the amount of budget available is agreed through assessment, but control over how it is spent is entirely in the hands of the individual. The concept of 'individual budgets' is rather like 'direct payments', but without the requirement to be an employer.

This places a whole new set of demands on organisations delivering services. The services that are commissioned must be flexible enough to meet the needs of individuals and to enable people to decide the outcomes they want to achieve and the ways they want the outcomes to be realised. Individuals are now able to choose when they want services and how and by whom they want them to be delivered. Organisations providing services have to 'square the circle'.

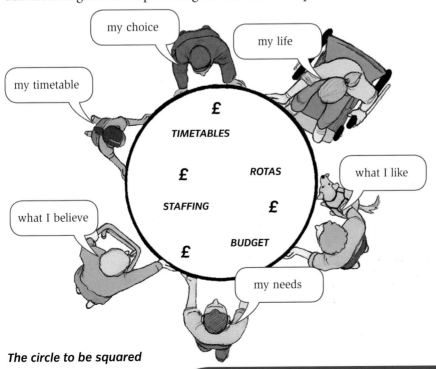

The circle to be squared

CASE STUDY: Empowerment

Reg is 82, and lives with his wife Enid. Although she is slow to get around, Enid still manages most domestic chores and personal care.

Reg has been diagnosed with the early stages of Alzheimer's disease, and he and Enid are aware that their way of life might change in the future. They have been receiving help twice a week with the cleaning and ironing, but after talking to Doreen, their support worker, they decide to discuss with the care manager the idea of getting in more support now, in order to avoid crises in the future.

1 *How should the care manager move the discussion forward in order to support Reg and Enid?*

2 *What additional support organisations could Reg access?*

3 *A diagnosis of Alzheimer's disease has frightening connotations for many people. How could the care manager address such fears sensitively as well as practically?*

Active knowledge

Using the list you made for the activity on page 167, make notes about the differences which could be made to the life of each individual you work with if he or she was able to make the choices you have identified.

Individuals' rights

 KS 1 3 6 8

Rights and responsibilities are a huge subject. In order to look at rights in terms of how they affect the people you work with and provide care for, it is helpful to discuss them under the following headings:

- rights under National Standards, codes of practice, charters, guidelines and policies
- rights provided by law.

Responsibilities are the other side of the coin to rights – most of our responsibilities are about protecting, improving or not infringing other people's rights. Responsibilities are the balance for rights, and it is impossible to consider one without the other.

Rights under codes, charters, guidelines and policies

These are rights which do not have the force of law, but which are enforceable within care work and designed to improve the services people receive.

National Minimum Standards

The Commission for Social Care Inspection (CSCI) now has responsibility for inspecting care services in England, and it is planned that this commission will take over the inspection of health services in the future. The CSCI uses a series of National Minimum Standards in order to inspect the quality of care. There are different sets of standards for different types of services. For example,

Did you know?

The CSCI has produced a booklet entitled 'Care Homes for Older People' detailing the rights that older people have within a care home. These rights include:

- privacy and dignity
- choice and control
- the meeting of cultural and spiritual needs
- health and well-being
- a social life and activities
- good food
- a clean, comfortable and safe home
- protection from harm and abuse.

Full details of national standards and booklets for service users can be found at www.csci.org.uk.

there are standards for care homes for older people, separate standards for care homes for younger adults, for children's homes and for fostering services. The standards documents provide a detailed set of definitions that outline the minimum quality of care that a service user may expect.

National Minimum Standards documents may appear rather technical; for example the standards for care homes for older people are 42 pages long plus appendices, and are intended to provide clear definitions to define quality care for inspection purposes. But the CSCI has now started to produce easy-to-read documents intended for service users.

Codes of practice

In 2002 the General Social Care Council in England published a code of practice for both employees and employers. Other regulatory bodies in Scotland, Wales and Northern Ireland have similar codes. A summary of the GSCC code of practice for employees is set out below.

Duties under the GSCC Code of Practice for Social Care Workers	
Protect the rights and promote the interests of service users and care workers Respect for **individuality** and support for service users to control their own lives. Respect for and maintenance of **equal opportunities**, **diversity**, dignity and privacy.	**Promote the independence of service users while protecting them from danger or harm** Maintenance of **rights**, challenging and reporting dangerous, abusive, discriminatory, or exploitative behaviour. Following **safe** practice, reporting resource problems, reporting unsafe practice of colleagues, following **health and safety regulations**, helping service users to make complaints and using **power** responsibly.
Establish and maintain the trust and confidence of service users Maintaining **confidentiality**, using effective **communication**, honouring commitments and agreements, declaring conflicts of interest and adhering to policies about accepting gifts.	**Respect the rights of service users while seeking to ensure that their behaviour does not harm themselves or other people** Recognising the right to take **risks**, following risk assessment policies, minimising risks, ensuring others are informed about risk assessments.
Uphold public trust and confidence in social care services Not abusing, neglecting or exploiting service users or colleagues, or forming inappropriate personal relationships. Not **discriminating** or condoning discrimination, or placing self or others at unnecessary **risk**. Not abusing the trust of others in relation to **confidentiality**.	**Be accountable for the quality of your work and take responsibility for maintaining and improving your knowledge and skills** Meeting standards, maintaining appropriate records and informing employers of personal difficulties. Seeking assistance and co-operating with colleagues, recognising responsibility for delegated work, respecting the roles of others and undertaking **relevant training**.

If you supervise other staff you may also need to consider the GSCC code of practice for employers, a summary of which is set out on the next page:

Code of Practice for Employers of Social Care Workers

1   Employers must make sure people are suitable to enter the social care work force and understand their roles and responsibilities.

2   Employers must have written policies and procedures in place to enable social care workers to meet the GSCC's Code of Practice for Social Care Workers. This includes written policies on:
- confidentiality
- equal opportunities
- risk assessment
- record keeping
- acceptance of gifts
- substance abuse.

Employers must also provide:
- effective systems of management and supervision
- systems to report inadequate resources
- support for workers to meet the GSCC code of practice.

3   Employers must provide training and development opportunities to enable social care workers to strengthen and develop their skills and knowledge, including:
- induction
- workplace assessment and practice learning
- supporting staff to meet eligibility criteria
- responding to workers who seek assistance.

4   Employers must put into place and implement written policies and procedures to deal with dangerous, discriminatory or exploitative behaviour and practice, including written policies and procedures on:
- bullying, harassment and discrimination
- procedures to report dangerous, discriminatory, abusive or exploitative behaviour
- policies to minimise the risk of violence and to manage violent incidents
- support for workers who experience trauma or violence
- equal opportunities
- assistance to care workers in relation to health needs.

5   Employers must promote the GSCC's codes of practice to social care workers, service users and carers and co-operate with the GSCC's proceedings. This includes informing workers of the code, informing social care users, using the code to assist in decision making, informing the GSCC of any misconduct, and co-operating with the GSCC in investigations.

If you supervise staff you may need to consider the GSCC Code of Practice for employers relevant to the country you work in

The table below lists some service-user rights, based on the English GSCC Code of Practice.

Moral rights of service users	GSCC standards
Diversity and respect for differences	1.1 treating each person as an individual 1.2 respecting and promoting individual views 1.6 respecting diversity and different cultures and values
Equality in care practice	1.5 promoting equal opportunities
Anti-discriminatory practice	5.5 not discriminating 5.6 not condoning discrimination
Confidentiality	2.3 respecting confidential information
Control over own life, choice and independence	1.3 supporting service users' rights to control their lives and make informed choices 3.1 promoting the independence of service users 3.7 helping service users and care workers to make complaints 3.8 recognising and using power responsibly
Dignity and privacy	1.4 respecting and maintaining the dignity and privacy of service users
Effective communication	2.2 communicating in an appropriate, open, accurate and straightforward way
Safety and security	Principle 3 promotes independence while protecting service users, including health and safety policies; appropriate practice and procedures 4.2/4.3 following risk assessment policies, taking steps to minimise risk 5.2 not exploiting service users 5.7 not putting self or others at risk
Right to take risks	4.1 helping service users to identify and manage risks

Your employer will have a range of policy and procedure documents that will also define how staff should behave towards service users.

Rights also involve responsibilities. Everyone has the responsibility not to infringe the rights of other people. Some responsibilities linked to the rights above are set out below:

Rights of service users	Responsibilities
Diversity and the right to be different Including an individual's right to express his or her own identity, culture, lifestyle and interpretation of life.	**Respect for diversity in others** Including an acceptance that other people have a right to interpret life differently. A responsibility not to discriminate against others on the basis that the individual's identity, lifestyle or culture is morally superior to that of others.
Equality and freedom from discrimination Including freedom from discrimination on the basis of race, sex, ability, sexuality or religion.	**Respect for the equality of others** Including respect for, and not discrimination against, members of other social groups.
Control over own life, choice and independence Including the freedom to choose lifestyle, self-presentation, diet and routine.	**Respect for the independence, choice and lifestyle of others** Including arriving at a balance between the impact of the individual's own choices and the needs of other people who may be affected by them – including care workers.
Dignity and privacy Including the right to be responded to in terms of the service user's own interpretation of dignity and respect.	**Respect for the dignity and privacy of others** Including issues associated with the identity needs of other users or carers.
Confidentiality Including rights as established in law and codes of practice.	**Respect for the confidentiality of others** Including others' legal rights, and rights established in codes of practice.

Continued

Rights of service users	Responsibilities
Effective communication Including appropriately clear and supportive communication that minimises vulnerability.	**Communication with others which does not seek to cause offence or threaten**
Safety and security Including physical safety, living in an environment that promotes health and emotional safety, security of property, and freedom from physical, social, emotional or economic abuse.	**Contributing to the safety and security of others** Including behaving in a way that does not threaten or abuse the physical or emotional safety and security of others.
The right to take risks Including taking risks as a matter of choice, in order to maintain the service user's own identity or perceived well-being.	**Not to expose oneself or others to unacceptable risks** Including a willingness to negotiate with respect to the impact of risk on others.

Rights provided by law

Most of the provisions of the UK's Human Rights Act came into force on 2 October 2000. This means that residents of the United Kingdom – this Act applies in England, Scotland, Wales and Northern Ireland – will now be entitled to seek help from the courts if they believe that their human rights have been infringed.

Organisations subject to Human Rights Act 1998	
Residential homes or nursing homes	These perform functions which would otherwise be performed by a local authority
Charities	
Voluntary organisations	
Public services	This could include the privatised utilities, such as gas, electric and water companies

It is likely that anyone who works in health or care will be working within the provisions of the Human Rights Act, which guarantees the following rights.

1 The right to life.

2 The right to freedom from torture and inhuman or degrading treatment or punishment.

3 The right to freedom from slavery, servitude and forced or compulsory labour.

4   The right to liberty and security of person.

5   The right to a fair and public trial within a reasonable time.

6   The right to freedom from retrospective criminal law and no punishment without law.

7   The right to respect for private and family life, home and correspondence.

8   The right to freedom of thought, conscience and religion.

9   The right to freedom of expression.

10 The right to freedom of assembly and association.

11 The right to marry and found a family.

12 The prohibition of discrimination in the enjoyment of convention rights.

13 The right to peaceful enjoyment of possessions and protection of property.

14 The right of access to an education.

15 The right of free elections.

16 The right not to be subjected to the death penalty.

Law, rights and discrimination

Discrimination is a denial of rights. Discrimination can be based on issues such as race, gender, disability or sexual orientation. The main Acts of Parliament which are related to discrimination are:

- the Equal Pay Act 1970
- the Sex Discrimination Act 1975 (amended 1986)
- the Race Relations Act 1976 (amended 2000)
- the Disability Discrimination Act 1995 and Disability Rights Commission Act 1999.

In addition it is important to note the regulations that provide a legal right not to be discriminated against on the basis of sexual orientation or religious belief. These are:

- Employment Equality (Sexual Orientation) Regulations 2003
- Employment Equality (Religion or Belief) Regulations 2003

Equal Pay Act 1970

This Act made it unlawful for employers to discriminate between men and women in terms of their pay and conditions of work. Before this law was passed it was possible for an employer to pay men more than women – even though they were doing the same job!

Equal pay legislation was updated in 1975 and 1983 to make it possible to claim equal pay for work that was considered to be of 'equal value'.

Active knowledge

As you consider these Acts of Parliament, make notes on whether your workplace and your own practice fully support this legislation. Be as critical as necessary. If there are gaps or problems with compliance, how could you make your workplace into a more anti-discriminatory environment? What could you do as your personal contribution?

Did you know?

Average male wages in the UK are still about 20 per cent higher than women's. In 1965, women's average wage was half that of men.

Sex Discrimination Act 1975

This Act made it unlawful to discriminate between men and women in respect of employment, goods and facilities. The Act also made it illegal to discriminate on the grounds of marital status. The Act identified two forms of discrimination: direct discrimination and indirect discrimination.

The Act tries to provide equal opportunities for men and women in getting jobs and promotion. In order to make sure that people's rights were protected, the government set up the **Equal Opportunities Commission** to monitor, advise and provide information on men and women's rights under the law. The commission will give help and advice to people who believe they have been discriminated against because of their gender. The law was updated in 1986 so that it also applies to small businesses.

Race Relations Act 1976

This Act makes it unlawful to discriminate on 'racial grounds' in employment, housing or services. This includes colour, race, nationality, ethnic or national origins. The Act makes it an offence to incite or encourage racial hatred. As in the law against sex discrimination, both direct and indirect discrimination are targeted.

The **Commission for Racial Equality** was set up in 1976 to make sure that the law against racial discrimination works. The commission can investigate cases of discrimination and give advice to people who wish to take legal action because of discrimination. The law was strengthened and widened by an amendment in 2000 in order to prevent discrimination in any public situation.

Active knowledge

Research the work of the Commission for Racial Equality and see whether you can find any recent cases relating to health and social care workers. Do they include any issues that could occur in your workplace?

Disability Discrimination Act 1995

This Act is designed to prevent discrimination against people with disabilities in employment, access to education and transport, housing and obtaining goods and services. Employers and landlords must not treat a disabled person less favourably than a non-disabled person. New transport facilities must meet the needs of disabled people and colleges, shops and other services must ensure that disabled people can use their services.

The **Disability Rights Commission** was set up by the Disability Rights Commission Act, 1999. This commission has the power to conduct formal investigations and to serve non-discrimination notices, make agreements, and take other action to prevent discrimination against people with a disability. The commission can give advice to people who believe they have experienced discrimination.

Disabled people need to be able to access premises and facilities

Providing support to meet the needs and preferences of individuals

Some service users may feel that they are as vulnerable because they feel that they cannot control the extent to which their needs are likely to be met. Some people with a learning disability see themselves as dependent on their care workers to organise appropriate daily activities to ensure their needs are met. Some older service users may be disorientated, and people with dementia may feel that they are unable to interpret and control their surroundings without appropriate support. Children are sometimes unable to make wise decisions or choices because of limited understanding of the world. Children may often have to rely on adult guidance in order to be safe. However, as people take control of their own services they are able to make their own choices with help from social care workers. Service users can also be at risk of exploitation, abuse and physical or emotional damage. It is, therefore, vitally important that care workers are actively concerned with promoting choice and independence and providing services to meet the outcomes that service users have identified.

Maslow's hierarchy of needs

A widely accepted model for interpreting human needs was developed by Abraham Maslow. Although Maslow's hierarchy may be perceived as a simplification, it provides a useful tool for summarising the range of human needs. There was a time when care was thought of as being about only the provision of food, shelter and warmth. Maslow's definition of needs covers social, emotional and intellectual needs as well as the need to maintain physical health.

According to Maslow's theory, people might be perceived as being vulnerable on different levels, as shown in the pyramid below.

Active knowledge

Look at Maslow's pyramid below. For each of the levels, what could you do within your role to help meet these needs?

Maslow's pyramid	The role of rights in meeting human needs
Development of full potential	Respect for individuality and support to help people take control of their own lives will often be necessary to help service users develop their full potential
Self-esteem needs	Respect for diversity, dignity and privacy will be important in helping people to develop or maintain a sense of self-esteem
Social needs	People need to be able to trust their care workers and receive effective communication in order to meet their social needs
Feeling safe	People need to be free from discrimination, have a right to confidentiality and be free from risks if they are to feel safe
Physical needs	Freedom from abuse and neglect will be important; as well as food and shelter, in order to meet physical needs

CASE STUDY: Care needs

Mrs Boswell is 84 and lives alone in an old terraced house. Her husband died five years ago, and since then she has been supported by her daughter and son-in-law who make regular visits. Recently Mrs Boswell has been increasingly forgetful and has left her front door open at night. Her daughter and son-in-law want to go abroad for a month or so and have arranged with Mrs Boswell that she should go into a care home for a short period.

1 *What kinds of care needs will Mrs Boswell have? Describe them in terms of Maslow's pyramid:*

   a *physical needs* **b** *safety and security needs*

   c *social needs* **d** *self-esteem needs.*

Keys to good practice: Providing support for rights

✓ Hold regular staff meetings and have a regular item on your agenda about rights.

✓ Ensure that service users are fully aware of complaints procedures and know how to follow them.

Continued

Keys to good practice: Providing support for rights (cont.)

✓ Make sure that you know your agency's policies and guidelines designed to protect and promote people's rights.

✓ Ensure that you share with your colleagues any information which relates to service users' choices, preferences and rights.

✓ Make sure that you discuss choices and preferences with service users.

✓ Support service users to maintain independence together with other rights if necessary.

✓ Never participate in or encourage discriminatory behaviour.

Supporting individuals to access information

Knowledge is power, and giving a person information empowers him or her. Working as a professional carer means that you will often work with people who are vulnerable and who have no confidence or power. Many people you work with will not have the information they need, because:

- they are unaware that the information exists
- they do not know how to find it

Did you know?

Age Concern receives around 16,000 requests for information in a six-month period. When the figures were last analysed, around 25% of the queries were found to be about health and social care, only slightly less about consumer issues (including wills), 10% about financing residential care, and about 20% respectively about income and housing.

Local authorities
Social workers
Home care assistants
Lunch clubs
Day centres
Housing advice
Street wardens
Sheltered housing wardens
Welfare advice units

Media
Radio
TV
Video/DVD
Newspapers
Books
Talking books
Magazines
Advertisements
The Internet

General advice agencies
Citizens Advice Bureaux
Age Concern

Education and leisure
Adult education centres
Community centres

Telephone support lines

Information sources

Family and friends

Specialist advice agencies
Housing advisory groups
Health-related groups/charities

Local community
Church
Local shops
Post offices
Libraries

Community services
GP
District nurse/Health visitor
Day hospital
Out-patient clinic
Dentist

Benefits Agency

- there are physical barriers to accessing information
- there are emotional barriers to seeking information.

If you are going to provide people with information, there are certain basic rules you must observe.

✔ Keys to good practice: Accessing information

✓ Make sure that your information is up to date. You may have to contact quite a few places to make sure you have the most accurate information possible. Check the dates on any leaflets you have and contact the producer to see whether it has been replaced.

✓ Go to the most direct source, wherever possible. For example, for information about benefits, contact the Benefits Agency. If you need to know about community care services, contact social services.

✓ Advice services such as the Citizens Advice Bureau are excellent and provide a wide range of information. Make use also of the specialist organisations such as Age Concern or Scope.

✓ Check whether the information you are providing has local, regional and national elements. For instance, if you are providing information about Age Concern's services for older people, it is important to provide the local as well as national contact points.

✓ The information you provide must be in a format that can be used by the person it is intended for. For example, there is little value in providing an ordinary leaflet to an individual with impaired sight. Obtain large print, audio or braille versions depending on the way in which the individual prefers to receive information.

✓ Consider the language used and provide information in a language which the individual can easily understand. Information is of no value if it is misunderstood.

✓ Provide information at an appropriate time when the individual can make use of it. For example, a man who has just had a leg amputated, following an accident, will not be ready to receive information about the latest design in wheelchairs or how to join in sports for the disabled. He may be interested in 12 months' time, but initially he is going to need information about support groups, and practical information about how artificial limbs work, and how to manage to use the toilet!

✓ The information you provide must be relevant and useful. For example, if an individual wants to make a complaint to the Benefits Agency, find out what the complaints procedure is and provide the relevant information and forms to be completed. A general leaflet about the services of the Benefits Agency would not be as helpful.

Offering further support where needed

There may be occasions when you have identified a person's rights and given him or her the information needed. However, the individual may not be able to exercise those rights effectively. There can be many reasons why people miss out on their rights:

- their rights may be infringed by someone else
- there may be physical barriers
- there may be emotional barriers.

When you need to support people to maintain a right to choice and independence it may be important to involve an outside advocate. An advocate is someone who argues a case for another person. An advocate tries to understand a service user's perspective and argue on his or her behalf. Your organisation may have procedures and advice to assist you in gaining the services of people who will act as an advocate for service users.

Key terms

Advocate: Person who is responsible for acting and speaking on behalf of an individual when he or she is unable to do so.

CASE STUDY: The right to make choices

Mrs Sullivan lives alone on just her state pension. She has never claimed any pension credit although there is no doubt she would be entitled to it. She struggles to survive on her pension and, by the time she has paid all her bills and fed the cat, there is little left for herself. She eats very little and is reluctant to turn the heating on. Despite being given all the relevant information by her home care assistant, Mrs Sullivan will not claim any further benefits. She always says: 'I shall be fine. There are others worse off than me – let it go to those who need it.'

1 *What are Mrs Sullivan's rights?*

2 *Should action be taken on her behalf?*

3 *Would the situation be different if she had a son with a learning disability who lived with her? Would her rights still be the same? Would her responsibilities still be the same?*

4 *What would your responsibilities be if you were a care worker for Mrs Sullivan?*

You may also need to defend people's rights in a more informal way during your normal work. For example, people have a right to privacy, and you may need to act to deal with someone who constantly infringes upon that by discussing other people's circumstances in public. You will have to balance the rights of one person against another, and decide whose rights are being infringed. You may decide that a right to privacy is more important than a right to free speech.

Active knowledge

An individual's right to rest may be infringed by someone who shouts all night. How would you balance the rights of one person not to be disturbed against the rights of another not to be given medication which is only for the benefit of others?

Complaints

An important part of exercising rights is being able to complain if services are poor or do not meet expectations. All public service organisations are required to have a complaints procedure and to make the procedure readily available for people to use. Part of your role may be to assist service users in making complaints, either directly, by supporting them in following the procedure, or indirectly, by making sure that they are aware of the complaints procedure and are able to follow it. You also need to learn to respond openly and appropriately to any comments or complaints you receive from people about their care. Most complaints procedures will involve an informal stage, where complaints are discussed before they become more formal issues.

Complaints to an organisation are an important part of the monitoring process and they should be considered as part of every review of service provision. If all service users simply put up with poor service and no one complains to an organisation, it will never be aware of where the service needs improvement. Similarly, if complaints are not responded to appropriately, services will never improve.

CASE STUDY: Dealing with comments and complaints

Sunny Ridge is a care home for older people. Many of the individuals in the setting are from a Chinese background and Chinese is regularly spoken, particularly during social activities like mah jong tournaments, which are very popular. Gerry, who is a new care worker, has become key worker to Mr Wong. Mr Wong's English is limited and he sometimes forgets that Gerry can't speak Chinese. There have been a number of misunderstandings where Mr Wong has become frustrated because Gerry does not understand him. Gerry also feels at a disadvantage because he can't take part in the social activities that are conducted in Chinese. One day Mr Wong's family came to complain to the supervisor that Gerry couldn't speak Chinese and wouldn't try. They want Mr Wong to have a Chinese-speaking key worker.

Gerry's response is that he is employed as care worker, not an interpreter, and as they are in the UK they should all be speaking English anyway.

1 *What are the communication issues here?*

2 *What are Mr Wong's rights in this situation?*

3 *What are Gerry's rights?*

4 *How could the supervisor resolve this situation while promoting choice and independence for the residents and the care workers?*

Active support

 KS ② ③ ④ ⑫ ⑮

The feeling of having achieved something is a feeling everyone can identify with – regardless of the size of the achievement or its significance when viewed from a wider perspective. Most achievements which give us pleasure are relatively small – passing a driving test, finishing a run, clearing a garden, passing an exam, putting together a set of flat-pack bookshelves ... Achievement does not have to mean reaching the North Pole or climbing Everest, or winning the World Cup. Achievements that are much smaller and closer to home are those that provide a sense of fulfilment for most people.

Working with individuals to help them have a sense of achievement is a key part of caring. It is tempting to undertake tasks *for* people you work with because you are keen to care for them and because you believe that you can make their lives easier. Often, however, you need to hold back from directly providing care or carrying out a task, and look for ways you can enable individuals to undertake the task for themselves.

For example, it may be far easier, less painful and quicker for you to put on people's socks or stockings for them. But this would reinforce the fact that they are no longer able to undertake such a simple task for themselves. Time spent in providing a 'helping hand' sock aid, and showing them how to use it, means that they can put on their own clothing and, instead of feeling dependent, have a sense of achievement and independence.

Sometimes you need to realise that achievement is relative to the circumstances of the individual. What may seem an insignificant act can actually be a huge achievement for a particular individual. Someone recovering from a stroke who succeeds in holding a piece of cutlery for the first time may be achieving something that has taken weeks or even months of physiotherapy, painful exercise and huge determination. The first, supported steps taken by someone who has had a hip replacement represent a massive achievement in overcoming pain, fear and anxiety.

One of the essential aspects of planning care services is to have a **holistic approach** to supporting people's needs and preferences. This means recognising that all parts of an individual's life will have an impact on his or her care needs and preferences. It will also put his or her achievements into the proper perspective.

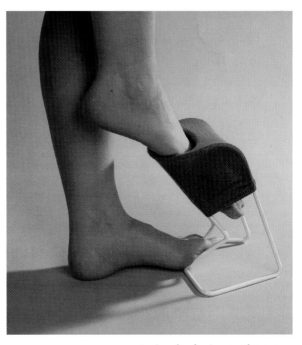

A simple device such as a sock aid can help maintain independence

Key terms

Active support: Support that encourages individuals to maintain their independence and to achieve their potential.

Key terms

Holistic: Looking at the *whole* person or situation.

Evidence PC 1 3 4 5 8

Think about a service user who you work with regularly.

Identify a task or activity which is carried out for them.

Why are they unable to do this task themselves?

Draw up a plan of active support to improve on this situation, this could be enabling them to carry out the task themselves or having more say in the way they are supported.

Where appropriate include the service user in writing this plan.

Make notes for your portfolio.

What you need to do

Supporting people's independence by encouraging and recognising their achievements is one of the best parts of being a professional carer. Sometimes you may need to spend time guiding individuals and encouraging them in order for them to achieve something.

- You may need to steady someone's hand while they write a thank-you note, but it is far better that you spend time doing this rather than write it for them.
- You could accompany a service user on many trips round the supermarket, and eventually wait in the car park while he or she goes in alone.
- You could demonstrate to an individual with poor motor control how to create pictures by painting with the fingers.

Make sure you always recognise and celebrate achievements. Think about it – whenever you achieve something, you usually want to share it with someone. Your enthusiasm and recognition are important to your service users.

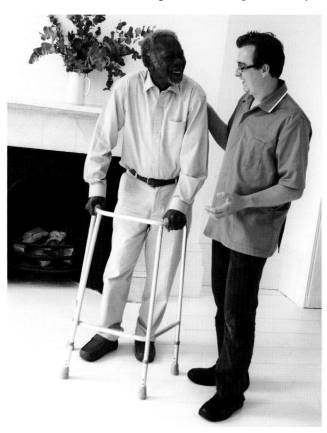

Always recognise and encourage achievements

Dealing with conflicts

 KS ③ ⑬

Not everything is plain sailing. There are inevitably times when stresses and strains show, and you can find yourself faced with conflict, arguments, angry people or even potential violence. These situations are always difficult, but you can develop skills in dealing with them.

Most care settings, whether residential or providing day-care services, involve living, sharing and working with others. Any situation which involves close and prolonged contact with others has the potential to be difficult. You only have to think about the day-to-day conflicts and difficulties which arise in most families to realise the issues involved when human beings get together in a group.

Disagreements between service users, particularly in residential or day-care settings, are not unusual and you may well find yourself being called on to act as referee. The conflicts can range from disputes over particular chairs or TV channels, to political disagreements or complaints about the behaviour of others. Conflict resolution is never an easy task, wherever you are and however large or small a scale you are working on. However, there are some basic guidelines to follow:

- remain calm and speak in a firm, quiet voice – do not raise your voice
- make it clear that neither verbal nor physical abuse will be tolerated
- listen in turn to both sides of the argument – don't let people interrupt each other
- look for reasonable compromises which involve both parties in winning some points and losing others
- make it clear to both sides that they will have to compromise – that total victory for one or the other is not an option.

Sometimes conflicts can arise about behaviour which is not anyone's fault, but is the result of someone's illness or condition. For instance, sometimes people experiencing some forms of dementia may shout and moan loudly, which may be distressing and annoying to others. Some people may eat messily or dribble as the result of a physical condition, which may be unpleasant and upsetting for those who share a table with them. These situations require a great deal of tact and explanation. It is simply not possible for the individuals concerned to stop their behaviour, so those around them have to be helped to understand the reasons and to cope with the consequences.

Test yourself

1 List some of the ways in which you can help to empower service users.

2 Why is it important that you do not provide a higher level of support than is really needed by an individual?

3 Why are relationships important to how you carry out your work?

4 Explain how you can support a service user in the exercise of his or her rights.

5 List the important factors in resolving conflicts and disagreements.

HSC 35b Respect the diversity and difference of individuals and key people

If you are going to make sure you always respond to individuals in a respectful way which ensures they are treated with dignity, you need to understand the range of ways in which people can fail to be treated with respect or can lose their dignity. It is also important that you recognise the ways in which good practice helps to protect people from discrimination and oppression.

Treating people as individuals

 KS 1 2 3 4 5 6 7 8 9 11 12 16 22 23

As discussed in Unit HSC 31, you should always consult the individual before you carry out any procedure, and explain everything you do. Everyone should be offered choices wherever possible. Below are examples of the kinds of choices you may be able to offer to people when you provide care.

Care service	Choices
Personal hygiene	Bath, shower or bed bath
	Assistance or no assistance
	Morning, afternoon or evening
	Temperature of water
	Toiletries
Food	Menu
	Dining table or tray
	Timing
	Assistance
	In company or alone

As we have seen, promoting choice and empowerment is about identifying the practical steps you can take in day-to-day working activities to give individuals more choice and more opportunities to take decisions about their own lives. Much of this will depend on your work setting and the particular needs of the individuals you care for. There are, however, some aspects of empowerment which are common to many settings and most individuals. Respecting people's dignity and privacy is always going to be an important factor in promoting their self-esteem.

If self-esteem is about how we *value* ourselves, **self-concept** (or self-image) is about how we *see* ourselves. These two are different, but both are equally important when you are working.

Self-concept is about what makes people who they are. Everyone has a concept of themselves – it can be a positive image overall or a negative one, but a great many factors contribute to an individual sense of identity.

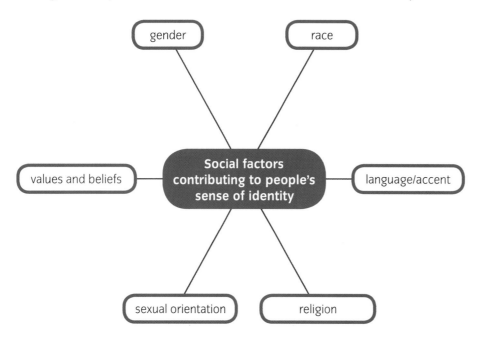

All of these are aspects of our lives which contribute towards our idea of who we are. As a care worker it is essential that you consider how each of the individuals you work with will have developed a self-concept and individual identity.

As part of empowering individuals, you will need to consider how you can promote their own sense of identity. This is not as difficult as it sounds! It is about making sure that you recognise that the values, beliefs, tastes and preferences which individuals have – the things that make them who they are – must be supported, nurtured and encouraged, and not ignored and discounted because they are inconvenient or don't fit in with the care system.

In your role as a care worker, you will come across situations where a little thought or a small change in practice could give greater opportunities for people to feel that they are valued and respected as individuals. For example, you may need to find out how an individual likes to be addressed. Is 'Mr' or 'Mrs' considered more respectful and appropriate, or is the person happy for a first name to be used? This, particularly for some older people, can be an important way of indicating respect.

You will need to give thought to the values and beliefs which individuals may have, for example:

- religious or cultural beliefs about eating specific foods
- values about forms of dress which are acceptable
- beliefs or preferences about who should be able to provide personal care.

What you need to do

You need to make sure that people have been asked about religious or cultural preferences and those preferences are recorded so that all care workers and others providing care are able to access them.

The National Standards Framework in England now requires that a single assessment process takes place involving a multidisciplinary, interagency assessment of the needs of service users. This process should result in a documented care plan. It will be important that you know where to find the information for every individual you work with.

How you need to do it

The prospect of having to ask people questions about their background, values and beliefs can be quite daunting. But it is rare for people to be offended by you showing an interest in them! Simple, open questions, asked politely, are always the best way:

Excuse me Mr Khan, I have read that you are a vegetarian. Can you tell me more about the types of food that you would like to eat?

You can obtain some information by observation – looking at someone can tell you a lot about their preferences in dress, for example. Particular forms of clothing worn for religious or cultural reasons are usually obvious (a turban or a sari, for instance, are easy to spot), but other forms of dress may also give you some clues about the person wearing them. Think about how dress can tell you about the amount of money people are used to spending on clothes, or what kind of background they come from. Clothes also tell you a lot about someone's age and the type of lifestyle they are likely to be used to. Beware, however – any information you think you gain from this type of observation must be confirmed by checking your facts. Otherwise it is easy to be caught out – some people from wealthy backgrounds wear cheap clothes, and some people in their seventies wear the latest fashions and have face lifts!

Active knowledge

Look at the form, or other means of recording information, which is used in your workplace to set down the cultural or religious preferences of individuals. Fill it in for yourself as if you were a service user. Note down all the factors that make you who you are. Think about:

- gender
- age
- background
- economic and social circumstances
- nationality
- culture
- religion
- sexual orientation
- food preferences
- entertainment preferences
- relaxation preferences
- reading material preferences.

Look at the form you have completed – would it tell care workers enough about you so they could ensure that you were able to be the same person you were before receiving a care service? If not, think about which other questions you would need to ask, and note them down. Make sure that, if appropriate, you ask those questions.

Overcoming barriers

Where individuals want to make choices about their lives, you should ensure that you do your best to help them to identify any barriers they may meet and then offer support in overcoming them. If you are working with individuals who are living in their own homes, it is likely to be easier for them to make day-to-day choices about their lives. In some situations they may require help and support in order to achieve the choice, but it is generally less restrictive than a residential or hospital setting, where the needs of many other people also have to be taken into account.

For many disabled individuals living in their own homes, the direct payment scheme has provided a far higher level of choice and empowerment than was possible previously. This system means that payments for the provision of services are made to the disabled individual, who then employs care workers directly and determines his or her own levels and types of service.

This changes the relationship between the disabled individual and the care workers, and puts the disabled individual in a position of power. Individual budgets also give people the chance to control their lives. Here they have control over how resources are used and how money is spent but do not have to be employers. You may need to offer some help initially, so people can get used to directing their own services.

Keys to good practice: Empowerment: enabling people to make choices

✓ Always ask individuals about their needs, wishes and preferences – whether this is the service they want and if this is the way they want to receive it.

✓ Ask if they prefer other alternatives, either in the service or the way it is delivered.

✓ Look for ways you can actively support individuals in achieving the choice they want.

The process of making choices can also be about simple things – it can just be a matter of checking with the individual as you work, as in the example below.

Mrs Jones, would you like to wear the blue dress today, or is there another one you would prefer?

Well, I did want to wear that grey spotty skirt with the pink blouse today, but I don't think it's back from the laundry, so I can't.

Let me go down to the laundry and find out if it's ready. If there's any way I can get it for you, I will.

Thank you.

The worker in this example has offered Mrs Jones a choice about clothes. Mrs Jones has indicated that she is not happy with the choice offered, and she has also identified the possible barrier to having the clothes she wants. The care worker has looked for a way that the barrier may possibly be overcome. This process can be used in a wide range of situations.

Sometimes individuals are not able, because of the nature of a particular condition or illness, to identify choices or to take part in decision making. In these circumstances, it is important that you make every effort to involve them as far as they are able. For example, if an individual communicates differently from you as the result of a particular condition, or there are language differences, it is important that you ensure the communication differences are reduced as far as possible so that the individual can take part in discussions and decisions. This may involve using specific communication techniques, or arranging to have help from an appropriate specialist. For example:

- if you are communicating with a deaf person, you may need to write things down or you may need to arrange for a sign language interpreter
- if you are communicating with someone who has speech difficulties following a stroke, you may need to use visual communication, or use cards that show a range of pictures such as food and drink
- if you are communicating with an individual whose first language you do not speak, you will need to use an interpreter.

All of these steps will allow people to make decisions about their case.

In other circumstances, you may be dealing with individuals who are not able to fully participate in all decisions about their day-to-day lives because they have a different level of understanding. This could, for example, include individuals with learning difficulties, dementia or brain injury. In this situation, it may be that the individual has an advocate who represents his or her interests and is able to present a point of view to those who are providing services. The advocate may a professional one such as a solicitor, social worker or a rights worker, or it could be a relative or friend. It is essential that you include the advocate in discussions, to make sure that the individual's decisions are followed.

People need to be offered choices because they are all different; don't fall into the trap of stereotyping individuals.

The effects of assumptions  KS ① ② ④ ⑤

'All apples are red.' That statement is clearly silly. Of course they're not – some are green, some are yellow. When it comes to people, everyone is different. However, there is a tendency to make sweeping statements (generalisations) which we believe apply to everyone who belongs to a particular group.

Active knowledge

Complete the following sentences.

Police officers are …

Teenagers are …

Nurses are …

Politicians never …

West Indians are all …

Asians always …

Men all …

Women are …

Americans are …

You can probably think of plenty of statements that you make as generalisations about others. Note some down, then think about how all these generalisations could affect the way you work.

Avoiding assumptions at work

Take the time and trouble to find out the personal beliefs and values of each individual you work with. Think about all the aspects of their lives: diet, clothing, worship, language, relationships with others, bathing. It is your responsibility to find out – not for the individual to have to tell you. It will be helpful for you, and for other workers, if this type of information is recorded in the individual's personal record.

For example, you may need to know that many Muslims will only accept medical treatment from someone of the same gender, that you will need to enable them to wash in running water, not a bowl, that they do not eat pork, and that any other meat must have been killed and prepared in a particular way – Halal.

If you are providing care for someone who is an Orthodox Jew, you need to be aware that they will not eat food unless it has been prepared in a specific way – the Kosher way. They do not eat pork. The Jewish Sabbath is a Saturday and Jewish beliefs forbid certain activities on that day.

Although you may hold a different set of values and beliefs from those of the individuals you are caring for, you do not have the right to impose your beliefs upon others. There may, in fact, be occasions when you will have to act as an advocate for their beliefs, even if you do not personally agree with them.

Remember

The most terrifying films and the scariest fairground rides are those where you do not know what is going to happen next, or you do not know exactly what you are afraid of. It is always not knowing and feeling unsure that makes you more likely to reject something new and different. Once you have information, it is much easier to welcome and value the variety that others can bring.

Keys to good practice: Valuing diversity

✓ The wide range of different beliefs and values which you are likely to come into contact with, if you work in a care setting, are examples of the rich and diverse cultures of all parts of the world.

Continued

Keys to good practice: Valuing diversity (cont.)

✓ Value each person as an individual. The best way to appreciate what others have to offer is to find out about them. Ask questions. People will usually be happy to tell you about themselves and their beliefs.

✓ The other key is to be open to hearing what others have to say – do not be so sure that your values and beliefs and the way you live are the only ways of doing things.

✓ Think about the great assets which have come to the UK from people moving here from other cultures, including music, food and entertainment, and different approaches to work or relaxation or medicine.

How to recognise your own prejudices

 KS 1 3 5 6 11

One of the hardest things to do is to acknowledge your own prejudices and how they affect what you do. Prejudices are a result of your own beliefs and values, and may often come into conflict with work situations. There is nothing wrong with having your own beliefs and values – everyone has them, and they are a vital part of making you the person you are. But you must be aware of them, and how they may affect what you do at work.

Think about the basic principles that apply in your life. For example, you may have a basic belief that people should always be honest. Then think about what that could mean for the way you work – might you find it hard to be pleasant to someone who was found to have lied extensively? You may believe that abortion is wrong. Could you deal sympathetically with a woman who had had an abortion? You may have been brought up to take great care of people with disabilities and believe that they should be looked after and protected. How would you cope in an environment which encouraged people with disabilities to take risks and promoted their independence?

 Active knowledge

Make a list of the things you believe in as values, and a second list of how they could affect your work. Then, examine whether they do affect your work – you may need the views of a trusted colleague or your supervisor to help you with this.

This exercise is very hard, and it will take a long time to do. It is often better done over a period of time. As you become more aware of your own actions, you will notice how they have the potential to affect your work.

Exploring your own behaviour is never easy, and you need good support from either your supervisor or close friends to do it. You may be upset by what you find out about some of your attitudes, but knowing about them and acknowledging them is the first step to doing something about them.

As a care worker, it will be easier to make sure that you are practising effectively if you are confident that you have looked at your own practice and the attitudes that underpin it. Don't forget that you can ask for feedback from service users and colleagues too, not only from your supervisor.

Beliefs and values of others

Once you are aware of your own beliefs and values, and have recognised how important they are, you must think about how to accept the beliefs and values of others. The individuals you work with are all different, and so it is important to recognise and accept that diversity.

The individuals you work with are all different

Evidence
PC 6

This exercise is best done with a group of colleagues, but you can do it on your own – it just takes longer!

1 Think of some ideas for a list of all the cultures and nationalities you know of. Write them down. Next to each one, write something that the culture has given to the world. For example, the Egyptians gave mathematics, the Chinese developed some wonderful medicines, and so on.

2 Next, think about people from the groups you care for. Note down the special angle of understanding each group can bring to society. For instance, someone who is visually impaired will always judge people on how they behave, not on how they look. Older people can often bring a different perspective to a situation based on years of experience and understanding.

Keep your notes as evidence for your portfolio.

Many workplaces now have policies which are about 'managing diversity' rather than 'equal opportunities'. This is because many people have realised that until diversity is recognised and valued, there is no realistic possibility of any policy about equal opportunities being totally effective.

Anti-discriminatory practice 🔗 KS ② ③ ④ ⑤ ⑩

Receiving a worse service than others because of his or her age, gender, race, sexuality or ability could damage a service user's self-esteem, and discrimination can reduce a person's ability to develop and maintain a sense of identity. As a care worker, you must practise in an anti-discriminatory way in your day-to-day work with service users, and challenge any tendency towards stereotyping and labelling people.

Stereotyping	Stereotyping leads to whole groups of people being assumed to be the same. It is often present when you hear phrases such as 'these sorts of people all …'. 'Old people love a sing song' or 'black people are good athletes' are stereotyping remarks.
Labelling	Slightly more complex than stereotyping, labelling happens when someone thinks the factor which people have in common is more important than the hundreds of factors which make them different. For example, the remark 'We should organise a concert for the elderly' makes an assumption that being older is what is important about the people concerned, and that somehow as you grow older your tastes become the same as all other people your age! It would be much better to say 'We should organise a concert for older people who like music from the shows' or 'We should organise a concert for older people who like opera', etc.
Discrimination	In care work, discrimination means treating some categories of people less well than others. People are often discriminated against because of their race, beliefs, gender, religion, sexuality or age. Treating everyone the same will result in discrimination because some people will have their needs met and others will not. In order to prevent discrimination, it is important to value diversity and treat people differently in order to meet their different needs.
Anti-discrimination	This means positively working to eliminate discrimination and to challenge it if you see it occurring in your place of work. For example, when weekly menus are being planned at a day centre, if no account is taken of the religious and cultural needs of individuals, you should challenge this and suggest changes.

Some obvious types of discriminatory practice are shown on the next page. You should monitor your own and others' behaviour in order to minimise the risk of such practices occurring.

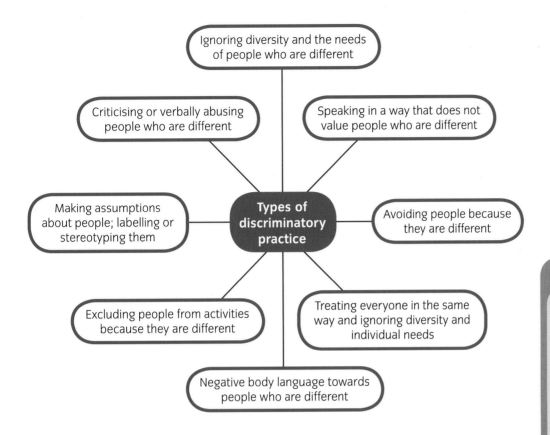

Types of discriminatory practice

- Ignoring diversity and the needs of people who are different
- Speaking in a way that does not value people who are different
- Criticising or verbally abusing people who are different
- Making assumptions about people; labelling or stereotyping them
- Avoiding people because they are different
- Excluding people from activities because they are different
- Treating everyone in the same way and ignoring diversity and individual needs
- Negative body language towards people who are different

Remember

- Stereotypes can influence how you think about someone. Be prepared to challenge your own thinking and assumptions.
- Don't make judgements about people – try to learn about different cultures, beliefs and lifestyles.
- Everyone is entitled to his or her own beliefs and culture. If you don't know about someone's way of life – ask.

Your day-to-day practice and attitudes are important in how effective your anti-discriminatory practice will be. You should be interested in learning about other people's lifestyle, culture and needs. Finding ways of meeting individual needs might provide a source of job satisfaction.

Supporting the work of colleagues

You need to support your colleagues, too, to work in ways that recognise and respect individuals' beliefs and preferences; your work setting should be a place in which diversity and difference are acknowledged and respected. You need to set a good example and to make it clear that behaviour such as the following is unacceptable:

- speaking about individuals in a derogatory way
- speaking to individuals in a rude or dismissive way
- undermining people's self-esteem and confidence
- patronising and talking down to people
- removing people's right to exercise choice
- failing to recognise and treat people as individuals
- not respecting people's culture, values and beliefs.

If you are having difficulty at any time in promoting equality and diversity, you need to seek advice from your manager or supervisor.

Steps you can take to reduce discrimination

Think about language. The words and expressions you use are important. Avoid using language that might suggest assumptions, stereotypes or discrimination about groups; for example:

Disability	Some words such as 'handicapped' can suggest the discriminatory assumption that disabled people are damaged versions of 'normal' people.
Race	Some words and phrases may be linked to the discriminatory idea that certain ethnic groups (white groups) are superior to others.
Age	Some words and phrases make fun of older people. Do not address an older person as 'pop' or 'granddad' unless you are invited to do so.
Gender	Some words and phrases are perceived as implying that women have a lower social status than men. Addressing women as 'dear', 'petal' or 'flower' may be understood as patronising or insulting.
Sexuality	Gay and lesbian people often object to being catalogued using the biological terminology of 'hetero'- and 'homo'-sexuality. Use the terminology that people would apply to themselves.

Encourage people you provide care for to achieve their full potential.
- Do not assume that older people are only capable of quiet activities that don't involve too much excitement.
- Avoid the temptation to over-protect people and therefore encourage dependence.
- Support people in challenging the barriers that stand in their way. If you work with people with disabilities, try to think of ways you can show employers what these people are capable of achieving.
- Try to work with the local community. If you work in a facility which is surrounded by neighbours, make sure that they get to know both service users and staff. Knowledge removes the fear which lies behind prejudice.
- Encourage people to behave assertively and to develop confidence in their own abilities.
- Refuse to accept behaviour which you know is discriminatory.
- Do not participate in racist or sexist jokes and explain that you are not amused by 'sick' jokes about people with disabilities or problems.
- If you are uncertain what to do in a particular situation, discuss the problem with your supervisor.

CASE STUDY: Dealing with prejudice

Garth is a care worker in a residential setting for adults with disabilities. He is gay but had never discussed his sexual orientation at work and it was not mentioned at the time of his appointment. His sexual orientation only became known when the parents of one of the residents spotted him in a photograph of a gay pride event printed in a national newspaper.

Garth had always been a popular member of staff and had an excellent work record, with appraisals which showed his skills and abilities were developing and progressing. However, following the discovery that he was gay the atmosphere in the setting began to change. Two of the residents complained about being cared for by someone who was gay and said they were not prepared to have Garth provide them with any personal care. Both of these residents were young men in their late 20s and their action was supported by their parents. Comments and jokes at Garth's expense began to circulate within the setting, particularly when Garth was on duty.

Garth felt that he was unfairly discriminated against and intended to obtain the support of his trade union.

1 *What are Garth's rights in this situation? Consider the Employment Equality (Sexual Orientation) Regulations.*

2 *What are the residents' rights? Consider the issue of rights and responsibilities.*

Test yourself

1 List at least three aspects of daily living where individuals may want to express a choice.

2 What would you do if someone told a racist joke:

   a laugh because it's only fun?

   b say nothing but feel awkward?

   c say that you find the joke offensive?

   Explain your answer.

3 Name three groups of people who are discriminated against.

4 What forms does the discrimination take?

5 How would you attempt to reduce the discrimination in those three instances?

6 What is stereotyping? Give an example.

HSC 35c Contribute to the protection of all individuals

In this element you will look at some of the most difficult issues that you will face as a care professional. For many people, starting work in care means coming to terms with the fact that some individuals will be subjected to abuse by those who are supposed to care for them. For others it will not be the first time that they have been close to an abuse situation, either through personal or previous professional involvement.

Regardless of previous experience, coming face to face with situations where abuse is, or has been, taking place is difficult and emotionally demanding. Knowing what you are looking for, and how to recognise it, is an important part of ensuring that you are making the best possible contribution to protecting individuals from abuse. You need to know how society handles abuse, how to recognise it, and what to do about it. It is a tragic fact that almost all disclosures of abuse are true – and you will have to learn to *think the unthinkable.*

The forms of abuse which you will need to be aware of and to understand are abuses which are suffered by individuals at the hands of someone who is providing care for them – abusers can be parents, informal carers, care professionals and/or the policies and practices of the care setting itself. (This element is not about abuse by strangers, which needs to be dealt with in the same way as any other crime.) If you can learn always to consider the possibility of abuse, always to be alert to potentially abusive situations and always to *listen* and *believe* when you are told of abuse, then you will provide the best possible protection for the individuals you care for.

Taking the right steps when faced with an abusive situation is the second part of your key contribution to individuals who are being, or have been, abused.

Forms of abuse

 KS ③ ⑰

Abuse can take many forms. These are usually classified under five main headings:

- physical
- sexual
- emotional
- financial
- institutional.

Abuse can happen to any individual regardless of his or her age or service needs. Child abuse is the most well-known and well-recognised type of abuse, but all service user groups can suffer abuse. Abuse of older people and abuse of people with learning difficulties, sensory impairment or physical disabilities is just as common, but often less well recognised.

Physical abuse

Any abuse involving the use of force is classified as physical abuse. This can mean:

- punching, hitting, slapping, pinching, kicking, in fact any form of physical attack
- burning or scalding
- restraint such as tying up or tying people to beds or furniture
- refusal to allow access to toilet facilities
- deliberate starvation or force feeding
- leaving individuals in wet or soiled clothing or bedding as a deliberate act to demonstrate the power and strength of the abuser
- excessive or inappropriate use of medication
- a carer causing illness or injury to someone he or she cares for in order to gain attention (this might be associated with a condition called fabricated and induced illness (FII)).

Remember

Abuse of vulnerable individuals can take many forms. An individual may be subjected to more than one type of abuse.

Sexual abuse

Sexual abuse, whether of adults or children, can also involve abuse of a position of power. Children can never be considered to give informed consent to any sexual activity of any description. For many adults, informed consent is not possible because of a limited understanding of the issues. In the case of other adults, consent may not be given and the sexual activity is either forced on the individual against his or her will or the individual is tricked or bribed into it.

Sexual activity is abusive when informed consent is not freely given. This might involve one service user abusing another more vulnerable service user. It is important to recognise the difference between the freely consenting sexual activity of adults who also happen to be service users, and those situations where abuse is taking place because someone is exploiting his or her position of relative power.

Sexual abuse can consist of:

- sexual penetration of any part of the body with a penis, finger or any object
- touching inappropriate parts of the body or any other form of sexual contact without the informed agreement of the individual
- sexual exploitation
- exposure to, or involvement in, pornographic or erotic material
- exposure to, or involvement in, sexual rituals
- making sexually related comments or references which provide sexual gratification for the abuser
- making threats about sexual activities.

Emotional abuse

All the other forms of abuse also have an element of emotional abuse. Any situation which means that an individual becomes a victim of abuse at the hands of someone he or she trusted is, inevitably, going to cause emotional distress. However, some abuse is purely emotional – there are no physical, sexual or financial elements involved. This abuse can take the form of:

- humiliation, belittling, putting down
- withdrawing or refusing affection
- bullying
- making threats
- shouting or swearing
- making insulting or abusive remarks
- racial abuse
- constant teasing and poking fun.

Financial abuse

Many service users are very vulnerable to financial abuse, particularly those who may have a limited understanding of money matters. Financial abuse, like all other forms of abuse, can be inflicted by family members and even friends as well as care workers or informal carers, and can take a range of forms, such as:

- stealing money or property
- allowing or encouraging others to steal money or property
- tricking or threatening individuals into giving away money or property
- persuading individuals to take financial decisions which are not in their interests
- withholding money, or refusing access to money
- refusing to allow individuals to manage their own financial affairs
- failing to support individuals to manage their own financial affairs.

Institutional abuse

Institutional abuse is not only confined to large-scale physical or sexual abuse scandals of the type which are regularly publicised in the media. Of course this type of systematic and organised abuse goes on in residential and hospital settings, and must be recognised and dealt with appropriately so that service users can be protected. However, individuals can be abused in many other ways in settings where they could expect to be cared for and protected. For example:

- individuals in residential settings are not given choice over day-to-day decisions such as mealtimes, bedtimes, etc.
- freedom to go out is limited by the institution
- privacy and dignity are not respected
- personal correspondence is opened by staff

- the setting is run for the convenience of staff, not service users
- excessive or inappropriate doses of sedation/medication are given
- access to advice and advocacy is restricted or not allowed
- complaints procedures are deliberately made unavailable.

You can probably begin to see that the different types of abuse are often interlinked, and individuals can be victims of more than one type of abuse. Abuse may be a deliberate act – something which someone actively does in order to demonstrate power and authority over another person. Abuse can also be motivated by the abuser deriving pleasure from his or her actions.

Neglect

Neglect happens when care is not given and an individual suffers as a result. The whole area of neglect has many aspects you need to take into account, but there are broadly two different types of neglect:

- self-neglect
- neglect by others.

Self-neglect

Many people neglect themselves; this can be for a range of reasons. People may be ill or depressed and unable to make the effort, or not feel capable of looking after themselves. Sometimes people feel that looking after themselves is unimportant. Others choose to live in a way that does not match up to the expectations of other people. Working out when someone is neglecting himself or herself, given all of these considerations, can be very difficult.

Self-neglect can show itself in a range of ways:

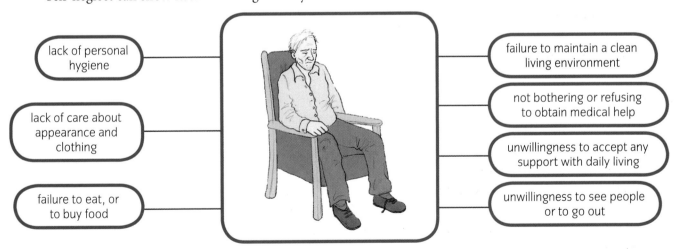

lack of personal hygiene

lack of care about appearance and clothing

failure to eat, or to buy food

failure to maintain a clean living environment

not bothering or refusing to obtain medical help

unwillingness to accept any support with daily living

unwillingness to see people or to go out

However, what may appear to be self-neglect may, in fact, be an informed choice made by someone who does not regard personal and domestic cleanliness or hygiene as priorities. It is always important to make a professional judgement based on talking with the individual and finding out his or her wishes, before making any assumptions about what may be needed.

Neglect by others

This occurs when either a care worker or an informal carer fails to meet the care needs of a person. Neglect can happen because those responsible for providing the care do not realise its importance, or because they cannot be bothered, or choose not, to provide it. As the result of neglect, individuals can become ill, hungry, cold, dirty, injured or deprived of their rights. Neglecting someone you are supposed to be caring for can mean failing to undertake a range of care services, for example:

- not providing adequate food
- not providing assistance with eating food if necessary
- not ensuring that the individual receives personal care
- not ensuring that the individual is adequately clothed
- leaving the individual alone
- not assisting an individual to meet mobility or communication needs
- failing to maintain a clean and hygienic living environment
- failing to obtain necessary medical/health-care support
- not supporting social contacts
- not taking steps to provide a safe and secure environment for the individual.

Remember

Neglect occurs when a person's needs are not being met.

In some care situations, care workers may fail to provide some aspects of care because they have not been trained, or because they work in a setting where the emphasis is on cost saving rather than care provision. In these circumstances it becomes a form of institutional abuse. Unfortunately, there have been residential care homes and NHS trusts where individuals have been found to be suffering from malnutrition as the result of such neglect. Individual workers who are deliberately neglecting service users in spite of receiving training and working in a quality caring environment are, fortunately, likely to be spotted very quickly by colleagues and supervisors.

However, carers who are supporting individuals in their own homes are in different circumstances, often facing huge pressures and difficulties. Some may be reluctantly caring for a relative because they feel they have no choice; others may be barely coping with their own lives and may find caring for someone else a burden they are unable to bear. Regardless of the many possible reasons for the difficulties which can result in neglect, it is essential that a suspicion of neglect is investigated and that concerns are followed up so that help can be offered and additional support provided if necessary.

As with self-neglect, it is important that lifestyle decisions made by individuals and their carers are respected, and full discussions should take place with individuals and carers where there are concerns about possible neglect.

Signs and symptoms which may indicate abuse

One of the most difficult aspects of dealing with abuse is to admit that it is happening. If you are someone who has never come across deliberate abuse before, it is hard to understand and to believe that it is happening. It is not the first thing you think of when a service user has an injury or displays a change in behaviour. However, you will need to accept that abuse does happen, and is relatively common. Considering abuse should be the first option when an individual has an unexplained injury or a change in behaviour that has no obvious cause.

Abuse happens to children and adults. Victims often fail to report abuse for a range of reasons:

- they are too ill, frail or too young
- they don't have enough understanding of what is happening to them
- they are ashamed and believe it is their own fault
- they have been threatened by the abuser or are afraid
- they don't think they will be believed
- they don't believe that anyone has the power to stop the abuse.

Given the fact that relatively few victims report abuse without support, it is essential that those who are working in care settings are alert to the possibility of abuse and are able to recognise possible signs and symptoms.

Signs and symptoms can be different in adults and children and you need to be aware of both, because regardless of the setting you work in you will come into contact with both adults and children. Your responsibilities do not end with the service user group you work with. If you believe that you have spotted signs of abuse of anyone, you have a duty to take the appropriate action.

Information on signs and symptoms comes with a health warning: none of the signs or symptoms is always the result of abuse, and not all abuse produces these signs and symptoms. They are a general indicator that abuse should be considered as an explanation. You and your colleagues will need to use other skills, such as observation and communication with other professionals, in order to build up a complete picture.

Signs of possible abuse in adults

Abuse can often show as physical effects and symptoms. These are likely to be accompanied by emotional signs and changes in behaviour, but this is not always the case.

Any behaviour changes could indicate that the service user is a victim of some form of abuse, but remember that they are only an indicator and will need to be linked to other factors to arrive at a complete picture.

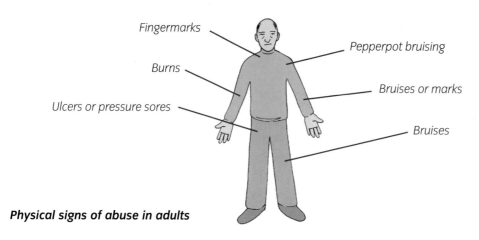

Fingermarks

Pepperpot bruising

Burns

Bruises or marks

Ulcers or pressure sores

Bruises

Physical signs of abuse in adults

Type of sign/ symptom	Description of sign/symptom	Possible form of abuse indicated
Physical	frequent or regular falls or injuries	physical
Physical	'pepperpot bruising' – small bruises, usually on the chest, caused by poking with a finger or pulling clothes tightly	physical
Physical	fingermarks – often on arms or shoulders	physical
Physical	bruising in areas not normally bruised such as the inside of thighs and arms	physical
Physical	unusual sexual behaviour	sexual
Physical	blood or marks on underclothes	sexual
Physical	recurrent genital/urinary infections	sexual
Physical	marks on wrists, upper arms or legs which could be from tying to a bed or furniture	physical/sexual
Physical	burns or scalds in unusual areas such as soles of feet, inside of thighs	physical
Physical	ulcers, sores or rashes caused by wet bedding/clothing	physical
Physical	missing cash or belongings, or bank accounts with unexplained withdrawals	financial
Physical	missing bank account records	financial
Emotional/behavioural	becoming withdrawn or anxious	all forms of abuse
Emotional/behavioural	loss of interest in appearance	sexual/physical/emotional
Emotional/behavioural	loss of confidence	sexual/physical/emotional
Emotional/behavioural	sudden change in attitude to financial matters	financial
Emotional/behavioural	becoming afraid of making decisions	emotional
Emotional/behavioural	sleeping problems	all forms of abuse
Emotional/behavioural	changes in eating habits	all forms of abuse
Emotional/behavioural	no longer laughing or joking	all forms of abuse
Emotional/behavioural	feeling depressed or hopeless	all forms of abuse
Emotional/behavioural	flinching or appearing afraid of close contact	physical

Signs of possible abuse in children

This is not a comprehensive list of every indicator of abuse. It is not possible to be exhaustive, neither does the existence of one of these signs mean that abuse has definitely taken place. Each is an indicator which needs to be used alongside your other skills, such as observation and listening. It is a further piece of evidence – often the conclusive one – in building a complete picture.

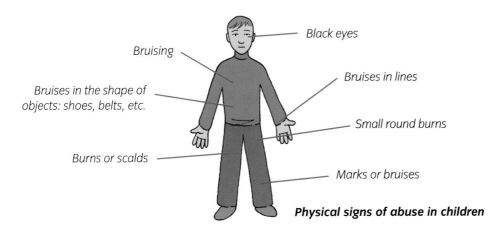

Black eyes

Bruising

Bruises in lines

Bruises in the shape of objects: shoes, belts, etc.

Small round burns

Burns or scalds

Marks or bruises

Physical signs of abuse in children

Type of sign/ symptom	Description of sign/symptom	Possible form of abuse indicated
Physical	bruising, or injuries which the child cannot explain	physical
Physical	bruises in the shape of objects – belt buckles, soles of shoes, etc.	physical
Physical	handmarks	physical
Physical	bruises in lines	physical
Physical	injuries to the frenulum (the piece of skin below the tongue), or between the upper and lower lips and the gums	physical
Physical	black eyes	physical
Physical	bruising to ears	physical
Physical	burns, particularly small round burns which could have come from a cigarette	physical
Physical	burns in lines, like the elements of an electric fire	physical
Physical	burns or scalds to buttocks and backs of legs	physical
Physical	complaints of soreness or infections in the genital/anal area	sexual
Physical	frequent complaints of abdominal pain	sexual
Physical	deterioration of personal hygiene	sexual/neglect
Emotional/behavioural	sudden change in behaviour, becoming quiet and withdrawn	sexual/emotional
Emotional/behavioural	change to overtly sexual behaviour, or an obsession with sexual comments	sexual
Emotional/behavioural	problems sleeping or onset of nightmares	sexual/emotional
Emotional/behavioural	a sudden unwillingness to change clothes or participate in sports	sexual/physical

Continued

Type of sign/symptom	Description of sign/symptom	Possible form of abuse indicated
Emotional/behavioural	finding excuses not to go home	physical/sexual/emotional
Emotional/behavioural	appearing tense or frightened with a particular adult	physical/sexual/emotional
Emotional/behavioural	excessive anxiety to please	physical/sexual/emotional

Carer behaviour which should alert you to possible abuse

Sometimes, it is not the behaviour of the service user that is the first noticeable feature of an abusive situation. It can be that the first behaviour you notice is that of the carer. The following are some indications of behaviour that may give cause for concern, although with the usual warning that each is only a *possible* indicator of problems:

- reluctance to allow visitors to see the individual
- insistence on being present with the individual at all times
- derogatory or angry references to the individual
- excessive interest in financial accounts or assets
- excessive requests for repeat prescriptions.

Who can abuse?

Abuse can take place at home or in a formal care setting. At home, it could be an informal carer who is the abuser, or it could be a neighbour or regular visitor. It can also be a professional care worker who is carrying out the abuse. This situation can mean that abuse goes undetected for some time because of the unsupervised nature of a care worker's visits to someone's home.

In a formal care setting, abuse may be more likely to be noticed, although some of the more subtle forms of abuse, such as humiliation, can sometimes be so commonplace that they are not recognised as abusive behaviour.

Abuse is not only carried out by individuals; groups, or even organisations, can also create

No dear, you can't go out now. You nearly slipped last time. You can't go on your own and I don't have anyone to send with you – can't you see how busy we all are?

abusive situations. It has been known that groups of care workers in residential settings can abuse individuals in their care. Often people will act in a different way in a group than they would alone. Think about teenage 'gangs', which exist because people are prepared to do things jointly which they would not think to do if they were by themselves.

Abuse in a care setting may not just be at the hands of members of staff. There is also abuse which comes about because of the way in which an establishment is run, where the basis for planning the systems, rules and regulations is not the welfare, rights and dignity of the residents or patients, but the convenience of the staff and management. This is the type of situation where people can be told when to get up and go to bed, given communal clothing, only allowed medical attention at set times and not allowed to go out. This is referred to as 'institutional abuse'.

Remember

Abusers can be:

- individuals
- groups
- organisations.

CASE STUDY: Appropriate ways to care

Julie, aged 43, had been a senior support worker in a residential unit for people with a learning disability for the past five years. Julie loved her job and was very committed to the residents in the unit. She was very concerned for the welfare of the people she supported and did everything she could for them. Many of them had been in the unit for many years and Julie knew them well. The unit was not very large and had only a small staff who were able to work very closely with the resident group.

Julie and the other staff were concerned that the residents could easily be taken advantage of, as some were not able to make effective judgements about other people and potentially risky situations.

Regular mealtimes were arranged so that everyone could share the day's experiences and talk together, and bedtimes and getting-up times were also strictly adhered to. The staff found that this was a good way of keeping the residents organised and motivated. Residents did not go out into the local town in the evenings because of the potential safety risk, but the staff would plan evenings of TV watching, choosing programmes that they thought would interest the residents. Sometimes simple games sessions or walks in the local park were arranged.

A new manager was appointed to the unit, and Julie and the other staff were very surprised to find that the new manager was horrified by many of these practices, and wanted to make major changes.

1 *What changes do you think the manager may have suggested?*

2 *Why do you think those changes may be needed?*

3 *Do you consider that Julie and the other staff members were practising in the best way for the residents?*

4 *Think about, or discuss, whether this situation was abusive.*

Up to this point, consideration has been given to abuse by carers, whether parents, informal or professional. But do not forget that in residential or hospital settings, abuse can occur between residents or patients, and it can also happen between visitors and residents or patients. People can also abuse themselves.

Self-harm

The one abuser it is very hard to protect someone from is himself or herself. Individuals who self-harm will be identified in their plan of care, and responses to their behaviour will be recorded. You must ensure that you follow the agreed plan for provision of care to someone who has a history of self-harm. It is usual that an individual who is at risk of harming himself or herself will be closely supported and you may need to contribute towards activities or therapies that have been planned for the individual.

Why does abuse happen?

One of the key contributions you can make towards limiting abuse is to be aware of where abuse may be happening. It is not easy to accept that abuse is going on, and it is often simpler to find other explanations.

Be prepared to *think the unthinkable*. If you know about the circumstances in which abuse has been found to occur most frequently, then you are better able to respond quickly if you suspect a problem.

It is not possible accurately to predict situations where abuse will take place – a great deal of misery could be saved if it were. It is possible, though, to identify some factors which seem to make it more likely that abuse could occur. This does not mean that abuse will definitely happen – neither should you assume that all people in these circumstances are potential abusers. But it does mean that you should be aware of the possibility when you are dealing with these situations.

Situations when vulnerable adults may be abused at home

Adults may be abused at home in situations where:

- carers have had to change their lifestyles unwillingly
- the dependent person has communication problems, has had a personality or behaviour change (such as dementia), rejects help or is aggressive
- there is no support from family or professional carers
- carers are becoming dependent on drugs or alcohol
- carers have no privacy
- the dependent person is difficult and inconsiderate.

Situations when child abuse can happen

Child abuse can happen in situations where:

- parents are unable to put a child's needs first
- parents or carers feel a need to show dominance over others
- parents or carers have been poorly parented themselves
- parents or carers were abused themselves as children
- families have financial problems (this does not just mean families on low incomes)
- families have a history of poor relationships or of use of violence.

Think about the last shift you did at your workplace. Write a summary of the tasks you completed that day.

For each of the tasks identify how:

Your practice and actions were sensitive to situations, issues and behaviour that may have led to danger, harm and abuse.

You provided necessary protection for individuals whilst taking in to account rights and restrictions.

CASE STUDY: Caring at home

Sunita is 48 years old. She has Parkinson's disease, which has recently begun to develop very rapidly. Her mobility has become very limited and she cannot be left alone because she falls frequently. The number of personal care tasks she can carry out has decreased significantly, and she is almost totally dependent on her husband for care.

Sunita has two grown-up sons who live and work considerable distances away. They both visit as often as they can, but are not able to offer any regular caring support. Sunita's husband has given up his career as a ranger in the local country park, a job he loved, in order to look after Sunita. She is very reluctant to go out because she feels people are looking at her. She is very angry about the way Parkinson's has affected her, and has alienated many of the friends who tried to help initially, by being unco-operative and refusing much of the help they offered.

1 *Are there any warning signs in this situation which would make you aware of the possibility of abuse? If so, what are they?*

2 *How would you try to relieve some of the pressures in this situation?*

Situations when abuse can happen in a care setting

Abuse can happen in a care setting when:
- staff are poorly trained or untrained
- there is little or no management supervision or support
- staff work in isolation
- there are inadequate numbers of staff to cope with the workload
- there are inadequate security arrangements

Active knowledge

Look at your workplace. Do any of the above points apply? If any of these are the case in your workplace, you need to be aware that people can be put under so much stress that they behave abusively. Remember that abuse is not just about physical cruelty.

If none of these things happen in your workplace, then try to imagine what work would be like if they did. Sit down with a colleague, if you can, and discuss what you think the effects of any two of the items in the list would be. If you cannot do this with a colleague, you can do it on your own by making notes.

- there is no key worker system and good relationships are not formed between staff and residents.

If you want to be effective in helping to stop abuse you will need to:

- believe that abuse happens
- recognise abusive behaviour
- be aware of when abuse can happen
- understand who abusers can be
- know the policies and procedures for handling abuse
- follow the individual's plan of care
- recognise likely abusive situations
- report any concerns or suspicions.

Your most important contribution will be to be *alert*. For example, an individual's plan of care or your organisational policy should specify ways in which the individual's whereabouts are constantly monitored – and if you are alert to where a vulnerable person is, and who he or she is with, you can do much to help avoid abusive situations.

Many factors are involved in building protection against abuse

How to respond to abuse and neglect

 KS 7 8 18 20 21

When you find out, or suspect, that a service user is being abused or neglected, you have a responsibility to take action immediately. Concerns, suspicions and firm evidence all require an immediate response.

There are several situations in which you may find yourself in the position of having information to report concerning abuse or neglect.

- A service user may disclose to you that he or she is being abused or neglected.
- You may have clear evidence that abuse or neglect is happening.
- You may have concerns and suspicions, but no definite evidence.

How to respond to disclosure

The correct term for a service user telling you about abuse or neglect is **disclosure**. If a service user discloses abuse to you, the first and most important response is that *you must believe what you are told.*

This is often harder than it sounds. If you have never been involved with an abusive situation before, it is hard to believe that such cases arise and that this could really happen.

You must reassure the person, whether an adult or a child, that you believe what you have been told. Another common fear of people who are being

Remember

One of the biggest fears of those being abused is that no one will believe them – do not make this fear into a reality.

abused is that it is somehow their fault – so you must also reassure them that it is not their fault and that they are in no way to blame for what has happened to them.

When a service user discloses abuse or neglect to you, try not to get into a situation where you are having to deal with a lot of detailed information. After reassuring the service user that you believe him or her, you should report the disclosure immediately to a senior colleague and hand over responsibility. This is not always possible because of the circumstances or location in which the disclosure takes place, or because the service user wants to tell you everything once he or she has started disclosing. If you do find yourself in the position of being given a great deal of information, you must be careful not to ask any leading questions – for example, do not say 'And then did he punch you?' Just ask 'And then what happened?'. Use your basic communication and listening skills so that the service user knows he or she can trust you and that you are listening. Make sure you concentrate and try to remember as much as possible so that you can record it accurately.

Another common problem that arises with disclosure is that you may be asked to keep the information secret. *You must never make this promise – it is one you cannot keep.*

What you can do is promise that you will only tell people who can help. You may well find yourself in this situation:

Remember

People disclose abuse because they want it to stop. They are telling you because they want you to help make it stop. You cannot make it stop if you keep it secret.

If I tell you something will you promise not to tell anyone?

I can't promise that until I know what you are going to tell me

You mustn't tell anyone. I'll get killed!

I can promise you this – I'll tell only people who can make you safe

The most important first step is to ensure that you know the procedures in your workplace for dealing with abuse and neglect. You should also receive training on abuse as part of your induction and staff development. All workplaces will have policies and procedures and it is vital that you are familiar with them and know exactly who you need to report to. Then you will be in a position to support the individuals you work with to understand that you must pass on information about actual or likely danger and abuse. You can also reassure individuals about how you can fulfil your responsibilities to protect them from such harm.

Situations where you have evidence

There may be situations where you have evidence of abuse, either because you have witnessed it happening or because you have other evidence such as bank slips, forged pension books, etc. These situations must be reported immediately to your supervisor, or the person identified in the procedures followed by your workplace for cases of suspected abuse. You should make sure that you provide all the detailed evidence that you have, with full information about how you found the evidence and how and where you have recorded it. If you have witnessed, or intervened in, an act of abuse that may constitute a criminal offence, you must *not* remove any possible evidence until the police have examined the scene.

Situations where you have concerns

It is more likely that you will not have evidence but you have noticed some of the signs or symptoms of possible abuse. You must report this as rapidly as you would if you had clear evidence.

It may be tempting to wait until you have more evidence or something happens to confirm your suspicions, but do not do this. You must report anything unusual that you notice, even if you think it is too small to be important. It is the small details that make the whole picture. Sometimes, your observations may add to other small things noticed by members of the team, and a picture may start to emerge. Teamwork and good communication are vitally important.

Teamwork and good communication are vital in preventing problems

Dealing with abuse in a care setting

One of the most difficult situations to deal with is abuse in a professional care setting, particularly if you believe it to be taking place within your own workplace, or elsewhere in your organisation. If you are concerned about possible abuse or neglect in your workplace you should follow the same procedures as you would for any other abuse or neglect concerns.

- Report the problem to your line manager or supervisor.
- If you suspect that your manager is involved, or will not take action, you must refer it to a more senior manager who is likely to be impartial.

- If you cannot report the abuse to anyone within your workplace or organisation, you should report your concerns to the Commission for Social Care Inspection, which is responsible for ensuring that standards are maintained in all care settings.

Whistle-blowing

Reporting concerns about practice in your workplace is known as 'whistle-blowing' and you cannot be victimised for doing this. An Act of Parliament protects you – it is called the Public Interest Disclosure Act (1998). It encourages people to 'blow the whistle' about malpractice in the workplace and is designed to ensure that organisations respond by acting on the message rather than punishing the messenger. It is important that you know the details of your organisation's 'whistle-blowing' policy.

The Act applies to employees reporting crime, civil offences (including negligence, breach of contract, etc.), miscarriage of justice, danger to health and safety or the environment, and the covering up of any of these. It applies whether or not the information is confidential, and extends to malpractice occurring in the UK and any other country or territory.

In addition to employees, it covers trainees, agency staff, contractors, home workers and every professional in the NHS. The Act means that your employer cannot take any action to victimise you because you have reported genuine concerns.

Recording information about possible abuse

Any information you have, whether it is simply concerns, hard evidence, or a disclosure, must be carefully recorded. You should write down your evidence, or if you are unable to do so for any reason, you should record it on audio tape. It is not acceptable to pass on your concerns verbally without backing this up with a recorded report. Verbal information can be altered and can have its meaning changed very easily when it is passed on. Think about the children's game of Chinese Whispers – by the time the whispered phrase reaches the end of its journey, it is usually changed beyond all recognition.

Sometimes your information may need to be included in an individual's plan of care or personal records, particularly if you have noticed a change in the way he or she is cared for, or if his/her behaviour could be an 'early warning' that the care team need to be especially observant. Your workplace may have a special report form for recording 'causes for concern'. If not, you should write your report, making sure you include the following:
- everything you observed
- anything you have been told – but make sure that it is clear that this is not something you have seen for yourself

- any previous concerns you may have had
- what has raised your concerns on this occasion.

> P was visited by her son this afternoon. She was very quiet over tea, did not join in conversation or joke with anyone. Just said she was tired when asked what was wrong. Went to her room without going into the lounge for the 'seconds evening'. Said she thought the clothes were too expensive and she couldn't afford them. Unusual for her. Similar to incident about a month ago when she said she couldn't afford the hairdresser – again after a visit from her son.
>
> Needs to be watched. Is he getting money from her? For discussion at planning meeting.

Discuss your report and your concerns with your supervisor and colleagues.

Evidence PC ③ ⑤ ⑧

Write a report on concerns about an abuse situation that could occur in your workplace. If you are aware of abuse situations that have happened, you could report on one of them, making sure you do not use service users' names or any other information that could identify them. If not, make up the details. State to whom, in your workplace, you would give the report.

In serious cases your written evidence may be needed by the social workers who will investigate the situation. It may be useful for a doctor if he or she has to conduct an examination, or it may be needed for the case conference or for court proceedings. So you must make sure you record all information accurately and factually, avoiding any statements (such as expressions of your personal opinions) which would make it difficult to rely on in future investigations or court proceedings.

The effects of abuse    KS ⑩ ⑫ ⑰ ⑱ ⑳

Abuse devastates those who suffer it. It causes people to lose their self-esteem and their confidence. Many adults and children become withdrawn and difficult to communicate with. Anger is a common emotion among people who have been abused. It may be directed against the abuser, or at those people around them who failed to recognise the abuse and stop it happening.

One of the greatest tragedies is when people who have been abused turn their anger against themselves, and blame themselves for everything that has happened to them. These are situations that require expert help, and this should be available to anyone who has been abused, regardless of the circumstances.

Some of the behaviour changes that can be signs of abuse can become permanent, or certainly very long-lasting. There are very few survivors of abuse whose personality remains unchanged, and for those who do conquer the effects of abuse, it is a long, hard fight.

The abuser, often called the 'perpetrator', also requires expert help, and this should be available through various agencies depending on the type and seriousness of the abuse. People who abuse, whether their victims are children or vulnerable adults, receive very little sympathy or understanding from society. There is no public recognition that some abusers may have been under tremendous strain and pressure, and abusers may find that they have no support from friends or family. Many abusers will face the consequences of their actions alone.

Care workers who have to deal with abusive situations will have different emotional reactions. There is no 'right way' to react. Everyone is different and will deal with things in his or her own way. If you have to deal with abuse, these are some of the ways you may feel, and some steps you can take that may help.

Remember

Everyone is different and will deal with his or her emotional reactions to an abusive situation in a different way.

Shock

You may feel quite traumatised if you have witnessed an abusive incident. It is normal to find that you cannot get the incident out of your mind, that you have difficulty concentrating on other things, or that you keep having 'flashbacks' and re-enact the situation in your head. You may also feel that you need to keep talking about what happened.

Talking can be very beneficial, but if you are discussing an incident outside your workplace, you must remember rules of confidentiality and never use names. You will find that you can talk about the circumstances just as well by referring to 'the boy' or 'the father' or 'the daughter'. This way of talking does become second nature, and is useful because it allows you to share your feelings about things that have happened at work while maintaining confidentiality.

These feelings are likely to last for a fairly short time, and are a natural reaction to shock and trauma. If at any time you feel that you are having difficulty, you must talk to your manager or supervisor, who should be able to help.

Anger

Alternatively, the situation may have made you feel very angry, and you may have an overwhelming urge to inflict some damage on the perpetrator of the abuse. While this is understandable, it is not professional and you will have to find other ways of dealing with your anger. Again, your supervisor or manager should help you to work through your feelings.

Everyone has different ways of dealing with anger, such as taking physical exercise, doing housework, punching a cushion, writing feelings down and then tearing up the paper, crying or telling your best friend. Whatever you do with your anger in ordinary situations, you should do the same in this situation (just remember to respect confidentiality if you need to tell your best friend – miss out the names). It is perfectly legitimate to be angry, but you cannot bring this anger into the professional relationship.

Distress

The situation may have made you distressed, and you may want to go home and have a good cry, or give your own relatives an extra hug. This is a perfectly normal reaction. No matter how many years you work, or how many times it happens, you may still feel the same way.

Some workplaces will have arrangements in place where workers are able to share difficult situations and get support from each other. Others may not have any formal meetings or groups arranged, but colleagues will offer each other support and advice in an informal way. You may find that work colleagues who have had similar experiences are the best people with whom to share your feelings.

There is, of course, the possibility that the situation may have brought back painful memories for you of abuse you have suffered in your own past. This is often the most difficult situation to deal with, because you may feel as if you should be able to help because you know how it feels to be abused, but your own experience has left you without any room to deal with the feelings of others. There are many avenues of support now available to survivors of abuse. You can find out about the nearest support confidentially, if you do not want your workplace colleagues or supervisor to know.

There is no doubt that dealing with abuse is one of the most stressful aspects of working in care. There is nothing odd or abnormal about feeling that you need to share what you have experienced and looking for support from others. In fact, most experienced managers would be far more concerned about a worker involved in dealing with abuse who appears quite unaffected by it, than about one who comes looking for guidance and reassurance.

Remember

- Feeling upset is normal.
- Talk about the incident if that helps, but respect the rules of confidentiality and miss out the names.
- Being angry is OK, but deal with it sensibly – take physical exercise, do the housework, cry.
- Do not be unprofessional with the abuser.
- If you are a survivor of abuse and you find it hard to deal with, ask for help.

How the law affects what you do

Much of the work in caring is governed by legislation, but the only group where legislation specifically provides for protection from abuse is children. Older people and people with a learning disability, physical disabilities or mental health problems have service provision, rights and many other requirements laid down in law, but no overall legal framework to provide protection from abuse.

The laws which cover your work in the field of care are summarised in the table below.

Service user group	Laws that govern their care	Protection from abuse
Children	Children Act 1989 Children Act 2004	Yes
People with mental health problems	Mental Health Act 1983 Mental Health Act 2007	No
Adults with learning disabilities	Mental Health Act 1983 Mental Capacity Act 2005	No Yes – some
Adults with disabilities	Chronically Sick and Disabled Persons Act 1986 Disability Discrimination Act 1995	No
Older people	National Assistance Act 1948 NHS Community Care Act 1990	No
All service user groups	Care Standards Act 2000	Yes, through raising standards

There are, however, a number of sets of guidelines, policies and procedures in respect of abuse for service user groups other than children, and you will need to ensure that you are familiar with policies for your area of work and particularly with those policies which apply in your own workplace.

Dealing with abuse is difficult and demanding for everyone, and it is essential that you receive professional supervision from your manager. This may be undertaken in a regular supervision or support meeting if you have one; if not, it will be important that you arrange to meet with your supervisor so that you can ensure you are working in the correct way and in accordance with the procedure in your setting.

Your supervisor will also need to be assured that you are coping on a personal and professional level with the effects of having to deal with an abusive situation.

Government policies and guidelines

The most important set of government guidelines which lays down practices for co-operation between agencies is called 'Working Together to Safeguard Children'. It was published in 1999 and forms the basis for child-protection work. This guideline ensures that information is shared between agencies and professionals, and that decisions in respect of children are not taken by just one person.

A similar set of guidelines has been published by the government about adults, called 'No Secrets'. These guidelines state that older people have specific rights, which include being treated with respect, and being able to live in their home and community without fear of physical or emotional violence or harassment.

The guidance gives local authorities the lead responsibility in co-ordinating the procedures. Each local authority area must have a multi-agency management committee for the protection of vulnerable adults, which will develop policies, protocols and practices. The guidance covers:

- identification of those at risk
- setting up an inter-agency framework
- developing inter-agency policy – procedures for responding in individual cases
- recruitment, training and other staff and management issues.

A government White Paper published in 2001, 'Valuing People: A New Strategy for Learning Disability in the 21st Century', sets out the ways in which services for people with a learning disability will be improved. 'Valuing People' sets out four main principles for service provision for people with a learning disability:

- civil rights
- independence
- choice
- inclusion.

The White Paper also makes it clear that people with a learning disability are entitled to the full protection of the law.

Recent policy approaches to protecting children and vulnerable adults in care environments have concentrated on improving and monitoring the quality of the service provided to them. The principle behind this is that if the overall quality of practice in care is constantly improved, then well-trained staff working to high standards are less likely to abuse service users, and are more likely to identify and deal effectively with any abuse they find.

What does the law say about protecting children?

The Children Act 2004 requires that local authority children's services departments provide protection from abuse for children in their area. The Act of Parliament gives powers to children's services departments, following the procedures laid down by the local Safeguarding Children Board, to take legal steps to ensure the safety of children.

What does the law say about protecting vulnerable adults?

The Acts of Parliament that are mainly concerned with provisions for vulnerable adults are the National Assistance Act 1948, the NHS and Community Care Act 1990 and the Safeguarding Vulnerable Groups Act 2006. They do not specifically give social services departments a 'duty to protect' but, of course, people are protected by the law. If a vulnerable adult is abused and that abuse is considered to be a criminal offence, then the police will act. It is sometimes thought that because someone is confused, a prosecution will not be brought – this is not so. All vulnerable adults will have the full protection of the law if any criminal offences are committed.

The Mental Health Act 2007 (and the draft Mental Capacity Act 2005) forms the framework for service provision for people with mental health problems or a learning disability. There are provisions within this legislation for social services departments to assume responsibility for people who are so 'mentally impaired' that they are not able to be responsible for their own affairs. This is called guardianship. However, like all other vulnerable adults, there is no specific duty to protect people from abuse.

'Valuing People' (see page 220) forms the basis for services to all people with a learning disability and provides rights, but no specific duty of protection.

While the Chronically Sick and Disabled Persons Act and the Disability Discrimination Act provide disabled people with rights, services and protection from discrimination, they do not provide any means of comprehensive protection from abuse.

As with all vulnerable groups, there is a long and tragic history to the physical and emotional abuse suffered by people with physical disabilities or a learning disability. The public humiliation and abuse of those with mental health problems is still visible today, so it is hardly surprising that abuse on an individual level is still all too commonplace.

Did you know?

The Safeguarding Vulnerable Groups Act 2006 brings the vetting and barring information together in one place. It integrates the current List 99 (for teachers), and the Protection of Children Act lists (for those working in childcare settings) and also provides for a new list of people barred from working with vulnerable adults to replace the Protection of Vulnerable Adults list. The list can be checked by all employers, including parents employing nannies, music teachers and private tutors and people in receipt of direct payments employing personal assistants.

Information on ways to protect individuals

Safeguarding and protecting vulnerable adults and children is an area of work that has been in the public eye for many years. As a result of this, a great deal of research has been carried out, and plenty of information is available in order to develop and improve your understanding of this difficult subject. You will be able to find training courses available in your local area – all social services departments provide training by their specialists, and many private agencies with specialist knowledge, such as the NSPCC and Action on Elder Abuse, produce very useful training materials and publications.

Your supervisor or manager will be able to advise you about the best way to find out information, and you should choose the way in which you find it easiest to learn – you may prefer to attend a training course, to read a book or to watch a training video. Ask your supervisor to find out what is available in your workplace.

Following the rules

Much of what you read about dealing with abuse may give you the impression that this is a subject full of rules and procedures. It is, and for very good reasons. Abuse is extremely serious – it is potentially life-threatening. Systems and rules have been developed by learning from the tragedies that have happened in the past. Many of these tragedies occurred because procedures were either not in place, or were not followed. You must make sure that you and any staff you supervise know what the procedure is in your workplace and follow it carefully.

Test yourself

1 What are the signs of financial abuse?

2 What factors may lead you to consider that a carer is abusing an individual?

3 What is the difference between abuse and neglect?

4 Why is it important to record information about suspected or actual abuse?

5 What is your position if an individual asks you not to tell anyone about abuse he or she has experienced?

6 What are the two key things to do when someone discloses that he or she has been abused?

Providing care for vulnerable people can be challenging and difficult, whilst at the same time rewarding. The more support you receive and information you gather, the better equipped you will be to cope with the demands and responsibility.

www.dh.gov.uk (Department of Health: Health and Social Care related topics – Dignity in Care, Vulnerable Adults, POVA, PoCA)

www.gscc.org.uk (General Social Care Council – Codes of Practice)

www.crb.gov.uk (Criminal Records Bureau)

www.pcaw.co.uk (Public Concern at Work)
tel: 02074046609

www.nspcc.org.uk (National Society for the Prevention of Cruelty to Children)

www.unison.org.uk (Unison – guides to POVA and PoCA including a leaflet called 'Reported')

www.csci.org.uk (Commission for Social Care Inspection: Care Provider – guidance related to the social care services you are researching)

www.elderabuse.org.uk (Action on Elder Abuse)

www.dh.gov.uk (No Secrets – Guidance on Developing and Implementing Multi-Agency Policies and Procedures to Protect Vulnerable Adults from Abuse)

www.valuingpeople.gov.uk (Valuing People: A New Strategy for Learning Disability in the 21st Century)

www.everychildmatters.gov.uk (Working Together to Safeguard Children – Every Child Matters)

www.dca.gov.uk (Department for Constitutional Affairs)

Arroba, T., Ball, L. (2001) *Staying Sane; Managing the Stress of Caring* Age Concern

Maclean, S., Maclean, I. (2001) *Social Care and the Law* Kirwin Maclean Associates

Maclean, S., Maclean, I. *Supporting You: Supporting Others Health & Social Care (Level 3)* Kirwin Maclean

Moore, R., Maclean, I. *Cultural Sensitivity in Social and Health Care* Kirwin Maclean

Contribute to care planning and review

Services are provided by a wide range of agencies in many different ways. These could be as different as providing a hospital bed for someone who is acutely ill, providing residential accommodation for a homeless young person or providing large-print books for someone who has a visual impairment. One of the most important aspects of the provision of a service is to ensure that it is meeting the needs of the individual.

Individuals' needs are not about what an agency or care worker believes to be needed; they are about what individuals understand their own needs to be. One of the most important roles of a care worker is to find out from individuals about the type of service needed and then to work alongside them and their family, and any other carers, to ensure that the best and most effective level of service is provided and that it meets the needs of all those concerned.

It is also important that a worker understands the limitations of the service that is provided by his or her agency. Sometimes it is necessary to explain these limitations to an individual, even though it may be disappointing not to be able to provide exactly what had been hoped for.

In this unit you will learn about the process of creating care plans for individuals, based on an assessment of their needs and preferences. You will also explore the the concept of person-centred care and how this can be applied when implementing and reviewing care plans. Finally you will learn about the process of managing and recording care plan reviews.

What you need to learn

- How care plans are created
- Your role in the assessment process
- Taking a holistic approach
- The importance of giving people choices
- Obtaining information from other sources
- Your role in developing and implementing plans of care
- How to communicate care choices to the individual
- How to record service-user plans
- How to support the care plan activities
- Ways of monitoring
- The purpose of reviews
- The review process
- How the review process is recorded.

HSC 328a Contribute to assessing the needs and preferences of individuals

How care plans are created

The process of assessing need in social and health care is currently very well defined in government policy and guidance. This guidance is associated with several key Acts of Parliament which give a framework for the help and services that people are entitled to receive and give people the ability to say how the services should be provided.

Section 29 of the National Assistance Act 1948 says that local authorities have responsibilities and duties to promote the welfare of people who have sensory, physical or mental difficulties. Local authorities must do this by making accurate assessments of how they meet the outcomes set by people.

The 1986 Disabled Persons Act (s.4) said that if a disabled person or his or her representative asked for an assessment, the local authority had a duty to carry it out. This legislation was strengthened by the NHS and Community Care Act 1990 (s.47 (2)) which says that if a person is disabled, he or she has an automatic right to an assessment and should be informed of this.

The White Paper 'Our Health Our Care Our Say', 2005 set out to change these practices dramatically. Putting power and control in the hands of people who use services was the key message of the White Paper. People were encouraged to control their own services through 'self directed support' where the amount of budget available is agreed through assessment, but control over how it is spent is entirely in the hands of the individual. The concept of 'individual budgets' is rather like Direct Payments, but without the requirement to be an employer.

Both the law and associated guidance make it clear that the three areas to be assessed are outcomes, risk and services. The resulting decisions are to be set out in the form of a **care plan**.

Such care plans must record the outcomes the service user wants, how this is to be done (the implementation plan), what to do if things don't go to plan (contingency arrangements), and how unmet needs will be identified and taken into account.

This system depends on good quality assessments of need and risk. Local authorities all have rules that set out how money and resources should be allocated to people with additional needs. Such rules are called **eligibility criteria**. Basically, the more disabled a person is, the greater his or her entitlement to all the services needed. In 2003, the government introduced

Key terms

Care plan: A formal document that sets out everything to be done to meet someone's needs. This document sets out objectives or goals, together with the services that will be provided to meet these objectives.

Key terms

Eligibility criteria: The rules that explain a person's entitlement to receive services. The greater a person's needs and risks to independence, the greater that person's entitlement to receive services.

Fair Access to Care Services, a system that sets out four categories of eligibility for services: critical, substantial, moderate and low.

The process of care management is a cycle. About six weeks after services have begun to be delivered, the care manager must review whether or not the service user is achieving the identified outcomes. If things are not working out as the service user wants, the plan will have to be changed.

Local authorities are obliged to carry on reviewing services, at least once every twelve months. When such a review is carried out, the outcomes of service provision will be evaluated to check whether the planned intervention is working. **Evaluation** and the re-setting of outcomes, goals and plans are critical aspects of care management.

Consider the following case study, in which an older person is at risk as a result of her physical disabilities.

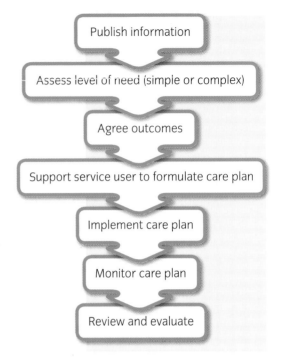

Publish information

Assess level of need (simple or complex)

Agree outcomes

Support service user to formulate care plan

Implement care plan

Monitor care plan

Review and evaluate

The seven steps of care management

CASE STUDY: Help to take a bath

Mrs Green is 68 and lives with her husband. She has severe arthritis which means that although she can manage to wash herself, she cannot get into the bath.
She is able to do all other personal care tasks, but unless she gets some help, she will have to give up taking baths. However, her personal hygiene and health are not at risk.

1   *What would be involved in the assessment of this situation?*

2   *What assistance do you think Mrs Green might want?*

Although Mrs Green, in the case study above, is fairly low risk in terms of the Fair Access to Care Services eligibility criteria, it is clear she could be helped by the provision of specialist equipment. In her case, if she wants to be able to use the bath, an assessment would be carried out (probably by an occupational therapist or a physiotherapist from an Older Persons' Team), and it is likely that a bath hoist would be ordered and installed. Mrs Green may also want to improve her ability to do household tasks, to walk and to travel (on public transport, for example) and services will be provided to assist her. After six weeks, the care manager allocated to Mrs Green would check whether the hoist had been installed, and whether Mrs Green was satisfied and able to use it safely and with confidence.

Key terms

Evaluation: A systematic review of what has happened. For a care plan, an evaluation would consider whether the objectives had been met, and whether the services given had been effective.

If Mrs Green decided she wanted any other services, these would be built into a revised care plan. The local authority would review her case, at least every twelve months, to see whether she or Mr Green had any further requirements.

Your role in the assessment process

 KS 1 2 5 6 7 10 11 12

Adult service users who decide they want services of a residential care home are now referred through a single assessment process that combines an assessment of health and social needs. Service users will therefore have a single care plan. Where service users are self-funding, care homes are required to carry out a needs assessment to ensure that services are appropriate.

Care homes have to develop an individual service-user plan which is based on the single care plan – and this service-user plan will need to be regularly updated.

In England, the Commission for Social Care Inspection (CSCI) uses a series of National Minimum Standards in order to assess the quality of service provision. There are different National Minimum Standards for different services. Currently there are standards for:

- care homes for older people
- care homes with adult placements
- care homes for adults 18–65
- adult placement schemes
- domiciliary care
- nurses' agencies
- children's homes
- adoption
- residential family centres
- boarding schools
- residential special schools
- accommodation of students under 18 by further education colleges.

Care homes have to develop an individual service-user plan

It will be important that you know the standards relevant to your own service and that you are aware of the regulations for assessment and updating of service-user plans. Copies of the National Minimum Standards appropriate to your service should be available at your place of work. You can also find the National Minimum Standards on the CSCI website at www.csci.org.uk.

Standard 6 of the National Minimum Standards for care homes for adults (18–65) is set out in full below in order to provide an example of what is expected in terms of the individual service-user plan.

6.1	The registered manager develops and agrees with each service user an individual plan, which may include treatment and rehabilitation, describing the services and facilities to be provided by the home, and how these services will meet current and changing needs and aspirations and achieve goals.
6.2	The plan is generated from the single care management assessment/care plan or the home's own assessment, and covers all aspects of personal and social support and health care needs as set out in Standard 2.
6.3	The plans sets out how current and anticipated specialist requirements will be met (for example through positive planned interventions; rehabilitation and therapeutic programmes; structured environments; development of language and communication; adaptations and equipment; one-to-one communications support).
6.4	The plan describes any restrictions on choice and freedom (agreed with the service user) imposed by a specialist programme (e.g. a treatment programme for drug or alcohol misusers); for mental health service users, in accordance with the Care Programme Approach and in some instances the Mental Health Act 1983.
6.5	The plan establishes individual procedures for service users likely to be aggressive or cause harm or self-harm, focusing on positive behaviour, ability and willingness.
6.6	The plan is drawn up with the involvement of the service user together with family, friends and/or advocate as appropriate, and relevant agencies/specialists.
6.7	The plan is made available in a language and format the service user can understand (e.g. visual, graphic, simple printed English, deafblind manual, explanation, British Sign Language video), and is held by the service user unless there are clear (and recorded) reasons not to do so.
6.8	A key worker (or personal tutor in specialist colleges; designated nurse if receiving nursing care) who can communicate with the individual and appreciates his/her racial and/or cultural heritage is allocated for each service user, with the full involvement of the service user.
6.9	The service user is made aware of the respective roles and responsibilities of the care manager/CPA care co-ordinator, key worker and/or advocate, and knows how to contact them.
6.10	The plan is reviewed with the service user (involving significant professionals, and family, friends and advocates as agreed with the service user) at the request of the service user or at least every six months and updated to reflect changing needs; and agreed changes are recorded and actioned.

The detail of your work will of course depend on the service in which you are working and the standards that apply to the service. However, whatever role you have as a worker and regardless of the kind of services your agency provides, there are some basic principles which apply to the work you do.

One of these is that you must carefully explain to the individual your role in the whole process. Before you can clearly explain your role to someone else in a way that they can understand, you must ensure that you understand it fully yourself.

Your role will include the need to ensure that:

- the needs of the person are met as far as possible by the service
- as much relevant information as is necessary is obtained about the person, in order to meet individual needs
- you provide the individual and his or her carers and family with as much information as you can about the nature of the service that can be provided in order to meet individual needs.

You will also need to explain to individuals the range of choices and possibilities open to them within your agency. It can sometimes be helpful to explain how your agency is funded and what the limitations may be on the types of services that can be provided.

Taking a holistic approach

 KS 1 2 5 6 7 10 12 14

One of the essential aspects of planning care services is to have a **holistic** approach to planning and provision.

This means recognising that all parts of an individual's life will have an impact on his or her care needs and that you need to look beyond what you see when you meet him or her for the first time.

Person-centred planning is mainly used in the area of learning disability and comes from the Valuing People (2001) White Paper. It contains some broad principles that are of relevance to work with all service users. Key aspects are set out below.

Key principles of person-centred planning assessment
- The person is at the centre
- Family and friends are full partners
- Person-centred planning reflects the person's capacities, what is important to the person (now and for their future) and specifies the support they require to make a valued contribution to their community.

Remember

- Give all possible information about your role and the role of your agency.
- You may have to give this information to several people if there are family members or other people involved in the individual's care.
- You may have to repeat the information, write it down or make it available in some other format if the person has hearing or learning difficulties.
- Information is very important and it empowers people. People cannot make informed choices if you fail to give them enough information.

Key terms

Holistic: Looking at the *whole* situation.

Key terms

Evidence-based decision making: Decision making that is fully informed by information. Social workers and care workers should not make plans based on guesswork.

A wide range of factors will have an impact on the circumstances which have brought an individual to request social care services. All of the following factors will directly affect a service user and they must be taken into account when considering the best way to provide services:

- health
- employment
- education
- social factors
- religious and cultural factors.

Health

The state of people's health has a massive effect on how they develop and the kind of experiences they have during their lives. Someone who has always been very fit, well and active may find it very difficult and frustrating to find his or her movement suddenly restricted as the result of an illness, such as a stroke. This may lead to difficult behaviour and the expression of anger against those who are delivering services. Alternatively, the individual may become depressed. Someone who has not enjoyed good health over a long period of time, however, may be able to adjust well to a more limited physical level of ability, perhaps having compensated for poor health by developing intellectual interests.

Someone who has been fit and well may find it frustrating to become restricted by an illness

Employment

Health is also likely to have had an impact on an adult's employment opportunities, either making employment impossible at times or restricting the types of jobs he or she could do. Whether or not adults are able to work can have a huge effect on their level of confidence and self-esteem. Employment may also have an effect on the extent to which individuals have mixed with others and formed social contacts. This may be an important factor when considering the possible benefits of residential care as opposed to care provided in a home environment.

Income levels are obviously related to employment, and these will have an effect on standards of living – the quality of housing, the quality of diet and the lifestyle people are able to have. Someone who has had a well-paid job is likely to have lived in a more pleasant environment with lower levels of pollution, more opportunities for leisure, exercise and relaxation, and a better standard of housing. It is easy to see how all of this can affect an individual's health and well-being.

Education

People's level of education is likely to have affected their employment history and their level of income. It can also have an effect on the extent to which they are able to gain access to information about health and lifestyle. It is important that the educational level of an individual is always considered so that explanations and information are given in a way which is readily understandable. For example, an explanation about an illness taken straight from a textbook used by doctors would not mean much to most of us! However, if the information is explained in everyday terms, we are more likely to understand what is being said.

Some people may have a different level of literacy from you, so do not assume that everyone will be able to make use of written notes. Some people may prefer information to be given verbally, or recorded on tape. Also, remember that some illnesses such as a stroke or dementia can affect a person's ability to understand, assimilate and communicate information regardless of their educational level.

Social factors

The social circumstances in which people have lived will have an immense effect on their way of life and the type of care provision they are likely to need. Traditionally, the social classification of society is based on employment groups, but the social groups in which people live include their family and friends, and people differ in the extent to which they remain close to others. The social circumstances of each individual who is assessed for the provision of care services must be taken into consideration, to ensure that the service provided will be appropriate.

Religious and cultural factors

Religious and cultural beliefs and values are an essential part of everyone's lives. The values and beliefs of the community people belong to and the religious practices which are part of their daily lives are an essential aspect for consideration in the planning of services. Some people may also have a specific ethnic identity and a sense of belonging to a specific ethnic community. Any service provision which has failed to take account of the religious, ethnic and cultural values of the individual may provide a poor quality of service to individuals.

The importance of people having choices

 KS 1 2 3 4 7 8 10 12 13

Active knowledge

Check out the processes used at your place of work for assessing the needs and preferences of individuals. Are there clear guidelines as to how information is obtained? Are the roles and responsibilities of managers and care workers clearly defined? Are all the key people consulted? If appropriate, you could propose improvements to the system.

One of the essential aspects of planning care services is to have a **holistic** You need to think carefully about the ways you influence people. It is not only your own personal style of communication that influences them, it is also the way you explain the possibilities of service provision. You will need to beware of pushing individuals and their families into a particular decision, simply because you happen to believe it is the best one.

Individuals will ask for your advice, and perhaps ask: 'What would you do?' You will have to learn to avoid answering that question directly, as it is not your role to give advice about a course of action, nor is it for you to explain what you think you might do if you were in a similar situation. This is not helpful.

What you can usefully do is provide information about services and empower people to make their own decisions. You should simply provide unbiased, accurate and clear information and then support individuals to achieve the best outcome with the decision they have made.

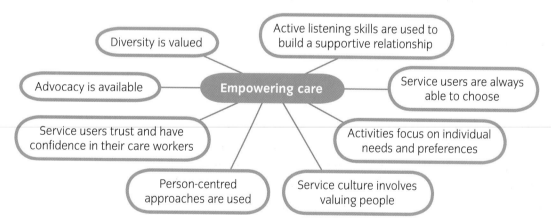

In your current role you may not be in a position to set up placements for a service user. However, the principle is the same, whether you are helping someone make a major decision such as this, or a relatively minor one such as what clothes to put on in the morning; giving people choice is an essential aspect of everyday care.

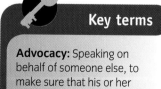

Key terms

Advocacy: Speaking on behalf of someone else, to make sure that his or her views and wishes are heard.

Woodville Day Centre is an excellent place. You've no idea how hard I had to work to get you an offer of a place there – of course, it's entirely up to you. If you want to just stay at home you can.
Oh well, if you went to all that trouble, and you think it's that good, I'd better go.
What would you do if you were me?
Well, I'm not you, so I wouldn't necessarily do the same thing as you. But what we could do is make a clear list of the pros and cons of each option.

Putting individuals in control

Throughout the process of obtaining information you should make sure you constantly check that individuals are fully aware of what is happening and feel they are in control of the process. One of the problems with the way services are provided, regardless of whether they are services for health, for social care or for children and young people, is that many service users feel they play only a passive role.

It is easy to see how this can happen. Agencies and service providers have well-organised systems which can often involve filling in a great many forms, attending meetings and working through the bureaucracy. If you work for such an organisation these things are a day-to-day part of your life. They do not represent a threat to you. But you need to remind yourself that many of the people you deal with will not be familiar with the workings of your agency and may not feel confident enough to question or challenge what is happening.

There are several steps you can take at each stage of the process to ensure that individuals feel they are in charge of their service.

Step 1

Individuals should make clear who needs to be involved in the process of thinking about and planning their service provision. You may need to prompt them to think about the people they would like to be involved. Sometimes it is helpful to make some suggestions. For example, you could ask 'What about your neighbour, Mrs Smith, the one who pops in with your dinner? Might it be a good idea to ask her?' Or, 'Your niece Susan might have some ideas about the sort of services you could use.'

Step 2

At each stage of the process you should check with the individual that he or she is in agreement with the steps that have been taken so far. You should do this using the means of communication which the individual prefers. For example, if your normal means of communication is to talk, then you could have a regular chat to ensure that the service proposed is what the individual wants and to ask whether there are any specific ways in which he or she wants tasks to be carried out. Alternatively, if the individual has any form of hearing impairment, your means of communication to establish the same information may be by writing or using signs. If any extra support is needed to enable an individual to communicate his or her views, such as interpreters, translators or signers, make sure that this is provided.

Step 3

The use of any additional sources of information, for example previous records from other agencies that may be involved with an individual, must be agreed in advance before you approach the sources for the information.

It is important you do not take this agreement for granted and that you explain exactly what it is you intend to do so it is clear what is being agreed to.

Step 4

Make sure that you record the individual's agreement to other people being approached for information. Some agencies require written confirmation of an individual's agreement before they provide information about him or her. If at any point during your initial assessment and checking of information an individual withdraws consent for you to approach a particular agency or person, you must respect that and not pursue that particular source of information.

Mr J, it would be helpful if we could talk to your doctor to find out exactly the kind of help we can give you to make sure that you're not putting your health at risk.

Are you happy for us to do this? It will mean me telephoning your doctor and asking her exactly how much you are able to do without aggravating your heart condition.

Do you understand the sort of information I'm going to ask for?

Step 5

Support the individual and his or her family, friends or carers to feed back their views about the assessments made. If the process goes smoothly the feedback will be positive, but you may also need to support people in challenging some points or in complaining about an assessment that doesn't meet their expectations. Make sure that you understand the appropriate channels to use for passing on any concerns, and that you communicate them not as your own views but as the views of the individuals in question.

Gretta is 85 years old. She lives alone and has recently become increasingly frail. She has no memory difficulties but finds shopping, cooking and coping with housework increasingly difficult.

Gretta has been widowed for some years and moved recently to live hear her daughter, who has grown-up children. She has always been independent and reluctant to depend on her daughter for care, although she very much enjoys her grandchildren's visits. Although comparatively well off, Gretta has always been very careful with money.

Before she moved, Gretta had a number of friends whom she met to have coffee with and to play bridge. She was also a regular attender at the local church, which had an active club for its older members.

However, since she moved home, Gretta has become increasingly isolated. Her daughter helps with her shopping and housework, and her grandchildren visit at least once a week, but she misses her own friends and the community of her church. So her daughter contacted the social services, who made an assessment of Gretta's needs. They arranged for a local taxi firm to provide transport to and from a church in the neighbourhood which maintains an active social circle, in the hope that Gretta would enjoy the company and the regular routine.

Gretta attended church once. When the taxi arrived for her the next Sunday she told the driver that she would not be going again. She told her daughter that she didn't like using a taxi, as it seemed 'extravagant' to be travelling in a taxi alone, and that the church was just not 'right' for her.

Some older people enjoy socialising in groups

1   *From what you know of Gretta's background, why do you think she was unhappy with the arrangements made for her?*

2   *Do you think the service provided was appropriate for Gretta? If not, why not?*

3   *What actions would you take next in this situation?*

4   *Suggest alternative support that could be offered to Gretta and her daughter.*

Obtaining information from other sources

 KS ① ② ③ ④ ⑤ ⑥ ⑦ ⑧ ⑩ ⑬

Once you have ensured you have an individual's agreement to do so, you may wish to consider accessing a range of other sources to complete the picture of the person and the way in which he or she can most benefit from the services your agency provides. Examples of sources are:

Bear in mind that information you gain, particularly from other professional sources, may be restricted by:

- the rules of confidentiality under which that professional operates
- the legal restrictions as to how information may be passed on.

Most professionals are bound by principles of confidentiality in respect of their service users. You know that there are limits to the information you can share with others about your service user, so you must expect that other professionals from whom you are seeking information will be bound by similar rules. Information can be protected under a range of different legislation, as shown below.

Type of information	Relevant legislation
Medical information/hospital records	Data Protection Act 1998
Information relating to children and young people	Children Act 1989, Children Act 2004
Information relating to people with mental health problems	Mental Health Act 2007
Information relating to people with a disability	Disability Discrimination Act 1995
Any information stored on a computer or in manual records	Data Protection Act 1998

All these Acts work on the basic principle that personal information given or received in what is understood to be a confidential situation and for one particular purpose, may not be used for a different purpose. They also contain the proviso that information may not be passed to anyone else without the agreement of the person who provided the information. The Data Protection Act ensures that individuals have access to their own health or social services records but that these are not available to anyone else without the individual's permission. This applies even after death where an individual has expressly forbidden any information to be passed to anyone else or to a specific individual.

Family and friends

Family and friends can be an invaluable source of information about an individual and his or her needs. However, you must be sure before you discuss anything with family or friends that this is being done with the consent of the person concerned. It is easy to assume that because someone is a relative or close friend there will be no objections over him or her giving information to you. Under the single assessment process the initial assessment details will indicate who the individual wishes information to be shared with, but you should always confirm with individuals that they have no objection to you discussing particular matters with family or friends.

Other sources

Sometimes you may find that you have completed all your discussions with individuals and their families, but are still unsure about how to best meet the needs that have been identified. You should discuss this with your supervisor, who will be able to advise you about the alternatives available and the best sources of further information. This could include voluntary or private sector organisations, carers' groups, other carers or individuals already receiving a service.

Evidence   PC 1 2 5 6

Prepare a record sheet which could be used for someone about whom you have to gather information. This should include the basic factual information required by your agency, but make sure you add to it information you have obtained through your own observation or through your understanding of the individual's values, beliefs and culture.

You could organise this as a checklist so that you can use it whenever you need to gather information. Check your list against any forms that are provided by your agency and see how many additional aspects you have included. This should give you some indication of the importance of obtaining information on all aspects of the needs of individuals, not just the basic factual information which is often all that is required on agency forms.

Test yourself

1   What are the key principles of a holistic approach to assessing individuals?

2   What information will you expect to have before you start to prepare a plan of care for an individual service user?

3   Why is it important to obtain information from a range of sources?

4   Why is it important to put individuals in control of their care?

HSC 328b Support the development and implementation of care plans

Your role in developing and implementing plans of care

KS ① ② ③ ④ ⑤ ⑥ ⑦ ⑨ ⑩ ⑫ ⑭

You may be involved in a care planning meeting organised to develop or review a service user's care plan.

The individual you are working with will have identified the outcomes they want and will have chosen the support to help achieve them. You need to be clear about what you need to do to ensure that the outcomes are achieved, but the way you relate to the person you are working for is also important, as many people will have had experiences that have damaged their confidence and self esteem.

If you are responsible for developing the initial service user plan and gathering the necessary information, you must make sure that you provide all the information to the participants in the meeting as early as possible. People need time to read and consider background information before coming to a meeting so that they are able to make firm decisions about the services which should be provided. If they receive information only when they arrive at the meeting it may not be possible for a decision to be made on the spot. This can result in delays, causing frustration and disappointment for your service user.

The responsibility for organising the meeting may lie with you, someone else in your agency or another agency. You must ensure that you contact whoever is responsible for the meetings and provide all your information as soon as possible so that the meeting may proceed smoothly.

The following table provides a list of care workers and their responsibilities.

Worker	Responsible for
Social worker	Managing and co-ordinating the delivery of service provision for an individual
Domiciliary services organiser	Managing and delivering domiciliary support services, such as home help, and for assessing service level requirements
Voluntary co-ordinator	Co-ordinating and organising volunteers who provide a wide range of support services to individuals in the community
Support worker	Providing direct support to a wide range of individuals in their own homes or in hostel accommodation. This support enables people with a range of different types of needs to maintain an independent or supported living situation
Health visitor	Working with GP practice and providing help with monitoring, review and promotion within the community
Occupational therapist	Assessing needs for aids and adaptations to enable independent or supported living

You might also find you are working with other professionals such as a specialist social worker (e.g. for older people, people with sensory needs or psychiatric needs), a day centre worker, nursing staff, a GP, consultant, physiotherapist, speech therapist, housing officer, teacher, education welfare officer, careers adviser, disability employment adviser, or benefits adviser.

How to involve the service user

Meetings held between health care professionals can be very intimidating for service users and they may feel that they do not have the confidence to participate. It is important that you work to encourage the service user and his or her family or friends to feel able to make an active and effective contribution to the process. If they are to attend a meeting, you can take actions beforehand to help them feel they have a useful and important contribution to make.

1   Go through the procedure of the meeting with them so that they know exactly who will be there, what will happen, in what order matters will be discussed and the type of contributions that all of those present at the meeting will make.

2   Help them to decide what they want to say and to work out the best way to present it. This could be in a written form or they could prepare some notes in advance to ensure that they cover all the points they want to make.

3   There may be special communication issues that you need to take account of in order to enable service users to express their opinions effectively.

4   Make sure they know the different results which could come from the meeting so that they will not be surprised by any of the decisions that could be made. Explain to them that there could be a range of options for the meeting to consider.

5   You may need to work with an advocate who is acting on behalf of the service user, or you may need to consider engaging an independent advocate in order that the service user's needs and wishes can be effectively understood and explained at the meeting. Your agency may have a procedure for engaging advocates.

6   Where necessary, make practical arrangements for a service user to attend. This could include ensuring accessibility of the meeting room, providing transport where necessary, or providing translation or other communication assistance.

Encourage the service user to make an active and effective contribution to the process

Putting forward the service user's views

An individual may feel confident and well able to put across his or her own point of view. If so, your role is simply to support and encourage. However, if an individual does not feel able to put his or her views across adequately, or if there is a difference of opinion as to how his or her needs are best met, it may be your role, or the role of an advocate, to ensure that the individual's views are clearly represented and understood.

Active knowledge

Try to remember a situation where you have felt you were not in control and that other people held the power. This may have been a medical situation, for example where you were a patient and felt that you were unable to ask all the questions that you wanted to because the doctor simply did not seem to have time to answer them. It may have been a situation that involved lawyers or other professionals, or your child's teacher or head teacher. Think how much easier it might have been if someone had been acting as a support for you.

Remember how you felt in those situations, and choose one of them to act as your 'trigger' to recall those feelings whenever you are in a care planning meeting, or similar situation, with a service user. This should remind you to encourage and help the individual to put across his or her views.

There is a fine balance between representing individuals' points of view and putting across your own views about what you think may be best for them. You will need to be careful to represent an individual's views even if you think they are not the most appropriate. When you are making contributions at a meeting you should always ensure that you introduce remarks with, 'Mr X has told me that …', or 'Mrs Y has explained to me that she would prefer …', rather than, 'I think that …' or 'In my opinion the best course of action would be …'. It is important not only for accuracy, but also to make sure the individual knows that his or her views are being represented, not your own, and that he or she is the person in control.

Difficult situations

You can find yourself in a difficult position when an individual's views and expectations of the service needed are different from the views of the other professionals, or of the individual's own relatives or carers, and particularly if they differ from the views of your own agency. Your role is to represent the views of your service user, but you should not get drawn into the role of attempting to manipulate the procedure to ensure that the individual achieves his or her desired outcome.

Neither should you become involved in disputes with other professionals; you should simply ensure that the individual's views are clearly expressed. You may also wish to add your own views as a professional, and these will be based on the service user's needs and wishes.

Your own agency may have a particular view on the type of service which can be provided, based on resource limitations or agency policy and guidelines. For example, you may have a service user who wants a regular home help but expects this service to provide window cleaning in addition to normal support. You would need to explain that the original contract for services does not include this provision and that your agency may be limited in the services it can provide by issues such as the health and safety policy. However, you may be able to suggest ways in which the service user can obtain the additional service.

Look at the case study below. You may not be involved in this level of decision making in your current role, but it is important to recognise that sometimes perceptions of need may vary.

CASE STUDY: Different perceptions of need

Mr Jessop is 72 years old. His wife has recently died and although he has children they do not live locally. He is insisting that he wishes to go into residential care. Mr Jessop is not disorientated, nor is he physically frail. He is a fit and healthy 72-year-old, but he is very lonely following the death of his wife and he finds it impossible to carry out domestic tasks. He never did any domestic tasks in the house as his wife did everything, and he has no idea how to cook, clean or shop. However, he is still able to maintain his garden, which he has always done, and is happy to carry out practical tasks around the house.

The key worker has suggested that services be provided for Mr Jessop in his own home and that it would be possible for him to have support to learn how to cook simple meals and how to maintain the cleanliness of his house. However, Mr Jessop has refused these offers of help, saying that he does not believe that it is a man's role to carry out these tasks and that he needs to be in residential care so that he can have women who will look after him.

1   *Identify Mr Jessop's needs.*

2   *Do you consider that his needs will be met by residential care?*

3   *What alternatives could be considered?*

4   *Do you think that Mr Jessop's demands mask other needs?*

5   *There are three suggested outcomes to this situation. Select the one you consider to be most appropriate, or develop one of your own.*

Outcome 1

Mr Jessop's request for residential care is agreed to and he is admitted into full-time care. All of his physical needs are met, he has his own room and appears to be very content with the way in which care is provided for him. He spends his days reading the newspapers and watching TV. He is gradually becoming more and more disorientated but appears happy in the residential setting.

Outcome 2

The key worker has another service user a few streets away whose husband died about nine months ago. She is very lonely and is finding that the maintenance of her house is increasingly difficult for her to manage. She has little idea how to maintain the garden and has never undertaken jobs around the house. She also misses having someone to cook meals for and look after. The key worker introduces the two and they develop a friendship and share the tasks of daily living between them. Mr Jessop maintains the gardens and

CASE STUDY: Different perceptions of need (cont.)

houses, and she shops, cooks, and does the washing and cleaning for both of them. Both appear to be very happy with the arrangement.

Outcome 3

Mr Jessop's request for residential care is refused. However, the key worker introduces him to a cookery course at his local college which also includes the basics of home management, shopping and cleaning. He attends very reluctantly but realises that he has little choice.

As a result of attending college he finds out about other courses which are available. He has bought himself a computer and discovered the Internet. He has also joined his local over-50s swimming club, which he found out about while at college, and goes there three mornings a week. He spends his time at home surfing the Internet and 'chatting' to a wide range of people from all over the world.

6 *List the advantages and disadvantages of each of these solutions. (In case you are curious, outcome 2 was what actually happened in this particular situation.)*

Person-centred care

Government policy is increasingly focused on the importance of putting service users in control of the services they receive. Many care services are developing a person-centred approach to their work. Person-centred care is care that places 'the person' at the centre of decision making and activities; in other words, it seeks to value the individual 'personhood' of service users.

For example, in the area of services for people with a learning difficulty, the government white paper 'Valuing People' (2001) argues that services should use person-centred approaches when planning care. Person-centred means that care must be focused on the specific needs and wishes of the service user. In person-centred care, service users plan their own lives and make their own choices using help from family, friends and professionals; service users are empowered (see page 229).

In the past few years, a number of different ways of including everyone in the planning process in a meaningful way have been developed. Some of these have already been mentioned above. They include:

- advocacy
- self-advocacy
- facilitated decision making
- providing mentors and/or other support for family members
- providing training for staff and family members.

The system of having a person to speak on behalf of another person is called **advocacy**. An advocate will go with a person to a meeting, for example, and make sure that his or her views are fully expressed. **Self-advocacy** involves empowering people to speak for themselves by building their confidence, self-esteem and communication skills.

Key terms

Self-advocacy: Speaking up for oneself.

Self-directed support: A process that involves the service user playing a key role in decision making about the services he or she wants.

A key element in achieving person-centred planning is to have a **facilitator** to help people not only say what they want, but also know what's available.

In your present work role, it may be possible to assist someone in the care planning process by acting as an advocate, or even as a facilitator or mentor.

Consider the following case study.

CASE STUDY: Learning about what's available

Ellen has a learning disability and regularly uses day services provided by her local social services department. Like many people with a learning disability, she isn't used to being asked to say what she wants, and usually gives answers that she thinks the staff want to hear. She also has a limited knowledge of what kinds of things are available to her.

Person-centred planning has recently been introduced by social services, and staff have investigated ways of finding out what each service user wants. One of the workers has been on a special training course to learn how to lead groups to do this, and there is now a weekly meeting at the unit where people are helped to discover what they like.

This week, the subject is fruit. Staff have brought in a very wide range of fruits for everyone to try. As each fruit is tasted, service users explain their reaction to it by pointing to a face symbol: a smiley face for 'love it', a grumpy face for 'don't like it', and so on.

Ellen discovers that she loves fresh pineapple, something she's never tasted before, but she's not very keen on kiwi fruit.

1 *What is the value of this type of exercise?*

2 *What is its long-term aim?*

3 *Describe the reasons for starting with an unthreatening subject such as preferences for different types of fruit.*

Personhood

Some of the most vulnerable people who receive care services are older people with Alzheimer's disease or dementia. Dementia is an illness that includes problems with making sense of what is happening around you. If care is seen as concerned only with 'looking after people', 'making people better' or meeting physical needs, working with people who have dementia can feel hopeless. In the past, people with dementia were often understood as having 'no cure, no help, no hope'. Kitwood (1997) argues that there is an alternative approach to caring for people based on the principle of 'personhood'. This involves establishing a relationship involving recognition, respect and trust. The first task of a care service is to maintain a service user's sense of being a person – not to find a cure for the dementia.

Kitwood (page 84) argues that: 'The prime task of dementia care … is to maintain personhood in the face of failing mental powers. Now it is possible to go further and suggest that this will occur through the sensitive meeting of this cluster of needs.' Kitwood's approach to maintaining personhood is summarised below.

Need	Explanation
Comfort	The soothing of pain and sorrow, the calming of anxiety, the feeling of security that comes from being close to another.
Attachment	Without the reassurance that attachments provide it is difficult for any person, of whatever age, to function well.
Inclusion	All people need a distinct place in the shared life of a group. Individual care plans may overlook the social needs of individuals.
Occupation	People need a sense of purpose, to be involved in personally significant activities that draw on their abilities.
Identity	To have an identity is to know who one is, to have a sense of continuity with the past, and hence a narrative, a story to present to others.

Kitwood's approach might be seen as arguing for person-centred relationships. A person-centred approach involves more than simply providing choice. It places great value on the social, emotional and identity needs of each unique individual.

A care setting may meet the needs identified by Kitwood in the following ways.

Comfort	Offering services such as foot massage and aromatherapy
Attachment	Trying to build supportive relationships with service users
Inclusion	Listening carefully to service users – despite the difficulties
Occupation	Reminiscence activities
Identity	Care workers learning about service users' history

If you do not work with people with dementia the type of support and activities provided in your place of work may be very different from the examples given above, but the basic principle of person-centred care – focusing on understanding the emotional needs and preferences of individuals – may translate into your service.

How to communicate care choices to the individual KS ① ② ③ ④ ⑤ ⑩ ⑫ ⑬

If a care planning meeting has gone well and there is sufficient information on which to develop a service user plan, you may be able to present the individual with a proposal for consideration. You may find that you need to explain in detail the choices available. Even if the service user and his or her family and friends have been present at the meeting, you may find that you need to go over the information that was discussed and the decisions reached. It is extremely important that you provide the individual with a record in written or other accessible form of the decisions taken at the planning meeting so that there is no misunderstanding about the choices available.

It is also important that you do not, by your behaviour, discourage individuals from commenting on the proposals. It is sometimes easy to give the impression that everything is already organised and agreed. Ensure that you always make it clear the individual has an opportunity to comment on any proposals. For example, you should always check that:

- you are not suggesting these are the only choices, and that if the individual does not agree to them no service can be provided at all
- you are not 'selling' the service-user plan by making it sound ideal, so that the individual feels you will be disappointed if he or she rejects it
- you are not making the individual feel guilty at being dissatisfied with the plan by implying, for example, that there are a great many others who would be grateful for the level of service that is being suggested.

Being aware of how you influence service users is an important part of working in an effective, caring way; you need to be aware of the effect your words and actions are having on others. Never assume that an individual will agree with your perspective.

Keeping all parties informed

One of your key roles in this process is to provide information to the service user and all those who are involved in the process about the precise services proposed. For example, if you are giving information to an individual about a proposal for providing day care, this will include details about:

- the exact nature of the day care proposed
- the location of the day care
- the type of care offered
- the general aims and atmosphere of the facility
- the number of people who attend
- what the transport arrangements will be.

One of your key roles is to provide information to the service user

Informed choice can only be made with this kind of detail. If necessary, you should offer to make arrangements for the individual and his or her relatives or carers to visit any establishments that are part of the proposal for care services.

How to record service-user plans

 KS ①②④⑤⑦

Once you have produced a plan that the service user is happy with, and any changes have been discussed with all the relevant people involved, you should ensure that those decisions are recorded in such a way that all of those involved with the process can access them readily. You may want to consider using a form for recording the outcomes of the planning meeting and simply add to it any subsequent changes made and agreed.

Keys to good practice: Maintaining good communication

✔ Communicate all information clearly and in a way that can be understood.

✔ Make sure individuals' views are clearly represented to any forum where decisions are being taken or proposals formulated.

✔ Support the individual to put forward his or her own views wherever possible.

✔ Clearly record information and planning proposals and ensure that all the relevant people involved receive them.

✔ Make sure the individual and his or her relatives, friends or carers receive the planning proposals in a form they can access and understand.

✔ Ensure they have the opportunity to comment in their own time on the proposals and in an atmosphere where they feel able to make criticisms if necessary.

✔ Ensure that all final proposals for care provision have the agreement of the individual and those who are involved in his or her care.

✔ Ensure that all of those involved with the process are kept informed of any changes and updates made to the proposals.

✔ Ensure that records are stored securely and that confidentiality is maintained.

Evidence   PC ①

Think about an individual you are currently working with. Consider all your actions in respect of that individual and whether he or she was given a choice in the services provided.

If you believe the individual was given every possible choice, then list the ways in which you ensured that was the case. If you believe the individual's choice was restricted unnecessarily, identify the reasons why this happened and the steps you could take to ensure that it does not happen again.

How to support the care plan activities

KS 2 3 4 10 11 13 16

When a care plan is in place, as well as carrying out your own duties under the plan you will need to support colleagues to carry out those activities that are their responsibility.

Monitoring the impact of the care plan

Monitoring is essential to ensure that any plan of care is continuing to meet the needs it was designed to meet. A plan of care will have originally been assessed, planned and put in place to meet a particular set of circumstances. The original service user plan should include plans for monitoring and review, because plans put in place with even the most thorough assessment and careful planning will not necessarily be appropriate in six months or a year's time, and continue to provide services of the quality or at the level originally expected.

Monitoring may seem a complex process but its principles are very simple. Most of us monitor many things in our lives on a regular basis without realising it.

Active knowledge

If you use a car and buy petrol for it regularly, then you probably monitor the cost. For example, you might compare the cost at your local garage with supermarket prices. Depending on whether you are in a hurry, you might choose the cheaper petrol at the supermarket, or the convenience of buying at the local garage.

Think of other examples of monitoring in your everyday life, for example the quality of the food you buy, and your own health and well-being. Make notes about how and why you monitor.

Monitoring of care services needs to pick up changes in the circumstances of those receiving the services, their carers and the service provider. The original care plan will include forms of care and support that reflect the individual's needs at the time. For example, someone recently discharged from hospital following treatment for mental health problems may receive quite extensive support under the care programme approach, consisting of day care, community psychiatric nurse visits, and access to a support group of carers. However, feedback on that individual's progress may show his or her mental health has improved to the point that day care is no longer needed on the previous level and that an alternative service, such as support in finding employment, is now far more appropriate. A service that is frequently monitored is likely to be one which is responsive to the needs of the individual, and is also an effective use of the resources of the health service or social services department responsible for funding.

Checking resources

Checking on resources can also be important if changes in the availability of those resources means that a care package will have to be altered in some way. A reduction in available funding or an increase in demand for a particular resource may mean that adjustments in the level of service provision will have to be made. Regular monitoring makes it easier to be aware of where resources are being used and where changes need to be made.

Steve, I'm really sorry but a decrease in resource availability coupled with an increase in the demand level for specific resources has led us to review your levels of access to particular services.

What on earth does that mean?

It means we're having to cut some of your services.

Communicating with carers

Regular monitoring and feedback should cover the needs of carers, to make sure the provisions are still meeting their needs. Carers should also be included in providing feedback about the service. Regular feedback from carers, and the knowledge that they will contact you if circumstances change, can be taken into account when monitoring.

However, it is not appropriate or reasonable to put all the responsibility on a carer to notify you when changes take place. Carers cope with tremendous demands on their time and energy, both physical and emotional. Whatever systems you agree in order to keep up to date with feedback from carers, you must make sure you are not placing even more demands on their time.

Ways of monitoring

 KS 1 2 4 8 10 11 12 13 15 16

Whatever approach your agency takes to monitoring, it will be decided at the outset how a particular plan of care will be monitored and the methods will be agreed with the individual and his or her carers. Your feedback will be an essential part of the process. A monitoring process will involve the following key people:

- the individual receiving the service
- his or her carers or family
- other health care professionals
- the service provider – whose performance will be monitored.

Monitoring by the individual

Obviously the most important person in any monitoring process is the individual receiving the service, so he or she must be clear about how to record and feed back information on the way the care package is working. This can be through:

- completing a checklist on a regular basis (weekly or monthly)
- maintaining regular contact with the care manager/co-ordinator, either by telephone or through a visit
- using an electronic checking and monitoring form which would be e-mailed on a regular basis to the care manager/co-ordinator
- recording and reporting any changes in his or her own circumstances or changes in the provision of the care package.

Opposite is an example of a feedback form from an individual in care.

Have there been any changes in your health since the last report? If so, please say what.	Not really - much the same
Have there been any changes in your circumstances since the last report? If so, please say what.	My sister has come to live a few streets away
Are the services you receive still giving the support you need?	Yes, still very good, but don't need day centre on Thursdays now as my sister takes me out every Thursday
How would you like the services to change what you receive?	Cancel Thursday at the day centre, but everything else is fine

A feedback form from an individual in care

Monitoring by carers and families

Carers and families are likely to participate in the monitoring of a care package in similar ways. You will need to make sure that carers are willing to participate in monitoring and they do not feel you are adding yet another burden to their lives.

Monitoring by other health care professionals

Maintaining contact between reviews with other professionals who may be involved with the individual is an essential part of the monitoring process. The most effective method of doing this is to agree the types of changes that will trigger contact. For example:

- the GP may be asked to notify the care manager of any significant health changes or hospital admissions

- the community nurse may be asked to notify any problems in compliance with treatment, or changes in the individual's ability to administer his or her own medication, or changes in home conditions
- the physiotherapist may be asked to notify any significant changes in performance.

You may be asked to report any significant changes in an individual's performance

There may be other professionals involved, such as occupational or speech therapists, depending on the circumstances of the individual. The principles of monitoring remain the same. Professionals will need to be particularly vigilant in reporting any changes which could mean that the individual is at risk of receiving inadequate care under the current plans.

Feedback from care professionals

Your role in administering the plan of care means that you are in an ideal position to identify changes in an individual's circumstances that may mean a service is no longer appropriate. It may need to be increased, decreased or changed in order to meet a new situation. The changes do not have to be major, but they can have a significant impact on a person's life.

How to identify significant changes that affect the care package

Throughout any monitoring and evaluation process you are looking for and responding to change. It is important you are clear about the difference between types of changes that require action, and those which are simply a part of everyday life and do not involve a major re-think of a care package. For example, an individual who inherits £50,000 will experience significant change, whereas someone who receives a £1.20 per week increase in Income Support will not! Both, however, have experienced a change in their financial circumstances.

Similarly, someone who changes from working two days each week to a full-time job experiences a significant change which will involve alterations in the care package he or she receives. But someone who changes from working two days each week as a telephonist to working the same two days as a receptionist is unlikely to need significant changes in any care package.

CASE STUDY: Acknowledging change

Miss Pugh is aged 73. She lives alone and is a retired floor manager from a large local department store. She has had support from the home help and mobile meals service since her mobility deteriorated with the increasing severity of her arthritis over the last five years. She was a fiercely independent lady who had always refused to accept any benefits or support in addition to her state pension. After finally getting her agreement to review her finances, her key worker had identified that she had some additional benefits due to her from her company pension scheme. This had increased Miss Pugh's monthly income considerably and had eased her financial situation. However, this change in circumstances had also put her income above the payment threshold for home-help service and she now has to pay for the service that she had previously received at no charge. Miss Pugh is angry at this and is considering cancelling the home-help service, although she would find it extremely difficult to manage without it.

1 *How would you explain the situation to Miss Pugh?*

2 *What are the skills you would need in order to successfully encourage Miss Pugh to continue using support services?*

3 *Should such a possibility have been discussed with Miss Pugh in advance of obtaining her agreement to review her finances?*

Active knowledge

Look at your own circumstances over the past 10 years and make a list of the ways in which they have changed. For example, you may have more children than you had 10 years ago, or some children may have left home and moved away. Members of your family may have died or been born in the past 10 years, you could be living in a larger or a smaller house, you could have more money or less money, you could be doing a different job. All these are major changes which have taken place in your life in just the short period of 10 years. Listing them will help you see the types of situations that change and affect people's lives.

Then take a much shorter period, for example the past year, and look at much smaller changes which may have happened to you during that time. They could be changes in your finances and your job role. You could now be undertaking a qualification, you may be driving a different car, you may have acquired digital television – any number of small changes have affected the way you are living your life. Again, make a list of these changes and consider the impact each of them has had. Although the second list may have had a smaller impact than some of the big changes you listed in your first reflection, they will nonetheless have combined to bring about some quite significant changes in your lifestyle.

Consider the results of this exercise when you are thinking about the importance of contributing to the monitoring of care programmes which are in place for people you work with.

Possible changes in service users' circumstances

There are many aspects of service users' lives that could change. Some examples are shown below.

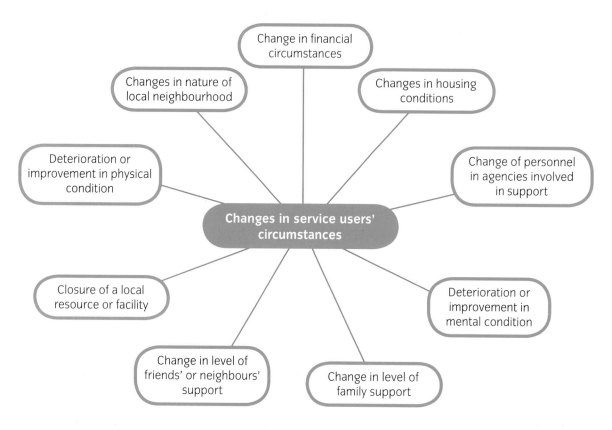

Change in financial circumstances

Changes in nature of local neighbourhood

Changes in housing conditions

Deterioration or improvement in physical condition

Change of personnel in agencies involved in support

Changes in service users' circumstances

Closure of a local resource or facility

Deterioration or improvement in mental condition

Change in level of friends' or neighbours' support

Change in level of family support

CASE STUDY: Changing levels of support

Katherine is a woman in her early 50s. She has Parkinson's disease, her level of mobility has been decreasing gradually over the past three years, and she has recently begun to fall frequently. She lives with her two sons aged 19 and 25, and her only contact with health and care provision so far has been through her hospital consultant and the primary care team. Her service requirements have been mainly medical with regular support from a physiotherapist.

Her increase in falling has coincided with a major change in her circumstances. Her younger son has been offered a place at an excellent university and her older son has been headhunted for his dream job in the United States on a two-year contract. Katherine does not want either of her sons to miss the opportunities they have been offered – so she now wants to discuss the ways in which she can arrange support that will allow her to remain as independent as possible.

1   *Who should be the first professionals Katherine holds discussions with?*
2   *Who else should be involved in planning?*
3   *How would you help to ensure that Katherine retained control of the process?*
4   *What feelings would you anticipate Katherine would have about her change in circumstances?*
5   *What steps do you think should be taken to make sure that Katherine remains independent?*

Keys to good practice: Developing and implementing care plans

✔ Support the individual in making a direct contribution to the process of planning his or her own care programme, and in expressing preferences.

✔ Check that proposals made by professional agencies meet with the agreement of the individual before starting any programme of care.

✔ Ensure that you are able to carry out the care plan activities for which you are responsible.

✔ Support colleagues to carry out the care plan activities for which they are responsible.

✔ Make arrangements to regularly feed back on the provision of the service.

✔ Contribute to arrangements for regularly reviewing the service and make sure that the individual is involved throughout the process.

Test yourself

1 What are the main points to remember about your role in developing and implementing care plans for the individuals you work with?

2 List three ways in which you could support individuals to comment on the content of the care plan.

3 Why is it important to monitor plans of care?

4 Describe three ways in which you could monitor a plan of care, and suggest the circumstances in which you would use the different methods.

5 What are some of the changes that could be made to a care plan as a result of monitoring?

HSC 328c Contribute to reviewing care plans

The purpose of reviews

 KS 16

Reviews are essential because care situations very rarely remain the same for long periods of time. As circumstances change, the package of care may need to be reviewed in the light of those changes. At agreed intervals, all of the parties involved should come together to reflect on whether or not the package of care is continuing to do the job it was initially set up to do. If there were no reviews, the arrangements could continue for years regardless of whether they were still meeting care needs.

A review will gather together all the information about the circumstances of the individual, the service provided and the service provider. It will give all those concerned with the care of the individual the opportunity to express their opinions and to be involved in a discussion about how effective care provision has been and the changes, if any, that need to be made.

The review process

 KS ① ② ③ ④ ⑤ ⑦ ⑧ ⑩ ⑪ ⑫ ⑬ ⑯

Any review should attempt to obtain the views of as many people as possible who are involved in the care of the individual. The most important people at the review are the individual and his or her carers or family. You, as the person (or one of the people) providing services from the plan of care, are a very important contributor. The key worker or care manager/co-ordinator is also central to the review process, as is any organisation providing the care.

It is also important that others with an interest in the care of the individual have the opportunity to participate in a review. For example, a GP, health visitor, community psychiatric nurse, community occupational therapist, physiotherapist, speech therapist, welfare rights support worker, representative of a support group, or anyone else who has been a significant contributor to the life and care of the individual concerned should be involved if at all possible. The status of all the participants should be equal, in that everyone has the opportunity to give a view and to contribute to the discussion. However, the key person who must agree to any review decision is the individual concerned.

Remember

Nothing stays the same – everything is subject to change. This includes all aspects of people's circumstances. You must make sure that the care people receive changes in line with any changes in their lives.

People who might be involved in a review

GP

Community psychiatric nurse

Key worker

Relative

Service user

Speech therapist

Health visitor

Representative from a support group

How the review process is managed

The care manager/co-ordinator or key worker is likely to be the person responsible for organising the review itself and making sure that it takes place at the appropriate time. If the individual receiving care is receiving direct payment, he or she is likely to take responsibility for initiating a review if it is felt to be necessary. Where direct payments are involved your role is very different; it is simply one of being there to provide support and assistance if it is required by the individual. You would only become involved in a review if that was requested by the individual.

The person managing the review is likely to go through a checklist similar to the one below to make sure that the review meets the needs of the individual concerned.

Review checklist

1   Does the individual understand what a review is?

2   Do the individual's carers also understand what a review is and its purpose?

3   Is the review arranged at an appropriate time to check progress?

4   Is this an annual review or has it been triggered by a change in the individual's circumstances?

5   Does the review cover whether the individual continues to need the same level of support and services, whether there have been any changes, what the original care plan intended, and the results of monitoring?

6   Has the individual been asked when and where would be convenient for the review?

7   Has it been explained to the individual which decisions the review is able to take in respect of his or her continuing care provision and the development of a new care plan?

8   Has the individual been offered an advocate in order to help him or her prepare for the review, to support or to speak for him or her at the review?

9   Does the individual know who is responsible for making sure that the review meeting is managed?

10   Does the individual know all of the people who will be at the review?

11   Can all of the participants contribute either in writing or verbally to the review?

12   Do all the participants in the care plan know that they can request a review?

13   Have carers been consulted about the appropriate time and location for the review?

14   Have crèche facilities been offered for anyone who needs them so that they can attend the review?

During the review everyone should be given a chance to contribute. If the individual receiving care has chosen to use an advocate to present his or her point of view, this person should have every opportunity to contribute on the individual's behalf. If some choose to communicate in writing or by other means, such as e-mail, then those comments must be taken into account. If there have been any changes in organisational policies or access to resources, or changes in the circumstances of the service provider, these are also key matters and should be fed into the review for consideration.

If any conflict or difficulty arises in relation to the care plan because of feedback or observations, you must ensure that organisational procedures are followed to address the issues raised.

Supporting people to contribute

You may need to support the individual to recognise the impact of significant change and to identify the differences between important and unimportant changes. You may wish to use a prompt such as:

> Sara, your sister coming to live nearby is something which has happened to you since the last review, isn't it? Do you think things will change much for you?

> John, have you found that your new job has made much of a difference to you?

> Marvin, has having an extra afternoon at the centre made the difference you hoped for at the last review?

You may also need to support individuals to complete any paperwork that is necessary for the review or for the implementation of any revised care plan.

Care workers and other members of your team may also need support in order to contribute to the review meeting. They may feel intimidated, particularly if they are unfamiliar with speaking in front of a roomful of people.

You can encourage them to prepare for the meeting by:
- putting together a list of all the records they have kept on the individual
- informing them of their role in the meeting and preparing them for questions they may be asked
- checking they are familiar with your organisational procedures and that they understand the process.

Making decisions

Once all the information has been gathered and all contributions have been made, those taking part in the review will need to make a decision about any necessary changes to the care plan and the care package for the next period of time. Decisions should clearly be based on the monitoring of evidence and should particularly take account of contributions from the individual and his or her carers.

A review should not take a decision about changing provision with which the individual fundamentally disagrees. If the proposed changes are because of a change in the level of available resources and result in a reduction in service to the individual, it may be that such a decision is inevitable. However, it is important that the alternative which will be in place is acceptable to the individual.

If the individual is dissatisfied at the end of the review, it is important he or she is informed about the complaints procedure and the process for asking for a further review of the resources available. Full access should be ensured by offering advocacy or any other support services that may be required for individuals to take full advantage of any complaints system or further routes to changing decisions, such as approaching decision makers or accessing pressure groups.

Setting the next review date

At the end of each review it is essential that the date is set for the next review and that all the participants, particularly the individual and his or her carers, find the date acceptable, both in terms of their own availability and the length of time before the review is due to take place.

Reviews must be undertaken at least once a year and if an individual is receiving a care package under the care programme approach system through the mental health services, any admission to hospital must generate a review within a month of discharge.

Evidence   PC 6 7

Carry out an analysis of the last care plan review in which you were involved. Consider:

- the roles and responsibilities of the people involved in the review
- the quality and detail of the feedback
- whether changes were identified
- whether the review was person-centred
- how any conflict was handled
- how the review was recorded.

Keep your notes for your portfolio.

How the review process is recorded

 KS ① ④ ⑤ ⑥ ⑦ ⑩ ⑪

 Keys to good practice: Recording a care package review

All reviews must be recorded in the individual's records. Confidentiality must be respected and the records must include:

✔ written reports from each care service included in the care package

✔ a record that all relevant staff have been invited to attend the review or to contribute in writing

✔ a record showing how the individual has been prepared for the review and the access he or she has to an advocate if required

✔ evidence that relevant carers and others who offer support have been invited to contribute

✔ a record of all those who attended or who contributed

✔ a careful record of any changes

✔ the revised care plan as a separate document.

Many organisations still have their own documentation (although under the single assessment process, joint records are increasingly being produced). They are likely to cover most or all of the above points.

It is important that all those who have contributed, even if they have not been present at the review, are informed of the outcome and that they know of any changes to the care plan for the individual.

Recorded reviews contribute to the overall quality of the service any organisation offers and they are likely to be included in any file audit undertaken during inspection processes. The review process, if it is well conducted, provides a vital opportunity for individuals to contribute and to make choices about the care package they receive.

Reviews that are badly prepared and carelessly undertaken rob individuals of the opportunity to take decisions which affect their lives significantly, and they also result in an ineffective use of scarce and valuable resources.

Test yourself

Mrs McPhail is a woman aged 91. She lives alone and is finding it increasingly difficult to get upstairs to the bathroom and also to bed. Fortunately her house has a downstairs toilet, but because of her difficulty in accessing the bathroom her personal hygiene has deteriorated, and she has also begun to sleep in an armchair instead of making her way upstairs to her bedroom.

1 What should happen now for Mrs McPhail?

2 Who should be involved in considering the next steps?

3 How can you make sure that Mrs McPhail is involved in the process?

4 In what ways can changes such as these be monitored?

5 Who is responsible for monitoring changes for Mrs McPhail?

HSC 328 FURTHER READING AND RESEARCH

Here are some books, websites and agencies you can go to for further information. When assisting to create a plan of care you should, however, remember that the first place to go for information should always be the individual.

www.dh.gov.uk (Department of Health)

www.directgov.co.uk (Direct Gov)

www.csci.org.uk (Commission for Social Care Inspection)

www.scie.org.uk (Social Care Institute of Excellence)

Local Authority/Social Services in your area (this can be found through an Internet search or in the Yellow Pages)

Bradley, A., Murray, K. Couman, L. (2007) *My Life Plan; Interactive Resource for Person Centred Planning* Pavilion Publishers

Heath, H., Watson, R. (2005) *Older People: Assessment for Health and Social Care* Age Concern

Leader, A. *Direct Power; A Resource Pack for People Who Want to Develop Their Own Care Plans and Support Networks* Pavilion Publishers

Maclean, S., Basnett, F., Drayton-Green, D., Blunn, C., (2004) *Health Care Issues for Social Care Staff* Kirwin Maclean Associates

Mansell, J., Beadle-Brown, J., Ashman, B., Ockenden, J. *Person-Centred Active Support* Pavilion Publishers

Unit HSC 330

Support individuals to access and use services and facilities

In this unit you will have the opportunity to think about how you can best support individuals to identify and communicate their needs and how you can pass information to individuals that will enable them to gain access to the most useful services and facilities. Regardless of your role and area of work, you will at some point need to provide information to those you work with or their relatives or friends. It is important that you understand how to access and update that information and how you can assist people, not only to consider services but to use them where they need support.

Information is knowledge, and it makes a huge contribution towards empowering people. Familiarity with the services and facilities that are available and accessible will provide service users with the opportunity to increase their level of independence.

What you need to learn

- How to establish the services needed
- How to obtain accurate information
- Legislation about information
- How information is stored
- Reviewing information
- How to make information accessible
- How to support people to use services
- Overcoming barriers
- Enabling people to use services and facilities
- How to evaluate services and facilities
- Methods of checking information
- How to give useful feedback on services and facilities.

HSC 330a Support individuals to identify services and facilities they need

How to establish the services needed

 KS ①②④⑪⑯⑱

The key word in the title of this element is 'individuals'. You need to be sure that you establish people's individual needs and wants in connection with services and facilities.

This is not about what you think would be best for someone, tempting as it may be to try to persuade people to make use of a facility you think would benefit them. That is not your role. Your role is to support individuals to identify and communicate what they want and need in order to improve their own health and social well-being. Their carers should also be encouraged to identify support that would help them fulfil their caring role. You need to give both individuals and carers the information that will help them to reach their own conclusions.

Do not assume that everyone will be in a position to ask directly for the information they need. In order to be able to ask for what you need, you have to know the right questions to ask and you have to know something about the solutions that exist. For example, how could an older person ask about attending a luncheon club unless he or she knew that such a thing exists? How could a carer looking after a parent with Alzheimer's ask about a local carers' support group unless he or he was aware of its existence?

Individuals need to know what is available before they can decide what they would like to do

Asking the right questions

To establish the type of information or services that an individual needs you may have to access records on the individual's needs, views and preferences, but you may also have to ask quite a few questions. You cannot rely on individuals being able to identify what it is they want. You will need to use your listening skills in order to pick up what it is that individuals are looking for.

It can also help if you ask some prompting questions. This may help to point people in the general direction of a service or facility that they would like to use. The type of questions to use are those beginning: 'Would you like …?', 'Would it help if …?', 'Would you enjoy …?'.

To give people the maximum possible choice in reaching their decisions it may be better to phrase your questions generally. 'Would you enjoy some company for lunch once or twice a week?' may be better than 'Would you like to go to the luncheon club at the community centre once or twice a week?'.

Posing a question in this way allows an individual to gradually get used to a new idea and to think about his or her preferences. It also allows people to stop at the point where they feel they have made enough commitment for the present. It may be sufficient for a first conversation to establish that an individual would like some company; it may take a little more time to decide that he or she would like to join with a group of other people at a luncheon club, rather than arrange for someone to visit once or twice a week. The general question has allowed the individual to make a decision about the idea of company. Later discussion can establish exactly the form and the setting in which company would be welcome. If you had begun the discussion with full details of the luncheon club and the community centre, this may have provoked a negative response from an individual who may not be keen on meeting a lot of strangers in a strange building.

Taking decisions

With careful thought and full information given at the right time, decisions can be taken at a pace that suits the individual. This careful pace will also enable you to be sure that the individual has understood any information you have shared with him or her.

Of course, you may not always be in the position of gradually widening the options for an individual. There may be circumstances where you are faced with the opposite. For example, if you work with a young, enthusiastic person with learning difficulties or a disability, who wants to know about a wide range of opportunities and facilities, you may find that you have to carefully assist him or her to achieve a realistic view of how many things can be undertaken at any one time.

Young people with disabilities may want to take advantage of a wide range of opportunities and facilities

The golden rule is to go at the individuals' pace, whatever that may be, and provide the information they require about the services they consider to be important. Be careful not to limit the information you provide, or the ways in which you provide it, because you believe that a particular facility or service is unsuitable for someone. The choice is theirs, and the job of supporting them to access the information is yours.

 Keys to good practice: Investigating wants and needs

✓ Get to know the individual's interests and needs.

✓ Proceed at the individual's pace.

✓ Do not impose your views about suitability or appropriateness.

✓ Be realistic about what is available.

✓ Keep your information accurate and up to date.

Identifying strengths and weaknesses

You should support individuals to identify their own strengths, and those of their current support network. Any gaps in the current arrangements and any opportunities to improve the individual's health and well-being should be investigated.

If you have worked with individuals for a period of time and have got to know them, and possibly their carers too, it will be much easier for you to know about their needs and interests and the types of services and facilities that are likely to be useful. It is then easier to raise questions about any new facilities or services that they may wish to try. Carers are likely to have ideas about the kind of support that would be most appropriate in helping them fulfil their caring role.

However, you will also need to take care that you do not encourage unrealistic expectations about services and facilities available in the local area. When you are asking questions about services and facilities that an individual and/or his or her carer would like to use, take care that you only provide definite information about those of which you are certain. If you have any doubt whether a particular service or facility is provided in your local area or is restricted because of lack of resources, you should say that you will find out more information and let the individual know.

Under the direct payment system, individuals may have access to funds so that they organise and pay for their own care. But it will still be an important part of your role to provide relevant information.

It may be useful to have a list which you check regularly in respect of all the individuals you work with about the services and facilities that may be of value to them. Facilities vary greatly from area to area and from setting to setting. However, the following table shows a general picture of the services and facilities which individuals may find useful, and which you should be able to provide information about.

Services and facilities checklist

What	Who	Where
Meals	Social services or voluntary organisation, commercial organisation e.g. supermarket	Social services department, Internet
Home care	Social services or independent provider, private care agencies	Social services department
Family support	Social services or independent sector	Social services department
Shopping	Local voluntary organisations, local supermarkets	Library, Citizens Advice Bureau, social services department, local church, Internet, local supermarkets
Lunch or social clubs	Social services or local voluntary organisations	Social services department, library, Citizens Advice Bureau, local church
Holidays and outings	Specialist travel companies (e.g. Saga, Winged Fellowship), social services, specialist voluntary organisations (e.g. Royal National Institute for the Blind, Mencap, Scope, Age Concern)	Social services department, library, Citizens Advice Bureau, Internet, travel agent

Continued

What	Who	Where
Pensions/benefits	Benefits Agency, social services, Welfare Rights Centre, voluntary organisations	Welfare Rights Centre, Claimant's Union, Benefits Agency, Citizens Advice Bureau
Education	Local education office, college of further education, library	Town or county hall, telephone directory, Internet
Sports	Leisure services department, specialist voluntary organisations (e.g. National Organisation for Sport for the Disabled, International Paralympic Committee, Riding for the Disabled)	Town hall, Citizens Advice Bureau, library, Internet, Yellow Pages
Mobile library	Libraries/leisure services department	Town hall
Cinema, theatre and entertainment, clubs and pubs	Leisure services department, theatres and cinemas, local tourist office	Town hall, library, Internet, What's On guide, tourist office, local newspapers

CASE STUDY: Finding out about needs

Vijay was a young man in his mid-twenties who used a wheelchair following a spinal injury. Vijay was provided with 24-hour care and had a team of support workers. Recently Vijay had appeared to be somewhat unhappy. He said he was bored and wanted something more exciting to do. His support worker suggested a range of options including visiting the cinema, the theatre, going to a social club or visiting an art gallery – all of which were interests of Vijay's. However, every suggestion was rejected without Vijay giving any clear reason why.

A few days later a different support worker decided to approach matters in a different way, and through questioning she established that Vijay would very much like to take up any of the suggestions made earlier, but had assumed that to do any of them he needed to take a taxi and this was something he felt unable to afford. Vijay had not liked to say that he could not afford the taxi and so had simply refused any of the suggestions.

The second support worker was able to explain to Vijay that the local authority operated a dial-a-ride service with a small bus specially adapted for wheelchairs, and that Vijay could book this service and use it for a nominal charge. There was also a taxicard scheme entitling eligible users to a certain number of taxi journeys per month at dial-a-ride prices. Vijay was delighted and began to make plans for a range of visits and activities.

1   *What was the mistake made in giving information to Vijay?*

2   *What may have happened if the second support worker had not spoken to Vijay?*

3   *What can you learn from this?*

How to obtain accurate information

 KS ② ⑤ ⑦ ⑪ ⑫

No one expects you to have your head full of information to pass on to people! However, you do need to know where to find information and the best and most efficient ways of doing so. You also need to know how to keep information so that you have access to it whenever you need to use or update it.

We now live in an information society – masses of information are available on more subjects than you ever knew existed. It is easy to become confused and end up with information that will not serve a useful purpose for the individuals you work with.

Local sources of information

One of the most useful sources of information is the 'one-stop shop' approach of organisations such as the Citizens Advice Bureau. You may also find that your local Council for Voluntary Service or your local authority may have an information point; these are often located in libraries, town halls, civic centres or other easily accessible places. At these points you can usually obtain leaflets and information, and staff are available to find out more for you and to offer advice on specific areas of need. Most advice centres will find information for you if they do not have it to hand.

You may be looking for specific information in response to an individual's request or you may be generally updating your own information so that you are ready to deal promptly with any information requests. In either case, any of these facilities provide you with a very good starting point.

Many excellent sources of information are available to you locally

Special interest groups

Another excellent source of information is the range of specific interest groups such as Age Concern, the Alzheimer's Society, Mencap, Scope, and so on.

These are a wonderful source of information about facilities and services, specifically related to those with a particular condition. The contact addresses and telephone numbers for these organisations will be found at your starting point advice centre, such as the Citizens Advice Bureau or your local library or voluntary services. All of these organisations also have websites with a wealth of information and links to other websites of interest. The websites can be found by typing the name of an organisation, or of a condition such as Alzheimer's, into a search engine such as Google.

The Internet

One of the best sources of information is the Internet. To use this you will need access to a computer connected to the Internet and some skill or experience in using the various search engines in order to locate relevant websites.

The information that you can obtain from the Internet is almost unlimited and covers every possible subject. However, you must be aware that this information is not subject to any form of verification or control, and therefore it is not always possible to confirm its accuracy. If you are finding information from the Internet to pass on to individuals, you should obtain it primarily from official websites of relevant organisations for the particular area of interest.

Other useful websites are official government sites and those of universities and research establishments. You may find that there are government reports and results of inquiries, or research findings, that are relevant to individuals with whom you work. Using the Internet can be a very quick and easy way of gaining accurate and up-to-date information, often before it has appeared in print or become readily accessible in other ways.

Encouraging individuals to use the Internet

For many individuals, accessing information for themselves over the Internet can be useful and can motivate them to explore the huge potential of the World Wide Web. This can provide many people with a new hobby, as can be seen from the massive interest in 'Silver Surfers' groups being run around the country by Age Concern. The take-up of these classes for older people has been huge, and many people now have the skills to access information for themselves. Beware of assuming that anyone over the age of 60 knows nothing about 'surfing the Net' – you may be surprised to find that they are much more able than you are!

The Internet can also provide many people with the opportunity to network with others who have similar interests and issues. This can help to broaden

Remember

When researching information on the Internet, be careful to use reliable websites such as official government sites and those of reputable organisations.

the social contacts of individuals who may otherwise find themselves with limited opportunities for such contact. However, you should make sure individuals are well aware of the basic precautions that should be taken when using the Internet in this way:

- remember that because of free and unrestricted access to the Internet, not every message is genuine and truthful
- never give out your address, telephone number or any financial information
- if you arrange to meet someone you have come into contact with via the Internet, meet in a public place and do not go alone.

There are also many useful opportunities for education and training via online learning materials. This can make learning more accessible and may offer the chance for new knowledge and understanding which may not be available through traditional teaching approaches.

There are increasing opportunities for people to access the Internet even if they do not have their own computers. Cyber cafés and many libraries, local town halls, colleges and universities have facilities for public access to the Internet, usually for a small fee. You might encourage people to take advantage of these if appropriate. As always, the best approach is to support individuals to be self-managing and to find out information for themselves.

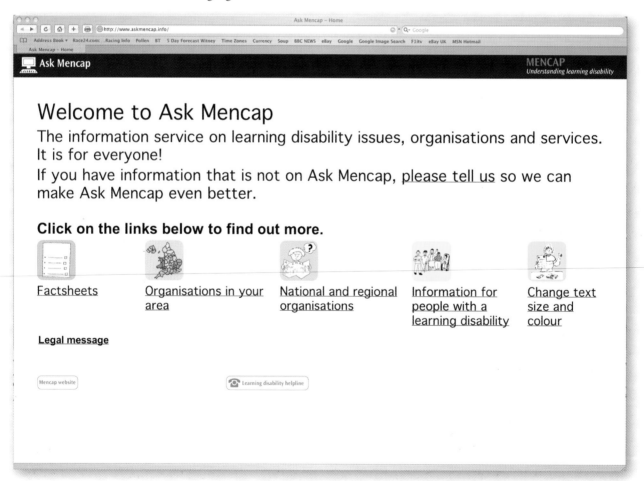

Mencap's website is an excellent source of easy-to-access information

Legislation about information

 KS ① ⑦ ⑧ ⑨ ⑩

Access to information is broadly governed by two Acts of Parliament. The first is the **Data Protection Act 1998**, which restricts the way in which personal information can be used and limits those who can access information about individuals. There are basic principles which govern the way information must be handled.

All information, however it is stored, is subject to the rules laid down in the Act; it covers medical records, social service records, credit information, local authority information – in fact, anything which is personal data (facts and opinions about an individual).

Anyone processing personal data must comply with the eight enforceable principles of good practice. As you saw in Unit HSC 31, these say that data must be:

- fairly and lawfully processed
- processed for limited purposes
- adequate, relevant and not excessive
- accurate
- not kept for longer than necessary
- processed in accordance with the data subject's rights
- kept secure
- not transferred to countries without adequate protection.

You will need to be aware of these restrictions in case an individual asks you for help in finding out information about someone else.

The other piece of relevant legislation is the **Freedom of Information Act 2000**. This Act is about accessing information held by public bodies such as local councils, the National Health Service and the government. It is concerned with records about the activities and plans of public bodies, not about individuals.

You need to be aware of the laws that are concerned with access to information

Each public body must set out the details of information it will routinely make available, how the information can be obtained and whether there is any charge for it. Each public authority must comply with requests for the information it holds unless an exemption from disclosure applies. Public authorities normally have a maximum of 20 working days to respond to a request.

This will be useful if you are helping someone find out about the policies and decision-making of a public body.

How information is stored  KS 2 12 18

Once you have obtained information for an individual, or to keep your own knowledge up to date and current, you need to be sure that you can store it in an accessible way. You can rely on your memory for many of the main facts, but clearly you need to record individual addresses, telephone numbers, website addresses and detailed information about the services provided.

It is a good idea to create an information store where you can keep leaflets, notes, telephone numbers and cuttings from newspapers or magazines which may be of interest either to people you are currently working with, or to others in the future. A simple filing system, either alphabetical or grouped by subject, in a concertina file or a filing drawer, is probably the easiest way to deal with this.

A small library of information is very useful provided that it is kept up to date. It is important that on a regular basis, perhaps every three months, you go through it, discarding information which has become outdated and replacing it with the most current. If you prefer to store information electronically, create a folder on a computer in which you record the website and e-mail addresses of relevant services. Remember to regularly back up your electronic records in case of accidental loss. It is also useful to keep important websites in the 'favourites' menu so that they are easily accessible.

Reviewing information  KS 2 4 11 12

You will need to support individuals, and the key people involved with them, to review the information obtained and to identify the services and facilities to be accessed. Identifying the options available to a particular individual and supporting him or her to assess the advantages and disadvantages of each will be an important part of your role.

You will also need to assess any risks involved in accessing and using the services and facilities. For example, if the individual has to travel to a facility, or will be involved in a new physical activity or in meeting new people, there may be associated risks that will have to be assessed and managed.

Sometimes, the options available may prove disappointing to an individual. Imagine someone who has become convinced that he or she can solve a current financial problem through receiving a particular grant; the individual has heard

Remember

Everyone has the right to take risks. If they have full information and decide that the benefits outweigh the risks, your role will be to assist in managing those risks, not to try to discourage individuals from taking them.

about the grant and has built up hopes of it. When you support the individual in finding out about the grant, you discover that he or she is not eligible.

In all such cases it is good practice to prepare the ground in advance by encouraging the individual to consider all possibilities and to make contingency plans in case of disappointment. Be ready to suggest alternative approaches to problems, and new areas to explore.

Test yourself

1   Why is it important to ask prompting questions when finding out about an individual's needs and wants?

2   What sources of finance are available to individuals in your area?

3   What precautions do you need to take when finding information on the Internet?

4   What are the two main pieces of legislation that cover information?

5   How would you prepare to pass on information about available services to an individual if you knew the information was likely to disappoint him or her?

HSC 330b Enable individuals to select, access and use services and facilities

How to make information accessible

 KS 1 2 6 7 18

Once you have found out what someone's needs are and referred to your own store of information or made further enquiries, you need to provide the information in a way that is useful to the individual concerned. When you are providing information you will need to give careful thought to:

● the needs of the person receiving the information

● the nature of the information.

The needs of the individual

First, you must be sure that you give the information in a way that can be understood by the individual concerned. You must ensure that any specific communication needs are met. For example, people may require information to be in a particular format such as large print or in braille, or to be communicated using signing. You will need to find out how to change the format of the information, or access it in a suitable format.

You will also need to consider the circumstances when you pass on information about a particular service or facility. You should take into account the situation of the individual at that particular time – remember to look at the bigger picture. An obvious example is that you would not pass on information about social clubs and outings to someone whose partner had just died. That sort of information may be appropriate in a few weeks or months, but it is unlikely to be of any value at the moment. This principle also applies in situations where you are aware that someone is particularly upset by problems or difficulties. You also need to take into account an individual's state of health and any medical treatment that may affect the relevance or usefulness of the information.

Make sure that information is accessible by:
- presenting it in the most useful format
- making it available at the right time
- taking all the circumstances into account.

There is also a right way and right time for supporting people to access information. From your work on communication skills, you will remember that it is important you do not rush what you say, and that people are more receptive to information if they are comfortable and at ease. Don't attempt to pass on information as you are rushing out of the door – it is unlikely that someone will remember the details of a hurried remark.

Oh Betty, I did check and there is a painting class on Tuesday afternoons at 2.30, or Thursday mornings at half-past 10, and you can go along to either of them if you just phone the library first ...

Care workers must take the time to pass on information clearly, not in a rush

Directly accessed information

If an individual is accessing information independently, he or she may come across other difficulties. Information may not be available in a format the individual can readily use. For example, information about a local theatre production may not be available in large print, or a poster advertising an exhibition may be at the top of a flight of stairs, making it inaccessible for some people. A local information office may not have a loop system, making it difficult for people with impaired hearing to access verbal information. Problems of this type will need to be addressed.

You may come across situations where services clearly discriminate against people on the grounds of race, gender or disability. For example, someone finding out information about a job may be told he need not apply because he has a disability. If you find any instances of discrimination, you should offer to support the individual concerned in informing the relevant bodies – see Unit HSC 35, page 165.

Problems with access to information, either because it is in an inappropriate format or location, or because it is inaccurate or out of date, need to be dealt with for two reasons:
- the individual still needs to find out the information
- it needs to be made available for others in the future.

The nature of the information

For many individuals it can be helpful if you write down basic information or give them a relevant leaflet. This may be enough for some people and they may undertake the next stages of research for themselves. Others may want you to do some further research with them.

For most people it is useful to have information in a form they can refer to again while they consider it or commit it to memory. Before meeting someone you should always make sure that you have prepared the information in the most useful form so that passing it on is straightforward.

Remember

Throughout this process, your role is to support and encourage people to deal with issues for themselves wherever possible, rather than relying on you to do it for them.

How to support people to use services

 KS ① ② ④ ⑤ ⑦ ⑪ ⑫ ⑬ ⑭ ⑮ ⑱

The range of services and facilities that individuals may want to use is large and varied. By no means all are provided by the health and care services. Many other services and facilities provided by commerce, industry, entertainment and retail organisations will also be useful for people. Once people have the information on what is available, the next stage is to support them to make use of it.

Support the individual to complete application forms or other paperwork

This may involve completing application forms or other paperwork, and you may need to support individuals to fill in any forms that are required to access their selected facilities or services. As always, your role will be to assist in gathering the information and, if necessary, to help with the writing involved. But you should not simply 'take over' the task; encourage the individual to contribute to it as much as he or she is able and willing.

Home services

Depending on circumstances, some individuals may wish to take advantage of services which can be supplied to them in their own home rather than having to travel. If you work with someone who is unable or unwilling to travel, you will need to support him or her in finding out whether services can be provided at home. Many organisations provide an off-site service. Examples are:

- mobile shops
- mail-order shopping catalogues
- mobile libraries
- solicitors
- homecare services
- meals services
- doctors and other health services
- pharmacists
- mobile hairdressers.

Most banks and building societies provide services online and by telephone, as do many large and small retail shopping facilities. Home delivery take-away food is readily available in most areas, as are films via rented videos or through satellite or cable television. Most local councils allow payments online, and one social services department is trialling a procedure of carrying out assessments for services online. The benefits are enormous for those people who have access to a computer and the skills to use the Internet.

Travelling to services

People have to travel if they want to participate in many forms of entertainment and culture, such as the theatre, concerts, art galleries, or sporting events. They will also have to travel to essential appointments, such as an appearance in court or a visit to the hospital. When you are encouraging individuals to make maximum use of services you may need to discuss travel arrangements with them. Information about travelling and access will be important, and you may need to work with the individual to identify any problems with accessing the services he or she wants to use.

Services such as meals can be provided directly to individuals' own homes

Taking a back seat

Many people may need to be encouraged to use services after finding enough information to make a properly considered choice. However, you must be careful not to cross the boundary between encouraging them and pressurising them into using a particular facility or service. Everyone has a right to choose not to take up services and facilities available to them.

You are unlikely to pressurise anyone into reading a particular book or seeing a particular film, simply because you think it is good – you would simply say how enjoyable you found the book or film, and strongly recommend it. However, it is easy to step over the boundary when you believe an individual needs to be encouraged to find out about and use a service that seems to be in his or her interests.

For example, you may feel that receiving additional support services, attending a physiotherapy session or making a claim for additional benefit would be of great advantage to the person concerned. But your role is limited to supporting the individual in finding the information necessary to make an informed choice. You should avoid putting pressure on the individual to take a particular course of action.

Similarly, you should not attempt to prevent someone from following a course of action because you believe it is risky or unsuitable. Professional carers can be faced with difficult situations when people have obtained information about facilities or activities that may expose them to risk of injury or other dangers. There is a fine line between neglecting your responsibilities for the individual's safety and imposing unfair restrictions. Most people working in health and care are likely to be cautious, rather than careless. Although this concern for the safety of individuals is well-intentioned, it can result in restricting people's rights to enjoy the facilities and services available.

CASE STUDY: The right to take risks

Jemma spent all her childhood in a residential facility for young people with learning disabilities. She is now 21 and has moved into supported group accommodation in the community. She is able to care for herself and has also started a job at the local supermarket where she collects and returns the trollies. Jemma has been very happy in the supported accommodation, and she enjoys her job and the independence it brings her. At work, Jemma has met a boyfriend who is now suggesting that she move out of the supported accommodation and into a bedsit with him on the other side of the town. Jemma is very keen to do this, but she still requires a considerable degree of protection as she has an extremely naïve view of the world and has very little understanding of any risk to her personal safety. Her boyfriend is very attached to Jemma, but he has had recurring problems with drugs in the past and finds keeping a job difficult. At the moment, however, he is free from drugs and has a steady job.

Staff at the supported accommodation are concerned that Jemma would be at risk if she moved in with her boyfriend because she has very little understanding of the issues to which she could be exposed. They are therefore considering whether they are able to, or ought to, prevent Jemma from moving out of the supported environment.

1   *Do the staff have any legal right to stop Jemma moving in with her boyfriend?*

2   *Do the staff have any moral right to stop Jemma moving in with him?*

3   *How do you think this situation should be handled?*

4   *To what extent should Jemma be allowed to make her own choices?*

5   *What might be the effect on Jemma of losing the opportunity to make this change?*

6   *Would the situation be any different if Jemma wanted to move in with another resident in the supported accommodation?*

Individual needs

As you saw in Unit HSC 31, one of the most significant influences on communication and the way people deal with decisions or stressful issues is the life stage they have reached (see pages 25–28). You will obviously need to take this into consideration when deciding the appropriate degree of support to offer an individual in accessing and using services.

People also vary in their self-image and the amount of self-esteem they have. Some may lack confidence in their own skills and abilities, and therefore find the prospect of accessing and using new services and facilities very daunting. In such a case, both informal and professional carers need to be prepared to offer considerable encouragement and support, while ensuring that they do not cross over the line into a situation where they misuse the power and influence they have over an individual.

Remember

- If you are using information about other people you should not identify them, in order to maintain their confidentiality.

- If you want to offer to introduce other people, don't forget to respect confidentiality, and never offer this without the express agreement of both parties.

Keys to good practice: Encouraging individuals to select and use services

✓ Make sure that you support individuals and key people to access a full range of information.

✓ Try to identify difficulties and answer as many questions as possible.

✓ If you do not have information or cannot answer questions, tell the person you will find out, and make sure you do.

✓ Give any information you have about the consequences of using the service or facility, including information about others who may have benefited.

✓ Encourage individuals to find out all the information they need to know about how to access the service or facility, such as whether the service is one they can use at home or have to travel to, and what the travel arrangements need to be.

✓ Offer to assist and support individuals in any way you can, such as offering to introduce them (by previous agreement) to others who may be using the service or facility.

✓ Make sure you do not use undue influence over an individual to persuade him or her to act in a particular way simply because you think it is best.

Overcoming barriers

There are many barriers which can restrict access or prevent people from using facilities or services. Information is one of the keys to overcoming barriers. An individual with plenty of accurate and current information, clearly understood and found well in advance, is far more likely to be able to challenge and overcome difficulties than someone who feels uncertain because of a lack of information, and is unprepared for any difficulties.

Barriers to access tend to fall into three categories: environmental, communication, and psychological. Environmental barriers are the most common.

Environmental barriers	• lack of disabled toilet facilities • high-risk or threatening location, e.g. near a busy pub or parade of shops which is a known hang-out for gangs of young men • narrow doorways • no ramps • no lifts • lack of transport or lack of access by transport • lack of wheelchair access
Communication barriers	• lack of loop system • poor quality communication skills in staff at the facility, e.g. an unhelpful or obstructive receptionist • lack of translators or interpreters • lack of information or publicity about the service or facility • lack of information in an appropriate language or format
Psychological barriers	• unfamiliarity • lack of confidence • fear or anxiety • concern at loss of independence • unwillingness to accept help

How to challenge and overcome barriers

Start by checking that all possible information is available about the facilities and services, the challenges and the alternatives. Work alongside an individual to help plan ways to challenge and overcome any discrimination and barriers. For example, you may need to support someone to search out alternative facilities if the ones originally found do not have wheelchair access.

If the local theatre does not have wheelchair access, encourage the individual to make arrangements to travel to one that does. Of course, you could also encourage the individual to raise the issue with the local theatre and point out to them that they are in breach of the Disability Discrimination Act.

If there are problems finding suitable transport, it will be necessary to find out about transport with provision for wheelchairs, by checking local taxi or public transport facilities which have the necessary adaptations. Most train companies have support services for people with disabilities, such as ramps and a porter service to enable people to get on and off trains. However, many trains that do provide porterage and ramps do not have readily accessible toilets for disabled people.

Any particular arrangements with a facility to provide access must be agreed with the individual concerned. If a person who uses a wheelchair has to make an important visit to a particular location which cannot be changed and there is no wheelchair access through the main entrance, it may be suggested that the individual use a back entrance or goods entrance and the goods lift. You should always check with the individual before agreeing to this type of arrangement, as not everyone is prepared to access a building through a goods entrance. Many disabled people take the view that they should have the right to access buildings in the same way as everyone else. In such a case, you may need to support the individual in arranging for the visit to take place at a different location. It is essential you never compromise the right of an individual to choose his or her own means of access and to set boundaries as to what is acceptable in terms of personal space and dignity.

An individual has the right to set boundaries as to what is acceptable in terms of dignity

Evidence

PC ③ ④ ⑤

Choose three different types of facility that individuals may wish to access in your locality.

For each, list the potential barriers to access and the ways in which you would begin to tackle the barriers.

Where appropriate, talk to the individuals you had in mind to access the facilities.

Find out their views on barriers and access.

Make notes for your portfolio.

Enabling people to use services and facilities

KS 2 5 18

The level of support that you need to provide to an individual will vary depending on the circumstances. Your support can range from handing someone an information leaflet to making all the arrangements to use a service and accompanying him or her to use it. Between these extremes are a wide range of alternatives. Some people may simply need you to make the initial contact for them. Others may need you to accompany them on a first visit to a new facility or to meet a new group of people, and then to gradually withdraw as they grow in confidence in using the service. On other occasions your role may be to enlist the support of other people who are better qualified, more experienced or who have the resources or time to provide a better service for the individual.

It is important you encourage people to dispense with your support as soon as they feel able to manage independently. You should do this when you notice them becoming more confident in using the facility or service. Do it by gradually and appropriately reducing the level of support.

For example, you may have accompanied someone on a first visit to a Welfare Rights Advice Centre. The individual needed you because he or she was unfamiliar with the service and did not understand the benefit system enough to be able to explain the information required. However, as the visits continue and the work of the Welfare Rights Advice Centre is under way, you may be able to withdraw from accompanying the individual as he or she becomes more familiar with the workers in the centre. Your involvement may then be limited to driving the individual to the centre, or holding a support session on his or her return.

It may take people a while to adjust with confidence to new social situations. For example, if someone has been supported by you to find out about and then visit a new day centre or social club, it may take a few visits before he or she is confident enough to go alone. As always your role is to do the minimum and to allow individuals the maximum opportunity to make their own lives and to be as independent as possible.

Test yourself

1   Give three points to consider when providing information about services and facilities.

2   Name three barriers to accessing and using services and facilities.

3   How could those barriers be overcome?

4   Describe an occasion when you provided support to an individual using services or facilities. Evaluate how successful this was for the individual concerned.

HSC 330c Enable individuals to evaluate services and facilities used

How to evaluate services and facilities

 KS 12 18

Key terms

Evaluate: To decide on the value of something.

Evaluation is often thought to be a difficult and complex process, but in fact it is straightforward. The process of evaluating an event or experience is extremely useful because it allows you to find out:

- what worked well
- what worked badly or didn't work at all
- what was wrong and can be fixed
- what was wrong and can't be fixed
- what you would do/use again
- what you would not do/use again
- what was better than you expected
- what was worse than you expected
- what needs to be changed
- what should stay the same
- what you need to do next time.

The simplest way to find out about any of the items on this list is to ask for feedback. In the case of a service, a product or a facility, all those involved in providing, recommending or using it need to know whether it is working well.

CASE STUDY: Compiling a directory

Students at a local college were studying for a health and social care qualification. For one of their assignments they were asked to produce a directory of information about entertainment and leisure facilities in the local area. When they had completed the project, the students decided to present the finished directory to the supported living unit at 24 The Avenue. This unit provides supported living for eight people with a disability, some of whom have complex needs.

The directory was printed out and stapled to form a booklet. The work had been done very neatly and each facility was identified in bold lettering, followed by a short description of the facilities, like this:

> **Royal Theatre**
> Plays, concerts and shows. Weekly programme of events. Seats 500. Tickets through box office 10.00hrs–20.00hrs 0123 45678. Café available 11.00hrs–18.00hrs. Facilities DT, WA, L, B, H (see key on p. 5)

A few weeks later, staff noticed that the directory was lying in the lounge and no one seemed to have used it.

1 *What do you think may be the reason why the directory was not used?*
2 *How could the directory be improved?*
3 *What sort of information should be in it?*
4 *How should it be presented?*
5 *What should the residents and staff of the unit do now?*

Methods of checking information

The basic requirement for any sort of information is that it should be:

- accurate
- relevant
- up to date
- easy to understand
- accessible to everyone
- within the law.

You need to encourage individuals to check that information is accurate and relevant for their purposes. It also helps if information is interesting!

People who provide information need to know whether it is all of those things, so feedback is essential. You should encourage and support people in providing feedback about information they have accessed or tried to access.

Information needs to be accurate, relevant and accessible

If you have tried to obtain information about welfare rights and it was not available in large print, this fact can be fed back to the co-ordinator of the Welfare Rights Centre. However, it will be important that you encourage the individual concerned to check that information has improved, otherwise the feedback will have been wasted.

In the case of commercial businesses, shops, supermarkets, cinemas, entertainment centres or theatres, feedback should be given to the manager on site. Some businesses may be part of a national or international chain and information may be handled centrally. Where this is the case, you should encourage and support people to seek out those who have responsibility for the information policy of the company and make sure they receive the feedback.

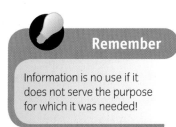

Remember

Information is no use if it does not serve the purpose for which it was needed!

How to give useful feedback on services and facilities

KS ② ⑤ ⑦ ⑫ ⑮ ⑱ ⑲

You will need to agree the methods and timescales you will use with an individual and his or her carers for evaluating how the use of services or facilities has contributed to his or her well-being. People's needs do not remain the same, so services and facilities that appeared to meet an individual's needs at one time may no longer be appropriate after quite a short period of time. Regular review and feedback will therefore be needed. Feedback should identify:

- the services and facilities the individual has selected and used
- any discrimination or exclusion that the individual has experienced
- which services and facilities have been beneficial to the individual's well-being
- which services and facilities have been less helpful
- the reasons for the helpfulness or lack of helpfulness in each case.

As a care professional you know that receiving feedback is not always easy and that criticism can sometimes make you feel resentful. So you should encourage individuals offering feedback to ensure they make positive suggestions alongside any complaints they may have. No one likes receiving a long list of complaints and criticism, even if it is well deserved. People are much more receptive to feedback if it is accompanied by useful suggestions about how matters could be improved. This will help them to improve the quality of the services they provide, and should mean that others will not experience the same problems in the future.

Evidence   PC ⑥

Explain the process of evaluating services and facilities used in your workplace including documentation used.

Where is the resulting information kept and who has access to it?

Identifying and implementing necessary changes

Constructive feedback involves identifying the changes necessary to improve the outcomes for individuals using services and facilities. Your role in supporting this process may include collating information, records and reports connected with the evaluation. You must follow organisational procedures and remember the rules of confidentiality when you are working with such information.

Evaluation is of no use unless it results in the appropriate changes being made. You will need to work with the individuals and key people involved to achieve the changes that have been identified as being necessary for the improvement of services and facilities. You will also need to support them in challenging any discrimination or exclusion they have experienced.

However, as with the selection of services, it will be important that you do not misuse your position of trust with the individual in order to influence the feedback he or she gives so that it reflects *your* opinion of services and facilities. There will be channels through which you can communicate your own experiences and opinions, and these will have their own value; but you must ensure they are kept clearly separate from the feedback given by the individual himself or herself.

Test yourself

1 How could you offer support to individuals in evaluating the services and facilities they use?

2 Why should individuals be encouraged to offer constructive suggestions alongside any criticisms?

3 What procedures are in place to ensure feedback is acted upon in your workplace?

4 Why is it important that feedback is seen to be taken seriously and acted upon?

HSC 330 FURTHER READING AND RESEARCH

You may find it most useful to research services and facilities in your area, as these will be easiest for access. Here are some ideas to help you start this process and build upon what you have already learnt in this section.

www.citizensadvice.org.uk (Citizens Advice Bureau)

www.goodaccessguide.co.uk (Good Access Guide) tel: 01452741585

www.disableddirect.co.uk (Disabled Direct) tel: 08714267715

www.drc-gb.org (Disability Rights Commission – Disability Equality Duty)

Leader, A. *Direct Power; A Resource Pack for People Who Want to Develop Their Own Care Plans and Support Networks* Pavilion Publishers

Sobczak , J. (2001) *Alive and Kicking* Age Concern

Stalker, K., Duckett, P., Downs, M. (1999) *Going with the Flow; Choice, Dementia and People with Learning Difficulties* Pavilion Publishers

Contribute to the prevention and management of abusive and aggressive behaviour

When people need care, difficulties and conflicts can arise that put individuals, their carers and those around them under great stress. If these situations are not dealt with constructively, aggressive and abusive behaviour can result. In other cases, the condition of individuals causes them to become frustrated and to lose the ability to control their reactions, or to consider the consequences of their behaviour. They can then become verbally or physically aggressive to those around them.

It is a vital part of your work that you contribute to the prevention and management of any abusive and aggressive behaviour. It is not always preventable, so when it occurs you need to be able to deal with it appropriately. You also need to help in the review of such incidents according to the policies of your workplace and in a way that satisfies legal requirements.

This unit does not address systematic abuse. It is concerned with incidents of verbal or non-verbal behaviour which is abusive and/or aggressive. But this is as difficult an area to deal with as the prevention of systematic abuse and neglect, discussed in Unit HSC 35, and you will need to be clear about your role and learn how to manage the feelings aroused by such incidents.

What you need to learn

- Ways of communicating appropriately
- Knowing yourself and your own behaviour
- How to listen
- How to maintain an emotionally safe atmosphere
- Causes of abusive or aggressive behaviour
- How to minimise the risk of aggression or abuse
- Behaviour that is unacceptable
- How to respond to unacceptable behaviour
- Physical restraint issues
- Recording an incident
- How dealing with abuse or aggression can affect you
- Encouraging those involved to contribute to a review.

HSC 336a Contribute to preventing abusive and aggressive behaviour

Good communication is vital in preventing the conflicts and frustrations that can lead to abusive or aggressive behaviour.

People communicate differently, and the varieties in communication styles can result from differences in culture and background. Culture is about more than the language people speak – it is about the way that they live, think and relate to each other.

Ways of communicating appropriately

 KS ① ② ⑤ ⑦ ⑧ ⑫ ⑬

You need to communicate with others in ways which:

- are appropriate for them
- encourage open exchanges of views and information
- minimise constraints to communication
- are free from discrimination and oppression
- acknowledge and support the rights of everyone involved.

In order for you to work as an effective communicator, you must know how to deal with people in a way which takes account of their individuality. When time is short and demands are high, it is often easier to treat everyone in a group in the same way, to make plans for a whole group of people or to assume that what is good for one person will be good for all. Learning how to avoid this is an important part of your job.

Each person you work with is an individual – completely different and unique. This may sound obvious but it is so important that it is worth repeating. Making judgements about people which are based not on knowledge and understanding of that person but on generally accepted stereotypes, often with little truth behind them, is a recipe for conflict.

Working in caring is not only about having good working relationships with colleagues, although good teamwork is essential; it is also about the relationships you make with the individuals you are caring for, and it is about understanding other relationships they have, with their friends and relatives.

Avoiding stereotypes

One of the most effective ways you have of helping people is by recognising them as individuals. As discussed in Unit HSC 35, it is vital never to make assumptions about people in groups.

Think about the number of ways in which people can be identified – they can be described by age, gender, eye colour, place of residence, job, special interests, and any number of personal characteristics. This will remind you of the number of different aspects there are to any one individual.

The problem with 'labelling' people by placing them in particular groups for particular purposes is that it is very rarely accurate. It may be very convenient when planning care to decide that 'all individuals will want …' or 'this age group will benefit from …', but the number of individuals contained within any group means that any planning that starts with a generalisation is doomed to be unsatisfactory.

Remember that people are different, enjoy different activities and have different needs

Active knowledge

Think of a way to describe yourself, starting with the most general – 'I am a woman' or 'I am a man'. So are other people, so that does not describe you. 'I have brown hair' – so do a great many others. Continue thinking of ways to describe yourself, getting closer all the time to finding a description that is unique to you (one that describes you, and no one else). Each time you think of another way to describe yourself, it will eliminate more and more people from the group, until finally you may (depending on how well you know yourself) come up with a description which applies to no one else but you.

Each time you are tempted to treat people as one of a group, remember how long this task took and how many descriptions you listed before you found a unique reference to you. Remember that everyone you deal with is unique – an individual.

It will be important to be aware of the risk of stereotyped thinking when you are assessing the degree of risk involved in working with someone who is distressed. Stereotyping might result in dangerous assumptions such as 'only men are violent, so I need not worry about the reaction of this woman' or 'I can relax with this person because he is like me – so nothing can go wrong'.

Equally, stereotyping may result in discriminatory assumptions such as 'I cannot possibly work on my own with people who have dementia in case they become violent'. The stereotype this reflects is the belief that all people with a mental health problem are potentially violent. The stereotype behind the judgement that 'I may be at risk if I work with people from a different ethnic group' is that people who are different from you are dangerous!

It is always important to check your thinking for assumptions and stereotypes – unless you become good at this you may expose yourself to risk and expose service users to discrimination.

Encouraging an open exchange of views

Valuing people as individuals means having respect for all of the people you deal with. Respect is usually something that develops as you form relationships. When you provide care for someone, you will get to know and talk to him or her, and a relationship will grow. This is not easy with all individuals you care for. When there appears to be no two-way communication, you may find that forming a relationship is difficult.

Remember

- Everyone has the right to make choices.

- All people are different.

If you accept these points, you will never be guilty of making generalisations or making prejudiced judgements about people again.

Keys to good practice: Respecting individuals

✓ Make sure that any service you provide for someone is with his or her agreement. People have a right to choose the care they receive and the way in which they receive it.

✓ Set a good example by being open to the views expressed by others. Encourage people to listen to and respect each other's views.

Of course, people cannot suddenly stop doing and thinking things which they have been doing and thinking all their lives, and begin to agree with each other on every point; but they can be encouraged to develop an awareness of everyone's right to a different point of view.

Once you realise how your own background and beliefs alter the way you think about people, you can begin to recognise the differences and see the value of other cultures and beliefs. It is inevitable that, by thinking carefully about what has influenced you, you will also consider what has influenced others with whom you come into contact.

You need to talk to people, whether they are colleagues or service users, about aspects of their culture or lifestyle you do not understand. As a care professional, it is your responsibility to make sure that you have considered the culture, beliefs and lifestyle of someone for whom you are providing care. It is not acceptable to expect that they will adapt to your set of cultural beliefs and expectations.

If you work to create the kind of environment in which everyone's contribution is valued, and where meaningful interactions can take place between people with very different needs or backgrounds, you will be making an enormous contribution to preventing inappropriate behaviour. The diversity of the human race is what makes living in our society such a rich and varied experience. If you welcome this diversity, and encourage others to do so rather than resist, condemn or belittle the things they do not understand, the relationships among colleagues and service users will be much more rewarding and the quality of your care practice will be greatly improved.

Knowing yourself and your own behaviour

  KS 5 7 8 12

It is vital, if you are to help people to live and work together effectively, that you understand how you affect any situation. Human beings do not react in the same way to everyone. You have doubtless had the experience of meeting people who make you feel relaxed and at ease – you find it easy to talk to them and feel as if you had known them for a long time. Equally, there are other people who seem much harder to talk to – in their presence you feel nervous, or unsure; you can't think of anything to say and feel generally uncomfortable. You are still the same person, but you have reacted in a totally different way to different people.

To be a good practitioner in caring, you have to learn to understand how people react to *you* and the way in which your own beliefs, background and prejudices will influence the outcome of an interaction with another person.

It is essential that you understand about interaction between people if you are working in caring. It is not always easy to understand how it works. It may help if you think about dealing with other people as being like looking in different fairground mirrors. All of the reflections look different – some are short and fat, some long and thin, some are wavy and curved; it all depends on the mirror. You are still the same, but the mirror makes everything appear different. In the same way, you will interact differently depending on the person you are talking to.

Dealing with different people is like seeing yourself in different fairground mirrors

Remember

- Stereotypes can influence how you think about someone.
- Don't rush to make judgements about people.
- Everyone is entitled to his or her own beliefs and culture. If you don't know about someone's way of life – ask.

Evidence PC 3 4

Think of a service user who you work with regularly and who may display abusive or aggressive behaviour.

Describe the actions you take to maintain calmness and safety around them.

Be honest, do any of your actions restrict movement or deny peoples rights?

If you feel they do, discuss this with your supervisor. Is there anything that can be done to improve the situation?

Learning about yourself is not an easy task. Often you never take the time to examine your own behaviour in depth. It can be a shock when someone points out something you are doing, or a way you have of behaving, which you had not realised.

If you intend to be effective as a carer, you will need to spend some time looking at your own behaviour, and try to look in the mirror of other people's reactions.

 Keys to good practice: Examining your own behaviour

- ✓ **Are your interactions sometimes unsuccessful?** If you are talking to someone and he or she suddenly seems to close down the conversation, or appear frustrated, try to think back to the point at which the atmosphere changed. Be honest with yourself. Did you react to something he or she said? Did you say something that was a little thoughtless? Did you laugh in a way that could have been interpreted as unkind? Or did he or she begin to back away when you looked at your watch, or spoke briefly to someone else who wanted your attention?

- ✓ **Do some individuals seem to find it easier to talk to you than others?** Do you find it easier to talk to some individuals than others? Of course, there are bound to be some people you like more than others, but when you are working as a professional carer it is not enough just to acknowledge that. You have to think about the reasons in order to make sure that it does not result in individuals being treated differently.

- ✓ **Only you can work at examining your own behaviour.** If you have a manager or colleague to work with you, that is a great help, but essentially no one can do it for you. You will need to be able to consider a series of questions: Which people do you find it hard to deal with? Can you work better with women than men? Do you find it hard to talk to young people? or to older people? or to people of a particular social class? or to people of particular races? or to anyone with a different accent?

- ✓ **Do you find that you have less patience with some people?** Can you identify which people? Is there a pattern? You may not always like the answers you come up with, but until you can work out how you behave towards others and why, you will never be able to make any adjustments to your responses.

Continued

 Remember

You can change the way you behave by reflecting on your own behaviour, deciding what you need to change and practising new approaches until they become natural to you.

Keys to good practice: Examining your own behaviour (cont.)

✓ **Look at your own culture and beliefs.** You may, for example, have grown up surrounded by people who believed that it was unthinkable to owe a penny to anyone, so you may find it difficult to offer empathy and support to someone who is desperate because he or she is deeply in debt. If you have lived in a culture which holds older family members in high regard and gives them great respect, you may find it hard to relate to the family of an older person if they hardly ever visit and do not appear interested in his or her welfare. Nevertheless, in your role as a carer you have to be aware of how your own background may influence you and to ensure that you include that factor in the analysis of any situation.

✓ **Don't be too hard on yourself.** If you acknowledge your own prejudices you will be more than halfway towards overcoming them. Just being able to understand why you behave in the way you do is more than most people achieve in a lifetime! So don't worry if it takes a while before you feel that you are really thinking effectively about what you do and how you affect others. Knowing how people respond to you and making allowances for that will, eventually, become second nature.

How to listen

 KS 7 12

The key areas of listening and talking are where people interact meaningfully. You may think that this comes naturally to most people, but everyone can learn some basic skills which will improve their communication significantly.

Active listening

Active listening is about doing much more than simply hearing the words which an individual is speaking. It includes encouraging someone to talk to you, letting him or her know that you are interested, concerned and supportive, and allowing him or her the space, time and attention to express feelings and concerns in a calm manner.

Remember

- To hear what someone is really telling you, you have to be a good listener.

- To help someone understand what you are saying and to tell you what he or she wants to say, you have to be a good communicator.

The way in which you listen to someone can make all the difference to how easy he or she finds it to talk to you. When someone is talking to you, keep encouraging him or her by responding – nodding and saying 'mm' or 'I see' are often all that is needed. There is nothing worse than receiving no response.

Sometimes people find it difficult to express what they want to say and need some encouragement. You can help by repeating back to them what they have been saying, not in parrot fashion but in an encouraging way, as in the following example:

Service user: 'My family are very busy, I don't see them much. They all have important jobs ...' [silence].

You: 'So your children don't have much time to come here because they all work so hard ...'

Paraphrasing what someone has told you can also be a useful way of showing that you have understood what he or she is saying. In paraphrasing you take what someone has been saying and repeat it in a slightly different way.

This can be used effectively to clarify what someone has said. For example, if an individual has just told you about feelings ranging from sadness and anger to relief at coming into residential care, a reply of something like 'so your feelings are very mixed – that's very understandable' demonstrates that you have heard what he or she said and also offers reassurance that this reaction is normal and only to be expected.

Asking the right questions

As you learned in Unit HSC 31, you can ask 'open' or 'closed' questions when you are talking to someone. Which questions you use makes a difference to the response you will get.

- Closed questions are those that allow people to answer 'Yes' or 'No'. For example, 'Are you worried about the tests tomorrow?' This may get only a one-word response. If you then want to find out any more, you have to ask another question. If you are not careful, individuals can end up feeling as if they are on 'Twenty Questions'.
- Open questions are those that do not allow for a one-word response. If you rephrase the question in the previous example, it becomes 'How do you feel about tomorrow's tests?' The difference is obvious, and there is a far greater chance that the person you are talking to will feel able to express his or her feelings.

Remember

There are many barriers to effective communication, as you learned in Unit HSC 31. These can be physical, environmental, or related to people's feelings and attitudes. In your work you should be constantly looking for the best ways to overcome them.

What you say

Make sure that you are not the one doing all the talking. Be careful not to tell someone what you think and keep giving your opinions. Telling someone 'If I were you, I would …' is neither good practice nor good communication.

Don't ever tell someone 'That's silly' or 'You shouldn't feel like that'. Such a remark effectively dismisses people's feelings or tells them that they have no right to feel that way. It invites anger or frustration in response.

How you say it

Think about the speed and volume of your speech. We often fail to realise how quickly we speak. It can often be difficult for someone who has some impairment of hearing or poor eyesight to catch what you say, if you speak too quickly.

Think about your accent, and the individual you are talking to. Local accents can be difficult to understand, if they are unfamiliar.

Volume is also important. There is no need to shout – it simply distorts what you say, plays havoc with your facial expression and makes you appear aggressive! You should, however, make sure that you speak clearly and at a reasonable level. Generally, speaking too softly can make it hard for you to be understood.

There are some occasions when you may have to balance the volume of what you say with the need to maintain someone's privacy. It may be worth having to repeat yourself a few times, if it helps to keep a discussion private.

How to maintain an emotionally safe atmosphere

 KS ① ④ ⑦ ⑧ ⑩ ⑪ ⑫

The Codes of Practice of the regulatory bodies emphasise the importance of treating each person as an individual and respecting the views, wishes and dignity of service users. Your workplace will have its own policies and practices, but effective communication based on active listening will be vital in order to build an understanding of the views of individual people, and essential for creating a supportive atmosphere. There is a saying that 'the communication is the relationship'; in other words, if time is spent listening and building an understanding of individual needs, a supportive relationship is likely to develop between care workers and service users.

If service users feel that they can communicate their emotional needs and that their dignity and self-esteem are not threatened, there is less likelihood of frustration and depression. Understanding each service user's plan of care and being involved in regular interaction with service users will help to create a safer emotional environment.

Active knowledge

You may not know how your own voice sounds. Try making a tape recording and listening to yourself. Or ask a friend or colleague to advise you honestly about the way you speak and the speed at which you talk. Do you need to make any changes?

 Remember

A supportive environment involving effective communication and listening is likely to be an emotionally safe environment.

Preventing aggression

One of the key ways of showing respect for other people is to be assertive. The word 'assertiveness' is often misunderstood. Many people see assertiveness as 'sticking up for yourself', but being assertive involves much more than this. It is about remaining calm, and showing respect for other people. Assertiveness involves being clear about your own needs and intentions and being able to communicate in a controlled and calm manner.

Fear and aggression are two of the basic emotions that we experience. It is easy to give into our basic emotions and either become submissive (fearful) or aggressive when we feel stressed. Assertiveness is an alternative way of coping, and it involves controlling the basic emotions that urge us to either run away or fight. Assertiveness involves a mental attitude of being willing to negotiate, and trying to solve problems rather than giving in to emotional impulses.

Winning and losing

During an argument an aggressive person might insist that he or she is right and other people are wrong. He or she will want to win while others lose. The opposite of aggression is to be weak or submissive; a submissive person accepts that he or she will lose, or be criticised.

Assertive behaviour is different from both these responses. In an argument an assertive person will try to reach a solution that involves no one losing or being 'put down'. Assertiveness is a skill that makes 'win–win' situations happen – no one has to be the loser. For example, suppose a service user is angry because the care worker is late. The following responses are possible.

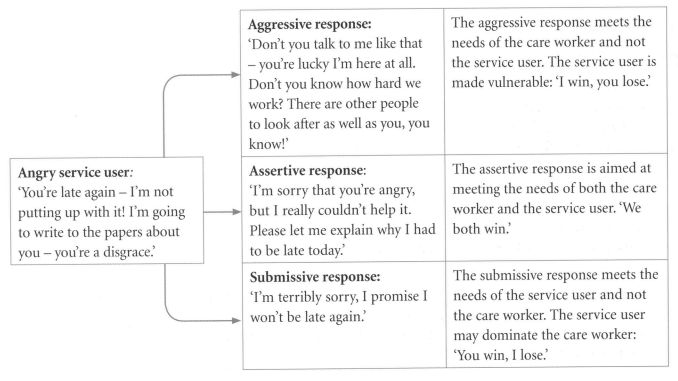

Angry service user:
'You're late again – I'm not putting up with it! I'm going to write to the papers about you – you're a disgrace.'

Aggressive response:
'Don't you talk to me like that – you're lucky I'm here at all. Don't you know how hard we work? There are other people to look after as well as you, you know!'

The aggressive response meets the needs of the care worker and not the service user. The service user is made vulnerable: 'I win, you lose.'

Assertive response:
'I'm sorry that you're angry, but I really couldn't help it. Please let me explain why I had to be late today.'

The assertive response is aimed at meeting the needs of both the care worker and the service user. 'We both win.'

Submissive response:
'I'm terribly sorry, I promise I won't be late again.'

The submissive response meets the needs of the service user and not the care worker. The service user may dominate the care worker: 'You win, I lose.'

How assertiveness enables everyone to win

Assertiveness can help care workers to cope with difficult and challenging situations. To be assertive a person usually has to:

- understand the situation he or she is in – including facts and other people's perceptions
- be able to control personal emotions and stay calm
- be able to act assertively using the right body language
- be able to act assertively using the right words and statements.

Some characteristics associated with assertiveness are contrasted with submission and aggression in the table below.

Submissive behaviour	Assertive behaviour	Aggressive behaviour
Main emotion: fear	Main emotion: confidence	Main emotion: anger
Letting other people win	Negotiating so that everyone wins	Wanting to win
Understanding and acceptance only of other people's needs	Understanding and acceptance of your own and other people's needs	Understanding only your own needs
A mental attitude that other people are more important than you	A mental attitude that it is important to negotiate in order to get the best outcome for yourself and others	A mental attitude that you are more important than other people
Not speaking, or only asking questions to find out what's wanted	Listening carefully	Not listening to others; making demands
Lack of respect for yourself	Respect for yourself and others	Lack of respect for others
Speaking quietly and/or hesitantly	Speaking in a clear, calm voice	Shouting or talking loudly
Submissive body language including looking down, not looking at others, looking frightened, looking tense	Relaxed body language including varied eye contact, looking confident, keeping hands and arms at your side	Threatening body language including fixed eye contact, tense muscles, waving or folding the arms and clenching fingers.

If you behave assertively your calm, respectful behaviour may help to prevent aggression in other people. This is because you will not set yourself up as a target for other people's emotions. If you lose control of your own emotions and become angry you may increase the threat experienced by another person, who may feel justified in abusing or even physically attacking you, because 'attack is the best defence'. If you appear weak and afraid you may invite abuse and attack because this may increase the frustration experienced by another person. A person who is weak and afraid may also appear to be an easy target – easy to dominate and control. If you listen and show respect for another person you may create an emotional environment where the person feels encouraged to respond by listening and showing respect.

CASE STUDY: Creating emotional safety

Frank is 89 and lives in a care home. He usually sits with a small group of other residents at teatime. He is often quiet and does not join in the conversation, although the other three residents on his table are quite talkative.

This afternoon one of the residents is dominating the conversation with a lengthy and rambling account of how he made ends meet during the war, and rationing. Janet, a care worker, notices that Frank is beginning to appear tense. Frank is clenching and unclenching his fingers, his face is tense and has a scowling expression. Frank is staring in a fixed way at the resident who is dominating the conversation. Janet senses that Frank may be about to lose his temper. She speaks to him as follows.

Janet Frank, I've got a new packet of biscuits. Can I open them and put them on a plate here?

Frank Do what you like!

Janet OK, do you think you could pass me the plate?

Frank Yeah.

Janet You were in the Navy during the war, weren't you?

Frank I don't talk about it.

Janet Did you live around here in the fifties? It's just that we've got this person coming tomorrow who wants to learn about people's memories of the time just after the war.

Frank Oh yes, I've always lived here.

Janet Would you like to talk to him? You could join in the group with me.

Frank Well if he wants to listen – I don't mind talking if you are there.

After this exchange, Frank appears more relaxed and decides to get up and walk away from the table.

1 *Why might Frank have been tense while sitting with someone who would not stop talking about himself?*

2 *Janet has skilfully worked with Frank's emotions without challenging or threatening him. She has managed to engage Frank's attention but her conversation is not just about distracting him. What is it about Janet's conversation that makes it so effective?*

3 *How does Janet use her knowledge of Frank to defuse tension?*

4 *How does she manage to make Frank feel valued?*

Causes of abusive or aggressive behaviour

 KS 11

Your role in reducing fear and frustration, and encouraging people to find an alternative outlet for their anger, is vital in preventing unacceptable behaviour.

When you are working you need to use your communication skills to constantly reassure people. You can help to maintain calmness and safety by always explaining your actions to individuals, even when they do not appear to understand the explanations.

The true source of anger or frustration may lie in an individual's condition or personal situation, but it can easily be displaced so that it becomes focused on people caring for the individual, or on visitors, fellow residents or people in authority. Having considered the likely original sources of such feelings, you also need to consider the triggers that may be the immediate cause of unacceptable behaviour, and how to avoid them. They might include the following.

- **The assumptions that people make.** People sometimes react badly to each other because of assumptions about appearance or language. A person who uses long words, for example, might be thought of as trying to be superior. A person with a particular accent might be seen as strange or inferior. It can be difficult to discover and understand some of the issues that result in tensions and conflict. Group experiences such as group reminiscence work, or even just sharing tea, sometimes help people to change their assumptions. As a last resort, you may have to maintain arrangements that keep to a minimum the necessity for them to interact at all.

- **Behaviour towards or in the vicinity of the individual.** Certain behaviours, even something as minor as someone mumbling aloud when he or she reads the newspaper, can cause irritation when people are living and working closely together. And of course, any behaviour which is disrespectful of an individual can cause extreme anger or frustration. In the case where, because of a person's condition, he or she cannot help behaviour that others find difficult – such as talking loudly or spilling food while eating – others will have to be helped to understand and cope with this. But no one should have to accept being treated disrespectfully by others, and this is an issue you will need to address.

- **Environmental factors.** When people live together in a residential setting, everyone has to make compromises about the way the environment is planned. In certain settings it may also be difficult always to provide as much privacy as people would like. In these circumstances you should work to maintain the environment in a way that encourages meaningful interactions between people, and that maximises the space and privacy each person can have when required.

- **Personal or social aspects of an individual's life.** Everyone faces difficulties and stresses in their lives, and people who are receiving care are likely to have health or mobility problems to cope with too. You will need to take factors such as financial worries or family problems into account when considering how best to promote a calm approach and constructive behaviour.

When people are living together in a residential setting, a planned shared environment can minimise any necessary compromises

Remember

- Learn to know yourself before you think you can know about others.

- Each person should be valued as a unique individual.

How to minimise the risk of aggression or abuse KS 8 11 12

No one can guarantee that all aggressive or abusive behaviour can be prevented – human beings have always abused each other in one form or another. However, using the information you have about the role of good communication and the possible triggers for aggression, you are able to work towards preventing abuse by recognising where it can happen. If a known trigger to unacceptable behaviour occurs, you may be able to act quickly to divert an individual to other activities, or take other preventive action. When risk situations occur in the community, you may be in a position to intervene directly or to report to your supervisor and offer suggestions about ways to reduce risks.

Try to ensure that people in potentially difficult situations are offered as much support as possible. However difficult the circumstances, a person is less likely to resort to aggression or abuse if he or she feels supported, acknowledged and appreciated. Showing sympathy and understanding for a person's situation can often defuse potential explosions. A care worker could express this by saying, for example, 'It must be so hard caring for your mother. The demands she makes are so difficult. I think you are doing a wonderful job.' Such comments can often help someone to feel that he or she is understood and that there are people who are able and willing to support him or her.

Keys to good practice: Minimising risks

✓ Always prevent a difficult situation from arising if you can. If you know, for example, that two people regularly disagree violently about everything from politics to whether or not it is raining, try to arrange that they are involved in separate activities and, if possible, have seats in separate lounges! Alternatively, you may decide to deal with the situation by talking to them both, and offering to help them resolve their disagreements.

✓ Only intervene directly if there is an immediate risk. You will need to use your communication skills to ensure that you handle the situation in a way that does not make things worse and will ensure that you protect the person at risk. Ask for support if necessary.

✓ If there is no immediate risk, report the incident and get assistance as soon as possible.

Providing support

Some situations require much more than words of support, and giving practical, physical support to an individual, a carer or a family may help to reduce the risk of aggression or abuse.

While your support is vital in preventing a potential aggressor from behaving unacceptably, you must also protect potential victims of such behaviour. When resources are provided within the community rather than at home, this also offers a chance to observe someone who is thought to be at risk. Day centres, training centres, schools, after-school clubs and youth centres also provide an opportunity for people to talk to staff and to feel that they are in a supportive environment where they can talk about any problems and they will be listened to and helped.

Remember

- Preventing abusive or aggressive behaviour is better than having to deal with it.

- Support may make all the difference to a person under stress.

- Only intervene directly if there is an immediate risk.

- Act assertively to stop any aggressive or abusive behaviour.

Test yourself

1 What could you do to show someone that you are interested in what he or she is saying?

2 How can your personality affect how you work?

3 People react in the same way, regardless of whom they speak to. True or false?

4 What is the difference between an open question and a closed question? Name situations where you would use each type of question.

5 Describe some triggers to abusive or aggressive behaviour that might occur in your workplace.

HSC 336b Deal with incidents of abusive and aggressive behaviour

Behaviour that is unacceptable

 KS 12

All abusive and aggressive behaviour is unacceptable. However, you may come across other kinds of behaviour which you may not be able to define directly as abusive, but which are close to it or could lead to such behaviour if not dealt with.

People have a right to express their views in an assertive way; in fact one could say it is a duty to act assertively to protect one's own or someone else's rights. The difference between assertive and aggressive behaviour is that the latter fails to treat other people with respect and infringes their rights. Generally, you can define behaviour as unacceptable if:

- it does not take into account the needs or views of others
- people are afraid or intimidated
- people are undermined or made to feel guilty
- the behaviour is likely to cause distress or unhappiness to others.

Examples of unacceptable behaviour include:

- threatening violence
- subjecting someone to unwelcome sexual attention
- seriously disturbing others, for example by shouting or playing loud music in a quiet area, or late at night
- verbal abuse, racist or sexist taunts
- spreading malicious gossip about someone
- attempting to isolate someone.

All of these types of behaviour are oppressive to others and need to be challenged. You can probably think of many other situations in your own workplace which have caused unhappiness. You may have had to deal with difficult situations, or have seen others deal with them, or perhaps you have wished that you had done something to challenge unacceptable behaviour.

Evidence PC 1

List three behaviours that you would find unacceptable. Check the policy of your organisation to see if these behaviours are to be challenged in your workplace.

Describe a situation where you have challenged one of these behaviours.

Be honest, did you follow organisational policy?

How to respond to unacceptable behaviour

What happens when people become aggressive?

Anger is a powerful emotion and it often seems as if people suddenly lose their temper without a reason. A service user might suddenly start shouting or making abusive comments. But this service user might have felt stressed long before the outburst of anger. Frustration and tension can grow as an individual loses control over his or her emotions and circumstances.

Triggers

As tension mounts it may take only a single remark or a small thing going wrong to push someone into an angry outburst. People who feel stressed may only need a minor incident to act as a trigger to set off an explosion of the anger that has built up inside them.

After an explosion of anger, stressed people can still feel tense. Very often they may feel that it is someone else's fault that they have been made to feel so angry. Anger can flare up again if the person is not given respect and encouraged to become calm. As time passes, tension may reduce as stress and levels of emotional arousal decrease.

Not all angry outbursts follow this pattern. Some people learn to use aggression to get their way, and some people can switch aggressive emotions on and off as they wish. Being angry can sometimes be a reaction that a person has chosen. But it is wrong to assume that most aggression and anger are deliberate; a great deal of aggression experienced by care workers is an emotional response to frustration or distress.

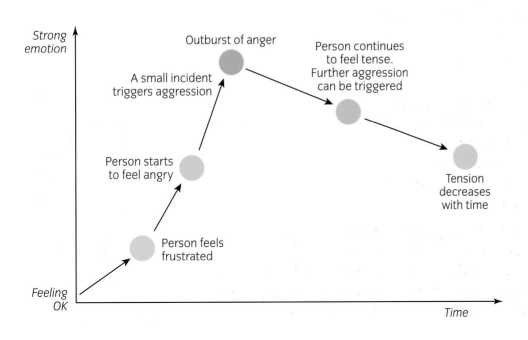

Stages in the development of aggression

The desire to fight or run

When people are aggressive or abusive they may make care workers feel threatened. The simple in-built emotional response to a threat is to want to run or fight. An unskilled response to aggression is to be aggressive in return. This will almost certainly escalate into a conflict situation, which is unlikely to have a positive outcome.

For example, imagine that an immobile resident in a care home has asked for assistance to get up but has been kept waiting. He or she may react aggressively with accusations such as: 'You don't care about me – you're too lazy to do your job properly', and so on. An unskilled response to this abuse might be to shout back at the resident, returning the abuse with statements such as 'You're not the only person here you know! I've only got one pair of hands' and so on. The problem with responding to aggression by being aggressive is that one or both people have to lose. The key purpose of care is to protect vulnerable people and meet social and self-esteem needs as well as basic physical needs. If a care worker is successful in being more aggressive than the service user, this is likely to increase the service user's sense of being out of control, lower his or her self-esteem and create increased helplessness in the individual. Depressed or withdrawn people may seem easier to manage than aggressive ones, but turning an aggressive person into a depressed person can never be acceptable.

Even in mildly aggressive encounters, one or both people are likely to feel resentment towards each other following the incident. You are unlikely to have job satisfaction if you develop resentment towards the people you work with.

There is of course, no guarantee that the care worker will be the winner if a conflict situation arises. Some members of the public can become physically violent and cause physical as well as emotional injury to staff. Other members of the public may make successful formal complaints if they have received abuse. The professional, skilled response is to stay calm, be assertive rather than aggressive, try to calm the other person, and resolve the situation without creating resentment. Of course, it is much easier to describe this formula than it is to implement it in practice.

Staying in control of your own emotions

We are all pre-programmed to either run away from or fight anyone who threatens us. Learning to be assertive and to take control of our instincts to run or to fight is a difficult task, but many people do learn to control their emotions. It is possible to stay in control and not allow the desire to run or fight to become overpowering.

We have two systems that guide our reactions. We can think and reason using the outer part of the brain, called the cortex, and we can react to experiences with emotion – a system built into our mid-brain. Emotion is designed to enable us to respond rapidly if we are threatened. If you switched on the lights as you entered a room in your house and saw a large bear coming towards you, your emotional system would make you respond with fear – you would attempt to run away. If you suddenly realised that this was a friend wearing a fancy dress costume, your fear response would switch off. You would probably laugh because your emotions had made you react inappropriately. Thought takes time and is much slower than your emotional responses, but thought can influence our perception of threat. You can use mental skills to control feelings of threat so that you can remain calm in situations involving people who are distressed or aggressive.

Control of emotion is therefore not a matter of willpower, but a matter of controlling whether we feel threatened or not. If someone is aggressive towards us it is often possible to rethink what is happening and not to feel threatened. Whereas an unskilled person faced by someone being aggressive may simply experience the emotions of threat and danger, a professional care worker may see that the person is distressed and overwhelmed by emotion – and that he or she can be helped. The professional person can therefore switch off the threat and think: 'This person is distressed, but I'm sure I can work with him; he will not harm me.' Learning to reinterpret threats means that professional people can choose the emotions they need to be able to work effectively with people. Many untrained and unskilled people may be controlled by their emotions, but people who have trained themselves in coping skills can often control how much threat they experience.

This is a threat – I'd better run!

I needn't feel threatened because:
- I can understand why this person is acting this way
- I know how to stay calm and to cope with this situation
- I've dealt with this type of incident successfully before – I'm a skilled worker.

In care situations the way we think controls what we experience

Care workers are unlikely to be able to switch off feelings of being threatened simply by wishing them away. Usually workers will switch off the threat by using positive thoughts about their own past experiences, their skills in being able to calm people, or just using their own professional role to protect themselves from feeling victimised. If a care worker can think 'This person is distressed because of his/her situation', rather than 'This person is out to get me', the emotions that create the feeling of being threatened can be switched off.

Staying calm

Being calm depends on the thoughts we have, but it is also a practical skill that can be learned and rehearsed. If a worker can appear to be calm, this behaviour may have a calming effect on others. Non-verbal signs of being calm are summarised in the diagram below.

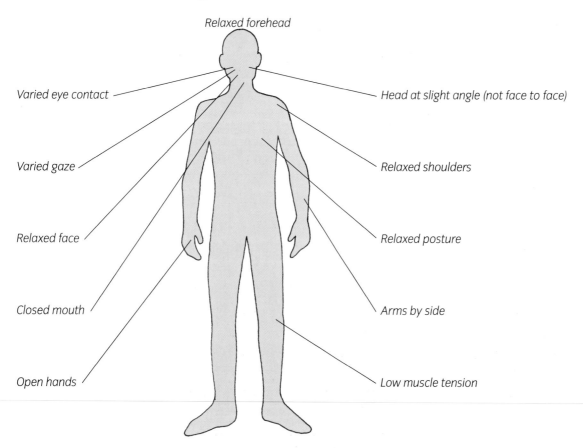

Relaxed forehead

Varied eye contact

Head at slight angle (not face to face)

Varied gaze

Relaxed shoulders

Relaxed face

Relaxed posture

Closed mouth

Arms by side

Open hands

Low muscle tension

Person creates inter-personal space

Non-verbal signs of being calm

It is important to remember to breathe gently and slowly. Slow, careful breathing can help to promote relaxation and calmness as well as making you look calm to others. Sometimes it is appropriate that body posture should be at a slight angle towards an angry person. A face-to-face posture is sometimes interpreted as an attempt to dominate or be threatening. The volume of speech should not be raised; it is important to talk in a normal tone and volume and to show that you do not feel threatened or angry.

Communicating respect and value

It is important to acknowledge the feelings that distressed people may be experiencing. If people feel they are being taken seriously and are being listened to, this may have a calming effect. Reflective listening skills and the ability to keep the conversation going will be very important. A professional would make sure the conversation is warm and sincere while also seeking to build an understanding of the situation. Thanking the person for clarifying issues may be one way in which a worker can reduce the frustration the person may feel. If a worker can communicate understanding of the person's point of view this may go a long way towards calming a situation and preventing further outbreaks of anger.

Assertiveness

Staying calm and in control of our own emotions, displaying respect for others, active listening and building an understanding of another person's viewpoint are all part of assertiveness. This involves being able to understand another person's viewpoint while being able to help him or her to understand your own viewpoint.

Assertiveness skills create a situation where negotiation is possible, and are therefore very important when working with distressed individuals. Assertiveness was discussed and compared with aggressive and submissive behaviour on pages 293–294.

Creating trust and negotiating with distressed people

If you can successfully calm an angry or distressed person, the next step will be to try to establish a sense of common ground. It is at this stage that a skilled worker will attempt to build an understanding of the other person's viewpoint.

Creating trust involves meeting the other person's self-esteem needs. In some situations it may be necessary to make the other person feel important; at other times it may be appropriate to say just a little about your own feelings, background and so on if this helps to build bridges and create a sense of safety for the other person. It is usually appropriate to come across as open-minded and supportive but it is important that you do not agree with everything the other person demands. It will be vital to keep the conversation going and to keep the person talking – perhaps using questioning and active listening skills.

Once you have built a level of understanding with a distressed person, it may then be possible to try to negotiate the kind of help or support you can offer. At this stage in the interaction it may be possible to take a problem-solving approach. Problem solving may start off by clarifying the issues that are involved and exploring alternative solutions.

Sometimes it may be necessary to structure expectations. This means gently introducing ideas of what is possible and not possible. Is important not to argue with a distressed person, as arguing may only force him or her into becoming aggressive or withdrawn. If you have to say 'no' to a demand, it may often be better to slowly lead up to the expectation that you must say no, rather than directly confronting a person with a rejection of their views. For example, say 'I understand what you're saying and I'll see what I can do, but it would be wrong to promise anything', or 'we can try, but I am not hopeful'.

Only after you have developed a sense of trust with the distressed person should you try to resolve the issues involved in the aggressive incident. During this stage of negotiation it may be important to bring factual information into the conversation. It will be important not to appear patronising when offering information, but also to clearly explain technical information that the other person may not understand.

Sometimes it will not be possible to reach agreement with a distressed person, and in these circumstances it will be important to conclude the conversation leaving a positive emotional outcome, even if agreement has not been reached. It may be possible to agree to resume a conversation tomorrow, or to thank the person for his or her time and offer to talk again. It will always be important to leave the person with an increased sense of self-esteem, even if he or she did not agree with your viewpoint.

Remember

While you can't always give other people what they want, you can always give respect and a little time in supportive communication. Listening and respect may go some way to creating a positive emotional environment.

1 Stay calm.

2 Try to calm the person using appropriate non-verbal behaviour.

3 Listen to the person.

4 Build trust and meet the other person's self-esteem needs.

5 Negotiate and try to solve problems.

> I'm glad you've talked about how unhappy you've been feeling. Now we can try to work at making things better.

Try to end the interaction on a positive note and leave the person with an increased sense of self-esteem

Real conversations do not always follow simple stages, but it is important not to attempt to negotiate and solve problems before listening and building trust.

Managing a difficult conversation

One way of developing skills in conversation management might be to analyse real conversations using the principles set out above. The brief example below is designed to illustrate some of these principles; real conversations may often be longer and more complex than this example, of course. The conversation takes place in a residential home for older people.

Relative What have you done to my mother! She's so much worse than before. You aren't looking after her properly. She can't eat because of the rubbish food you give out!

Worker Your mother does look worse today. Perhaps you would like to sit down and we can talk.

Relative Well, you tell me what's going on then, and why the food is such rubbish!

Worker I'll explain what we're doing if you like, and I'm sorry that your mother doesn't like the food. Could tell me what sort of things she really likes to eat?

Relative Not the rubbish here!

Worker Sometimes it's possible to increase a person's appetite by just offering a very small, tasty piece of something they really like. Perhaps fruit, or a tiny piece of bread and jam?

Relative What, and you are going to sort that out, are you?

Worker I've found that it works for a lot of people – but can you give me some ideas of what your mother would like?

Relative Well, she likes pears and cherry jam, but good stuff – not like here.

Worker OK. Could you possibly bring some of her favourite things in and we could try and see if that would help?

Relative Why should I?

Worker Well, it might help. Everyone is different and you are the person who would really know what your mother is likely to enjoy.

Relative Can't you do something about the food here?

Worker I'm afraid that the choice of food is limited, but we might be able to work together to improve your mother's appetite as a first step to making things better.

Relative I suppose it's not up to you to change the food. I'll bring the jam in but I still think it's not right.

Worker I'm sorry that you're not happy about the food, but perhaps we can talk again tomorrow.

Relative Well, thank you for your time. At least I could talk to you.

This conversation starts with the relative making aggressive accusations. The worker responds by remaining assertive and not arguing, and not going straight into discussing the complaints the relative has raised. Instead, the worker attempts to calm the situation and invites the relative to sit down. By inviting the relative to sit down the worker is taking control of the conversation and creating a situation where she can use her listening skills.

At several points the angry relative is still challenging the worker with complaints and aggressive statements. The worker is careful not to respond to these challenges and risk triggering more aggression. The worker is able to stay calm and to build a sense of trust by keeping the conversation going. She is able to ask the relative questions about his mother's needs, and also to meet his self-esteem needs by pointing out that he is the person who would really know what his mother likes.

In this conversation the worker negotiates with the relative to bring some food. The worker structures the relative's expectations by mentioning the limited choice of food. Because the relative has been listened to, he is willing to stop complaining – he compliments the worker with the statement that at least she listened.

The conversation ends on a positive emotional note, even though the problems of catering in this care setting have not been resolved. The point of this conversation was to meet the emotional needs of the distressed relative, and not to find technical solutions to catering problems.

Dealing with challenging behaviour

Each workplace will have policies to deal with challenging behaviour, and you must make sure that you are familiar with them. You should also discuss with your supervisor the types of behaviour you are likely to come across in your workplace.

Many care workers have to deal with verbal abuse or aggression from service users. This may be related to anger and frustration, or it may be caused by the medical condition of the service user. Clearly, reasonable communication is not possible with someone who is being aggressive and abusive, and the situation needs to be calmed before communication can begin.

Dealing with people who are extremely angry is difficult and, as a general rule, should be undertaken by highly experienced and skilled staff. You should never try to deal with a violent situation alone – you should always get help.

Remember

The basic rule is to follow the policies of your workplace in dealing with the particular behaviour, but do not be concerned about trying to resolve a problem until the situation is calm enough for discussion to be possible.

Steps in dealing with difficult situations

Step 1 Considering possible issues involved in the situation

- If you have some knowledge of an individual's background, culture and beliefs, it may be easier to see why he or she is behaving in a particular way. This does not make it acceptable, just easier to understand. For example, an individual who has been in a position of wealth or power may be used to giving people instructions and expecting to have immediate attention, and may be quite rude if it does not happen.

There are many reasons why people may become aggressive, as shown below.

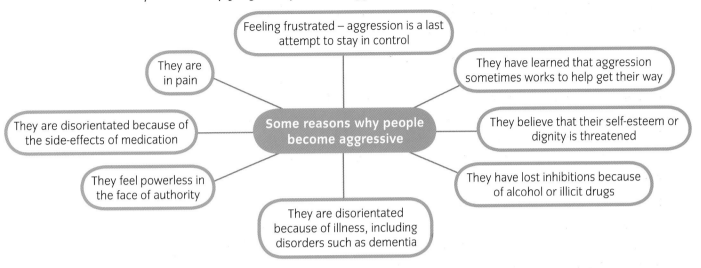

None of these reasons means that aggression should be tolerated, but if you can understand why a person is behaving in a challenging way it may help in two respects. First, the more that you can understand a situation the more you may feel able to assess the degree of risk involved. Second, the more you understand a situation the more ideas you may have for ways of managing it.

Step 2 Being aware of everyone's needs

If you are in a work situation, this can be complicated by the fact that the person whose behaviour you are challenging may also be one of your service users. It is important to ensure that you challenge the behaviour without becoming aggressive or intimidating yourself, and that you do not undermine the individual.

Step 3 Deciding on the best approach

How you decide to deal with an incident of unacceptable behaviour will depend on:

- whether the behaviour is violent or non-violent – if the behaviour is violent, what the potential dangers of the situation are, who may be in danger, and what needs to be done to help those in danger
- who is involved, and how well you know them and know how to deal with them
- whether you need help, and who is available to help you
- whether the cause is obvious and the solution is easy to find.

Clearly, you will need to weigh up the situation quickly, in order to deal with it promptly. You will, no doubt, feel under pressure, as this is a stressful situation to be in, whether you are experienced or not. Try to remain calm and think clearly.

Case study: Dealing with aggressive behaviour

Nathaniel is a care worker in a home for older people, and he works closely with Alf. Alf has been diagnosed as having dementia, and he often becomes disorientated and frustrated. One morning, Alf stands at the entrance to a lounge and starts shouting: 'Who are all these people? I want them out of here now – this is my home!' Alf becomes increasingly agitated and raises his walking stick, threatening to hit the other residents in the lounge. Nathaniel immediately calls to Alf as follows.

Nathaniel Hello Alf – I'm Nathaniel. You remember me.

Alf Who the **** are you? Get out of my house!

Nathaniel We talked about your daughter Janice yesterday. Janice said she would be coming to visit you, do you remember?

Alf Are you a friend of Janice, then?

Nathaniel Yes, we had a very friendly conversation last week.

Alf Well you can help me get these people out, then.

Nathaniel Well, I was wondering if we could leave that for the moment – I was wondering if you could spare me some time to talk about your daughter's visit. I'd be ever so grateful if you would come with me and we could talk about it down at the office – just down the corridor here.

Alf Well if it's important – but these people have to go, you know …

Nathaniel Well perhaps we can talk about it over a cup of tea and biscuits. What do you think?

Alf All right then, as long as you're a friend of Janice's.

1 *How is Nathaniel able to protect other service users and himself in this situation?*

2 *Why does Nathaniel not confront Alf or argue with him?*

3 *What are Nathaniel's immediate aims?*

In the case study above (in real life, it might take a little longer!) Nathaniel is able to protect the other service users and himself by using the following strategy.

- He remains calm, confident and assertive. He is able to do this because he understands the tension and frustration that Alf is experiencing – he knows that Alf is unable to make sense of the setting he is in. Nathaniel also has a supportive relationship with Alf, and he is able to predict that he will be able to safely manage the situation by mentioning Alf's daughter. Nathaniel knows that Alf will feel safer if he is with people who know his family.

- Nathaniel does not confront Alf and argue with him, because an increase in threat might trigger a violent reaction.

- Nathaniel tries to focus Alf's attention on him in order to protect the other service users.

- Nathaniel talks about Janice in order to create a sense of liking and trust, which may prevent aggression.
- Only after creating a calmer atmosphere where they are talking to each other does Nathaniel try to get Alf to agree with him to move away. This phase of negotiation only comes when Alf feels calm and supported enough to cope with it.

Limitations on methods of preventing aggression

The method described above can often be bypassed when you know that you are in a relationship where the person accepts your role and the boundaries that you set. For example, sometimes service users expect to be challenged by members of staff – children, for example, may feel safer where adults establish clear boundaries as to the kind of behaviour that is acceptable. In a setting where you can predict that a person will respond appropriately to authority, you might be able to speak loudly (without shouting), firmly and clearly to issue short instructions such as 'Stop shouting – now', 'Move way from Jim', 'Go into my office', and so on. Within a predictable relationship this type of short, firm instruction might have a chance of defusing the situation and restoring enough calm for problems to be investigated.

At the other extreme, attempting to create a sense of trust and to negotiate might be entirely inappropriate where a person is motivated to be aggressive or violent. For example, if you were confronted by an intruder with a weapon who demanded money, it might be inappropriate to try to talk the person out of his or her demands. Instead, the issue of your own safety and the safety of service users should take priority over defending the organisation's property.

If you are confronted by a situation where you cannot meaningfully assess the degree of risk that you face, then you must always put your safety and the safety of others first. This means that it may be best not to try to use the management technique of staying calm, creating trust, and negotiating, as this may put you at risk. Some situations need to be handled by specially trained members of staff, or even the police in the case of intruders. If you are the only person at risk it is often better to try to escape from a situation and raise the alarm rather than to attempt to manage an unpredictable situation.

Dealing with non-violent behaviour

If the behaviour you have to deal with is not physical aggression or violence, then you will need to ensure that you challenge it in a situation which provides privacy and dignity. You should challenge assertively; remain calm and quietly state what you consider to be unacceptable about the behaviour. Do not try to approach the subject from various angles, or drop hints. Be clear about the problem and what you want to happen.

For example: 'Bill, you are playing your radio very loudly late at night. Other residents are finding it difficult to get to sleep. I would like you to stop playing it so loudly if you want to have it on late.' You may well have to negotiate with Bill about times, and the provision of headphones, but do not be drawn into an argument and do not be sidetracked into irrelevant discussions. Keep to the point:

Bill   Who's been complaining? No one's complained to me. Who is it?

You   Bill, this is about your radio being too loud. The issue is not about who complained, but about the fact that it is upsetting residents and I want you to stop doing it.

By the end of this discussion, Bill should be very clear about what is being required of him and be in no doubt that his behaviour will have to change.

Evidence   PC ④

Think of a situation where you have had to act to challenge aggressive or abusive behaviour, or intervene to prevent such behaviour when it seemed likely to occur. Make a note of how you handled the situation. Could you have dealt with it in a better way? What else could you have done? Would it have turned out differently?

If you have never had to act in such a situation, ask an experienced colleague to tell you about an incident he or she has had to deal with. Then answer the same questions, based on what your colleague has told you. Remember, your colleague may not want to hear the conclusions you draw! Keep your notes for your portfolio.

Calming a potentially violent situation

It is always better to avoid a violent situation than have to respond to one, so you need to be aware of the signals which may indicate that violence could erupt. Be on the lookout for signs such as verbal aggression; raised volume and pitch of voice; threatening and aggressive gestures; pacing up and down; quick, darting eye movements; prolonged eye contact.

Try to respond in ways least likely to provoke further aggression.
● Use listening skills, and appear confident (but not cocky).
● Keep your voice calm and at a level pitch.
● Do not argue.
● Do not get drawn into prolonged eye contact.
● Attempt to defuse the situation with empathy and understanding. For example: 'I realise you must be upset if you believe that George said that about you. I can see that you're very angry. Tell me about what happened.'

Be prepared to try a different approach if you find you are not getting anywhere. Always make sure that an aggressor has a way out with dignity, both physically and emotionally.

Dealing with aggressive or violent behaviour

Be aware of the situation you are in and take some common-sense precautions: make sure that you know where the exits are, and move so that the aggressor is not between you and the exit; notice if there is anything that

Did you know?

There is a technique recommended for use in situations which become violent. It is called 'Breakaway' and is approved by the Home Office for use in all types of care settings. It provides you with methods for dealing with a physical threat or attack without causing injury. Ask your employer to arrange for you to attend a course with an approved trainer.

could be used as a weapon, and try to move away from it; make sure that the aggressor has enough personal space, and do not crowd him or her. Stand at a slight angle to the aggressor – this may appear less confrontational and it also provides you with the chance of shifting your weight and running to an exit more quickly than if you have to turn around in order to run.

If you are faced with a violent situation, you should try to remain calm (even though that is easier said than done!) and not resort to violence or aggression yourself.

It is possible that a distracting technique such as holding up a hand in front of you, as if you were directing traffic, and shouting 'Stop' or even 'Mind the table!' may confuse an attacker, or delay him or her long enough for you to get away. You should remove yourself from the situation as speedily as possible.

If there are other, vulnerable people at risk, you must decide whether you can summon help more effectively from outside or inside the situation. If you decide to remain, you must summon help at once. You should do one of the following.

- Press a panic alarm or buzzer, if one is provided.
- Shout 'help!' very loudly and continuously, if it is possible to do this without provoking physical assault from the aggressor.
- Send someone for help.
- Call the police, or security, or shout for someone else to do so.

Do not try to be a hero – that is not your job.

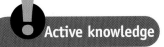

Physical restraint issues

KS 3 4 5

Physically restraining individuals is very much a last resort and restraint should be used only if it is absolutely unavoidable. If you are likely to need to use physical restraint as part of your work with adult service users, then it is critically important that you should have appropriate practical training in the use of safe restraint techniques. It is quite possible to cause serious injury, or even to kill someone by using inappropriate techniques. Your workplace will have a policy on the use of physical restraint, if permitted, and you will need to be sure that you know what it is for your own setting. The policies vary, but are likely to include the following principles.

- Before using restraint, staff should have good grounds for believing that immediate action is necessary to prevent an individual from significantly injuring himself/herself or others, or causing serious damage to property.
- Staff should take steps in advance to avoid the need for physical restraint, such as by discussing or providing diversion from the problem; and the individual should be warned that physical restraint will be used unless he or she stops.
- Only the minimum force necessary to prevent injury or damage should be used.
- Every effort should be made to have other staff present before applying restraint. These staff can act both as assistants and witnesses.

Active knowledge

Your workplace should have a policy on dealing with aggression and violence. Ask to see it and make sure that you read it carefully.

Remember

- Everyone is different and will react differently to each situation.
- You are the factor that makes the difference.

● As soon as it is safe, restraint should be gradually relaxed to allow the individual to regain self-control.

These are the general principles, but you must also act within the law. Any use of physical restraint can be viewed as assault, and result in a criminal charge. This is why it is essential that you follow your workplace policy, and discuss with your supervisor exactly what steps you must take.

Recording an incident

Once the immediate risk has been averted, you must report the incident to your manager, and the correct procedures for dealing with it must be followed. You are not in a position to take a decision about what is and what is not serious enough to be followed up. That decision will be taken after discussion with the agencies involved.

It is important that you write a report of any incident of abuse or aggression as soon as possible. You may think that you will never forget what you saw or heard, but details do become blurred with time and repetition. Your workplace may have a special form or you may have to write a report.

Your report of any incident of abuse or aggression must be in line with your workplace policy

Regulation 37 of the Care Homes Regulations 2001 requires any 'event which results in a serious injury to a service user' or any 'event in the care home which adversely affects the well-being or safety of any service user' to be reported to the Commission for Social Care Inspection. If you have been involved in a serious incident it will need to be reported using the two-sided form currently available on the CSCI website.

Remember

Think about the children's game of Chinese Whispers. The players sit in a circle and a message is whispered from one person to the next around the circle. The last player speaks the message aloud; it has usually changed quite a lot as it has been passed around the circle!

It is easy to see how verbal information can become distorted, or messages lose their emphasis, as they are retold. Always make sure you record information as soon as you can.

If there is a reason why writing a report is not possible, then you should record your evidence on audio tape. It is not acceptable to pass on the information verbally – there must be a record that can be referred to. Your evidence may be needed by the social workers and police officers who will investigate the situation. It may be useful for a doctor who will conduct an examination, or it may be needed for a case conference or for court proceedings.

If you have witnessed, or intervened in, an act of aggression which may constitute a criminal offence, you must *not* remove any possible evidence until the police have examined the scene. If there are injuries, or the possibility of physical evidence, a medical examination must be arranged. If an adult has been affected, he or she must consent to an examination before one can be carried out. In the case of a child, the parents must consent, unless they are the suspected abusers.

Test yourself

1   List the important factors in resolving conflicts and disagreements.

2   What is the difference between being assertive and being aggressive?

3   List some examples of unacceptable behaviour that may occur, or have occurred, in your workplace and the steps for dealing with them.

4   What should you do if faced with a potentially violent situation?

HSC 336c Contribute to reviewing incidents of abusive and aggressive behaviour

How dealing with abuse or aggression can affect you
KS 5

Being involved in an incident of violence or aggression can be very distressing and you should ask for support from your supervisor if you find that you are affected by an incident you have witnessed or been involved in.

Do not underestimate how upsetting it can be to deal with someone who is displaying powerful emotions. Feeling concerned, upset or even angry after a particularly difficult experience with a service user is perfectly normal. The fact that you continue to have an emotional response after a situation is over is in no way a reflection on the quality of your work or your ability as a care worker.

After dealing with any difficult or emotional situation most people are likely to continue to think about it for some time. One of the best ways to deal with this is to discuss it with your line manager or supervisor; or you could talk to a close friend or relative, always ensuring that you never compromise an individual's right to confidentiality. If you find after a period of time that you are unable to put a particular incident out of your mind or you feel that it is interfering with your work, there are other sources of help available to you, both within your workplace and outside it. Talk to your line manager or supervisor to ensure that you have access to any help you need.

Abuse and aggression will always be distressing for the person who deals with them. But if you are able to develop your skills and knowledge so that you can identify the causes of unacceptable behaviour, contribute towards reducing it and offer effective help and support to individuals, then you are making a useful contribution to the provision of quality care. The best way to channel your thoughts and feelings following an incident will be to make clear and constructive contributions to team discussions, and to undertake a careful review.

Encouraging those involved to contribute to a review KS ④⑤⑥⑦⑧⑨⑪⑫

There needs to be a process of review following an incident of abusive and aggressive behaviour to identify any action that needs to be taken, and for lessons to be learned so that such situations can be avoided in the future. You will need to offer time, space and support so that everyone involved can express their feelings and examine their behaviour.

The review should explore constructively the reasons for, and consequences of, the incident. You may need to offer support to individuals before, during or after their contribution to the review. The support you give can range from straightforward reassurance and information to relieve anxiety and apprehension about the process, to using basic counselling skills to resolve some of the issues and concerns which have resulted from the incident.

EvidencePC ① ② ⑥

Describe the feelings you experience from dealing with incidents of abuse and aggressive behaviour.

How do you manage your feelings?

How do you encourage others involved to manage their feelings and review the incident?

Remember

Those affected by an incident may include people who were not present, such as relatives, friends or carers of the individuals involved. They should be invited to contribute to the review.

Keys to good practice: Encouraging individuals to speak about an incident

✓ Follow the principles of good communication. Remember to talk to the individual in an appropriate environment where he or she can feel relaxed and secure.

✓ Remember that you are doing the listening, not the talking.

✓ Listen actively to what the individual tells you and prompt him or her by nodding and using encouraging words.

✓ You may need to repeat back what the individual tells you to check that you have understood and to show that you are listening well.

✓ Avoid giving direct advice if possible, but try to encourage the individual to understand for himself or herself what has happened and to look at options for the future.

If you find yourself having to offer extensive support, you should talk to your supervisor or line manager for advice or guidance. In many cases it may be necessary to make referrals to appropriate professionals for specialist help to be provided.

Self-confidence and self-esteem

Being involved in an abusive or aggressive incident can be a huge blow to someone's self-confidence and self-esteem, and low levels of these may have contributed to the fact that the incident arose in the first place. If someone is not very confident or does not have a high opinion of himself or herself, you will need to offer extra support in order for him or her to contribute to a review.

Being the victim of abuse or aggression often creates a major threat to self-esteem. For many people, being shouted at or being pushed, for example, will have little impact on their physical well-being. However, being subject to abuse can be a threat to your dignity. Being disrespected (or 'dissed' in teenage slang) can damage your emotional well-being. When people have been assaulted, the degree of physical injury may sometimes be less damaging than the emotional damage to their self-confidence and self-esteem.

Many service users in care are vulnerable people; they come into care because of a loss of health, the loss of a partner, or the loss of physical, sensory or mental abilities. Many people in care may already have low self-esteem or feel vulnerable because of their situation. Becoming the victim of abuse or aggression provides an additional threat to self-esteem.

One of the most straightforward defences that people use when their self-esteem is threatened is to withdraw from, or deny the significance of what has happened. You may find that service users do not wish to talk about an event that has damaged their self-esteem.

Key terms

Self-esteem: How people value themselves; how much self-respect they have.

Counselling

In some situations people who have been victims of abuse or assault may need the support of a professional counsellor in order to assist them to make sense of events and to rebuild their self-confidence and self-esteem. It is likely that your organisation will have a procedure for contacting counselling services where staff or service users need such support.

Sometimes, skilled active listening may be enough to help a person make sense of what happened and re-establish self-esteem and confidence. It may be that by offering to talk an issue through you will be able to support a person to report or review an incident.

If you find that you are unsure about the best ways to meet the needs of particular individuals, you should discuss this with your supervisor, who will be able to give you advice based on knowledge of the individual concerned and the local facilities available.

Exploring the reasons for the behaviour

An individual may find it difficult to accept and describe the feelings of fear, frustration or anger that caused him or her to behave aggressively. Because of people's beliefs, values and culture they may not find it easy to understand or to express in a constructive way how they feel. It is important to create as many opportunities as possible for people to express their feelings openly, and the review of the incident should be conducted in such a way that people feel supported in doing this.

The stressful or angry feelings that led to the behaviour could have many causes, but the individual can be supported in finding constructive ways of coping with stress or managing anger, such as:

- talking things over with a carer, friend, relative or counsellor
- doing something to take his or her mind off the problem, if only temporarily
- using relaxation techniques such as controlled breathing, which can be taught
- undertaking physical activity such as walking, gardening or simple exercises, if possible.

Managing your own feelings

Aggression can create a high level of threat to your own self-esteem as well as a threat to your physical well-being. Even verbal abuse can be very upsetting if we do not have a clear understanding of why we became a victim. We may have thoughts such as 'Why did they pick on me?', 'Did I do something wrong?', or 'Is there something about me that encourages attack?'

Aggressive and threatening behaviour usually has a strong emotional impact. Part of the process of coping with challenging behaviour is managing the emotional response following the events. It is natural to feel emotions involving hostility and resentment towards people who have threatened your own self-esteem or well-being. Part of the process of coping is to recognise your own feelings and to work out a way in which your emotions can be used positively to increase your confidence in coping with challenging situations.

While some people feel anger at being threatened, other people may experience feelings of guilt. You may have thoughts such as these: 'Perhaps I handled it badly – I'm sure there is something I could have done better. Perhaps I'll never be any good at this work.' It is easy to convince yourself that experts can predict and control everything and that highly skilled people never have difficulties. But not all incidents can be prevented. Self-blame can sometimes be useful if it leads us to reflect on our behaviour, but the problem with self-blame is that it can lead to the negative emotional conclusion that you cannot improve anything because you are a 'bad' or 'incompetent' person.

The desire to punish people who have threatened us, or the desire to punish ourselves, needs to be understood as one expected result of emotionally charged experience. So it is important to acknowledge the feelings you have,

> **Remember**
>
> Be sure that, following the review and all discussions of the incident, you complete accurate records about decisions taken and actions that are recommended for the future, and that you store your records according to workplace requirements.

but then to move on and do something constructive that might improve your self-confidence and self-esteem. Sometimes professional counselling is needed in order to help people achieve this difficult task.

Talking through the experience with a trusted colleague or supervisor may help you to cope with your reactions

For many people it will be important to be able to understand and interpret why the event may have happened in the way that it did. Theory has a role to play in helping us to understand events. If we can understand some of the ways in which frustration, and feeling out of control, can cause people to become aggressive, this may help us to think positively and be able to improve self-confidence as a result of an experience.

CASE STUDY: Understanding an aggressive incident

Rick works in a day centre for people with learning difficulties. He runs cookery classes for small groups of service users. He enjoys very good relationships with all the service users in the centre and usually there is a very happy and supportive atmosphere in the teaching sessions.

Two weeks ago, however, Rick reported an incident where one of the service users – Tia – became very aggressive and threatened to stab Rick and other service users with a knife she was using. Although Rick was eventually able to talk Tia into putting down the knife, and although no one was injured, the incident keeps going through his mind. During his supervision session, Rick discusses the incident as follows.

Rick The thing that is really worrying me is I still don't know exactly what happened. I mean – I thought we had a good understanding. She has always responded well to me before but on this day she didn't. I don't know what triggered her to become so aggressive. Did I do

Continued

CASE STUDY: Understanding an aggressive incident (cont.)

something wrong – was I just not observant enough? I mean, it should be possible to stop these things happening, right? So I must have not been paying attention. It scares me to think that this could happen again and I don't know how to stop it.

Supervisor What possible reasons might there have been for Tia to become aggressive?

Rick Well, that's the problem – I don't know, but I ought to know.

Supervisor Why do you think it's your responsibility to know this?

Rick Well – an expert would be able to spot these things and prevent aggression, wouldn't they?

Supervisor No, perhaps they wouldn't. No matter how much you have studied and no matter how much experience you've had, you have to remember that people are immensely complicated. Most of the time we can guess what other people are feeling – perhaps we can often predict how they might react – but there will always be situations that even the most expert person cannot predict. We can't know exactly what Tia was thinking, and we can't know what was happening in terms of her physical state. The thing was that you handled the situation very effectively. You stayed calm, you made things safe for the other service users and you used your understanding of Tia to help her cope with the emotion she was feeling. So, well done – perhaps that's all anyone can do!

1 *Rick is using reflective skills (see Unit HSC 33) in order to try to find an answer to the problem of preventing aggression. How effective is the supervisor in helping Rick to develop his skills?*

2 *Why does Rick believe that there must be a simple answer to preventing aggression?*

3 *The supervisor confronts Rick with the idea that all we can do is to develop skills for managing situations – we cannot always predict how people will behave. Is Rick's supervisor right about this?*

4 *If Rick feels confident that he can manage aggressive behaviour, how will this help him in working with service users in future?*

Not always about you!

It may also be important to understand that sometimes you can become a target for 'displaced anger'. For example, some people have had the experience of being dominated and bullied by authority figures. Sometimes this might start with an authoritarian father in the family, and as a result some people view all authority figures as their enemies. Even though you may have been calm, assertive and friendly, your behaviour may have been viewed with suspicion. One long word that the other person did not understand may have been interpreted as an attempt to dominate and belittle them. The abuse or aggression you experienced may not really be a direct consequence of the word you used, but the word may have acted as a trigger for pent-up anger and aggression – perhaps harboured for many years.

Discussing a stressful event with your supervisor can be very helpful, provided your supervisor is able to support you to make sense of what happened. It is important to be able to resolve your understanding of incidents of aggression without needing to resort to blaming others, or holding on to the feeling that either you or the people who have wronged you are in some way 'evil' and should be punished.

Test yourself

1 Why should all those involved in an abusive or aggressive incident contribute to a review?

2 Why is it important to record information about the decisions taken following a review?

3 How would you access professional help for someone needing support after an incident involving aggression or abuse?

4 How would you access support for yourself, should you need it?

HSC 336 FURTHER READING AND RESEARCH

Below are some books, websites and agencies you can look up to continue your study of this subject.

www.alzheimers.org.uk (Alzheimer's Society)

www.rethink.org (Rethink)

www.scope.org.uk (Scope)

www.thecbf.org.uk (the Challenging Behaviour Foundation)

www.nas.org.uk (National Autistic Society)

Age Concern (DATE) *Supporting People with Dementia* Dementia Voice

Woodward, P., Hardy, S., Joyce, T. (DATE) *Keeping it Together: A Guide for Support Staff Working with People Whose Behaviour is Challenging* Pavilion Publishers

Support individuals to manage their financial affairs

In this unit you will learn about ways of supporting individuals in managing their finances in the most independent way possible.

This unit is most likely to be of importance to those working in the community supporting individuals in their own homes, but many supported living environments and some types of residential setting provide for individuals to have a significant degree of financial independence. Even within a residential setting it is important that you are aware of some of the financial regulations in case you are asked questions by service users or their relatives.

A list of useful contacts is provided at the end of this unit (pages 349–350).

What you need to learn

- How to provide active support
- How to find out about benefits and allowances
- Budgeting
- Managing debts
- Overcoming problems
- How to help individuals apply for benefits and allowances
- Methods of collecting benefits and allowances
- Supporting individuals to make payments
- Methods of making payments
- Ways of recording payments made
- Ways of dealing with potential conflicts
- Reviewing effectiveness.

HSC 345a Work with individuals to access information and advice about their financial affairs

How to provide active support

Your first step, as always when working with service users, should be to establish with the individual the level of help he or she is going to need. Obviously, this will depend partly on the individual's stage of life and experience in dealing with money matters, and partly on current circumstances. You will need access to any relevant records and information.

The first thing that you should do in any situation where an individual has requested financial management assistance is to discuss the exact type and level of assistance required and how much information the individual feels comfortable with you being given about his or her financial affairs. For example, some individuals may be happy for you to collect their pension or to pay their TV licence or gas bill, but would not consider showing you their bank statements. The level of involvement must be established and agreed with the individual.

When an individual cannot deal confidently with his or her financial affairs, you may need to help

It is important that you understand the difference between needing support to manage financial affairs and being incapable of managing financial affairs. It is one thing to agree a level of support you will provide for an individual and quite another to take over the administration of his or her affairs completely because of incapacity. Administering all the financial affairs of another person is not part of your role – there are strict legal provisions about who may undertake this and in what circumstances. If you feel that you are working with an individual who is not capable of understanding money matters, this must be reported to your supervisor at once. The appropriate legal steps to protect the individual can then be taken.

The Mental Capacity Act 2005 has brought about changes in the Power of Attorney process. All Powers of Attorney are now controlled by the Office of the Public Guardian and there are two different powers: an Enduring Power of Attorney and a Lasting Power of Attorney.

You could find in working with an individual for several years that his or her abilities deteriorate and you are doing more and more. It is important that from time to time, particularly where you are working with an individual with a degenerative condition such as Alzheimer's disease, you check his or her level of understanding of financial matters and that you report any concerns as soon as possible. And of course you must always ensure that you are working within the relevant codes of practice and strictly following the guidelines laid down by your workplace.

Where individuals are in need of support in managing financial matters, it may well be that they, their carers or other key people in their lives will have relevant skills and abilities, and it will be an important part of your role to encourage individuals to identify the skills that are available to them. Each individual should be encouraged to access and use the information and support already available that will help the person to manage his or her financial affairs efficiently. Where there are gaps in skills or support is where your role in providing assistance begins.

The first step may be to find out about any benefits and allowances to which individuals or their carers may be entitled.

How to find out about benefits and allowances KS ① ⑥ ⑨ ⑩ ⑮ ⑰ ⑲

It is always preferable to encourage and enable individuals to find out as much information for themselves as possible. You should only intervene in the provision of information when the individual is unable to carry out the research and it is not possible for you to empower him or her.

Sources of information about benefits and allowances are extremely varied throughout the country, and are different depending on whether you are working in a rural or urban area. The most comprehensive advice and information is usually available at centres such as the local Citizens Advice Bureau, at a welfare rights centre or a money advice centre.

Key terms

Power of Attorney: Legal power and responsibility given to a person or persons to administer the financial affairs of someone who is incapable of doing this for himself or herself.

Key terms

Enduring Power of Attorney (EPA): a legal process in which a person (the Donor) hands over to someone else (the Attorney) the power to decide what is done with their financial affairs and property.

The Attorney can use the power straight away if that is what the Donor wants. Or the Donor can make it clear that the EPA is only to be used if they become mentally unable to manage their affairs in the future.

In this way, an EPA allows the Donor to choose someone they trust now to deal with their affairs if they become mentally unable to manage them themselves in the future. An EPA only covers decisions relating to a Donors financial and property affairs.

Key terms

Lasting Power of Attorney (LPA): a legal document that someone (the Donor) makes using a special form. It allows that person to choose someone now (the Attorney) that they trust to make decisions on their behalf at a time in the future when they either lack the mental capacity or no longer wish to make those decisions themselves.

The decisions could be about the Donor's property and affairs or about their personal welfare. Making an LPA is the only way to make plans for a time in the future when you may lack the capacity to make decisions for yourself. An LPA can only be used after it is registered with the Office of the Public Guardian.

The Citizens Advice Bureau is a national organisation with branches in most towns and cities throughout the UK. It also has a comprehensive website (www.citizensadvice.org.uk) and telephone advice lines. Welfare rights centres and money advice centres are often run by local authorities, so your local council should be able to tell you the nearest location of these. The local library is always a good source of information about advice centres and it will also be able to advise on the nearest Citizens Advice Bureau.

The Benefits Agency provides a benefits helpline where information about specific allowances and benefits can be obtained. However, this relates only to state benefits. Any broader or more general advice will need to be obtained from a Citizens Advice Bureau or a money advice centre.

Active knowledge

Visit the Citizens Advice Bureau website at www.citizensadvice.org.uk and find out about the information it offers and how it operates.

Welfare rights centres are a source of comprehensive advice on benefits and allowances

Offering help in researching benefits and allowances

In many circumstances you will find that offering some additional support in researching possible benefits and allowances may be all that is required to allow an individual to gather and assess information. Below is a list of reasons why people may need help, and ways of offering appropriate assistance.

Possible difficulty	Assistance that could be offered
Mobility	Arrange transport, check in advance about access to information centre, library, etc.
Lack of confidence	Offer to accompany individual to find out information.
Unable to use telephone	Explore use of telephone adaptations if appropriate.
No access to Internet	Arrange support to visit library, cyber café, or computer centre to access information on the Internet.

Individual entitlements

Depending on his or her circumstances, an individual may be eligible for a number of state benefits or allowances. However, state benefits are not the only source of income you may need to assist in investigating. If the individual has been in employment, he or she may have access to a company or private pension scheme, or may be eligible for financial support from a charity or benevolent fund specifically for retired or former members of particular occupations. The *Charities Digest*, a copy of which should be available in your local library, gives information about every charity in the country and explains the help provided by each charitable organisation.

Individuals may be entitled to other kinds of help because of age or level of disability. These benefits can make a significant difference to a person's financial situation, so it is important that you ensure individuals obtain information about their entitlements. You don't have to have full knowledge of welfare rights and all the allowances available; but it is helpful if you know in general terms what an individual may be eligible to receive. The main points of the most important benefits are set out below.

All this information is intended only to provide you with a guide as to the range of benefits that may be available for any individual you are working with. It is not an exhaustive list, so it is vitally important that you obtain information from expert sources, either at advice centres or directly from the Benefits Agency, about any benefits to which an individual may be entitled.

Most importantly, you should be able to advise people where they can obtain further information.

General information on benefits

Pensions

Women over 60 and men over 65 are entitled to the state retirement pension. (From 2010 the pension age will begin to rise from 60 to 65 for women also.) This basic pension is paid to people who have reached the applicable age and who have sufficient National Insurance contributions.

People who do not have sufficient National Insurance contributions made or credited throughout their working life may get a reduced pension, or possibly no pension at all. Married women, if they do not have sufficient contributions of their own, can claim a pension based on their husband's contributions. In 2007 the full basic pension is £87.30 a week for an individual. The reduced rate for married women whose claims are based on their husband's contributions is £52.30.

Help with residential or nursing home fees

People wishing to enter residential or nursing home care will have their care needs assessed by their local authority. Assistance with nursing home fees will be provided on a sliding scale after a financial assessment or means test is carried out. The rules differ in different parts of the UK.

- In **England and Northern Ireland**, people with capital below £20,000 may be entitled to some state assistance towards care costs. The social services department will carry out an assessment of the person's care needs under Section 47 of the NHS and Community Care Act 1990. Anyone assessed as needing nursing home or residential care will be asked to claim any income support benefits or pension credit he or she may be entitled to and these will be taken into account in a means test to ascertain how much the person can afford to pay. Normally the person will have to pay all income towards the fees, less £18.10 per week that must be retained for personal expenses. If the person has capital below £12,250, he or she will receive the maximum help. A person with capital of between £12,250 and £20,000 will have to make a contribution of £1 for each £250 of capital between these two figures.

- In **Scotland** a person with capital below £11,750 receives maximum help. A person with capital between £11,750 and £19,000 will have to make a contribution of £1 for each £250 of capital between these two figures.
- In **Wales** a person with capital below £13,500 receives maximum help. A person with capital between £13,500 and £20,500 will have to make a contribution of £1 for each £250 of capital between these two figures. In Wales the personal expenses allowance is £18.40.

NHS nursing contribution

NHS nursing contributions are not means tested. Again, the rules differ in different parts of the UK.

In **England**, people living in a care home which provides nursing care are entitled to a contribution towards these costs from the NHS. This is paid directly to the care home. An NHS nurse assesses the person and the level of care required. There are three bands for payments.

- Those who require low levels of nursing care receive £40 a week.
- Those who have moderate needs receive £77.50 per week.
- People who require high levels of nursing care receive £125 per week.

In **Wales**, people requiring nursing care receive a flat rate of £105 a week. In **Northern Ireland**, they receive a flat rate of £100 a week, and in **Scotland** £65 a week plus an allowance of up to £145 a week for personal care.

Continuing care

Continuing care is not means tested. If a person has complex health needs or requires palliative care, he or she may be entitled to NHS continuing care funding. The person will be assessed by a range of NHS professionals and by a care manager. A panel then assesses the case. If the person meets continuing care criteria, the NHS meets all costs of care. A reassessment normally takes place every three months.

Prescription charges

People over 60 are entitled to free prescription charges and free sight tests regardless of their level of savings or their income.

Transport

The government now requires local authorities to offer free or reduced bus/ train fares to local older people. The provisions vary, so you should ask your local council what its arrangements are. Many rail companies give reductions on national rail fares to people aged 60 or over, and some of the national bus companies provide similar discounts.

Attendance allowance

This allowance is designed for people who need assistance with washing, dressing, mobility or feeding, or who need supervision so they are not a risk to themselves. In 2007 this is paid at two different rates: one is a weekly rate of £43.15 for individuals who need help during the day or night and the other, higher rate is currently £64.50 for help needed round the clock.

Individuals are eligible to claim attendance allowance regardless of their living circumstances – they can claim even if they live alone. The requirement is that the individual needs help, but he or she does not have to be getting help in order to qualify for the allowance. As a general rule, individuals must meet the conditions for the allowance for a period of at least six months before it is payable. However, special rules apply for individuals who are terminally ill.

Child benefit

Child benefit – which was called Family Allowance until 1977 – is payable as a universal benefit, regardless of income or savings, to the mothers of all children who are in full-time education. Since its introduction in 1946, child benefit has risen from 5 shillings (25p) a week for each child after the first one to £1 a week in 1977, when it began to be paid for the first child as well as others, to the present rate of £18.10 for the first child and £12.10 for the second and subsequent children.

Benefits for those on low incomes

All the benefits designed to support people with low incomes are based on a means test, which takes savings and income into account. Some of these benefits are also related to the National Insurance contributions that have been made.

Income support or pension credit

Income support is a benefit available to those who are under 60 and are on a low income. For people of pensionable age it has been replaced by pension credit.

Income support is available for people who have no more than £6,000 in savings. The level at which income support is payable is set by Parliament, as the minimum amount on which people should be required to live. All income and savings are taken into account, and then items such as housing costs are deducted. Full details of the current income support and pension credit rates can be obtained from the Benefits Agency or any advice centre.

Did you know?

Three million pensioners in the UK receive pension credit to make up their pensions to an agreed minimum level.

Housing benefit and council tax benefit

Housing benefit provides assistance towards rent for those on a low income, and council tax benefit provides support for the payment of council tax. Both of these benefits are only available to claimants with less than £16,000 in savings. A broad guide is that if an individual is eligible for income support, he or she is also likely to be entitled to housing benefit and council tax benefit. Those in receipt of income support will automatically be sent the appropriate forms to complete for housing and council tax benefit. Otherwise, the forms will be available from the local authority.

As in the case of income support, all the circumstances of an individual are taken into account, including income, savings, the number in the family, level of disability and so on.

There are also schemes that provide a reduction in council tax for people who live alone and for those who live with another person who has a low income.

Health costs

People in receipt of income support will receive free prescriptions, free dental treatment, help with travel costs for hospital visits, free sight tests and help towards the purchase of glasses. Those who do not receive income support, and who earn less than a set earnings limit, can still get some help towards these costs by completing a form available from a dentist, optician or hospital.

Social fund

The social fund can provide lump sum cash payments to cover large, necessary expenses that cannot be met from normal weekly incomes – for example, the purchase of an item of furniture such as a bed or cooker, or funeral costs. The social fund can also make loans in an emergency, but it is important to remember that these loans must be repaid.

Working families tax credit

This is a tax credit to ensure that wage earners in low-income families receive an income that meets the minimum income guarantee. Further information on this benefit, which is calculated according to levels of wages, allowances for housing and other costs, and the number of dependent children, can be obtained from the Benefits Agency.

Benefits for people with disabilities and for carers

Disability living allowance

This is a benefit for those who are disabled and require the same sort of care and assistance that qualifies people for the attendance allowance. It provides benefit for those who are unable to walk or have great difficulty walking outdoors. The calculations for the rates at which it is paid are complex. Information should be obtained from the Benefits Agency or a local advice centre.

Carer's allowance

This is paid to carers who spend at least 35 hours a week providing care to someone. Carers are eligible to claim this allowance if the person they are caring for qualifies for an attendance allowance or disability living allowance. To qualify, carers must not be earning more than £79 a week. Carers who are receiving other benefits may not be eligible for the carer's allowance.

Incapacity benefit (previously called invalidity benefit)

This is paid to people who cannot work because they are sick or disabled. It is based on the National Insurance contributions made, and the rates at which it is paid depend on the length of time that a person is unable to work. Incapacity benefit stops when a person reaches pensionable age.

Severe disablement allowance

This benefit is paid to severely disabled people who cannot work but do not have sufficient National Insurance contributions to quality for incapacity benefit. It is only applicable to disabled people aged under 65. The Benefits Agency requires a medical examination and there are strict guidelines as to the definition of 'severe disablement'.

The rate is the same as income support, but it is not means tested, so is available to people with a severe disability regardless of any income or savings they have.

Independent living fund

This helps severely disabled people who need to pay for care or support in order to remain living at home. Local authorities can also make payments as an alternative to providing community care services, thus enabling a disabled individual to make his or her own arrangements for care and support. Payments are available to anyone aged over 16 who is severely disabled.

Disabled person's tax credit

This benefit is designed for people with disabilities who are in work but earn a low income. Through the tax credit they are able to ensure that their income does not fall below the minimum income guarantee level.

Active knowledge

Investigate the different benefits that might apply to a person you work with who has a disability. Access copies of the relevant application forms and consider the range of information needed to fill them in.

If you do not work with adults with a disability, use a case study considering someone you know, or make up the details.

Being aware of other benefits

You should also ensure you are aware of any benefits or concessions individuals can receive on payments they need to make. For example, since November 2000, people aged 75 and over have qualified for a free TV licence, and since April 2000, people who are registered blind have received a 50 per cent reduction in the cost of their licence. If you are working with an individual who lives in sheltered housing or other supported living, you should check whether it is a scheme that qualifies for a concessionary licence.

Many older people, people with disabilities and people on low incomes are entitled to concessions for travel, use of local leisure facilities and libraries. There are also reductions in council tax for people who live alone and those with severe disabilities. It is important that you are aware of these concessions, and that you encourage individuals to take full advantage of them. You should keep your knowledge updated through regular contact with local advice centres and Citizens Advice Bureaux.

Budgeting

 KS 1 2 3 9 10 14 17 19 20

Where you are working with an individual who has found managing his or her financial affairs difficult and who is experiencing financial difficulty, either because of problems with management and organisation or because of low income, then assisting him or her in budget planning could be extremely valuable. Naturally this can only be done with the agreement of the individual.

Remember

You should also consider the possibility that a person is in difficulty because he or she is suffering from financial abuse at the hands of a relative, carer or friend. Sometimes people are pressurised or tricked into giving away money. Refer to Unit HSC 35 for information about financial abuse and how to deal with this situation.

If the individual does agree to a budget planning process, be careful not to impose your own values and beliefs. For example, if you were brought up to believe that you should never owe money, that you should always 'pay your way' and pay all bills as they fall due, then you may find it difficult to accept the philosophy of someone who never pays bills until the bailiffs arrive at the doorstep, or who is happy to allow debts to mount and bills to go unpaid.

However, if an individual wants to work to resolve financial difficulties or simply to organise his or her finances in a better way and is happy to plan a budget with your assistance, there are various ways in which you can do this. The following approach is simple, easy to understand and works in most circumstances.

An 'income and expenditure' budget chart

These are the steps you can take in filling in an income and expenditure budget chart such as the one on page 331.

- **Step 1** List the income the individual has, from any source. The headings given cover the individual circumstances of a wide range of people, so simply select the sources of income which are appropriate for the individual with whom you are working.

- **Step 2** List expenditure. Again, the types of expenditure listed are designed to cover the circumstances of a wide range of individuals, and you should list those that relate to the individual. Completing the weekly, monthly and yearly columns means that you are less likely to miss any payments that occur less frequently, and it also allows an overview of the individual's complete financial position to be arrived at.

- **Step 3** Look at the total yearly income and take away total yearly expenditure. This will show you whether the individual is able to live within the income he or she currently receives. If not – if expenditure is greater than income – you need to look at ways of either increasing the income or reducing the expenditure. This may be through claiming additional benefits or, if the individual is working, considering whether it is possible to work additional hours, or exploring the possibility of finding additional sources of income.

  For those on a low income, make sure they are receiving all the government support to which they are entitled. If an individual is dependent upon income from pensions and savings, he or she may wish to consider moving savings to an account that will provide a higher rate of interest. If this step is to be considered, you must strongly advise the individual to consult a financial adviser before making such a decision. You should not, under any circumstances, offer financial advice of this nature unless you are qualified to do so.

  The other alternative for any individual whose expenditure exceeds his or her income is to review expenditure and to examine where reductions can be made.

Active knowledge

Try completing an income and expenditure chart like the one on the next page, either for an individual you work with or for yourself or a member of your family. Evaluate how useful it was to do this.

Income and expenditure budget chart			
Step 1 – Income	**Weekly**	**Monthly**	**Yearly**
Salary/wage			
Other income			
Pension			
Jobseeker's allowance			
Income support/pension credit			
Housing benefit			
Other benefits			
Interest on savings			
Total			
Step 2 – Expenditure			
Mortgage or rent			
Second mortgage/secured loan			
Council tax			
Water rates			
Ground rent			
Repairs & maintenance charges			
Buildings insurance			
Contents insurance			
Gas			
Electricity			
Telephone			
Food			
Clothing			
TV rental and licence			
Prescriptions			
Health insurance			
Car tax and insurance			
Petrol/diesel			
Car repairs and servicing			
Public transport			
School uniforms, etc.			
Holidays			
Credit cards and loans			
Maintenance payments			
Contribution to pension			
Reserve for emergencies			
Regular savings			
Total			
Step 3 – Financial position			
Total income			
Total expenditure			
Financial position			

Research using the Internet

When you are supporting an individual to manage his or her financial affairs, you may need to research information on financial matters. The Internet is a fast and easy tool for finding up-to-date specimen costs, such as for insurance premiums or a comparison of the charges made by utility companies. It also offers a wealth of information on matters such as benefits, investments, taxation and pensions. But remember that the Internet is unregulated and not every source of information can be relied upon.

Be sure you access information only from the websites of dependable, well-established organisations and from universities, charities and government departments, and that you always cross-check any information you are using for financial planning with an appropriate source.

You may find government reports and the results of inquiries, or university research reports, have relevant information that you could follow up.

Managing debts

If you are supporting an individual who is in debt, you should encourage him or her to enlist the support of an experienced debt counsellor. These can be contacted through the Citizens Advice Bureau, welfare rights advice centres and local money advice centres. However, just as it is useful for you to know the general outline of the way the benefits system works, it is helpful if you understand the steps that a debt counsellor will take in order to resolve an individual's problems.

Citizens Advice Bureaux can provide the support of an experienced debt counsellor

The first thing that a debt counsellor will do is establish the nature of the debts an individual has. Debts are divided into **priority debts** and **non-priority debts**. Priority debts include:

- mortgage or rent
- council tax

- water charges
- gas
- electricity
- payments ordered by courts
- maintenance payments ordered by courts or the Child Support Agency.

Non-priority debts include:
- hire purchase debts.

The difference between the two kinds of debt is that failure to pay priority debts could mean the loss of an individual's home, or having to live without heat or light if services are disconnected. The consequences of failure to meet non-priority debts, while unpleasant, are not as serious. The repossession of goods by a hire purchase company may make life awkward but does not make it impossible. If a television or satellite system is repossessed, the family may feel bored; but the failure to purchase a TV licence could result in a large fine and an even higher amount of debt to be repaid.

Once the debt counsellor has established the level of income, probably on both a weekly and a monthly basis, he or she will look at basic expenses – those required for the basics of living, such as food and essential clothing. The counsellor will then identify priority debts, look at the amount of debt there is and what that represents in terms of repayments over a period of time. The counsellor will concentrate on ensuring that the priority debts are met in the first instance.

Once this information has been gathered, the counsellor will negotiate with all of the creditors involved and agree a schedule of repayments. Creditors are usually happy to

Failure to pay non-priority debts may have unpleasant consequences, but they are not as important as priority debts

agree deferred payments of outstanding debts as this is preferable to not receiving any payment at all on the debt.

Debt counsellors are trained and experienced in this type of debt management and you should encourage individuals to make use of their services if necessary. However, if they are unwilling to do so and wish you to carry out the negotiations or to do it themselves, you may wish to consult your local Citizens Advice Bureau or a money advice centre for further information and guidance before you begin negotiation with creditors.

It is important that you encourage individuals to abide by any arrangements made for the repayment of their debts. It frequently happens that once arrangements have been negotiated for repayment, an individual believes that the problem has somehow 'gone away' and it is no longer a matter to be concerned about.

Budget repayment plan for those in debt

Here is an example of a form to use for budgeting the repayment of debt.

Income/expenses	Weekly	Monthly
List income per week/month		
List basic expenses per week/month		
Deduct basic expenses from income		
Total money for debt repayment plan		
List priority debts		
Deduct priority debts from repayment plan		
Total money for other debt repayment		

Overcoming problems

 KS ① ② ④ ⑤ ⑦ ⑩ ⑭ ⑮ ⑯ ⑰

In the course of your work with an individual accessing advice and information about financial affairs, you may identify areas where you are unable to support the individual because of a lack of knowledge or expertise. In these cases you will need to call on specialist help, or support the individual to do so, on particular financial matters that are beyond your competence or levels of responsibility.

Evidence
PC ① ② ③ ⑥

Think of a service user who you support to manage their own finances.

How can you check the benefits and allowances they may be entitled to?

Describe the information this person has required about finances since you have worked with them and how you have provided it in a format they have understood.

Did you know?

The reason why many individuals and families are in debt is because they receive such a low income. In the UK today, 17 per cent of the population lives in poverty. Poverty is officially defined as 60 per cent or less of average national income. More than one in five, or 21 per cent, of children live in poverty. If housing costs are taken into account, the percentage of children living in poverty rises to 32 per cent.

You may also identify areas where the information and support you have helped to access does not meet the needs of the individual. This may be because:

- information is generally inaccessible
- information is not available in a format that the individual can access, e.g. braille or large print
- information or support is only available in a place that the individual is unable to access, for example one without an entrance suitable for wheelchair users
- the individual appears to be ineligible, under the relevant rules or regulations, to receive the support or information offered.

In these situations you should provide feedback (or support the individual to do so) to the appropriate people and organisations. Indicate the problem areas you have encountered, and ask for guidance.

Test yourself

1   What is the first step to take when starting work with individuals to manage their financial affairs?

2   Where would you find out about the benefits that might be available to a person aged 75 with no disabilities?

3   How would you explain the advantages of using a budgeting chart to an individual you were working with who had no experience of budgeting?

4   What does a debt counsellor do?

5   What should you do if you find that the information or support available on financial matters does not meet the needs of the individual you are working with?

HSC 345b Support individuals to manage and monitor their financial affairs

How to help individuals apply for benefits and allowances

 KS ① ② ③ ⑤ ⑥ ⑦ ⑨ ⑭ ⑮ ⑯ ⑰ ⑱ ⑲

An individual may choose not to claim benefits to which he or she is entitled. This can be extremely frustrating if you are trying to support someone who is surviving on a limited income; it can often be difficult to encourage people to claim their entitlements.

Many people, particularly older people, may feel that benefit is a form of charity and something they are not prepared to contemplate. Others may feel it is an admission of failure or defeat that they are unable to provide their own income through working. Some find it hard to acknowledge that a change in their circumstances or the development of a disability means they are no longer able to earn a living independently. For many in these circumstances the claiming of a benefit seems like the final admission and acknowledgement of their disability or illness.

You should also be aware that a person may have literacy difficulties. If there appears to be no logical explanation as to why a person is refusing to claim a benefit, you should consider the possibility that the individual is intimidated by the reading and form-filling involved. If you suspect this is the case, and that the individual is too embarrassed to discuss a literacy problem with you, try to find ways of overcoming the difficulty. You could offer to complete the relevant application form for the individual – perhaps on the grounds that the forms are lengthy – or you could advise him or her that there is a telephone application line for people who do not wish to complete a written form. If you find that the person responds positively to such suggestions, reinforcing the possibility of literacy problems, you should look for a way of finding out whether the individual would like support to improve his or her literacy.

Despite the frustrations that it may cause you as a worker attempting to support an individual who does not want to claim benefits, you must be prepared to support him or her in that decision. This does not mean you should not continue encouraging individuals to claim the benefit and to ensure they have all the necessary information, but you should recognise the point at which encouragement becomes harassment or bullying and allow people to make their own informed decisions.

Once the decision has been made, you must support individuals to manage their finances on the level of income they have. Decisions can be periodically reviewed and revisited, and this is something you should encourage individuals to do from time to time in the hope they may have changed their views. If they do change their minds about claiming a particular benefit, you should offer an appropriate level of support in assisting them to make the claim.

Did you know?

It is estimated that about 20 per cent of pensioners entitled to pension credit do not claim it. Government policies aim to reduce this percentage in the coming years.

You must support individuals to manage their finances on the level of income they have

Case study: Entitlement to benefits and allowances

Mrs Flanagan has lived alone since her husband died 25 years ago. She keeps her small house neat and clean and has always been very independent, doing all her own shopping, gardening and cleaning. She has a son in another part of the country who visits about twice a year. She is friendly with her neighbours and attends her local church where she has a wide circle of friends.

Mrs Flanagan has been finding it increasingly difficult to manage on her single state pension. Until she was admitted to hospital for investigations for a bowel condition she had no idea that she may have been entitled to additional support. Despite having a wide circle of friends and contacts in the local church she never considered discussing her personal financial circumstances with anyone outside her family, and on the occasions when she saw her son she did not want to burden him with discussions of her financial affairs. It was a passing comment she made to one of the support workers at the hospital, about the hospital food being a considerable improvement on what she could afford at home, that prompted a few further questions to Mrs Flanagan, and led to the discovery of the small pension she was receiving.

Mrs Flanagan was advised about what she could claim and was supported to make a claim for pension credit. As a result she received additional income, bringing her weekly income to the guaranteed minimum level. This made a huge difference to Mrs Flanagan, who was now able to run her home and do her shopping without the worry and anxiety she had endured for many years.

1   *What steps could have been taken to provide Mrs Flanagan with this information much earlier?*

2   *How would you organise an information campaign for people like Mrs Flanagan?*

3   *What sources would you target for information to help people such as Mrs Flanagan?*

Completing the paperwork

Benefit claim forms are usually very long. Great improvements have recently been made in the way they are structured to make them much simpler to understand, but it is often the length of these forms that inhibits people from filling them in.

Completing the forms is not as arduous as it appears, however, as for the vast majority of people large parts of the forms will not need to be filled in. These are the sections asking about investments, property owned and other sources of income. Even so, the mere appearance of the form makes some people feel unable to complete it.

Filling in a form may not be as difficult as it looks

The Benefits Agency has a system for filling in forms over the telephone and sending them to individuals for checking and completing. This is a valuable service for many people and ensures the information is entered in the correct places on the form. However, where individuals do not want to do this by telephone you may be asked to assist them in completing application forms.

Don't just take over the filling in of the form; an individual may only need you to check that it has been completed correctly. One important point to note when checking is to make sure that an individual with no income or no savings writes 'none' in the appropriate boxes.

You may need to make sure that an individual making a claim fills in the form legibly. This is important, as any difficulty in making out the details may cause a delay in processing the claim. Also, the information could be interpreted wrongly and the wrong decisions made in respect of benefit. If an individual's writing is not clear, you will need to handle this with tact and care – a person may well be offended if you imply that he or she cannot complete a form legibly.

Where individuals have literacy problems, you could offer either to assist or to complete the form on their behalf. Another approach is to encourage them to use the telephone application line.

You may have to deal with individuals who refuse to complete the whole form because they feel it is too long and complex, or because they are not willing to provide all the information the form asks for, such as information about their savings. You can only explain to them what the consequences will be of not providing that information. For example, if the individual is claiming a means-tested benefit the claim will not be considered unless all financial information is provided. The individual must be aware of the consequences of actions in order to make an informed decision about whether to pursue the claim for a particular benefit by providing all the necessary information.

Potential difficulties

If you are aware that an individual is attempting to make a deliberately fraudulent claim for a benefit or is making a deliberate attempt to mislead an agency providing a benefit about his or her circumstances, you must:

- explain that you cannot support this action and that you will be unable to assist in making the claim
- make it clear that if the individual persists in making a fraudulent or misleading claim you will have to record the matter and report it to your agency
- report the matter to your line manager, who will advise you on your agency's policy.

Active knowledge

Obtain a copy of a benefits claim form (such as a form for income support). Check it through to familiarise yourself with its style.

Methods of collecting benefits and allowances

KS 2 5 6 7 15 17 19

Payment into bank accounts

You will need to discuss and agree with the individual the best way you can support him or her in collecting any benefits or allowances. State benefits and many other payments from private pensions or employer pensions are now paid directly into people's bank accounts. If the individual does not have a bank account, it may be helpful if you can explain the value of having one, and give him or her information on how benefit is paid directly into it and how relatively easy it is to access it.

> You really should trust a bank to look after your money for you. It will be safer there.

Advise individuals on safer places to keep money

Where help may be needed

Where payments are being made directly into a person's bank account, you should encourage him or her to check bank statements regularly to make sure that all the necessary payments are being recorded in the account.

If you are dealing with money for individuals in residential care, your work setting will have its own form for recording money received on behalf of each individual and how much is spent. This will have to be recorded carefully, as will any payments made into bank accounts held in the individual's name.

Ways of ensuring individuals keep their money safe

In settings where you are working with vulnerable adults, whether they are residential or in the individual's own home, it is necessary to discuss with them the safety and security of any money they have. Many vulnerable people who continue to live in their own homes, particularly those who are elderly or with disabilities, are at high risk of being robbed if they keep cash in the house. Elderly people are more likely to keep large amounts of cash and you should discourage this wherever possible. They and their money will be much safer if they can be persuaded to keep it in a bank, building society or post office savings account.

In a residential setting there will be arrangements for the safe keeping of individuals' valuables and money. They should be encouraged to use this facility rather than keep money in their room, handbag or wallet. If an individual refuses to use the safe-keeping facility provided by a residential establishment, it is likely that he or she will be asked to sign a disclaimer form to acknowledge being offered the facility and having chosen to take care of valuables personally.

If you are aware of any cash being lost or stolen from an individual you must immediately report the loss – to your line manager if you are in a residential setting or to the police if you are working with individuals in their own homes. People are likely to be distressed by the loss of valuables, so you will need to offer them a lot of support during this time.

Evidence PC ① ⑤

Think of a service user who you support to manage their own finances.

List the documentation that you are required to complete and any documentation that they complete.

What support do you provide them to complete this documentation?

This will be easy – you know what old people are like – they keep their cash stashed away in the house because they don't trust banks

Older people who keep large sums of money in the home risk being robbed

Supporting individuals to make payments

Much of what you need to do in supporting individuals to make all the payments they need to make will depend upon the circumstances of the individual. You could be carrying out this type of task for a wide range of service users, each with varying levels of ability to manage their own financial affairs.

Establishing the level of help and support

One of the best ways to work out with an individual the level of support required is to look at the reasons why he or she needs assistance to make payments. It could be because the person is:

- specifically unable to make payments
- confused and too forgetful to make payments
- unsure what payments have to be made
- unlikely to be able to motivate himself or herself to make payments on time
- unable or unwilling to recognise the importance of making payments.

Once you have established the reasons why support and help are needed, it is much easier to agree the level of support. For example, if your assistance is required simply because someone is physically unable to write a cheque or to walk to the post office or the bank, it may be quite sufficient for you to write out cheques (if your employer's policy permits this) or to take things to the post office. There may be no need for you to assist with the process of identifying payments due or to become involved in any financial planning.

If an individual is unable to make payments because he or she is confused or unable to recognise the importance of making payments when they become due, he or she may be happy for you to become involved at a more detailed level in financial budgeting and planning.

Be aware at all times, however, that feeling unable to manage their own financial affairs may have an adverse impact on the self-esteem and self-image of individuals. Your work should always make it clear that the individual is the decision-maker on his or her own money issues, and that your role is only to assist in practical matters. Also, make sure individuals know you are conscientious about respecting confidentiality in all financial dealings, so that they do not feel their financial affairs have become 'public property'. Your professionalism, your understanding and the reassurance that their affairs are being taken care of in an efficient manner will do much to help individuals accept the situation while retaining their self-confidence.

Encouraging individuals to be self-managing

One of the keys to working effectively with individuals, whatever your role, is that you should always encourage them to take as much active responsibility as possible. Never assume that they will always require assistance at the level you currently provide. You should always review progress and wherever possible, either because their condition has improved or because they have learned from working with you, individuals should resume as much responsibility as possible for their financial planning, budgeting and payments.

Keys to good practice: How to encourage self-management

✓ Always begin by asking the individual to do as much as possible of the preparation for planning finances. Find out what the individual can do first, then support where necessary.

✓ Always check with the individual on everything you are doing, and ask 'What do you think?'

✓ Always make a regular review time for any financial support plan. This could be three or six months, depending on circumstances. At this stage you should review your level of support to see if the individual's needs have changed.

✓ If you notice changes between reviews, for example bills that have not been paid which the individual used to deal with, follow this up and make changes if necessary.

✓ If the individual is beginning to take more interest in financial matters and makes suggestions, check whether he or she would like to take more responsibility and reduce your involvement.

Range of payments

We all have our own range of payments to make, either regularly or as one-offs. While everyone has different financial demands made on their income, there are some types of payments that are more likely to occur for most of the individuals you work with.

When you are looking at the payments that need to be made by particular individuals, you should first ask them to identify, if they are able, which payments they need to make. It can be helpful to have a written checklist to try to make sure no payments have been forgotten. The list on the next page is a suggestion only, and it will obviously vary for each individual.

An individual may have trouble remembering all the payments that have to be made

Checklist of payments

Regular payments (which could be weekly/monthly/annually):

Rent	Mortgage
Food	Council tax
Heating and lighting	Water
Repair or maintenance charges	Telephone
TV licence	TV/video/satellite rental
Catalogue payments	Credit card payments
Insurance	Hire purchase or loan payments

Occasional payments:

Clothes	Furniture
Entertainment	Holidays

Such a checklist can be used for any individual, and additional items may be included to meet each person's circumstances. Once you have identified all the payments individuals need to make, you should discuss with them which payments they wish you to undertake and which payments they will continue to undertake themselves.

At this stage it is also useful to discuss methods of payment with the individual and to look at the advantages and disadvantages of the range of payment methods available.

Methods of making payments  KS 20

The following table lists the different methods of payment for goods and services and the advantages and disadvantages of these.

Method	Advantages	Disadvantages
Cash	Easy for those who receive wages or benefits in cash. Easily understood. Allows people to see their exact financial position.	Safety – keeping cash represents a serious burglary risk. Loss – cash is easy to lose, particularly if an individual is confused or forgetful. Inconvenience – cash cannot be sent in the post, so cash payments have to be made directly or through a bank, and this can mean having to make arrangements to visit the offices or the bank of the payee.

Continued

Method	Advantages	Disadvantages
Cheque	Convenient – can be sent by post. More secure than cash. Generally accepted (with a cheque guarantee card).	Requires bank account. Can incur considerable bank charges. Becoming less used with the advent of electronic bank cards. Cheque book can be lost or stolen. Cheques can be misused.
Electronic bank card, e.g. Switch or Delta	Convenient, generally accepted. Easy to carry and use. Easy to stop if stolen.	Requires bank account. May confuse some individuals. Can be stolen and misused.
Standing order – set up by individual	Regular payments made by bank. No action needed by individual. Makes payments directly.	Requires bank account. Individual needs to remember to alter it if payments change. Incurs bank charges.
Direct debit – set up by payee	Regular payments made by bank. No action needed by individual. Makes payments directly.	Requires bank account. Can incur bank charges.
Credit card	Enables payments to be made even if individual is temporarily short of money. Convenient.	Can accumulate large amounts of debt. Has higher interest charges. Is easily stolen and misused. Not accepted for all types of payment.
Telephone/ online banking	Can be used by individuals who have bank accounts with access via telephone/Internet/satellite TV. Can be used without leaving the house. Does not require any permanent arrangement. Is safe and secure.	Only available to those with the necessary hardware and level of technological understanding to use the equipment.

Cash can be a convenient method of payment, but it raises safety and security issues

Active knowledge

Carry out this exercise on your own personal finances. Make a list, as above, of all the payments you make and the range of methods you use to pay. Check which items you pay using which methods. If you include grocery and general household shopping, you may find that the balance of methods you use alters. Similarly, if you look at methods of payments for large items you may also find that this alters the balance of the different types of payments you use.

Review the payment methods that you currently use and consider whether you could benefit by changing any of them in order to save on charges or interest rates, or to improve convenience or safety.

Case study: Support with making payments

Rosa has suffered from severe depression since the birth of her third child, now one year old. Her other children are aged two and four. Her husband left six months ago as he felt unable to cope with her depressed state. Rosa has been receiving medication from her GP for her depression, which helps to some extent, but she finds it very difficult to cope on a day-to-day basis.

She was referred for support by her health visitor who was concerned about her motivation and her seeming lack of ability to organise the basic requirements of living for herself and her three children. Rosa had neglected to pay the mortgage on the house, not because of a lack of income but because she had not been motivated to make the required arrangements to transfer the payments after her husband left. She was being threatened with repossession of the house, and as she had not paid recent utility bills there were various threatening letters from the companies.

A support worker began to work with Rosa and her family, and following agreement with her made arrangements for all of her utility bills and mortgage payments to be made via direct debit. The support worker negotiated with the building society to extend the mortgage period by the missing six months and negotiated with the utility companies to allow Rosa to pay off the excess amounts over a period of time.

1   *What could have been the consequences for Rosa and her family had the support worker not begun to work with them?*

2   *What alternative ways could have been used to resolve Rosa's problems?*

3   *What other effects might you reasonably expect to see from the improvement in Rosa's financial situation?*

4   *What skills would the support worker need to have used in order to improve Rosa's circumstances?*

Ways of recording payments made KS 20

All payments made for any goods or services require a receipt. It is important that you encourage individuals always to obtain and keep receipts for any payments made. By doing this it will always be possible to resolve any disputes about the timing and amounts of payments, and it avoids confusion over which bills have and have not been paid.

Good grief! I've really got to sort this out. I just don't know where I am with all this stuff.

Individuals may need to be advised how to organise their records for easy access

If you are making a payment on behalf of an individual, it is essential you obtain a receipt and keep a copy in the individual's case notes or receipts file. This protects you and the individual if any question about the payment is ever raised.

Receipts can come in a range of formats. Payments made via a bank will be recorded on a bank statement, so an individual receipt will not be needed. However, payments made by cheque, debit card or credit card need a receipt of individual transactions, which are kept until the transactions appear on either the bank statement or credit card statement. This makes it easy to identify any unexpected or unauthorised payments. Also a transaction receipt helps to resolve any dispute over the transaction.

Receipts should be maintained in a system where they are easily accessible – the sideboard drawer does not qualify as easily accessible! A simple filing system where receipts are categorised as utility bills, food, TV licence, clothing, holidays, etc. may be the easiest way of ensuring they can be located when they are needed.

Receipts should not be kept indefinitely, and the system will have to be maintained. Receipts for any item under guarantee should be kept at least for the life of the guarantee. Other receipts should be kept until the payment shows on a statement of that particular account.

Many individuals do not see the importance of keeping receipts or may forget where they have put them or lose them. You should try to obtain agreement to set up a system which they can use or, if that is beyond what they feel able to undertake initially, ask them to hand receipts to you until they become more familiar with the system. This is likely to prove the most effective way of recording financial transactions.

Ways of dealing with potential conflicts

 KS ③ ⑤ ⑥ ⑦ ⑨ ⑯

You may be faced with a dilemma if individuals ask you to make payments in certain situations or tell you they intend not to make certain payments. This could involve:

- making payments for illegal items
- making payments for items of which you personally disapprove
- deliberately avoiding making payments that are due.

Illegal payments

If someone asks you to make a payment that you know is illegal, for example to pay for stolen goods or any other illegal items, then you should explain that it will not be possible for you to assist and that it is inappropriate for you to be asked to undertake this. If you become aware that an individual is involved in criminal activity you must report this to your line manager and follow your agency's policies and procedures.

Payments of which you disapprove

On the other hand, an individual may ask you to assist with making payments for an activity that is perfectly legal but is in conflict with your own beliefs and values. An example would be if you were strongly opposed to gambling and someone asked you to place a bet with a bookmaker on his or her behalf. In such a case you must be sure that you do not allow your own beliefs and values to influence the level of service you provide for the individual. However, your agency will have a policy on whether you may make payments to place bets or purchase alcohol. It will be important to check your agency's policy on any issue that you are uncomfortable with.

Put it on Starlight Express in the 3.30 for me, mate

You cannot allow your beliefs and values to affect the service you provide to individuals

The intention not to make payments

If individuals advise you that they are not going to make payments for goods or services or to meet their legal requirements, then you can find yourself in a difficult position. For example, someone could advise you during the budgeting process not to include an allowance for a TV licence as he or she does not intend to purchase one, despite having a TV. In this situation you should advise the individual of the consequences of his or her actions and the levels of fines that are imposed on those who fail to purchase a TV licence.

You are not, however, in a position to insist on a certain action or to override the individual's wishes. You are only able to advise and ensure that any decisions made about failing to maintain or make payments are based on an informed choice. You should record this information and advise your line manager accordingly, and explain to the individual that you are doing this.

You should never actively condone or encourage people to avoid making payments that they are required to make. Be careful that you do not give the appearance of encouragement by failing to comment. You do have a responsibility to ensure that an individual is informed of the potential consequences of any actions.

EvidencePC 6 7 8

Describe your role in supporting individuals to monitor their financial effectiveness.

What methods are used to monitor and how can you support them to make changes when required?

Reviewing effectiveness

 KS 2 8 9 10 14 15 17

Regular reviews will be necessary to monitor the effectiveness of the support provided to individuals in connection with their financial affairs. The methods and services selected may not continue to be appropriate, either because of a change in the individual's needs – individuals may need more or less help as time goes on – or because of a change in circumstances.

It is important that, at the outset of providing support for individuals, you work with them to decide how and when to review the effectiveness of the procedures put in place. At each review you will need to consider:

- what is working well
- which procedures need to be changed in order to improve support
- what is not working and needs a complete rethink
- any support that is no longer appropriate and can be discontinued
- any further support that has become necessary.

You will need to support the individual to identify the specific changes that need to be made, and work with the individual and other key people to make sure the agreed changes are implemented as soon as possible. Then make sure that future reviews are planned for an appropriate date.

1   List the different ways in which payments can be made.

2   Identify four reasons why people may refuse to claim benefits to which they are entitled.

3   How would you support an individual who felt it was impossible to complete a benefit claim form, because it was so long?

4   Why is it important regularly to review the effectiveness of the methods and services individuals use to manage their financial affairs?

Useful contacts

Benefit Enquiry Line (BEL)
Telephone: 0800 88 22 00
Fax: 01772 23 89 53
E-mail: Bel-Customer-Services@dwp.gsi.gov.uk
National, free telephone advice and information service on benefits for people with disabilities, their carers and representatives. It is available from 8.30 am to 6.30 pm weekdays and from 9 am to 1 pm on Saturdays. People who are deaf, hard of hearing or speech impaired and who use a textphone can call the benefits enquiry line free on 0800 24 33 55. Advisers can send out forms and give advice but they have no access to personal records. The Department of Work and Pensions has a helpful website: www.dwp.gov.uk

Counsel and Care
16 Bonny Street
London NW1 9PG
Advice line: 0845 300 7585
General enquiries: 020 7241 8555
E-mail: advice@counselandcare.org.uk
Website: www.counselandcare.org.uk

Provides free and confidential advice to older people, their carers and professionals. The advice line is available from 10 am to 1 pm on weekdays. Fact sheets on topics ranging from benefits to care homes are also available. Useful fact sheets include 'Choosing a care home: fees and funding', 'Paying care home fees: community care' and 'Community care and the NHS: a guide to making a complaint'.

Help the Aged
207–221 Pentonville Road
London N1 9UZ
Telephone: 020 7278 1114
Seniorline: freephone 0808 800 6565
E-mail: info@helptheaged.org.uk
Website: www.helptheaged.org.uk

Gives advice by letter or telephone on topics affecting older people, such as benefits, community care and home safety. Useful information sheets include 'Paying for residential care' and 'Residential care: problems with local authority funding'. Seniorline is available on weekdays from 9 am to 4 pm.

Help the Aged Care Fees Advisory Service
St Leonard's House
Mill Street
Eynsham
Oxford OX29 4JX
Freephone: 0500 76 74 76 (9–5 weekdays)
Fax: 01865 733 001

Citizens Advice Bureau
The National Association of Citizens Advice Bureaux
Myddelton House
115–123 Pentonville Road
London N1 9LZ
Website: www.citizensadvice.org.uk
Information and advice website: www.adviceguide.org.uk

HSC 345 FURTHER READING AND RESEARCH

Below are some books, websites and agencies you can look up to continue your study of this subject.

www.citizensadvice.org.uk (Citizens Advice Bureau)

www.csci.org.uk (Commission for Social Care Inspection)

www.helptheaged.org.uk (Help the Aged)

www.directgov.gov.uk (Direct Gov)

www.mind.org.uk (MIND) tel: 0845 7660163

Local Authority/Social Services in your area (this can be found through an internet search or Yellow Pages)

Gallache, Y., Gray, J. *Managing Debt: A Guide for Older People* Age Concern

Rowntree (J.) Foundation *Making Direct Payments Work*

Move and position individuals

The level of assistance individuals need in moving and achieving the correct position can vary from needing help to get out of a chair to being completely dependent on others to move them, to turn them over and to alter their position in any way, for example if they are unconscious or paralysed.

When individuals require this degree of care it is essential that they are moved and handled in the most sensitive and safe way. Safe procedures are also vital for you as a worker, and the people you work with – the commonest causes of people being unable to continue to work in health or social care are that they suffer injuries, usually back injuries, from lifting and moving individuals. It is possible to minimise the risk to yourself, to colleagues and to individuals for whom you provide care by following the correct procedures and using the right equipment.

The first element is about preparing the equipment, environment and individuals themselves for being moved. In the second element you will need to ensure that you know the way to carry out the move correctly and safely, and offer all the support people need.

What you need to learn

- Health and safety measures
- Working with the individual to be moved
- Suitable clothing and equipment
- How to encourage independence
- Equipment for moving and handling
- Methods for manual moving and handling
- Recording and passing on information.

HSC 360a Prepare the equipment, the environment and the individual for moving and positioning

Health and safety measures

 KS 4 5 6 9 20 25 28

As you learned in Unit HSC 32, all aspects of health and safety are covered by legislation. Moving people safely is no exception. The Health and Safety Executive guidance states:

1. The Manual Handling Operations Regulations 1992, which implement the Manual Handling of Loads Directive, came into effect on 1 January 1993 under the Health and Safety at Work Act 1974, and enable UK legislation to implement a European Community Directive on the manual handling of loads. They apply to all manual handling activity with a risk of injury.

2. The Regulations impose duties on employers, self-employed people and employees. Employers must avoid all hazardous manual handling activity where it is reasonably practicable to do so. If it is not, they must assess the risks in relation to the nature of the task, the load, the working environment and the capabilities of the handler and take appropriate action to reduce the risk to the lowest level reasonably practicable. Employees must follow appropriate work systems introduced by their employer to promote safety during the handling of loads.

Ensuring safety for both yourself, your colleagues and the person being moved is the joint responsibility of you and your employer.

The HSE provides guidelines about weights that can be safely lifted – these are very general guides and are not a substitute for a risk assessment, because many factors can affect the risks in each situation.

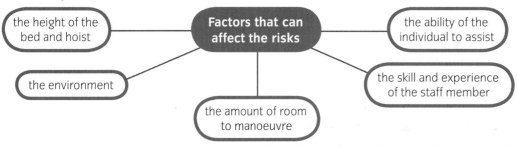

The HSE guidelines are based on moving inanimate objects, not people – who can move, wriggle, complain and co-operate (or not)! But these guidelines are useful in showing how little weight can be lifted safely, and serve as a useful warning to THINK RISK.

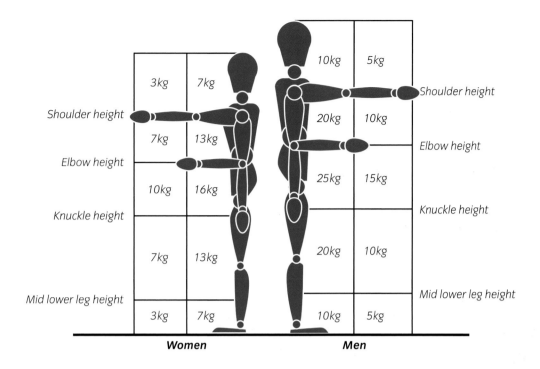

The diagram shows guideline weights for lifting and lowering, with figures for Women and Men at various heights.

Women:
- Shoulder height: 3kg / 7kg
- Elbow height: 7kg / 13kg
- Knuckle height: 10kg / 16kg
- Mid lower leg height: 7kg / 13kg
- (floor): 3kg / 7kg

Men:
- Shoulder height: 10kg / 5kg
- Elbow height: 20kg / 10kg
- Knuckle height: 25kg / 15kg
- Mid lower leg height: 20kg / 10kg
- (floor): 10kg / 5kg

Women | **Men**

Each box in the diagram above shows guideline weights for lifting and lowering.

Observe the activity and compare to the diagram. If the lifter's hands enter more than one box during the operation, use the smallest weight. Use an inbetween weight if the hands are close to a boundary between boxes. If the operation must take place with the hands beyond the boxes, make a more detailed assessment.

The weights assume that the load is readily grasped with both hands, and the operation takes place in reasonable working conditions with the lifter in a stable body position.

Any operation involving more than twice the guideline weights should be rigorously assessed – even for very fit, well-trained individuals working under favourable conditions.

There is no such thing as a completely 'safe' manual handling operation. But working within the guidelines will cut the risk and reduce the need for a more detailed assessment.

Source: HSE 1998

Infection control

Hygiene is also an important safety factory to consider, as the possibility of cross-infection is always present when you are working closely with and handling individuals. See Unit HSC 32 for advice on infection control, especially how to ensure your own hygiene – including standard precautions and the correct procedure for washing your hands.

How to assess risks

As you will remember from Unit HSC 32, your employer has a responsibility under health and safety legislation to examine and assess all procedures which take place in your working environment involving risk. All risks must be noted, assessed and steps taken to minimise them as far as possible. Your employer is responsible for providing adequate equipment for such tasks as moving and handling individuals who require assistance.

There are responsibilities on both the employer and the employee. The process of reducing risk is a joint responsibility – you must make your contribution in the interests of your own safety and that of your colleagues, as well as that of the person you are moving.

The employer's duties are to:

- **avoid** the need for hazardous manual handling as far as is reasonably practicable
- **assess** the risk of injury from any hazardous manual handling that can't be avoided
- **reduce** the risk of injury from hazardous manual handling, as far as reasonably practicable.

Employees' duties are to:

- follow appropriate systems of work laid down for their safety
- make proper use of equipment provided to minimise the risk of injury
- co-operate with the employer on health and safety matters; a care assistant who fails to use a hoist that has been provided is putting himself or herself at risk of injury, and the employer is unlikely to be found liable
- apply the duties of employers, as appropriate, to their own manual handling activities
- take care to ensure that their activities do not put others at risk.

Remember

The process of reducing risk is a joint responsibility of employer and employee.

Look after your back

Ideally every workplace should have, or have access to, a Back Care Advisor (BCA). These are people who are trained in manual handling and are able to provide expert advice to managers, manual handling supervisors and to members of staff who are involved in manual handling.

You must ensure that you follow the information provided by the BCA for your workplace, and take every opportunity to attend information and education events to make sure you are up to date on manual handling techniques and policies.

If you are supervising other staff, or have a responsibility for training, you must ensure that staff are trained and regularly updated. The health and safety officer in your workplace should also be able to provide up-to-date information regarding moving and handling.

Active knowledge

Find out who the BCA is for your workplace, and ask him or her when the next education sessions are planned.

Checklist

1 Is individual weight-bearing? Yes ☐
   No ☐

2 Is individual unsteady? Yes ☐
   No ☐

3 What is the general level of mobility? Good ☐
   Poor ☐

4 a What is the individual's weight? _____

   b What is the individual's height? _____

   c How many people does this lift require? _____

   (Work this out on the scale devised by your workplace)

5 What lifting equipment is required? Hoist ☐
   Sling ☐
   Trapeze ☐
   Transfer board ☐

6 Is equipment available? Yes ☐
   No ☐

7 If not, is there a safe alternative? Yes ☐
   No ☐

8 Are the required number of people available? Yes ☐
   No ☐

9 What is the purpose of the move? _____

   _____

10 Can this be achieved? Yes ☐
    No ☐

A checklist for assessing risks before moving an individual

The risk assessments your employer carries out are, however, general risks for your work environment. Each time you move or lift any individual, you too must make an assessment of the risks involved in carrying out that particular manoeuvre. Even if you have moved this individual every day for the past six months, you should still assess the risks on each occasion before you put anything into practice. If you are acting in a supervisory capacity, you must ensure that staff are fully aware of the procedures they are required to follow.

No two lifts are ever the same – there are always some factors that are different. These factors could be to do with the individual and his or her mood or health on that particular day; they could be about the environment; or they could be about you and your current physical condition.

You should run through the same checklist each time before you carry out any activity which involves you in physically moving a person from one place to another. A suggested checklist is shown on the previous page. You may need to adapt it to fit your own place of work and the circumstances in which you work.

Any changes in an individual's condition may influence the moving and handling procedures required. These should always be recorded in the care plan and a new risk assessment carried out whenever necessary.

This checklist system is best remembered as TILE – Task, Individual, Load, Environment. You should carry out a TILE assessment each time you move a service user.

You need to consider the environment carefully when you are assessing risk. You should take into account all of the following factors.

- Is the floor surface safe? Are there wet or slippery patches?
- Are you wearing appropriate clothing – low-heeled shoes, tunic or dress that has enough room to stretch and reach?
- Is the immediate area clear of items that may cause a trip or a fall, or items that could cause injury following a fall?
- Is all the equipment, both to carry out the lift and in the place to which the individual is to be moved, ready?
- Does the individual have privacy and can his or her dignity be maintained during the move?
- Is there anyone you could ask for help, for example a colleague, a porter or member of the ambulance service?

Remember

T	Task
I	Individual
L	Load
E	Environment

Working with the individual to be moved

Make sure you wash your hands and ensure your own hygiene before and after moving individuals. Bacteria on bed linen can easily be transferred from individual to individual unless care is taken to observe infection control procedures.

Consult the care plan and assess any immediate risks to individuals. If there is a risk you cannot deal with, seek advice from the appropriate people.

The individual who is going to be moved is the key person to be actively involved, as far as possible, in decisions about the best way to carry out the move. Unless the person concerned is unconscious or semi-conscious or so confused as to be unable to contribute to any discussion about the best way to proceed, then it is essential that you discuss with the person the method that he or she would feel most comfortable with.

Discuss with the person concerned the way that he or she would prefer to be moved

Encourage the individual to communicate the level of support he or she requires. Many people who have a long-standing disability will be very experienced in how to deal with it. They are the best people to ask for advice as they know the most effective ways for them to be moved, avoiding pain and discomfort as far as possible.

If you are caring for an unconscious or confused individual who has been admitted to residential accommodation after a period of being cared for at home, you might wish to consult with the home carers, general practitioner or district nurse for information about any moving and handling procedures that have been found to be effective, and which you can adopt in your workplace.

Active knowledge

Your workplace probably uses an assessment form similar to the one on the next page. Find the one your workplace uses and make sure you know how to fill it in. It may be similar to the checklist on page 355.

Patient's name		District nurse	

Body build   Obese ☐   Above average ☐   Average ☐   Below average ☐   Tall ☐   Medium ☐   Short ☐

Weight (if known)		**Risk of falls** High ☐ Low ☐

Problems with comprehension, behaviour, co-operation (identify)

Handling constraints, e.g. disability, weakness, pain, skin lesions, infusions (identify)

Tasks (see examples)	Methods to be used (see examples)	Describe any remaining problems, list any other measures needed (see examples)

Date(s) assessed:			
Assessor's signature:			
Proposed review dates:			

	Finishing date:	

Examples of tasks:
- ✔ sitting/standing
- ✔ toiletting
- ✔ bathing
- ✔ transfer to/from bed
- ✔ movement in bed
- ✔ sustained postures
- ✔ walking
- ✔ in/out of car

Examples of methods/ control measures

Organisation
- ✔ Number of staff needed?
- ✔ Patient stays in bed

Equipment
- ✔ Variable height bed
- ✔ Hoists
- ✔ Slings/belt
- ✔ Bath aids
- ✔ Wheeled sani-chair
- ✔ Monkey poles
- ✔ Patient hand blocks
- ✔ Rope ladders
- ✔ Turntable
- ✔ Sliding aids
- ✔ Stair lift

Furniture
- ✔ Reposition/remove

Examples of problems/ risk factors

Task
- ✔ Is it nesessary? Can it be avoided?
- ✔ Involves stretching, stooping, twisting, sustained load?
- ✔ Rest/recovery time?

Patient
- ✔ Weight, disability, ailments, etc.

Environment
- ✔ Space to manoeuvre, to use hoist
- ✔ Access to bed, bath, WC, passageways?
- ✔ Steps, stairs?
- ✔ Flooring uneven? OK for hoist?
- ✔ Furniture: moveable? height? condition?
- ✔ Bed: double? low?

Carers
- ✔ Fitness for the task, freshness or fatigue?
- ✔ Experience with patient and with handling team?
- ✔ Skill: handling, using equipment?

A risk assessment form for manual handling

The individual's physical condition

Because of the individual's condition, the normal range of movements in joints may not be possible. You need a working understanding of the way muscles attach to the skeleton and the way healthy joints work, in order to accommodate any difficulties in moving and positioning an individual.

The diagrams on pages 359 and 360 show how the skeletal muscles are arranged within the body and how they are all interlinked.

Remember

Your first port of call for advice on how to carry out a movement, after you have checked out the safety aspects and the risk factors, should be the individual himself or herself.

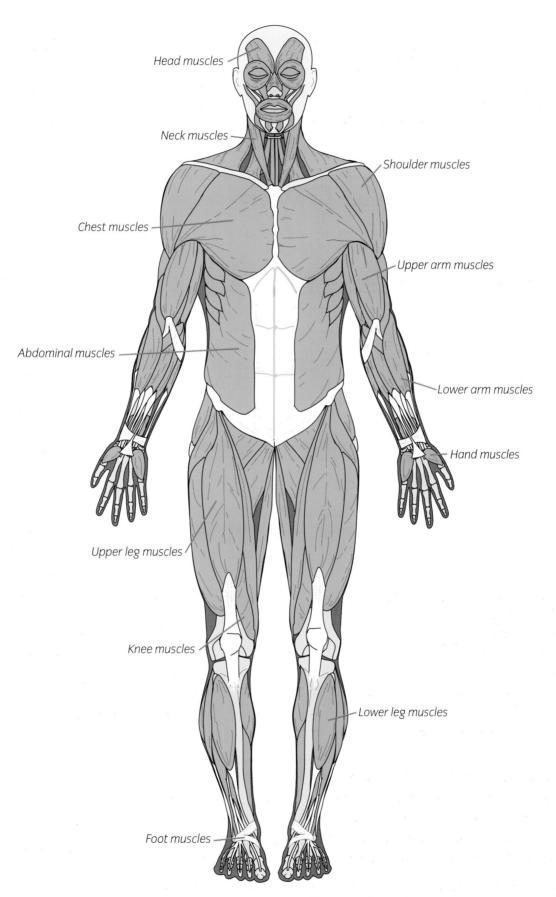

Head muscles

Neck muscles

Shoulder muscles

Chest muscles

Upper arm muscles

Abdominal muscles

Lower arm muscles

Hand muscles

Upper leg muscles

Knee muscles

Lower leg muscles

Foot muscles

The muscular system

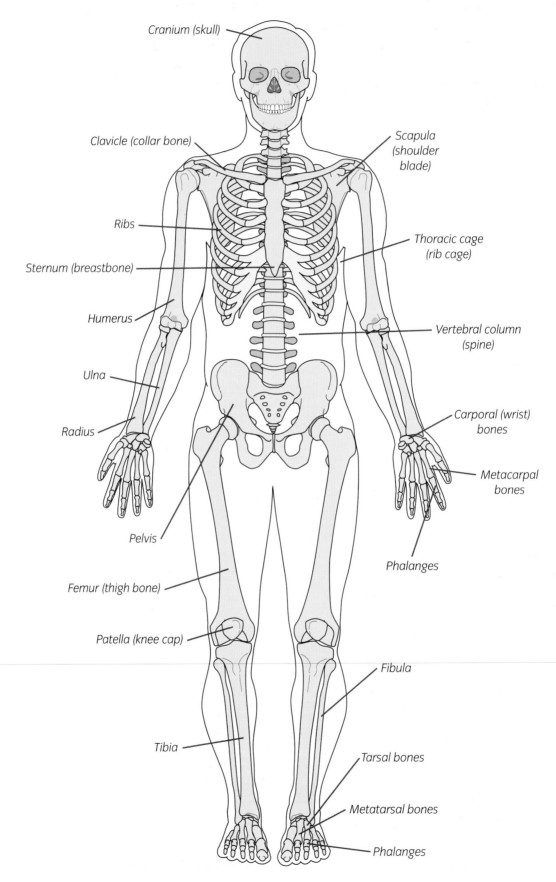

Cranium (skull)

Clavicle (collar bone)

Scapula (shoulder blade)

Ribs

Thoracic cage (rib cage)

Sternum (breastbone)

Humerus

Vertebral column (spine)

Ulna

Radius

Carporal (wrist) bones

Metacarpal bones

Pelvis

Phalanges

Femur (thigh bone)

Patella (knee cap)

Fibula

Tibia

Tarsal bones

Metatarsal bones

Phalanges

The skeleton

Muscles are attached to the bony skeleton. They work like hinges or levers – they pull and move particular joints. When a muscle contracts (gets shorter), it pulls a joint in the direction that it is designed to move. Pairs of muscles move antagonistically; that is, when one contracts, its opposite number relaxes to allow movement. Muscles can become slack and make movement slower and more difficult, but when muscles are regularly used they are toned and easy to move.

Types of joint

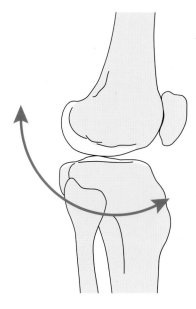

The knee is a hinge joint

- **Hinge joints**, e.g. the knee or elbow joint, can straighten or bend in the same way as a door hinge opens or closes.
- **Pivot joints**, e.g. the vertebrae in the neck, allow movements from side to side.
- **Saddle joints**, e.g. the thumb, allow back-and-forth and side-to-side movements, but rotation is limited.

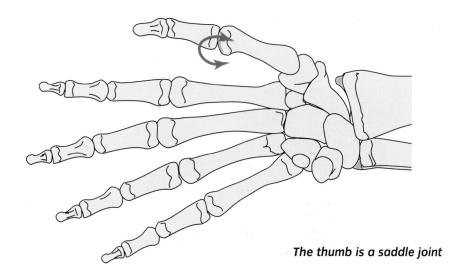

The thumb is a saddle joint

- **Ellipsoidal joints**, such as the joint at the base of the index finger, allow bending and extending, and rocking from side to side, but rotation is limited.
- **Gliding joints** occur between the surfaces of two flat bones that are held together by ligaments. Some of the bones in the wrists and ankles move by gliding against each other.
- **Ball and socket joints** are the most flexible free-moving joints, e.g. the shoulder and hip.

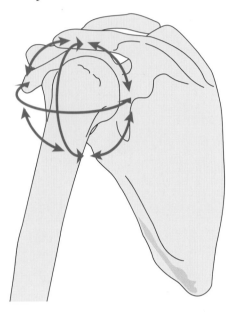

The shoulder is a ball and socket joint

How the knee moves

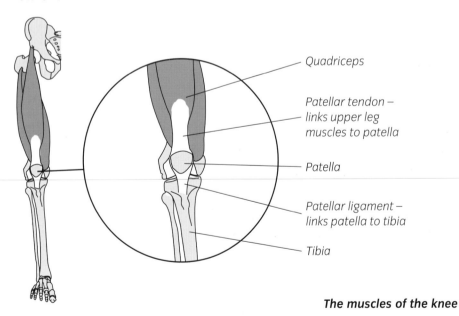

Quadriceps

Patellar tendon – links upper leg muscles to patella

Patella

Patellar ligament – links patella to tibia

Tibia

The muscles of the knee

The muscles responsible for moving the knee run from the upper to the lower leg. Those in the front of the upper leg (the quadriceps) pull on the tibia (lower leg bone) to straighten the leg. The muscles at the back of the upper leg make the knee joint bend.

How the upper arm moves

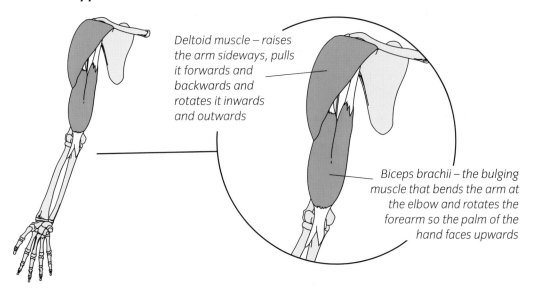

Deltoid muscle – raises the arm sideways, pulls it forwards and backwards and rotates it inwards and outwards

Biceps brachii – the bulging muscle that bends the arm at the elbow and rotates the forearm so the palm of the hand faces upwards

The muscles of the upper arm

The large muscles in the upper arm work together to raise and bend the arm. The most powerful arm muscle is the biceps brachii. If you bend your arm up and down, you will feel the biceps working.

Improving particular conditions

Exercise can be specifically designed to improve particular conditions. A physiotherapist would make an assessment and design a particular programme for an individual with this in mind. Some examples are shown below.

- Following a stroke, an individual will often have weakness in a limb or the whole of one side of the body. A mobility activity will be designed by a physiotherapist to work on strengthening the areas weakened by the stroke.

- Following surgery to replace a hip joint, an individual may have muscle weakness of the whole of the leg because of lack of exercise caused by osteoarthritis. In addition, he or she will have pain and stiffness following surgery. The key to recovery and regaining full use of the joint will be the plan devised by the physiotherapist.

- Many people who use wheelchairs may have special mobility activities to ensure that their muscles remain active as far as possible, and to promote their general fitness levels.

Explaining the move

Once you have carried out all the necessary assessments in an individual case, you should explain carefully to the individual exactly what you intend to do and what his or her role is in contributing to the effectiveness and safety of the move. This will vary according to the person's ability, but nonetheless most individuals will be able to participate to some extent.

Even where individuals are unconscious or appear to have no understanding of what is going on, you should still explain exactly what you are doing and why you are doing it and what the effects will be. We have a limited understanding of what a state of unconsciousness means to the person experiencing it; however, it is acknowledged that individuals who appear to be completely unconscious may be able to hear what is going on around them. Every individual has the same right to be treated with dignity and respect and to have procedures explained rather than simply having things done to him or her by care workers who believe that 'they know best'.

Each stage of the proposed move should be explained in detail before it is carried out, and it is essential to obtain the individual's consent before you move or handle him or her in any way. If you move an individual without his or her consent this could be considered to be an assault. So you should always be sure that you are carrying out the individual's wishes before you commence any move.

Keys to good practice: Preparing for moving and handling

✓ Wash your hands and ensure you are wearing suitable clothing and footwear.

✓ Check the care plan and assess risks to the individual and to yourself before starting any move.

✓ If the risk assessment states that more than one member of staff is required to perform the procedure, ensure that one or more colleagues are available to assist you.

✓ Remove potential hazards and prepare the immediate environment.

✓ Ask the individual about the best way of moving, or assisting, him or her.

✓ Explain the procedure at each stage, even where it may not be obvious that you are understood.

✓ Explain how the equipment operates.

✓ Check that you have the agreement of the person you are moving.

✓ Stop immediately if the individual does not wish you to continue – you may not move a person without his or her consent.

Never be tempted to drag an individual up the bed or chair, instead of ensuring that he or she is properly moved. Dragging someone can cause friction and break the skin, promoting the development of pressure sores, especially on the sacrum (the bottom of the back) and heels.

Suitable clothing and equipment

 KS ④ ⑤ ⑥ ⑲ ⑳

Your clothing

The type of clothing you wear when you are moving individuals is very important. It can make the difference between carrying out a procedure safely and doing it with difficulty and possible risk of injury. Footwear should be supportive and flat, with soles that grip firmly.

Recommendations in respect of uniforms are that dresses should have a pleat in the skirt and in the back, and a similar pleat in the sleeves. These are to allow space so that you do not find that your own movements are restricted by your clothing, possibly forcing you to move in an awkward way. It may be necessary, for example, to place one knee on a bed. This is impossible if you are wearing a straight skirt, or at least very difficult to manage at the same time as maintaining dignity – yours, not the service user's!

If you are in a situation where you do a great deal of moving and handling, it is a good idea to wear trousers, with a tunic top that has plenty of room in the sleeves and shoulders to allow free movement. Your employer should have carried out a risk assessment and ensured that the clothing that is provided for you to wear is appropriate and complies with current best practice and requirements in terms of moving and handling.

Work clothing should allow for free movement when handling individuals

Equipment

The use of equipment is covered by the Lifting Operations and Lifting Equipment Regulations (LOLER) 1998.

LOLER covers risks to health and safety from lifting equipment provided for use at work. LOLER requires that equipment is:

- strong and stable enough for the intended load
- marked to indicate safe working load
- used safely: the equipment's use should be organised, planned and executed by competent people
- subject to ongoing examination and inspection by competent people.

Hoists, slings and bath hoists are covered by the regulations. The regulations state that lifting equipment should be thoroughly examined by competent people at least every six months in the case of equipment used to lift people, and at least annually in the case of other equipment.

In your work you may use many different types of equipment, including several types of lifting and moving equipment. It is important that you check every time you use a piece of equipment that it is safe and that it is fit for use for that particular individual.

If you do find equipment has become worn, damaged or appears to be unsafe in any way, you should immediately stop using it, label it as being damaged, take it out of service and report it to your supervisor. You must do this even if it means having to change your handling assessment for the individual you were about to move. You should also ensure that other members of staff are aware that the equipment should not be used until it is repaired or replaced.

Under no circumstances is it acceptable to take a risk with equipment that may be faulty. It is better that the individual waits a little longer for a move or is moved in an alternative way rather than being exposed to risks from potentially unsafe equipment.

Make sure that you have read the instruction manual for each piece of equipment you use. It should give you a safety checklist – make sure you follow it, and that colleagues do so too.

Also make sure you seek any assistance you need in order to carry out a move correctly using any type of equipment. Safety procedures will specify how many workers are needed for each type of move.

Evidence

PC 3 6

Find out the procedure in your workplace for reporting faulty equipment. Check whether there is a file or a book where you need to record the fault. You may only need to make a verbal report, or you may have to enter the details of the fault into a computer. Make sure that you know what the correct procedure is, and make notes on it for your portfolio.

How to encourage independence

There are many ways in which an individual can assist and co-operate with care workers who are handling or moving him or her. It is important that this is encouraged and that individuals are not made to feel as though they are simply being transported from place to place 'like a piece of meat'. Co-operation from the individual is invaluable, both for maintaining his or her own independence and for assisting those who have to carry out the move. For example, you may be transferring an individual from a bed to a wheelchair. The first part of the process – getting to the edge of the bed and sitting on it – may well be possible for the individual to accomplish if he or she follows a correct set of instructions, rather than having to be moved by care workers.

Any independence that can be achieved is vitally important in terms of the individual's self-esteem and sense of well-being. A person may be able to transfer himself or herself from a wheelchair to a chair, to a car seat or into bed, either by the use of transfer boards or by simply being able to use sufficient upper body strength to slide across from chair to wheelchair, and vice versa, once the wheelchair arm is removed.

You may be able to use self-help techniques when an individual needs a bed pan. Rather than having to be lifted manually, he or she can be encouraged, with some simple instructions, to bend the knees and raise the bottom to allow the bed pan to be slid underneath him or her.

Techniques like this involve the active co-operation of the individual. Obviously they are not suitable for use where individuals are unable to co-operate, either because of their state of consciousness or because they have almost total paralysis. Some individuals may not be able to co-operate for emotional reasons – they may lack the confidence to make any moves for themselves because of fear of falling or fear of pain or discomfort. Where the plan of care has identified that the individual is capable of co-operation in moving and handling, this should be gently encouraged and any reasons for his or her reluctance to co-operate should be discussed with the individual.

Where there is any conflict between the individual's wishes and health and safety issues, it is important that these are discussed and that you explain to the individual that you must abide by statutory regulations to protect him or her, as well as yourself and your colleagues. Every attempt must be made to reach a compromise so that you can carry out any moving and handling procedure according to the guidelines, while meeting the needs of the individual as closely as you can.

Good preparation is the key to a successful move or transfer. Where the individual and the worker are working together, there is likely to be maximum safety and minimum risk, pain and discomfort.

Remember

If an individual can achieve any part of a move or transfer, with or without support, this will be invaluable both for the individual's self-esteem and in assisting the care worker.

CASE STUDY: Planning a move

Shireen is the care worker for Mrs Gold, who is 80. Shireen needs to move Mrs Gold from a bed into a chair. Mrs Gold is only able to assist a little as she has very painful joints and is unable to bear weight. She weighs 16 stones (101 kg).

1 What would you expect to see in Mrs Gold's care plan in respect of moving procedures? Give reasons.

2 What factors should Shireen take into account before starting to move Mrs Gold?

3 What should Shireen say to her?

Test yourself

1 Name three factors you would take into account when assessing the risk of carrying out a move.

2 In what sort of situations would you consider asking an individual to move himself or herself across the bed?

3 What type of clothing is most suitable for carrying out lifting?

4 What steps should you take if you have concerns about the safety of equipment?

HSC 360b Move and position the individual

You are ready to begin the moving and positioning of individuals when you have consulted the care plan and individuals themselves (where possible), assessed all risks and applied precautions for infection control.

Equipment for moving and handling

 KS 19 20

A wide range of equipment is available, and technological advances are being made continuously in the field of medical equipment. But regardless of the individual products and improvements that may be made to them, lifting and handling equipment broadly falls into the following categories:

- hoists, slings and other equipment, which move the full weight of an individual
- equipment designed to assist in a move and to take some of the weight of an individual, such as transfer boards
- equipment designed to assist the individual to help himself or herself, such as lifting handles positioned above a bed to allow individuals to pull themselves up. This category also includes grab handles, raised toilet seats, patient hand blocks and lifting-seat chairs.

Lifting handles above a bed can help individuals to move themselves

Depending on the setting in which you work, you may have to use some or all of the different types of equipment. If you work with individuals in their own homes, your access to equipment may be more limited, although there is now an extensive range of equipment that can be used very effectively within an individual's own home, often removing the need for residential care.

Using equipment

Each piece of equipment will have an instruction manual. You must read this and be sure that you follow the instructions for its use. There are some general points about how to use particular types of equipment, but you must know how to use the particular equipment in your workplace.

Hoists

- Make sure that you use the correct sling for the hoist and for the weight of the service user.
- Most slings are colour-coded. Check that you have the right one for the weight of the service user.
- Ensure that the seams on the hoist are facing outwards, away from the service user, as they can be rough and can easily damage the skin.
- Only attempt to manoeuvre a hoist using the steering handles – do not try to move it with the jib, as it can overbalance.
- Place the sling around or under the service user. Lower the bed to its lowest position. Then lift the service user. It is only necessary to have a small clearance from the bed or chair – there is no need to raise the service user a great distance.

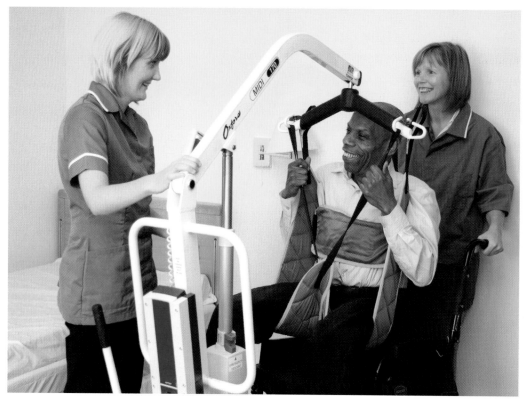

Completing a move: place the wheelchair in position and make sure it is steady

You cannot learn to use a hoist safely by reading a book – you must familiarise yourself with the hoists in your workplace and ask to be shown how to operate them. You should also ensure that junior staff are fully trained and familiar with the use of hoists.

The service user also needs to be comfortable with the procedure for using the hoist. Familiarise him or her with the hoist and the way the move is to be achieved before beginning.

- Ensure the hoist is appropriate for the service user, in terms of his or her needs as well as body weight.
- Explain fully to the individual what will happen at each stage of the move.
- Explain what you would like him or her to do.
- Take your time – don't rush the service user or the move.

Transfer boards/sheets

These require at least two people standing on opposite sides of the bed. They allow people to be moved from bed to trolley and vice versa. They can be used regardless of the level of consciousness of the individual.

They all work on the same principles. They are made of friction-free material which is placed half under the person and half under the sheet he or she is lying on. One worker then pulls and the other pushes. The sheet, complete with person, then slides easily from one to the other. There are several types available: 'Pat-slide', 'Easy-glide' and 'Easy-slide' are among the most common.

Slideboards

The slideboard is a small board placed between a bed and a chair or wheelchair. It is designed for use by service users who are able to be quite active in the transfer and only require assistance. The board allows the service user to slide from bed to chair, and vice versa, with some assistance in steadying and some encouragement.

Turn discs

These are used to swivel service users, in either a sitting or standing position, and can be useful for service users who are able to stand. They are particularly useful for getting in and out of vehicles.

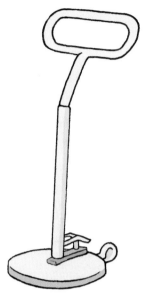

Turn disc

Monkey pole or lifting handle

This is a handle which is fixed above a bed, and swings from a metal frame (see the photograph on page 369). It is designed to allow people to assist themselves. They have to pull on the bar to lift the upper part of the body off the bed. This can enable people to help themselves to sit up, turn over and change position without having to call for assistance.

Handling belts

These enable you to assist a service user to rise from a chair, or provide a steadying hand, by holding onto the handles on the belt. It gives you a firm grip without risking bruising the service user or slipping and causing an injury to either of you.

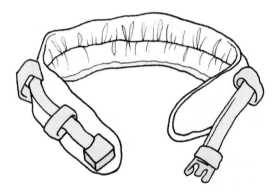

Handling belt

Patient hand block

This is a relatively new piece of equipment that will allow individuals to move themselves up and down the bed. It consists of large plastic handles with a non-slip base and has the effect of lengthening the arms and preventing them from sinking into the mattress. Hand blocks are particularly good for individuals using bedpans, although they will need to have quite strong hands and arms in order to use them.

Patient hand blocks allow individuals to move themselves in bed

Assessing equipment

When you are assessing how to assist a person to move and which equipment to use, you need to consider:

- the potential risks
- what the person can do to help himself or herself to move, and what he or she cannot do – remember that it is important to encourage as much independence as possible
- what the person knows from experience to be the best method, or the method he or she prefers.

If the person's preference conflicts with safe practice, you should tactfully explain this, pointing out the potential risks and suggesting the best method. Reassure the person, if necessary. If there is still a problem, you will need to tell your supervisor immediately.

You need to observe the individual throughout the activity and stop immediately if there are any adverse effects such as pain or anxiety for the individual. If any problems occur, seek help from other professionals.

When you are carrying out a moving procedure, it may be necessary to move items of furniture so that you can work safely. Remember that this also requires assessment: How heavy is the furniture? Is it on wheels? How many times will you need to move it? Whether you are working in a care setting or in an individual's own home, it is important that furniture is returned to its original position afterwards, so the individual can easily locate personal items in their usual places and feel reassured by the familiar surroundings.

Remember

You should never move anyone without his or her agreement.

Evidence   PC 1 4 6

Think of a service user who requires equipment and support to maintain a required position.

Describe the equipment needed and how you ensure that is it used safely, including standard precautions you use for infection control.

Explain what action you would take if any adverse effects occurred during moving or positioning.

Methods for manual moving and handling

 KS 1 3 9 12 16

There are very few situations in which manual lifting should be carried out. Unless it is an emergency or a life-threatening situation, there should be no need to move anyone without the correct equipment. It is important that service users are encouraged to assist in their own transfers and movements.

This means that even shoulder lifts (like the Australian lift) are no longer considered to be safe. There is no safe weight limit for lifting, so the only workplaces where manual lifting should now take place are units caring for babies and small children. Even there, it is important to ensure that risk assessments are carried out to avoid the likelihood of injury, as height differences between the care worker and the child, or the surface involved, present other safety issues.

Care workers in a hospital or residential setting should never have to lift or move service users without the necessary equipment. This is sometimes more of a problem in community settings, where it may not be easy to use equipment in the service user's home, or the equipment may not be available.

The Disability Rights Commission has highlighted the issues in relation to the human rights of people with disabilities. They argue that if disabled people are unable to live in the way they wish because of a 'no lifting' policy – for example, some people have had to remain in bed because no equipment was available to move them, or they did not wish to be moved using equipment – then the agency refusing to provide the care is in breach of both the Human Rights Act 1998 and the Disability Discrimination Act 1995.

There is no direct instruction in the Manual Handling Regulations not to lift, but they do state that all personnel should 'avoid hazardous manual handling where reasonably practicable', and many organisations, particularly within the NHS and social services, instruct their employees not to lift at all. However, guidance from the Health and Safety Executive – 'Handling Home Care', 2002 – states that while all risk assessments must be undertaken and equipment used wherever possible, 'no lifting' policies are likely to be incompatible with service users' rights.

The NHS 'Back to Work' guidance also states that 'no lifting' is a misleading term as it is often used to mean that lifting most, or all, of a service user's weight should not be undertaken. In no circumstances, however, should the service user or care worker be put at risk.

Evidence   PC 1

Check the policy in your workplace about moving individuals against the Health and Safety Executive and NHS guidelines. Does it conform? If not, what changes need to be made? Check the most recent information from the Disability Rights Commission. Are all the staff you are responsible for aware of this? Make notes on your findings for your portfolio.

If you need to move someone manually in order to change his or her position or to provide assistance, you should follow the principles of effective manual moving and handling.

- Risks must be assessed *every time*.
- The procedures should be well-planned and assessed in advance. Technique rather than strength is what is important.
- The procedure should be comfortable and safe for the individual – creating confidence that being moved is not something to be anxious about and that he or she can relax and co-operate with the procedure.
- The procedure should be safe for the workers carrying it out. A worker who is injured during a badly planned or executed transfer or move is likely in turn to injure the individual he or she is attempting to move. Similarly, an individual who is injured during a move is likely to cause an injury to those who are moving him or her.

Team work

Most moving and transfer procedures, whether manual or assisted, are carried out by more than one person. If you are to work successfully as part of a team, you need to follow some simple rules.

- Carry out a risk assessment.
- Decide who is going to 'shout', or lead the manoeuvre.
- That person will check that everyone is ready.
- He or she will say '1-2-3 lift' or '1-2-3 move'.
- Everyone must follow the count of the person who shouts.

Transfer

If you are assisting an individual to transfer from a bed or chair to a wheelchair, this can be done with one person providing assistance to steady the person as he or she uses the transfer board, provided that there are no complicating factors such as an individual who is particularly heavy or tall, or who has serious disabilities. In that case, the person should be moved using a hoist or a turntable.

Rolling or turning

If you need to roll or turn someone who is unable to assist, either because of paralysis, unconsciousness, serious illness or confusion, you should:

- follow the care plan and risk assessment
- carry out the procedure with at least two workers
- roll the person using a transfer sheet or board, or use the bottom sheet to roll the person onto his or her side (make sure the sheet is dry and intact!)
- support the person with pillows or packing.

When the person needs to be turned again, remove the pillows, lower him or her onto the back and repeat the other way.

Overcoming 'pyjama-induced paralysis'

One of the key factors in a safe handling policy is to encourage people to help themselves. There is a great temptation for people to believe that they can do far less than they are capable of. This is often encouraged by staff who find it quicker and easier to do things rather than wait for people to help themselves.

If you encourage individuals to make their own way out of bed, for example, they need to follow the simple set of instructions shown on the next page.

You may wish to encourage an individual to roll over in the bed, rather than having to be manually rolled by a care worker. This could be necessary to allow for a change of bedding, a bed bath or to change clothes. The instructions for achieving this are quite simple, and can be carried out by all but the most severely ill or disabled individuals, as shown on the next page.

Remember

The interests and safety of the individual and the workers are so closely linked that you must consider them both together.

Getting out of bed

1 Roll towards the edge of the bed

2 Swing your legs over the side of the bed while continuing to lie the top half of your body on the bed

3 Push with your hands to sit upright

Rolling over in bed

1 Turn to face the direction in which you are rolling

2 Bend the leg on the other side and keep your foot flat on the bed

3 Reach across your body with the opposite arm. This uses the counterweight of moving the arm across the upper body to assist with achieving a roll

If you need to get someone to raise his or her bottom from the bed in order to give a bedpan, or to prepare for rolling or turning, then you should ask the person to follow the instructions below.

1 Bend both knees

2 Keep your feet flat on the bed and push up on your feet and hands, so that your bottom is raised

Recording and passing on information

 KS 8 18 23 28 30 31

Information about the most effective ways of moving someone, or techniques that have proved effective in encouraging a person to assist himself or herself, should be recorded in the plan of care.

The plan of care should contain information on the moving needs of each individual, and it is vital that these are followed. However, you may notice a change in behaviour or response. This could be:

- a person finding movement more painful
- a loss of confidence in a particular technique
- an improvement in how much assistance a person can give
- a changed reaction following being moved.

Any change of this type, or anything else you notice, is significant and must be reported to your supervisor. Any changes may be indications of overall changes in the person's condition and should never be ignored. The risk assessment should be revised to take into account any changes in an individual's condition, as different equipment may need to be used.

The information you record should be:

- clear
- easily understood
- a good description of the person's needs.

Date	No.	PATIENT'S NURSING NEEDS/PROBLEMS AND CAUSES OF PROBLEMS (NB Physiological, Psychological, Social and Family Problems)	Objectives	Nursing Instructions	Review On/By	Date Resolved
1.5.07	8	Mobility:			8.5.07	
		Due to suffering from a congenital foot deformity, Mr K is unable to bear weight and needs the hoist to be used when moving and handling	To prevent complications of immobility and maintain Mr. K's safety as far as is reasonably practicable	a) Encourage Mr K to be as independent as possible.	15.5.07	
					22.5.07	
				b) Always give clear, consise instructions when moving and handling to gain full co-operation.	29.5.07	
					5.6.07	
					12.6.07	
					19.6.07	
				c) The hoist must be used at all times with either the Quickfit deluxe sling or the toiletting sling - depending on circumstances.	26.6.07	
					3.7.07	
					10.7.07	
					17.7.07	
					24.7.07	
				d) Ensure safe practice maintained when moving and handling.	31.7.07	
					7.8.07	
				e) Observe for any problems and reassess appropriately.		
				f) Review problem weekly		

An example of notes on an individual's mobility in his plan of care

Your records should include notes about when the next positioning manoeuvre is due, if appropriate.

CASE STUDY: Encouraging independence

Mrs Hinds had knee replacement surgery three months ago. Since her discharge from hospital she has been reluctant to move, complaining of severe pain in her leg and side. She asks for help to move from her bed to her chair and uses the wheelchair to go to the toilet. Mrs Hinds has been seen again by the orthopaedic surgeon, who can find no physical reason for the pain and believes the surgery was successful.

1 *Why do you think Mrs Hinds might want help?*

2 *What should the plan of care be in order to support her?*

3 *How could the issue be approached with Mrs Hinds?*

Test yourself

1   Describe the steps you would take before moving or handling an individual using equipment.

2   In what situations is it *not* safe to move an individual?

3   What is 'pyjama-induced paralysis' and how can it be overcome?

4   Name the key information to be recorded in an individual's plan of care concerning moving and handling.

HSC 360 FURTHER READING AND RESEARCH

Below are some books, websites and agencies you can look up to continue your study of this subject. You may also find it useful to make contact with local physiotherapists and occupational therapists that visit your workplace or are based in your local area.

www.backpain.org Back Care (Charity for healthier backs) tel: 0845 1302704

www.csp.org.uk Chartered Society of Physiotherapy

www.hse.gov.uk Health and Safety Executive tel: 0845 345 005

www.drc-gb.org Disability Rights Commission

www.manualhandlingguide.co.uk Manual Handling Guide

www.nric.org.uk (National Resource for Infection Control)

www.neli.org.uk (National Electronic Library of Infection)

BackCare (2005) *The Guide to the Handling of People* 5th Edition

BackCare (1998) *The Handling of Patients* 4th Edition

Oddy, R. (1998) *Promoting Mobility for People with Dementia* 2nd Edition Age Concern

Glossary of key terms

Abuse Causing physical, emotional, sexual and/or financial harm to an individual and/or failing or neglecting to protect him or her from harm.

Abusive and aggressive behaviour Behaviour that causes harm; it may be verbal or non-verbal and can be social, physical, sexual or emotional in nature.

Accidents Unforeseen major and minor incidents where an individual is injured.

Active support Support that encourages individuals to do as much for themselves as possible to maintain their independence and physical ability and encourages people with disabilities to maximise their own potential and independence.

Care plan A plan including all aspects of the individual's care needs that must be adhered to within any setting in which the individual is placed. It addresses the holistic needs of the individual.

Colleagues People with whom you work, including those for whom you have some supervisory responsibility.

Communication and language needs and preferences The individual's needs and preferences in terms of preferred language and ways of communicating with you, and the way you communicate with and respond to him or her.

Danger The possibility that harm may occur.

Emergencies Immediate and threatening danger to individuals and/or others.

Facilities Goods and environments that can be provided to an individual to promote his or her health and social well-being; they can be offered at a distance or taken to the place where the individual lives.

Harm The effects of an individual being physically, emotionally or sexually injured or abused.

Hazard Something with the potential to cause harm.

Individuals The people requiring health and care services. Where individuals use advocates and interpreters to enable them to express their views, wishes or feelings and to speak on their behalf, the term covers the individual and his or her advocate or interpreter.

Key people Those people who are key to an individual's health and social well-being; the people in the individual's life who can make a difference to his or her health and well-being.

Moving and handling Techniques that enable the worker to assist individuals to move from one position to another. Moving and handling must be consistent with current legislation.

Personal protective clothing Items such as plastic aprons, gloves (clean or sterile), footwear, dresses, trousers and shirts, or all-in-one trouser suits. They may be single-use disposable clothing or re-usable.

Protective equipment Equipment that provides extra protection, including visors, protective eyewear and radiation-protective equipment.

Reactions Non-verbal and verbal cues that indicate the individual is distressed, does not understand, etc.

Rights The rights that individuals have to:
- be respected
- be treated equally and not be discriminated against
- be treated as an individual
- be treated in a dignified way
- privacy
- be protected from danger and harm
- be cared for in the way that meets their needs, takes account of their choices and also protects them
- access information about themselves
- communicate using their preferred methods of communication and language.

Right to enter   The right to be on a property. People without the right to enter include those who may have a court order against them or those who have no need to be on the premises.

Risk assessment   A document that identifies actual and potential risks and specifies actions related to specific activities and functions.

Risks   The likelihood of a hazard being realised. Risks can be to individuals in the form of danger, harm and abuse, and/or to the environment in danger of damage and destruction.

Services   Personal and other amenities provided in the individual's home or in other places that promote the individual's health and social well-being.

Signs and symptoms of danger, harm and abuse   Physical, behavioural and emotional indicators that may signify possible danger, harm or abuse.

Specific aids   Aids that enable individuals with speaking, sight or hearing difficulties, additional needs or learning difficulties, to receive and respond to information.

Standard precautions and health and safety measures   A series of interventions that will minimise or prevent infection and cross-infection including: hand-washing/cleansing before, during and after the activity; the use of personal protective clothing and additional protective equipment when appropriate.

Working environment   All environments in which you work.

References

Akehurst, R. (1991) *The Health of the Nation* The University of York

Bonomini, J. (2003) *Effective Interventions for Pressure Ulcer Prevention* Nursing Standard 17, 52, 45–50

Clark, M. (1998) *Repositioning to Prevent Pressure Sores: What is the Evidence?* Nursing Standard 13, 3, 58–64

Collins, F. (2001) *Sitting: Pressure Ulcer Development* Nursing Standard 15, 22, 54–58

Griffith, R., Stevens, M. (2004) *Manual Handling and the Lawfulness of No-Lift Policies* Nursing Standard 18, 21, 39–43

Hawkins, S., Stone, K., Plummer, L. (1999) *An Holistic Approach to Turning Patients* Nursing Standard 14, 3, 52–56

Hayman, M. (1998) A *Protocol for People with Hearing Impairment* Nursing Times, October 28, Volume 94, No. 43

Honey, P. and Mumford, A. (1982) *The Manual of Learning Styles* Ardingly House

Kitwood, T. (1997) *Dementia Reconsidered* Open University Press

Mace, N. (1985) *The 36-Hour Day: A family guide to caring at home for people with Alzheimer's disease* Hodder and Stoughton

Moonie, N., Spencer-Perkins, D., Bates, A. (2004) *Diversity and Rights in Care* Heinemann

Richards, J. (1999) *The Complete A–Z Health & Social Care Handbook* Hodder and Stoughton

Thompson, N. (1996) *People Skills* Macmillan

Wills-Brandon, C. (2000) *Natural Mental Health* Hay House

www.RNIB.org.uk (Royal National Institute for the Blind)

www.seeitright.co.uk (See It Right, RNIB)

www.RNID.org.uk (Royal National Institute for the Deaf)

www.dlf.org.uk (Disabled Living Foundation)

www.mencap.org.uk (Mencap)

www.alzheimers.org.uk (Alzheimer's Society)

www.directgov.uk (Directgov – government information)

www.hmso.gov.uk (HMSO – government publications)

www.helptheaged.org.uk (Help the Aged)

www.ageconcern.org.uk (Age Concern)

www.scope.org.uk (Scope)

www.ukconnect.org (Connect)

www.speakability.org.uk (Speakability)

www.afasic.org.uk (Afasic)

www.stjohn.org (St John Health)

www.cyh.com (Children, Youth and Women's Health Service)

www.hse.gov.uk (Health and Safety Executive)

www.carers.gov.uk (Caring about Carers)

www.doh.gov.uk (Department of Health)

www.bettercaring.co.uk (Better Caring)

www.nursingtimes.net (Nursing Times)

www.dataprotection.gov.uk (Information Commissioner's Office)

www.nvqcareuk.com (NVQs in care)

www.cpa.org.uk (Centre for Policy on Ageing)

www.csci.org.uk (Commission for Social Care Inspection)

www.dlcc.org.uk (Disabled Living Centres Council)

www.mstrust.org.uk (Multiple Sclerosis Trust)

www.arc.org.uk (Arthritis Research Campaign)

www.arthritiscare.org.uk (Arthritis Care)

www.osteoarthritis-symptoms.co.uk (Osteoarthritis Symptoms)

www.activemobility.co.uk (Active Mobility)

www.painsociety.org (British Pain Society)

www.acupuncture.org.uk (British Acupuncture Council)

www.sleep-deprivation.co.uk (Sleep Deprivation Information)

www.sleepcouncil.org.uk (Sleep Council)

www.ec-online.net (Elder Care Online)

www.llmedico.com (LL Medico USA Inc)

www.incontinence.org (Bladder Advisory Council)

www.medinfo.co.uk (Medinfo – medical information and advice)

www.backcare.org.uk (Back Care)

http://spine-health.com (Spine Health)

www.diabetes.org.uk (Diabetes Organisation)

www.asthma.org.uk (Asthma Organisation)

Appendix

ACCIDENT REPORT FORM

	Book number		Page number		Date completed		Person completed sheet handed to.
	Book number		Page number		Date completed		Person completed sheet handed to.

A SEPARATE RECORD SHOULD BE FILED FOR EACH PERSON INVOLVED. It should then be removed and handed to the person or Department noted on the front cover of the book for safekeeping.

1. Details of person involved in accident.

Name:..

Address:...

....

Postcode:...

Occupation:..

Department:..

2. Details about person filing this report.
If you did not have the accident but are filing the report, place your details below.

Name:..

Address:...

....

Postcode:...

Occupation:..

Department:..

3. Description of incident. *(Use the back of this form if more room required.)*

A) Give time and date when accident occured   Date: /   /   Time:...................................

B) Give place of accident (Room/Dept./Area):...

....

C) Give details of how the accident occured with cause if known:...

....

....

D) Give details of any injury suffered by person involved:...

....

E) Sign and date this record before handing to nominated record keeper, whose name is on the front of book. Please also write the date and the name of the person you handed this record to in the 2 boxes at the top of the sheet. You may take a copy of this record for your own records

Signed:... Date: /   /

4. To be completed by employer only.

Only complete this section if you need to report under RIDDOR. After satisfying yourself about the facts, you should decide whether a further risk assessment is necessary and whether the accident should be reported under the Reporting of Injuries, Diseases and Dangerous Occurrences Regulations 1995 (RIDDOR). How was the report notified to the HSE?

Date notified: /   /   Name (Capitals):...................................... Signature:...............................

Knowledge specification

In the unit specifications, the required knowledge points are detailed under the headings 'Values', 'Legislation and organisational policy and procedures' and 'Theory and practice'.

The following grid shows how to pinpoint material relating to these knowledge points (specifications) in the text. The points are addressed on and following the page numbers shown. (Values point 1 is common to most units and is not included in the grid, since its content is fundamental to the information given in the whole unit.)

HSC 31

Values

2	2, 10, 33, 50
3	2, 20, 40

Legislation and organisational policy and procedures

4	35, 72
5	57, 64

Theory and practice

6	9
7	9
8	2, 25, 33, 40
9	25, 46
10	10, 50
11	11
12	12, 42, 49
13	20, 33, 46
14	22, 46
15	22, 50
16	25
17	54, 64, 73
18	64
19	9, 54, 64, 72

HSC 32

Values

2	84, 98

Legislation and organisational policy and procedures

3	79, 87, 110
4	87, 110
5	81, 87

Theory and practice

6	79, 90, 110
7	126
8	98, 107
9	84, 98
10	84, 107

11	80, 98, 103
12	90, 95
13	100
14	98, 108
15	79, 110, 113
16	80, 110, 113
17	80, 110, 113
18	84, 107

HSC 33

Values

2	129

Legislation and organisational policy and procedures

3	130, 151
4	151
5	143

Theory and practice

6	143, 147, 154
7	129, 135, 149
8	147, 154
9	145, 147, 154, 160
10	155
11	138, 145, 147, 150, 159

HSC 35

Values

2	167, 178, 183
3	170, 185, 194
4	178, 187, 197
5	187, 196

Legislation and organisational policy and procedures

6	170, 196, 219
7	170, 215, 219
8	170, 196, 219
9	189
10	213, 217

10	322, 332
11	332
12	321, 341
13	347
14	321, 329, 341
15	321, 329, 341
16	334, 339, 347
17	321, 329, 341
18	335
19	332, 334
20	329, 332, 339, 346

HSC 360
Values

1	356
2	356
3	356, 363

Legislation and organisational policy and procedures

4	352, 366, 373
5	352, 366, 373
6	353
7	354

Theory and practice

8	356, 363, 374
9	352
10	356, 358
11	354, 374
12	367, 372, 373
13	359
14	363
15	356, 363
16	363, 367
17	356, 358
18	376
19	368
20	366
21	352, 364, 372
22	364, 372
23	356
24	374
25	352, 369
26	364
27	352, 369
28	354, 356
29	372
30	376
31	376

Index

Units 369 and 375 are indexed separately. The index for each one is located at the end of the relevant unit on the CD.

lifting and handling 100–103, 351–377
   encouraging independence 367
   methods for manual 372–376
   recording information 376–377
   risk assessments 354–358
   suitable clothing and equipment 365–366
   using equipment 368–372
Lifting Operations and Lifting Equipment
   Regulations (1992) 101, 366
listening 37, 40–54, 290–292
loss of consciousness 118–119

M

manual filing systems 74–76
Manual Handling Operations Regulations (1992) 87,
   89, 101, 373
manual lifting and handling 101–102, 372–376
Maslow's hierarchy of needs 178–179
medical records 69–71
Mencap 267–268
Mental Health Act (1983), draft Mental Health Bill
   219, 221, 228, 236
monkey poles/lifting handles 371
motivation 107–108
moving service users *see* lifting and handling
muscular system 359, 361–363

N

National Assistance Act (1948) 219, 221
National Minimum Standards 60, 170–171, 227–228
needles 96
neglect 203–204
NHS and Community Care Act (1990) 219, 221, 325
NHS nursing contribution 325
non-verbal communication 23, 40–46, 51–52

O

observation charts 69–71

P

patient hand blocks 371
payments, making 341–348
pension credit 327
pensions 324

person-centred care 242–244
personal development 150–151, 160–163
personal effectiveness, developing 153–156
personal safety 108–109
physical development 25–27
physical disabilities and communication 5, 15
physical restraint 311–312
poisoning 122
post, communication by 56–57
power of attorney 322
prejudices 194–198
prescription charges 325, 327
pressure sores 364
professional development
   planning 160–163
   and training 145, 150–153, 163
Protection of Vulnerable Adults scheme (POVA) 221
protective clothing 106
proximity and personal space 42–43
Public Interest Disclosure Act (1998) 215
'pyjama-induced paralysis' 374

Q

questions
   prompting 262
   using open and closed 53, 291–292

R

Race Relations Act (1976) 176, 177
records and reports 54–76
   confidentiality of 57–71
   of mobility methods 376–377
   storing and retrieving 73–76
recovery position 118–119
reflective practice 135–142
register, language 2–3
Regulation of Care (Scotland) Act (2001) 151
relationships 166–167
   developing 22–23
   respect in 287–288
reporting
   abuse 212–216
   accidents 92–95
   emergencies 124, 125